# NEW WORLDS OF
# VIOLENCE

# NEW WORLDS OF **VIOLENCE**

## Cultures and Conquests in the Early American Southeast

*Matthew Jennings*

The University of Tennessee Press / Knoxville

First Edition.

The paper in this book meets the requirements of American National Standards Institute / National Information Standards Organization specification Z39.48-1992 (Permanence of Paper). It contains 30 percent post-consumer waste and is certified by the Forest Stewardship Council.

**Library of Congress Cataloging-in-Publication Data**

Jennings, Matthew, 1976–
New worlds of violence: cultures and conquests in the early American Southeast / Matthew Jennings. — 1st ed.
p. cm.
Includes bibliographical references and index.
ISBN-13: 978-1-57233-756-5 (hardcover)
ISBN-10: 1-57233-756-7 (hardcover)

1. Southern States—History—Colonial period, ca. 1600–1775.
2. Southern States—Discovery and exploration—Spanish.
3. Southern States—Discovery and exploration—British.
4. Violence—Southern States—History—17th century.
5. Violence—Southern States—History—18th century.
6. Indians of North America—First contact with Europeans—Southern States.
7. Indians of North America—Southern States—History—Colonial period, ca. 1600–1775.
8. Indians of North America—Wars—1600–1750.
9. Indians of North America—Wars—Southern States.
10. Whites—Southern States—Relations with Indians.

I. Title.

F212.J46 2011
975'.01—dc22
2011002608

*To my parents, Joyce and David Jennings, my wife Susan, and our sons Henry and Oliver, and to the memory of Grandmama and Granddaddy, Glenn and Sarah Holt*

# Contents

# Figures

# Maps

# Acknowledgments

This book attempts to puncture some timeworn myths: among them that Native American history before the advent of Europeans was simply a prelude and that the English engaged in a relatively benign process of "settlement," and not the harsher conquest carried out by the Spanish. Another myth is that of the lone scholar, a heroic, or weird, figure who spends days in archives and libraries far from home and, even when home, might as well not be. This myth has some truth to it, but, honestly, this book would not exist without the assistance of hundreds of people, who taught me how to write history, guided me through archives and special collections, located images, edited the text, and reminded me that some things matter more than history. Of course, any errors of fact or interpretation are mine alone.

This book was based on a dissertation completed at the University of Illinois in 2007. Dr. Frederick Hoxie, Dr. S. Max Edelson, Dr. James H. Merrell, and Dr. Daniel C. Littlefield served on the committee. In addition to providing insight and guidance for the dissertation, these historians led by example. Through their work, they showed me how powerful and beautiful the study of history can be. They also told me to try to write a dissertation that somebody might like to read, and I have tried. Beyond the dissertation committee, the faculty at Illinois was extremely generous with its time and intellect. Anyone who attended Illinois around the same time I did will also recall the crucial contributions of Jan Langendorf and the late Judy Patterson. I also recall fondly a Native American history reading group consisting of Fred Hoxie, Mike Sherfy, Rebecca McNulty and Kerry Wynn, and an early American history reading group made up of Max Edelson, Robert McColley and Jen Mylander, among others.

Financial assistance from the Committee on Institutional Cooperation's American Indian Studies Program and the Bartram Trail Conference helped underwrite visits to archives, including the P. K. Yonge Library at the University of Florida, the South Carolina Department of Archives and History, the Georgia Division of Archives and History, the Georgia Historical Society, and the South Caroliniana Library at the University of South Carolina. The staffs of these archives were all professional and courteous, but James Cusick at the P. K. Yonge Library and Charles Lesser at the South Carolina Department of Archives and History stand out in my mind. They took a rushed, relatively inexperienced scholar seriously, and I am grateful.

My students at the University of Illinois, Illinois State University and Eastern Illinois University, and Macon State College have improved my scholarship and teaching over the past decade (and counting). I set out to teach them that history matters, but I learned more from them than they know. Special thanks go out to the students in the Native American History, Colonialism and the Modern World, and the Atlantic World courses, who struck the right balance between encouragement and critical questioning. I'm not sure that the stammering and long pauses as I tried to answer your questions would make a college-teaching highlight reel, but I hope you all recognize that some of the ideas in this book were a product of our time together. You inspired to me to try to write a book that you might have liked to read (even if it were recommended and not required).

The University of Tennessee Press and Thomas Wells in particular have been helpful and kind. Thomas found my dissertation abstract on the internet and contacted me (I'm not making this up) the very day that I had gotten somewhat discouraging news from another press. He also placed the manuscript in the capable hands of James Carson. I first met Jamey when he commented on a conference paper of dubious value I gave in Chicago in 2004. He took me to task, but in an evenhanded manner that made me a better historian. He read the entire manuscript twice and improved it immeasurably with sharp comments on both form and content. Thanks to Karin Kaufman for her thorough and beneficial copyediting.

I was hired at Macon State College in 2007, and have found the environment at the college and in town positively inspiring. Macon State faculty members teach a lot, and we love our students, but we hold ourselves to high standards of scholarship as well. This is true of every member of the Department of History and Political Science (listed here in alphabetical order to avoid awkward moments at department functions): Bob Burnham, Jeff Burson, Jim Decker, Larry Israel, Julie Lester, Andy Manis, Carol Melton, Naomi Robertson, Stephen Taylor and Matt Zimmerman. Debra Slagle and Chad Dent keep most of us in line most of the time, and keep things running smoothly. Off campus, at the Washington Memorial Library, Muriel Jackson, Willard Rocker, and Christopher Stokes maintain an archival collection that would make some more well-to-do towns blush. The staff at Ocmulgee National Monument was also quite helpful, especially Lonnie Davis, whose picture of the "Moore's Raid" diorama graces the book.

Finally, special thanks are due to my friends and family. The friends I had in graduate school prove that people with sharp minds don't have to have dull personalities. Most of us have left Champaign now, but it hasn't left us entirely. Listing them all runs the risk of missing somebody, but here goes: Jill Baer, Will Cooley, Paul Droubie, David Hageman, Stephen Hageman, Jason Hansen, Debbie Hughes, Brian Ingrassia, Melissa Kath, Tom Mackaman, Kate Meehan (now Pedrotty), Matt Moon, Kristen Nash, James Nelligan, Michael Pedrotty, Kristen Nash, Paul Ruth, Melissa Salrin, Beth Savage, Cris Scarboro, Bryce Shields, Jason Tebbe, Jamie Warren, and Kerry Wynn.

My parents, Joyce and David Jennings, encouraged my intellectual curiosity from an early age and provided more assistance into middle age than they probably expected to. I can't thank them enough. I've also benefited from the guidance and support of my mother-in-law, Becca Gay, and Laif Forslund. My wife Susan and sons Henry and Oliver kept me from thinking about school and work too much and showed me that there are more important things. Henry and Oliver's arrivals, in 2005 and 2007 respectively, made writing the book take much longer than it probably should have, but for all the right reasons. When I started writing the dissertation that became *New Worlds of Violence,* Henry was not yet born. As I write these words, Oliver, our Georgia boy, who will be three by the time the book is finally published, is pulling my sleeve, demanding that I shell yet another handful of peanuts.

# INTRODUCTION

# Cultures of Violence

## Looking Back from Ocmulgee

Violence in the colonial Southeast could be generative as well as destructive, and stories people told about violence mattered. William Bartram's peregrinations through the Southeast were, from his point of view, a rather depressing journey. His travels can be read as a meditation on the futility of trying to tame lands that will eventually revert to their wild, overgrown status; his own rice plantation in East Florida had failed miserably in 1766.[1] At Ocmulgee—a Mississippian mound site near present-day Macon, Georgia—the naturalist William Bartram noted ancient traces of long-dead civilizations. To the Creeks, though, Ocmulgee was the place where their violent past could help build a modern Indian nation and stake a territorial claim to the Southeast.

Visiting Ocmulgee National Monument in Macon, Georgia, is a good idea. Apart from the obvious attractions (a large complex of ceremonial mounds), the visitors' center houses a collection of fascinating artifacts, and boasts a helpful staff that will start the educational film, "People of the Macon Plateau," for an audience of one. The National Park Service brochure suggests that "spring and fall are the best seasons to tour the park on foot," and that is probably true.[2] Visiting Ocmulgee National Monument in the middle of a humid August morning is not a particularly good idea. Still, standing on top of the Great Temple Mound, squinting through eye-stinging sweat, it is not difficult to see what has drawn people to the site for thousands of years. Apart from the modern city of Macon, stretched out to the north, the entire vista is lush and green. It seems like anything could grow there. William Bartram, the famed American naturalist, described the area in the 1770s as "rich low lands," noting that ancient fields extended "up and down the river, fifteen or twenty miles from this point."[3] People began to take advantage of this fertile landscape in the Woodland period (roughly 1,000 BCE to 900 CE) by cultivating squash and eventually corn and beans. Later, skilled Mississippian farmers planted extensive corn crops in the region, and large villages appeared.

By the time Bartram arrived here in 1773, the Macon Plateau already had a long, rich human history. Paleo-Indian, as well as Archaic and

Woodland-era artifacts have been found there, signaling that the site has been continuously occupied for thousands of years. But the most impressive era of occupation came between 900 and 1200. At that time, Mississippian people constructed a number of large mounds on the Macon Plateau, including a temple mound, a burial mound, and an earthlodge, which probably functioned as the seat of their government. A later Mississippian culture, the Lamar culture, had its center along the Ocmulgee River, less than three miles away, where its people built a unique spiral mound. The Ichisi province visited by Hernando de Soto in 1540 probably had its principal town at the Lamar site. In 1690, English traders set up a post on the Macon Plateau, the footprint of which is visible today. Some Muskogees migrated from the Chattahoochee River for easier access to English trade goods. Early English visitors to the Southeast referred to these people as "Creeks," since they lived on Ochesse Creek (the Ocmulgee). During the Yamasee War (1715–18), the British burned what they called Ocmulgee Town, and many Creeks returned to the west.[4]

While archaeologists might trace these communities through time by plotting settlements and tracking ceramic motifs, the Native people who occupied the plateau tell their own stories. For the Creeks, the Macon plateau was literally the seat of their history. Upon reaching the mound complex, Bartram relates the following story, which bears more than a passing resemblance to other legends concerning the origins of the Creeks. According to Bartram, "this place [Ocmulgee] is remarkable for being the first town or settlement, when they sat down (as they term it) or established themselves after their emigration from the west, beyond the Mississippi, their original native country." Bartram went on to retell the legend of the journey before the Creeks "sat down": "On this long journey they suffered great and innumerable difficulties, encountering and vanquishing numerous and valiant tribes of Indians, who opposed and retarded their march." Following a valiant last stand, the Creeks "recovered their spirits," achieved victory in a "memorable and decisive battle," and "subdued their surrounding enemies, strengthening themselves by taking into confederacy the vanquished tribes."[5]

At this point, the English, who established Carolina in 1670, entered the Creek narrative. The Creeks, according to the story told to Bartram, understood that the English were "a powerful, warlike people," and immediately dispatched diplomats to the colonial capital at Charles Town to "offer their friendship and alliance." Bartram also wrote of a treaty, established between the Creeks and South Carolina, which was never violated. The Creeks did not simply promise peace, they offered valuable services to the

English in the early years of the eighteenth century; "they never ceased war against the numerous and potent bands of Indians, who then cramped and surrounded the English plantations," according to the story told Bartram. During the harrowing years of the Yamasee War, the Creeks remained staunchly allied to the English, fighting off numerous enemies, and pursuing the defeated hostile Indians "to the very gates of St. Augustine."[6]

The "Bartram legend" signals the Creeks' attachment to the Macon plateau. But it also demonstrates the link between a community's history and its identity. The story Bartram's Creek consultants related accomplished more than asserting a claim to this land. It also explained the group's understanding of its past. For example, Bartram's associates were correct in their assertion that the Creeks and English had signed a treaty. The treaty, dated at Coweta on August 15, 1705, used strictly formulaic language to bind the Creeks, represented by twelve leaders—the English called them "Kings, Princes, Generals, etc."—in "Hearty Alliance with, and Subjection to the Crown of England."[7] But this event was clouded by other events not mentioned in 1773, most notably the eruption of the Yamasee War. As "Emperor" Brims of Coweta rose to prominence within the Creek Confederacy, the Lower Creeks pursued a policy of neutrality, playing the English, French, and Spanish off of one another in an effort to maintain control over the terms of trade, their land base, and their position of power over other Native communities in the region.[8] That the Creeks were a subject people was more English fantasy than reality in the early eighteenth century. In 1715, in the early phase of the Yamasee War, some Creek communities joined the Yamasees and killed the traders stationed in their towns. After a short-lived alliance between the Creeks and Cherokees broke down, and the English and Cherokees became military allies and trading partners, the Creeks broke off their attacks on English plantations, and chose instead to launch a series of devastating attacks on the Cherokees that would last three decades.[9] Fighting between Creeks and Cherokees helped define national territory and identity in ways that would foreshadow the fight between southeastern Indian nations and the United States in the early nineteenth century.[10] These actions do not match the language of the 1705 treaty, in which the Creeks declared that "all the *English* Friends and allies are in like manner ours, and all their Enemies are hereby Our declared Enemies."[11]

There was a distinct advantage in removing incidents of conflict between the English and Creeks from the oral historical record. By 1773, the British victory in the Seven Years' War had taken away the Creeks' ability to play European powers off of each other, and Georgia's non-Native population had risen sharply. The Creeks confronted a new demographic order in addition to a new political order. According to one estimate, there were 11,000 Creeks in 1730 and approximately 100 white settlers; in 1775, after the New Purchase cession, a population of about 14,000 Creeks faced down around 18,000 white colonists and 15,000 African American slaves.[12] In a 1763 conference at Augusta, British superintendent John Stuart promised that "all past offences shall be buried in oblivion and forgiveness."[13] Stuart hoped to usher in a new era of peaceful relations with the Creeks. By 1773, the Creeks who greeted Bartram at Ocmulgee had buried past offenses in oblivion remarkably well. Bartram readily accepted the legend's emphasis on English and Creek cooperation, and its amnesia regarding certain acts of violence. Memory loss on a historic scale held distinct advantages for the Creeks, and their portrayal of themselves as partners in the English colonizing project should be read as one "powerful, warlike people" allying itself with another. The origin story told to Bartram combined two histories the Creeks saw as parallel: their own violent establishment in the Southeast, and the establishment of English colonies. The Muskogees and the English were just two of the communities fighting in the international contest for the North American Southeast.

Warfare between Europeans and Native Americans in the Southeast plays a large role in the book that follows, but this is more than a history of war. War was one of many violent options available to the people of the Southeast before 1740. War also conjures certain images—especially when Native Americans and Europeans and their descendants face off against each other. The long shadow cast by the stereotyped "Indian War" can have a distorting effect on intercultural violence that was more complex and contingent than most people realize. *New Worlds of Violence* looks at slave raiding, skirmishing, and touches on the violent rhetoric that accompanied the physical violence associated with colonization.

The framework of the "culture of violence" is extremely useful in helping us understand the conflict over the early American Southeast. It places concrete violent acts and rhetorical acts of violence within multiple larger cultural contexts. Also, cultures of violence lend themselves to comparative and historical study, since multiple cultures of violence may be in play, interacting and changing each other at the same time.

Violence was a fact of life in the colonial Southeast, and it emanated from several quarters. England and Spain vied for supremacy over what is now the Southeastern United States; their hemisphere-wide struggle simmered in South Carolina as bands of Europeans and their Native allies fought over territory. One scholar has described this conflict as "giants wrestling with their fingertips."[14] The English and Spanish "giants"—and in one striking instance a band of French Huguenots—thumb-wrestled over the Southeast repeatedly from the sixteenth to the eighteenth century, and often engaged in tactics frowned upon in European combat. In the 1560s, for instance, the Spanish commander Pedro Menéndez de Avilés executed as many as 300 captured French people asking for quarter.[15] During Francis Drake's June 1586 attack on St. Augustine, English forces spent a week pillaging the town, carrying off all portable property, cutting down the fruit trees, razing the fields, and finally burning the outpost to the ground upon their exit.[16] A little more than a century later, a combined army of Native Americans and white Carolinians under the leadership of South Carolina's Governor James Moore would succeed in destroying Florida's most populous mission town, Apalachee, carrying off thousands of Indian slaves—most of them women and children—in the process.[17]

Native communities fought European invaders at the same time as they engaged in conflict against other Indian polities. Individual warriors and groups competed for cultural goals—prestige, masculinity, and religion—as well as more material aims, such as slaves, firearms, and trade goods. Hernando de Soto's 1539–43 *entrada* met with responses ranging from hospitality to indifference to fierce resistance, such as the pitched battle at Mabila (in present-day Alabama) in 1540. In the Tuscarora War (1710–12) and the Yamasee War (1715–18), Native groups employed violence to great effect; the Yamasee War severely hampered the white settlement of lands south of Charles Town, the colonial capital, for years, and also brought the Creeks and Cherokees into nearly thirty years of conflict (a number of Creek headmen were assassinated after the Cherokees joined the English as trading partners).

Planters used violence to control their African slaves, and African slaves used violence to resist their owners. South Carolina's elite planters acted out their dominion over slaves in public, state-sanctioned acts of violence which legitimated their high status.[18] Though the lash was a constant threat to all African slaves, those who ran away or violated slave codes in other ways faced especially swift and severe punishment. Of course, the same slave codes reigned in English violence as well. Public maiming, castration, and other forms of corporal punishment marked the early English slave regime in the Southeast.[19] Runaways and rebels, the most visible threats to slaveholding society, were often killed as examples. Slave resistance in colonial South Carolina took many forms, from insolent language and dress, to feigned simplemindedness, and occasionally to violence—the severity of which ran the gamut from striking a master or poisoning a mistress to the Stono Rebellion of 1739.[20]

The English, or Anglo-American, culture of violence that developed in the Southeast had three main components: a heavy reliance on Indian trade carried out in a lopsided power relationship, an intense land hunger and a desire to produce valuable crops for export. This last trait all but assured that slavery would be the labor regime of choice for the region's planters. The violence of slavery and the violence of trade were often connected in concrete ways, since the same Europeans who dominated the trade were often engaged in setting up plantations, which could not function without the threat of violence. Carolina's planter class, especially around the turn of the eighteenth century, showed little compunction about owning either African or Native American slaves, or about sponsoring and participating in long-range slave raids into Florida.

## Interpretive Problems and Solutions

Despite its centrality to life in the early Southeast, violence has proven a difficult theme for historians to track and interpret. Many general histories of the colonial Southeast suffer because the study of the Southeast's Native peoples lags behind other regions, most notably New England. The tendency not to integrate Indians into larger historical narratives has resulted in a situation in which the pervasive violence of the Southeast has been under-reported and poorly understood. Recreating the worldviews and attitudes of people who lived and died in the early modern Southeast presents an array of interpretive obstacles, not all of which can be overcome. The framework of the "culture of violence" suggests a constructive way to move past many of these old problems.

In its popular usage, the phrase "culture of violence," in the singular, refers to a time and place of heightened violence, when the rules governing violence are weak, and violence spins out of control. In this sense, a "culture of violence" could refer to anything from gang violence to sniping and school corridor murder to genocides in Darfur, Bosnia, and Rwanda. This book takes a different approach and historicizes multiple "cultures of violence" operating in the North American Southeast before 1740.

Before discussing the specific, comparative case studies of violence that make up this book, it makes sense to define a scholarly concept of a "culture of violence," as it appears below. Evan Haefeli, a historian whose ideas about violence lean on anthropology, employs the phrase "cultures of violence" in a piece about Kieft's War, which pitted Dutch colonists on Manhattan against several local peoples in the 1630s and 1640s. Haefeli explains the intense violence of Kieft's War by noting that Manhattan's natives and newcomers had differing sets of ideas about violence, and that these differing interpretations of violence led to bloodshed: "the real clash was between the

European and Native American cultures of violence, between their ways of interpreting and coming to terms with violent acts."[21]

In his often-overlooked 1956 work *The Militant South,* John Hope Franklin examined a specific Anglo-American culture of violence that developed in the antebellum era. Although Franklin did not use the phrase "culture of violence," he noted that the white man of the South was "the product of his experiences as a frontiersman, Indian fighter," and "slave-holder."[22] All of these activities involved violence, and all were present at the birth of the Anglo-American South. This book seeks to explain violence in the Southeast from multiple perspectives, at the same time as it traces the gradual English domination of the region and the formation of an Anglo-American culture of violence that would spread with English colonization to points west.[23]

Native Americans living in the Southeast had their own ideas about violence. Europeans and Africans who entered into this contested territory came into contact and collision with established cultural inheritances that defined the role of violence within Native American society. These inheritances influenced what acts of violence Native groups were prepared to direct against others and shaped them to understand violence directed against them in certain ways. Competing cultures of violence structured the encounter between natives and newcomers in the Southeast before 1740, but they did not predetermine the outcome of the contest for the region.

So different "cultures of violence" existed, and each of these would play a role in the violent drama of colonization in the Southeast. A useful undertaking at this point may be to attempt to define "culture" and "violence," while recognizing that any definition of such slippery terms will leave some people unsatisfied. My understanding of culture is grounded in the work of anthropologist Clifford Geertz. Geertz perceived culture as "an historically transmitted pattern of meanings embodied in symbols, a system of inherited conceptions expressed in symbolic forms by means of which men communicate, perpetuate, and develop their knowledge about and attitudes toward life."[24] This broad, semiotic view of culture works well as it relates to a history of cultures of violence. Not only is violence "historically transmitted," but violent acts can be read as signs, even as they have different meanings for perpetrators, victims, and onlookers.

"Violence" first appeared in English around the turn of the fourteenth century, and initially referred solely to physical acts; by 1600, the meaning of violence had expanded to acts committed against texts.[25] The fact that the category of violence is expansive enough to include not only physical acts, but also words and performances creates substantial interpretive difficulties.

One of the more influential definitions of violence in the 1980s and 1990s was provided by David Riches, in his book *The Anthropology of Violence.* Riches proposed that violence was "an act of physical hurt deemed legitimate by the performer and illegitimate by (some) witnesses."[26] Recently, Bettina E. Schmidt and Ingo W. Schröder, editors of *Anthropology of Violence and Conflict,* made a case for studying violence comparatively: "Violence is a basic form of social action that occurs under concrete conditions, targets concrete victims, creates concrete settings and produces concrete results. All of these dimensions are clearly accessible to comparative analysis."[27]

All this emphasis on the concreteness of violence can obscure the fact that violence may be committed by pens as well as swords. Colonial schemers carved up North America from a great distance, often with violent results, for instance. Of course, it is possible to focus entirely on the performative or rhetorical aspects of violence and overlook the fact that in the colonial Southeast, real wars were taking place, and real people were beheading other real people. Neil Whitehead, author of several important works on warfare and violence, proposed the framework of a "poetics of violence" in 2004. He hoped to account for the fact that "a violent death cannot be entirely understood by reference to biological origins, sociological functions, or material and ecological necessities but has to be appreciated for the way in which it is also a cultural expression of the most fundamental and complex kind."[28] Violence is fundamental and complex in our own times, and we should not expect the violence of the past to be any different. Try explaining any of the conflicts simmering around the world in our own times, and the pitfalls are apparent. Even with the benefit of historical perspective, the violent acts of the past are not easy to interpret.

Even where documentary, archaeological and oral historical records exist, there are serious problems of interpretation that riddle the historiography of the colonial Southeast. Herbert Bolton and Mary Ross, the earliest advocates of Spanish borderlands history, combined Spanish and English sources to tell the story of what they termed "the debatable land"—an area roughly concurrent with modern Georgia.[29] Since their work in the 1920s, few scholars have followed their lead. Verner Crane's *The Southern Frontier,* made some use of Spanish sources, and J. Leitch Wright's *The Only Land They Knew* drew more extensively on them.[30] Claudio Saunt, author of *A New Order of Things,* provides an even more balanced account, and even goes so far as to eschew the term "borderlands" itself.[31] To the Native people living in the early modern Southeast, far from Mexico City and Charles Town, and farther still from Madrid and London, the region was not divided between English and Spanish spheres of control.

Further problems arise in the translation of many of the sources which form the basis of this book. Many Native names are rendered differently in the English and Spanish documents, and some names have changed or disappeared entirely. The temptation to use modern or nineteenth-century ethnographic information, or to "upstream," in the jargon of anthropology, is great, and in some cases unavoidable. Scholars are sometimes forced by a dearth of documentary evidence to fill gaps by inferring information from nearby or culturally similar groups. These practices, while regrettable—and used sparingly in the work that follows, are part of any historical undertaking.

Beyond the difficulty of identifying who was where at what time in the Southeast, and what they were doing, there exists the difficulty of explaining what people said and wrote about violent acts. European colonizers in the Southeast typically reported Native attacks as "massacres" and refused to recognize Indians had complex reasons and methods for using violence to fight colonization. This Eurocentric tilt lived on well into the twentieth century, and general histories of colonial America often recycle the imagery of a group of hardworking English people arriving to make new lives for themselves in an unforgiving wilderness inhabited by savage strangers. Alternately, modern scholars eager to correct Eurocentrism and racism in earlier works often recast Europeans as savages and Native Americans as virtuous victims, thereby playing into the long-lived "noble savage" stereotype. The debate over how to portray the violence of colonization is not likely to be resolved any time soon.

Perhaps it is best to recognize that life in the colonial Southeast was violent, no matter one's tribal affiliation, and move on from there. Ian Steele, in the introduction to *Warpaths,* noted that "Colonial North American history was not created in peace and interrupted by war; wars, rumors of war, and costs of war affected every generation of Amerindians and colonists. It is disturbing to recognize that modern North America was established amid such violence, but this sobering realization is better than accepting sanitized myths that make modern levels of violence seem like moral degeneration from some peaceful colonial or pre-colonial Arcadia."[32]

The long shadow cast by the image of the "Indian War" needs to be acknowledged and dealt with. No major conflict in American history pitted only Native Americans against only Europeans or their descendants. To lump all sorts of conflicts into this category runs the risk of blaming violence solely on Native peoples, and to ignore the complexities of colonial violence. The phrase "Indian Wars" carries on the outmoded civilized-savage dichotomy, and implies the existence of two monolithic peoples destined to try to destroy one another in North America. Richard Slotkin called this "the fatal opposition, the hostility between two worlds, two races, two realms of thought and feeling."[33] In the Southeast, as elsewhere, Indian people chose to fight for many different reasons. The Yamasees, for instance, were the largest single group present in the South Carolina army that invaded Tuscarora country, in North Carolina, under the leadership of the colonist John Barnwell. During the turmoil of the Yamasee War, some Native Americans sided with the English. There were no "Indian Wars" in the colonial Southeast, as many of the English colonists, and historians sympathetic to their goals, might have claimed.

Works of Native American history must also deal with the fact that the United States itself, though born in a fight against colonialism, was, and in many ways remains, a colonial power. To be sure, the people who fought in the Southeast in the period under consideration in this book did not know or care about the United States. But the descendants of the people who invaded the Southeast, the descendants of those forced to labor on its plantations, and the descendants of those whose lands were invaded inhabit the same United States today. The present location of some of the nations discussed below—Creek, Cherokee, and Choctaw—points to the long-term implications of the processes that began in the 1500s and 1600s.

In an essay which has had a profound effect on my approach, Donald L. Fixico has put forward some ethical guidelines for the study of Native American history. Fixico envisions a combination of external and internal understandings of that history. In the case of the study of violence, it is essential to attempt to understand what the violence of the early Southeast meant to the people caught up in it. The best histories combine—though they will probably never transcend—the insider and outsider perspectives that have vexed many attempts to write Indian history.[34]

The relationship between the largely, though not entirely, non-Native academic community and Native communities is not always a smooth one, but both parties stand to learn from each other, and from the mistakes and biases of the past. In the eastern half of the United States, the specter of removal looms large, and many nations are struggling to assert their unique identities in comparison to larger groups further west. The non-Native belief that there are no Indians east of the Mississippi River is dying out slowly. Moreover, members of Southeastern nations in Oklahoma and elsewhere still remain closely tied to their ancestral homelands in the Southeast. The Muscogee (Creek) Nation of Oklahoma, for instance, has joined with environmentalist groups and preservationists to protect the sacred Ocmulgee site.

The colonial Southeast has been chronically understudied, and as a result, the region is among the least understood in colonial America. There are a number of reasons for this lack of knowledge. Early American history, as piles of high school and undergraduate exams can attest, is the story of the contrast between Massachusetts and Virginia. Also, because the Southeast, with its large Native and African population, as well as Spanish and French presence, does not lend itself to America's national myth, it is sometimes given short shrift in textbooks. Historical interpretation of the Native Southeast, while it picked up steam in the 1990s and 2000s, still lags behind the Chesapeake, and even farther behind New England. King Philip's War, which engulfed southern New England in the second half of the 1670s, was the subject of four monographs in the 1990s alone. Quality books and articles do exist on the colonial Southeast, but they are fewer and farther between than for the Chesapeake and New England. Some even treat violence, but usually not from the kind of perspective afforded by a "cultures of violence" approach.

Many colonial histories begin in the late seventeenth or early eighteenth century, though European colonization began with the Spanish expeditions of the 1520s and 1530s. The gap is so shocking that one leading scholar has labeled the intervening period "the forgotten centuries."[35] In fact, Native societies were changing rapidly in the decades leading up to contact with Europeans, so any full treatment of violence in the Southeast must begin in the Mississippian era. The large polities of the Mississippian era informed later political developments, even as they dispersed into villages and towns. These towns, many of them heterogeneous and multi-ethnic, would realign to form the basis of the Indian nations of eighteenth- and nineteenth-century America.

Two recent works, both of which came out as I was finishing *New Worlds of Violence,* make serious attempts to remember these forgotten centuries. Robbie Ethridge and Sheri Marie Shuck-Hall's *Mapping the Mississippian Shatter Zone* contains a number of essays that demonstrate how the legacy of the Mississippian World informed the coalescent Native American communities of the Southeast.[36] Joseph Hall's fine book, *Zamumo's Gifts: Indian-European Exchange in the Colonial Southeast,* traces the practice of gift-giving and the eventual rise of European-style trade from the Mississippian period to the establishment of the English.[37] Hall's chronology parallels that of the current undertaking, but emphasizes a rather different aspect of the meeting between Europeans and Native peoples. Indeed, one might even argue that Hall proffers a "cultures of exchange" framework to counter the "cultures of violence" approach laid out in this work. The story of European colonization and Native persistence in the Southeast is vast and complex, and no one should come away from *New Worlds of Violence* with the impression that violence is the only way to understand the region during this time period.

The question remains as to how a single narrative can correct the oversights of earlier works and the exhibit the political sensitivity necessary for writing about colonial situations. Ethnohistory, a discipline at the crossroads of anthropology and history, provides some useful ways of dealing with these problems, and the best recent work on colonization in the Southeast has adopted some of its methods. Relying on a variety of artifacts, whether material, cultural, or documentary, historians have begun the arduous task of reconstructing the American Southeast. Frederic Gleach, an anthropologist whose work is discussed below, has used the term "controlled speculation" to describe the process. When studying particularly poorly documented situations, it is necessary to move around in time and space to find analogous situations.[38] On one level, this is something that all historians must confront, but colonial-era history and particularly colonial Native American history seem like especially good candidates for controlled speculation.

Unfortunately, ethnohistory has also had the effect of "ghettoizing" American Indian history, separating it from the rest of early American history.[39] By isolating Native communities from their non-Native neighbors, ethnohistory has made it difficult to compare people across seemingly wide cultural divides. It has also, in a valiant effort to produce Native-centric versions of colonial history and make them relevant to the present, ascribed a certain timeless set of values to Natives and non-Natives alike. One way of avoiding this segregation of the past is to write about both Native and non-Native peoples on their own cultural terms. The changes occurring in the Southeast in the sixteenth through the eighteenth century are not wholly Native or European, so neither group can be the center of the narrative. Frederic Gleach decentered the traditional narrative of early Virginia cleverly in *Powhatan's World and Colonial Virginia* by presenting both English and Powhatan worldviews before the two cultures collided, and then describing the changes wrought as each group tried to civilize the other on its own terms. This multivocal history complicates the "big picture" of early American history, which is often seen simply as a prelude to the War for Independence.

The framework of the culture of violence offers a method for connecting incidents of violence across cultural lines. Every community has a culture of violence in this reckoning. That is, every community is capable of determining when violence is necessary and prescribing the most appropriate way of carrying it out. Each individual community's approach to violence reflects its worldview and its history. As a consequence, a community's approach to violence is rarely random. Violence can reinforce social values and create cultural unity at the same time as it disrupts and destroys one's enemies. Violence—understood here not only as a physical act—can become an integral ingredient of a community's lifeways.

Understanding an individual community's culture of violence, and tracing the interaction of cultures of violence in a single narrative presents a number of challenges. The "cultures of violence" approach enables scholars to rewrite the history of the colonial Southeast across cultural lines, since each group had its own culture of violence. Not only did people compete over the Southeast's land and resources, they struggled to show other competing groups that their culture of violence was superior, was the "right" way of living in the region. The history of the Southeast becomes the story of the emergence of various distinct cultures of violence, their contact, interaction—including alliances across cultural lines, conflict, and their eventual destruction by the English, or more properly, an Anglo-American, culture of violence.

The best way to study a culture of violence would be to obtain intimate, firsthand knowledge of a culture, and then proceed to a scholarly interpretation of that culture's ideas on violence and the role of violence in its participants' worldviews. Obviously, this type of cultural knowledge—the type that supports the work of scholars like Clifford Geertz, Keith Basso, and Julie Cruikshank—is impossible to obtain for the sixteenth through eighteenth centuries. However, historians can learn from anthropology and ethnohistory, and the lessons are particularly applicable to the study of violence.[40] Anthropology offers a useful theoretical framework for dealing with violence in history. Anthropological and ethnohistorical discussions of violence as performance are essential to understanding violence in an imperial, Anglo-Indian context. Violence occurs when one person or party asserts its power over another. As Bettina E. Schmidt and Ingo W. Schröder put it, violence is "an act of physical hurt deemed legitimate by the performer and illegitimate by (some) witnesses. Since the violent act is relatively easily performed, and at the same time highly visible and concrete, it is a very efficient way of transforming the social environment and staging an ideological message before a public audience."[41] Schmidt and Schröder borrow heavily from *The Anthropology of Violence*. In that work, David Riches argued for a cross-cultural interpretation of violence: "Violence is understood best when it is examined over a range of cultural settings, and in a full variety of social situations."[42] Violence on the southern Anglo-Indian frontier involved discrete, violent events and their reverberations, retellings, and responses. But, as Neil Whitehead pointed out, to limit violence to only physical acts is too restrictive. Other forms of violence, bundled together in a specific culture of violence, should also be fair game for comparison. It follows, then, that a comparative study of violence is possible; to push this even further, comparison between English and Native cultures of violence is necessary in order to understand why the Southeast looked the way it did by the eighteenth century. Violence in the colonial Southeast has yet to receive a culturally specific cross-cultural analysis.

One danger inherent in such a project is that the historian, operating at a great chronological remove, will impose, even accidentally, an ahistorical, externally delineated definition of violence. For instance, a Carolina planter's repeated whipping of a slave might not have been perceived by the planter as exceptionally violent, even though by twenty-first-century standards it would. Considering legitimacy is one way of approaching this problem. Planters, in all likelihood, recognized that their actions were violent, but they constituted a legitimate form of violence, since they coerced labor or punished bad behavior. Conversely, the slave might perceive the whipping as illegitimate, but her subsequent poisoning of her owner entirely justifiable. Determining legitimacy is fraught, but doing so is crucial and can enrich our understanding of violence.[43]

Until relatively recently, interpreters of violence have seen it as a disruptive force, one that weakened communities and threatened order.[44] This long-held theory of violence, based on the writings of thinkers like Hobbes, Descartes, Rousseau, and Machiavelli—men who believed that violence, especially when beyond the control of the state, existed outside the natural order of society or the way things ought to be, does not work that well for the colonial Southeast. Drawing on a more contingent definition of culture, Deborah Poole, who studies violence in the Peruvian highlands in the twentieth century, has argued that "violence, as a form of power, has come to be viewed as productive of subjectivities, truths, histories, and identities—productive, in short, of the social order itself."[45] In the colonial Southeast, violence did not disrupt any sort of broadly defined social order, except from the English perspective (and the English certainly did their share of disrupting other peoples' social orders). In some cases, the study of the violence of colonization in the Americas has stressed Native American victimization, a model that distorts in much the same way as the narrative of Native savagery and European civilization that it replaced.

African slaves brought to the Southeast to labor had their own cultures of violence; they combined traditions remembered from their diverse homelands into a uniquely African American culture of violence. During the period before 1740, African American identity was in a state of flux. Accordingly, it is hard to pin down many of the specifics of an African American way of perceiving and deploying violence. The dearth of documentary evidence makes the prospect all the more daunting. Still, recent preliminary work by John Thornton suggests that the rebels at Stono drew on military training acquired in Kongo as they engaged the South Carolina militia in their 1739 uprising. In a similar vein, Michael Gomez and Gwendolyn Midlo Hall have posited the continuation of Bambara warrior cults in Louisiana, an area where Bambara population was concentrated.[46] Other forms of violence such as poisoning, though less dramatic than the Stono Rebellion, also relied on older African models.

The English and Spanish brought their own cultures of violence to the colonial Southeast, forged in centuries of nearly ceaseless warfare between themselves and other Europeans, and shaped by previous colonial experiences in Ireland, West and West Central Africa, the Caribbean, and Central and South America. Until the close of the twentieth century, scholars did not really consider the cultures of violence of the various colonizing nations of Europe. This oversight is especially intriguing in light of how much it mattered to the English that they not replicate the atrocities of the Spanish Black Legend. Spanish, English, and Native peoples in the Southeast recognized the differences between their cultures of violence, and later historians have largely ignored this fact. Each of the various relevant cultures of violence will receive in-depth treatment in the pages that follow. Each contributed to the violence that shaped the colonial Southeast. Some scholars have focused on the changes in tactics or weaponry that occurred as different groups of people fought each other. The work which follows treats tactics sporadically because it is more concerned with the culturally specific meanings of violence, and the level of violence that various groups thought proper to employ in the Southeast. Rather than attempting to catalogue every single incident of violence that occurred in the Southeast from Mississippian times to the 1730s, *New Worlds of Violence* attempts to illuminate a few key episodes from each time period.

It may seem at first that the phrase "cultures of violence" is really nothing more than an unnecessarily elaborate way of describing war. Indeed, many of the events interpreted below would fall within the parameters of "war" to modern observers, but "war" and "peace" themselves are culturally specific notions, whose meaning can change over time and from group to group. Using "violence" between groups of people frees the work which follows to treat pitched battles as well as smaller-scale fights, raids, rape, and torture.

For every group in the Southeast, ideas about gender and violence were connected in some way. The most obvious example is that both European and indigenous men were expected to prove their masculinity through committing communally sanctioned acts of violence, and questioning a male enemy's masculinity was an insult that crossed cultural lines. Women could, and did, commit acts of communally sanctioned violence as well, though women's presence could also indicate peaceful intentions on the part of negotiators. As English men came to dominate the region and held larger numbers of Native American and African women in bondage, their sexual aggression toward such women provided another layer of complexity in the relationship between gender and violence.

The violence of the North American Southeast from 1500 to 1740 was not unique; other sites of colonialism and colonial violence existed before and after around the Atlantic world. The North American Southeast offers a fascinating backdrop for this colonial drama because of the diverse players involved, the Mississippian legacy, and the fact that the English mode of colonization born there was transported west rapidly through the eighteenth and into the nineteenth century.[47]

One of the well-worn stories of American history insists that English colonists were changed by their encounters with Native American warfare, so that when their cousins arrived from across the ocean to suppress their rebellion in the 1770s, they had combined European weaponry with Native American tactics to frustrate the efforts of the British to bring them to heel. A common approach in Native American history, less well known to laypeople, posits that Native Americans adopted English ways of war, and increased the intensity of their violence as their interaction grew more intense over the years of colonization.[48] There is something to be said for both of these perspectives, but *New Worlds of Violence* treats tactics only occasionally. I am more concerned with the ideas that informed the use of violence and the cultural connotations and implications of violence.

*New Worlds of Violence* is not the first book to consider the cultural connotations and implications of violence. In recent years a spate of books have appeared treating similar topics, though in different regions and different time periods: James Brooks's *Captives and Cousins*, Jill Lepore's *The Name of War*, Peter Silver's *Our Savage Neighbors*, Ned Blackhawk's *Violence over the Land*, and Karl Jacoby's *Shadows at Dawn* have informed *New Worlds of Violence* in various ways and to differing degrees, but all share one key assertion with the current undertaking.[49] Violent episodes from the North American past, even those that occurred a very long time ago, continue to resonate through the years, informing more recent historical developments and echoing into the present. Acts of violence can teach us about the peoples of the past, especially when we try to understand them from multiple perspectives—victim, perpetrator, onlooker, insider and outsider. Writing about violence is itself a part of long historical process. Karl Jacoby wrote in the introduction to *Shadows at Dawn,* a multi-sided account of the Camp Grant Massacre, that violence "often ends as a contest over meaning, as the participants struggle to articulate what has happened to them—and what they have, in turn, done to others."[50] In this sense, past American historical scholarship has compounded acts of physical violence with acts of rhetorical violence which have downplayed Native American and African American roles and reduced complex, historically contingent situations to morality plays about "Manifest Destiny" and "Westward Expansion."

## New Worlds of Violence

Edward Countryman interpreted America as a "collision of histories" in his 1996 book *Americans.* The term collision is particularly appropriate for the early modern Southeast. Cultures of violence collided in the region. As this occurred, community leaders interpreted events according to their own culturally specific ideas concerning violence. To borrow from James Merrell's and Colin Calloway's "New Worlds" idea—that colonization created "new worlds" for Europeans, Africans, and Native Americans—old, highly developed cultures of violence confronted and adapted to each other to form "new worlds of violence." In the years from the earliest Spanish forays into the region to the eventual—not inevitable—English domination of the region, various cultures of violence interacted and changed each other. Each group in the Southeast seemed to believe with George Rodd, South Carolina's future attorney general, who wrote during the Yamasee War in 1715 that the region was "worth the trouble of going to war to keep it."[51] By 1740, the English conquest was all but complete, and the twin English engines of trade and the plantation had drowned out other voices of violence.[52] African, Spanish, and Native cultures of violence still existed, but they were forced to move in circles defined by English plantations and trading houses.

The notion that the English conquered the Southeast may be discomfiting to some people. After all, any high school student knows that the Spanish came to the Americas as conquerors, the French came as traders and missionaries, and the English simply "settled." What could be more peaceful? Of course, each group of Europeans traded, each group sent colonists, and each committed acts of violence. The English conquered the Southeast as surely as the Spanish conquered the Aztecs. Of course, both of these conquests remained frustratingly incomplete from the conquerors' perspective, as Native peoples continued to carve out space in the various European empires. The English conquest looked somewhat different than its Spanish counterpart. It occurred later and relied on different tools, but by the 1740s, an Anglo-American culture of violence dominated the Southeastern seaboard and was poised to spread westward with white colonists.[53]

Each of the following chapters explores an important aspect of violence in the colonial Southeast. "Violence in the Mississippian World" traces the contours of the first cultures of violence in the ancient Southeast. "Spanish and Mississippian Violence" treats Spanish ideas about violence, examines how those ideas were put into practice, and shows how the towns of the Southeast responded to the Spanish threat. "The Fight for Florida" focuses on the events of 1565, the year in which the Spanish under Pedro Menéndez de Avilés and the French under Jean Ribaut engaged in a remarkably vicious fight for a foothold on the southeastern coast of North America. The next chapter, "Violence after the Entrada," shows how Native communities adapted their cultures of violence to suit the realities of repeated European incursions and demographic decline. In "Creating English Conquest," the English enter the narrative, and forge their own distinct culture of violence. "Violence and the Founding of English Carolina" follows that culture of violence across the Atlantic and shows how Native Americans dealt with the English from 1670 to the early 1700s. The penultimate chapter, "Violence in the Era of the Yamasee War," recasts the "Indian Wars" of the 1710s as contests between cultures of violence. "American Nations, American Violence," the book's concluding chapter, discusses the post–Yamasee War situation, the full-blown development of plantation slavery, and the long-term significance of the triumph of the Anglo-American culture of violence.

*New Worlds of Violence* ends in the aftermath of the Yamasee War. Indigenous people in the Southeast did not cease to resist the English at this time, but new forms of resistance were in the offing. Native Americans adopted some aspects of European culture; in this instance, the most important was the idea of the nation. When Creeks and Cherokees squared off against the United States, whether in battle or court, in the early part of the nineteenth century, they considered themselves nations. They had defined their nationhood in opposition to each other and the English; they had defined national territories, and they developed national histories which legitimized their nationhood.[54]

Looking back from Ocmulgee now, it is clear that both the Muskogees and the English used violence to establish themselves in the Southeast. Other recorded Creek oral histories confirm this fact. The Bartram legend, the Chekilli legend, and the Taskaya legend all mentioned the great violence that it took to establish the Creeks in the southeast. The Creeks saw themselves as a "powerful, warlike people," and by describing the English in similar terms, they placed themselves on an equal cultural footing. Having categorized the English as powerful and warlike, the Creeks opened the way for diplomacy, alliance, and, most importantly, trade between the two groups on their terms. The Chekilli legend is rife with supernatural and human violence on an epic scale. The Kasihtas' western migration is forced because "the earth became angry and ate up their children."[55] Red, the Creek color of war, appears repeatedly in the Chekilli legend. The Kasihtas come upon a "red, bloody river"; they witness a mountain emitting "red smoke"; they cover red poles with the scalps of slain enemies, noting that Kasihta, which had gathered the most, was the oldest.[56]

The Chekilli legend, red imagery notwithstanding, speaks of physical violence as well. The nations figure out which is the oldest by going to war. In an effort to kill a wild beast tormenting the Coosas, the Kasihtas use a motherless child as bait.[57] The legend also boasts of some conquests against people with flattened heads, in which the Kasihtas killed all but two villagers and, significantly, a white dog (white is the Muskogee color of peace). Eventually, they are persuaded by another group, the Apalachicolas, to lay down their arms.[58] The story concludes with Creeks and Georgians reaching a tenuous peace, but with the admission that "the Cussetaws first saw the red smoke, and the red fire, and make bloody towns, they cannot yet leave their red hearts, which are, however, white on one side and red on the other."[59] This refers to Coweta, a "red" town that broke off from Kasihta and crossed the Chattahoochee. After the speech concluded, the Creek delegation gave a version of the talk to the interpreter for Georgia, painted in red and black on a buffalo skin. The hide painting made its way to the Georgia colonial office in London, where it disappeared from the historical record.[60]

The version of the legend given to Benjamin Hawkins by Taskaya in 1798 is shorter, but still focuses on the role of violence in the origins of the Creeks. After the principal Creek towns chose which clans would lead them, "some other Indians came from the west, met them, and had a great wrestle with the three towns; they made ball sticks and played with them, with bows and arrows, and the war club. They fell out, fought, and killed each other."[61] After these hostilities subsided, as in the Chekilli legend, the Creek towns agreed to go to war against a common enemy for four years, counting the scalps accumulated to determine which would be the principal town. The next trial for the Kasihta people involved the flat-headed people, though in this particular legend, mounds factor in as well. The flat-headed people were "in possession of the mounds in the Cussetuh fields."[62] The Kasihtas attacked and took the mounds, and from that location moved out along the rivers of Georgia, including the Ocmulgee. The Creeks established themselves violently in the Southeast, and the English would do the same.

From Ocmulgee, William Bartram and the Creeks could look back on the violence that had helped establish both the Creek Confederacy and the English colonies of Georgia and South Carolina and use their versions of violence to inform their present and future. The legacy of this crucial period in American history reaches far beyond the initial forays of Europeans in the Southeast and their attendant Native responses. From a base of operations at Charles Town, the English came to control a wide swath of land to the west and southwest. Early conflict paved the way for the eventual English domination of an entire region. The forces that shaped society in the colonial Southeast, intercultural conflict, commercial conquest, and plantation conquest, would continue to shape lands far to the west, and far into the future.

# CHAPTER 1

# Violence in the Mississippian World

The history of violence in the Southeast does not begin with the arrival of Europeans in the sixteenth century. Europeans flattered themselves when they believed they had come across a primitive world inhabited by innately inferior non-Christians, ripe for conquest and exploitation. Equally flawed was the notion that native peoples inhabited an earthly paradise devoid of violent rivalries between communities. The people of the Southeast had organized themselves into sophisticated societies, capable of doing all the things that groups of people do. They engaged in trade over short and long distances, sometimes intermarried, conducted diplomacy, and, of course, went to war against one another. The role that violence played in eastern North America before Europeans arrived is still debated by scholars. Was warfare just one part of a larger competition between elite lineages and their associated communities for prestige and sacred power? Was violence an all-encompassing pursuit that raged through whole regions? The answer is more subtle than might be assumed. The communities of ancient North America were fully capable of committing acts of great violence against those they perceived as outsiders. They were equally capable of engaging in low-casualty raids or skirmishes to take captives, gain civil or religious prestige, or prove masculinity. In short, each community in the world we call Mississippian had its own set of rules governing intergroup conflict, its own culture of violence. Mississippian societies shared some basic characteristics, and probably a general group of ideas concerning violence, but recent archaeological work has gone a long way to dispelling the notion that the Mississippian world was culturally monolithic.

The most common word used to refer to these early American polities is "chiefdom." The word "chiefdom" is the product of a certain anthropological mindset that divided human societies according to their level of organization, from bands to states. According to this logic, chiefdoms were more complex than bands but less complex than states. The category of "chiefdom" is extremely broad when it comes to describing the lived experience of people. Chiefdoms also became something of a self-fulfilling prophecy in archaeological work. If scholars set out to find evidence of chiefdoms, many different kinds of artifacts could be used to prove that chiefdoms existed.[1] This chapter uses "chiefdom," "town," "community," and "polity" to describe Mississippian era political developments in recognition of the fact that the scholarly debate over what to call these developments is far from settled. Scholars also have disagreed over whether to use the term "state" to describe Cahokia and other major Mississippian centers. The study of violence may be instructive here. The theorist Max Weber noted that one of the characteristics of a state was its claim to a monopoly on the legitimate use of violence.[2] This was almost certainly the case at Cahokia, and it was likely the case at other Mississippian centers. In terms of the use of violence, there is no reason to doubt that Cahokia functioned as a state, though it may not meet other specific criteria in that regard according to those who care about such things.

A couple of interpretive issues have complicated our approach to Mississippian era America. First, most of the research has been done at large mound complexes, which may not have been representative of the full variety of the Mississippian world. Second, for a long time it was assumed that organizational complexity was a choice that any people would make, almost as a form of social evolution. According to this model, societies progress from simple bands, through chiefdoms, and arrive at the modern state. Recent research has complicated this notion considerably. In Mississippian America, for example, people who had been organized into chiefdoms may have chosen to decentralize. Also, chiefdoms could "cycle" local domination between them without making any substantive moves toward creating a state. Might native North Americans have taken a different path toward political development? Of course, but Europeans intervened and altered native America immeasurably.

## Violence at Cahokia

The Mississippian way of organizing people, planning towns, building monumental architecture, and even committing violence emerged at Cahokia, the first and largest Mississippian center. The elites at Cahokia planned and built their city in the fertile farmland along the Mississippi River across from present-day St. Louis. At Cahokia and in surrounding communities, sophisticated farmers accumulated large stores of food, built major earthworks, played a game called chunky, smoked tobacco from beautiful pipes, practiced a complex religion, created an elaborate government, and committed acts of violence.[3] The Cahokians left behind no written accounts of their achievements, but archaeologists, anthropologists, and modern historians, including those in native communities, have assembled a rich, if incomplete, understanding of what life at Cahokia was like. We know more about the world the Mississippians made at this point than at any time in the past. Unfortunately, scholars, native communities, and allied activists also find themselves in a race against time and tight budgets to preserve and investigate important sites that could fill in even more of the picture, as these places are in grave danger of being lost forever beneath urban sprawl and development.[4]

Though there had been large planned settlements in the heart of North America previously (Poverty Point, in Louisiana, for example), Cahokia eclipsed its predecessors with a period of explosive growth beginning around 1050. Timothy Pauketat, one of the leading scholarly interpreters of the site, refers to this date as Cahokia's "Big Bang."[5] It was around this time that the Cahokians built an enormous three-platform mound, today called Monks Mound, the site's most arresting visual feature. Resting on a base about the size of twelve football fields, Monks Mound towered approximately one hundred feet over the north end of an open ceremonial space, the Grand Plaza. Other plazas and more than one hundred other mounds flanked the Grand Plaza. Within a matter of decades, between ten thousand and sixteen thousand people lived in the core of the settlement, and thousands more inhabited the surrounding area, including related mound complexes near present-day St. Louis, Missouri, and East St. Louis, Illinois. By contrast, the next largest Mississippian town, Moundville, Alabama, which flourished later than Cahokia, featured a quarter as many mounds as Cahokia and a population one-fifteenth to one-twentieth the size of its predecessor.[6]

The Cahokians showcased human creativity and adaptability to a high degree, creating more than one hundred mounds. The earthworks were not randomly placed. Their layout and alignment clearly follow a plan. One recent treatment persuasively argued that the layout of the city itself reflected the world view of its planners, that Cahokia was in essence a "mirror of the cosmos" as Mississippians understood it.[7] In the vicinity of Monks Mound, archaeologists have unearthed evidence of "sun circles" or "woodhenges," which featured posts placed vertically in the ground and spaced evenly around a central pole, almost always in multiples of twelve.[8] Special classes of artists at Cahokia worked beads out of shells and fashioned brilliant pipes (see figure 1) and other ceremonial objects (see figure 2) using a variety of materials.[9] Both the Corn Mother effigy pipe and copper repoussé plate were produced at Cahokia during the height of its cultural influence but were found in distant locales, indicating two crucial facts about

**Fig. 1.** The Corn Mother effigy pipe, which dates to between 1100 and 1200 CE, relates to the Cahokian notion of the Under World and fertility. In this case, corn stalks grow out of the woman's outstretched hands and a sunflower lays across her back. Corn Mother is providing sustenance to her people. Courtesy of Kent Westbrook. Photograph by John Pafford.

**FIG. 2.** Birdman (the figure on the copper plate created between 1200 and 1300 CE) is related to the Upper World and takes a violent stance. He resembles a bird of prey, perhaps a falcon, wields a ceremonial mace, and carries a severed head. Both of these themes run throughout Cahokian art, though fertility themes are more prominent in the city's early years. This particular version of the Birdman appears on one of the Rogan plates, associated with Mound C at the Etowah Site. Photograph by D. E. Hurlbert. Catalog no. A91117. Courtesy of the Department of Anthropology, Smithsonian Institution.

Cahokia. First, that people moved special items great distances in ancient North America, and second, that Cahokia had a lasting influence in the Mississippian world which followed it.

Cahokian art contains violent imagery, like the Southeastern Mississippian art it prefigures. The copper plate in figure 2, one of a pair of artifacts called the Rogan Plates, references a culture hero known alternately as Birdman, Morning Star, or Red Horn. In various guises, some of which blur the distinction between men and falcons, and thus earn the sobriquet falcon-impersonator, this culture hero appears in many areas of ancient eastern America. He also predates Cahokia and appears on the Adena tablets, created between 400 BCE and 1 CE in Ohio.[10] Birds of prey have fascinated people of various epochs (witness the appropriation of the bald eagle by the early United States), and falcons were especially revered for their daring midair assaults that knocked their prey out of the sky for easier eating.[11] The copper plate was part of a leader's regalia at the Etowah site in northern Georgia, but it was fashioned at Cahokia. The artifact connects the person wearing it to the powerful Birdman at the same time as it contains some violent images or references to military matters. The most obvious is the fact that Birdman wields a ceremonial mace with one hand and holds a severed trophy head in the other; this could be a reference to some cosmic event, or it could be a not-so-subtle reference to the price of resisting chiefly authority. More subtle is the bilobed arrow headdress the figure wears. Scholars have offered various interpretations of the bilobed arrow, and, indeed, the symbol would have meant different things to different artists and communities; still, most of the ways of looking at the bilobed arrow, whether as a bow and arrow, an atlatl with its dart, or even as male genitalia, suggest a connection between masculinity, violence, and religious matters.[12]

Cahokian ideas about violence are both crucial to understanding later developments and extremely difficult to pin down with anything approaching precision. Mississippian religion had two distinct elements running through it, often in opposition to each other. The first of these was the Upper World, associated with structure, order, chiefly power, and violence. In contrast, Under World themes included fertility and agriculture.[13] In the early Southeast, many native peoples conceived of themselves as inhabiting This World, located between the Upper and Under Worlds. In This World, the trick was to maintain a balance between the orderly Upper World and the chaotic Under World.[14] Violence is a part of the orderly Upper World, not part of the chaotic Under World. Violence also might have been used to maintain balance between these worlds in a cosmic sense. The remains at Cahokia's Mound 72, described below, testify to the human price of the order that the Cahokians imposed on their most sacred site. The gender dynamics at play here may be recognizable to many students of Southeastern native America. Agriculture was almost always the exclusive province of women, while hunting, warfare, and associated activities were the domain of men. This division was played out repeatedly in the artistic expression of Cahokia and the Mississippians.

The nature and extent of Cahokia's power can provide hints to the culture of violence that the site's elites articulated in the years after 1050. Any history of violence and coercion is difficult enough to trace with documentary evidence, so conclusions based upon the Cahokian example must necessarily be tentative. Archaeologists have managed to combine some hard evidence with more speculative findings to paint an incomplete, though fascinating, picture of the role of violence in the rise of Cahokia after 1050. As Cahokia rose to prominence, it might seem that the communities closest to Cahokia would have suffered accordingly, as the lives of their people came increasingly under the influence of their rapidly growing neighbor. Contrary to that assumption, communities in the immediate vicinity of Cahokia experienced rapid transformation from autonomous villages to Mississippian-style towns with relatively little evidence of violent conquest. Life may not have gotten worse, and it may have gotten better as a result of Cahokia's influence over its hinterland. In fact, almost no hard evidence exists that Cahokia's armies conquered surrounding areas outright. Work at the Fred Edwards site in far southwestern Wisconsin has shown that the site was connected to Cahokia, providing that city with galena and deer and elk hides and receiving Cahokia-linked items, such as pots, in return. What evidence exists shows a mutually beneficial relationship with little to indicate violent subjugation.[15]

One of the most convincing explanations for the apparent lack of violence accompanying Cahokia's arrival on the scene lies in Cahokia's location. Cahokia got so big so quickly, and in such a well-chosen place, that taking on Cahokia directly must have been perceived as foolhardy. Greater Cahokia, which featured mound complexes on both sides of the Mississippi, controlled traffic and commerce on that most important artery, but not evidently too far beyond it, since canoes were the main means of water transport. Its positioning on trade routes also gave Cahokia an advantage in dealing with other polities that might have risen to challenge it.[16]

In the decades immediately following Cahokia's Big Bang, the city seems not to have constructed any kind of defensive wall. By contrast, many Mississippian towns in the later Southeast featured defensive walls during their ascents. The contrast is most clear with Moundville, which developed on Alabama's Black Warrior River in the decades after Cahokia. Moundville built a wall as it was rising. Once it dominated neighboring polities, it abandoned the wall, apparently confident in its security. Beginning about 1150, Cahokians built four walls around the city's center. These massive public works projects—one of which was three kilometers long and contained twenty thousand or so logs, complete with bastions—guarded the sacred space within from attack, by either outsiders or, perhaps, dissatisfied common Cahokians. One scholar has estimated that one of the defensive walls may have taken as many as 180,000 work hours to complete, and another has suggested that it probably took between two thousand and four thousand individuals working on the walls, though others, particularly those labeled Cahokian "minimalists," dispute these figures.[17] One of these minimalists, George Milner, has written that the palisade might have been constructed rather quickly, given that both elites and commoners at Cahokia would have received its protection.[18]

Since expansionist warfare played no significant role in the development of Cahokia, there is little in the way of violent iconography to be found from Cahokia's earliest phase. The theme of fertility features in many of the earliest pieces made at Cahokia. When Cahokia felt threatened by other regional powers, though, violent artistic imagery began to appear with increasingly regularity.[19] It was after 1100, for example, that the terrifying image of the Birdman was painstakingly hammered out of a copper sheet to produce the chief's regalia seen in figure 2. Both fertility and warfare themes are present, and indeed fertility and warfare-inspired art predate Cahokia, but fertility-themed works prevail in the years just after the Big Bang, and warfare-themed works prevail during the era in which Cahokia reached the height of its power and began to decline.

Cahokia was a religious center as well as a site of secular power, so taking on Cahokia directly might have been very difficult for people to conceive of doing, let alone execute. According to this viewpoint, Cahokia did not engage in widespread violence against its rivals because it did not have to, even though it might have been able to defeat nearby challengers quite easily.[20] There is some evidence that even after Cahokia began to decline in population, its leaders managed to keep their spiritual influence alive for several generations. In the meantime, though, people appear to have moved away from Cahokia.

It is possible that a "Pax Cahokiana" existed in the years of Cahokia's phenomenal rise. Cahokia's size and power, and perhaps its cultural significance, would have made it very difficult for other towns to challenge Cahokia's preeminence. Cahokia appears to have struck out against other sites upriver and downriver. Most of the violence was directed at places rather than people, and the evidence of attacks consists of burned town sites and houses.[21] Cahokia's army would have had an increasingly difficult time keeping the peace as its government fragmented or weakened through some other means in the years before 1200, and smaller rival chiefdoms could have emerged as military powers on a more regional scale. Sites in the Cairo Lowlands, though not as thoroughly studied as their Cahokian counterparts, built fortifications after the year 1100, perhaps indicating an increase in the mutual threat level between the Cairo Lowlands and Cahokia.[22] However, walls need not be interpreted as solely "defensive" in the traditional sense of the word. Well-protected cities required fewer defenders and might have freed up soldiers to attack enemies farther away from home, projecting a town's power in the process.[23] It is possible that these future smaller communities might have tried to suppress possible rivals in the same way that Cahokia had previously. Competition between towns, which could produce violence, was part of Cahokia's legacy to the Southeastern Mississippians of later generations.

In spite of the fact that violence played a minimal role in Cahokia's rise, Cahokia was a site of ceremonial violence, as evidenced by the findings at Mound 72. A ridgetop mound set off at an angle from the other surrounding earthworks, Mound 72 was excavated by Melvin Fowler, among others, in the late 1960s and early 1970s.[24] A prominent man was buried face up, laid out on a platform consisting of approximately twenty thousand drilled shell beads in the shape of a bird; another prominent man was buried face down beneath the beads, feet-to-head with the first burial, suggesting something of the dualism of Cahokian religious belief. Three men and three women, perhaps retainers who had been sacrificed, joined these powerful individuals in death. The grave goods associated with the burial were nothing short of astounding: twelve hundred exquisite arrowheads knapped from materials found at widely scattered sites throughout central North America, a sheet of rolled-up copper from the shores of Lake Superior, sheets of mica from North Carolina, and fifteen polished chunky stones. These rolling stones were at the center of a game played throughout much of eastern North America and may have had religious significance as physical artifacts that connected modern Native Americans to their Cahokian ancestors. Four men were buried nearby, all missing their heads and hands. Most striking of all was a nearby burial consisting of over fifty women, likely killed between their late teens and early twenties. Three more mass burials of women included more than sixty sets of remains in all. Subsequent analysis showed that Mound 72 was constructed in stages, and apparently, as succeeding generations of elite individuals died, their bones rested near those of their ancestors and were accompanied by human sacrifices on a scale unknown north of Mesoamerica. The women who were killed at Cahokia exhibited different sorts of dental features, indicating that they may have not been from Cahokia at all but perhaps from an outsider group whose leaders had offended Cahokia in some way or that the women were owed as tribute to Cahokia. The victims of such sacrifices may have been actors in moundtop dramas meant to teach religious lessons as well. The public nature of the killings suggests as much, and similar, better documented events were staged by other native North Americans, most notably in Mesoamerica. Violent imagery in Cahokian art, the inclusion of projectile points in elite burials, and the large number of likely human sacrifices would seem to indicate that violence served a ritual purpose, or at least that violence and Cahokian spirituality were connected in some way.[25] Mound 72–style violence was extremely rare in the centuries after Cahokia's dispersal, but human sacrifice was not unknown. In the Natchez chiefdom, which lasted into the era of French colonization, key relatives of prominent leaders joined those leaders in death. When a military leader named the Tattooed Serpent, the brother of the Great Sun, as Natchez leaders were known, passed away in 1725, eight people, including two of his wives, were sacrificed.[26]

Cahokia entered into a period of decline after maintaining its cultural dominance for just a few generations. Such appears to be the unstable nature of hereditary chiefdoms, in which many close relatives of leaders can vie for power, creating competition and factionalism.[27] There are any number of reasons that the site could have declined, dispersed, or fallen out of use. There may have been an environmental catastrophe or a prolonged series of lean agricultural years.[28] Leaders at Cahokia might have engaged in a disastrous public works plan that diverted nearby waterways and caused an unacceptable level of flooding.[29] It is also possible, to put it simply, that whatever had drawn people to Cahokia in the years around 1050 ceased to have the same effect on them, so they stopped coming or moved away. Some of them went north, where they adapted Mississippian ways to historical and environmental circumstances up the rivers that fed into the Mississippi. Small groups of Mississippians had been going south and southeast, too.[30] While these "missionaries" probably did not rely too heavily on Cahokian military might, they did spread Cahokian ideas, including the proper role of ordinary men and women as well as elites, the game of chunky, and certain forms of maintaining influence through violence or the threat of violence.

Cahokia did commit acts of violence, such as the mass killings at Mound 72, but there is also plenty of evidence that indicates that Cahokia did not *dominate* its neighbors in the sense that that term is usually understood. Violence was one aspect of Cahokia's rise, but the efficacy of Cahokian religion and the desire of nearby groups to contribute to Cahokia could also be used to explain its rise. Cahokia's elites committed strategically planned acts of violence aimed at maintaining their influence, perhaps punishing subordinates who had gotten out of line, as a function of Cahokia's religion or even as a brutal reminder of who was in charge. A certain culture of violence was part of Cahokia's legacy to the later towns of the Southeast, but it should not be understood as the sum total of Cahokia's legacy. Later Mississippian towns in the Southeast would follow this example. They did commit acts of violence, and may have even existed in constant tension with one another, but violence was only one of the ways in which they interacted and should not be considered a defining feature of Mississippian life.

## Violence after Cahokia

Conclusions about Mississippian violence after Cahokia rest on somewhat more solid ground than those about early Mississippian violence. In one sense, this is literally true, as the moist, heavy soils in the Mississippi River valley are crushing artifacts and remains from Cahokia. More important, though, post-Cahokia Mississippian life lasted for a longer time, from 1100 to 1700 in some places, and over a wider terrain. Finally, Mississippian forms of violence survived into the time period for which historical documentation is available. The written record pertaining to Mississippian violence figures more prominently in the next chapter, however, while the remainder of this chapter relies more on archaeology and treats the diversity of Mississippian cultures of violence after Cahokia. It is also important to note that while actual Cahokian power may not have extended over a huge territory, Cahokian ideas, including a Cahokian culture of violence, did exert influence over a considerably wider area.

Mississippian centers were usually near waterways to capitalize on maize-growing potential, and they included mounds, but these facts alone aren't enough to distinguish them from their predecessors. Their size is crucial in setting them apart from other developments. Mississippian towns were not just larger than other polities in their vicinity, they dwarfed them.

Archaeologists consider some Southeastern Mississippian sites, such as Ocmulgee, mentioned in the Introduction, to be site intrusions, meaning that Mississippians moved into an area, designed a town, usually from the central plaza outward, and began to practice what they remembered from their Mississippian hometowns with modifications to suit them or their environment. For Ocmulgee, this may have happened around 1100, when

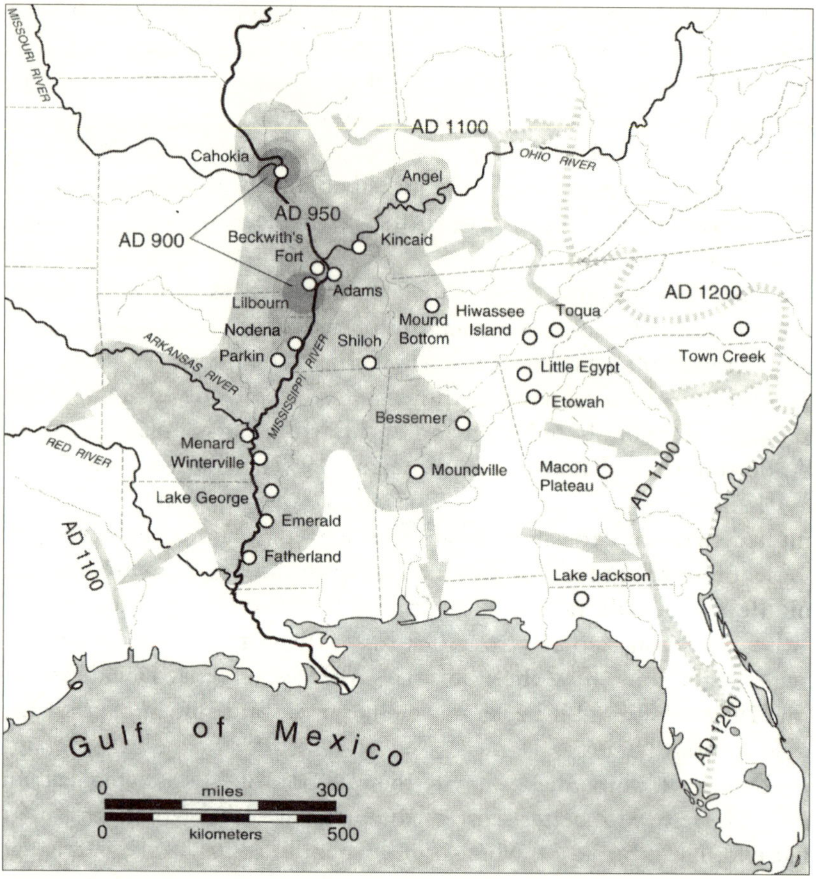


**Map 1.** By 1100, Mississippianism had spread east to present-day Georgia, west through what is now Louisiana into Texas and Oklahoma, and up the Ohio River valley into Indiana. By 1200, the end of the Pax Cahokiana, communities in the Carolinas, Florida, and Ohio reflected Mississippian influence. From Timothy Pauketat, *Chiefdoms and Other Archaeological Delusions*, 88, courtesy of Altamira Press and David G. Anderson.

migrants, probably from what is now eastern Tennessee, settled near the Ocmulgee River and constructed a plaza and platform mounds, the heart of today's Ocmulgee National Monument. Other Mississippian-inspired features include elaborate mortuary practices for elites and a striking bird design in the floor of what was likely a council house.[31] In other places, preexisting communities might have borrowed Cahokian ideas, including ideas about violence, as they accepted missionaries from Cahokia bearing stories and fantastic objects to explain those stories, demonstrated in part by the discovery of the objects like those in figures 1 and 2 far from the place they were made.

Most Mississippian societies combined floodplain agriculture of beans and maize with foraging and hunting. In fact, since Cahokia came of age as a maize-producing behemoth, the ideas it spread about fertility and violence might have been readily adaptable to other societies that were situated in similar places, such as the fertile agricultural lands along the river systems of the Southeast. The practice of corn agriculture was by no means universal, and some Mississippians varied their dependence on corn or did not grow it at all. Even in places like this, the long-term effects of a broadly Mississippian culture of violence could be felt. Mississippians in Oklahoma and western Arkansas—the Caddoan peoples associated with the Spiro archaeological site—did not rely as heavily on corn as other Mississippians but created and collected some of the most striking examples of early American art with violent imagery.[32] On the peninsula of Florida, the stratified and militarily effective Calusa chiefdom—who defeated Juan Ponce de León's 1521 expedition, killing him in the process—developed wholly without the benefits of agriculture.[33] All of this speaks to the diversity of Mississippian life.

The mound centers at Spiro, Moundville, Etowah, Ocmulgee, and elsewhere inherited many things from Cahokia or similarly designed sites. Sometimes the inheritance was physical. Spiro, for example, exchanged ritual gifts with Cahokia for multiple generations, and many items of Cahokian manufacture have turned up in Oklahoma. The cultural and ideological legacy of Cahokia is harder to trace, but some case studies demonstrate that there was not a single legacy but multiple legacies. Mississippian communities that came after Cahokia share some broad design principles and aspects of religion, but each town interpreted Cahokia in a way that made sense to it.

Etowah, in northern Georgia, may have turned to Mississippian-style governance as a way to break a cycle of chaotic violence. As corn agriculture spread into the region, groups fought one another for access to the most productive land. Rather than a single polity winning out and dominating the others, though, several smaller groups made alliances to bring the hostilities to a stop. The result was the Etowah chiefdom. The mounds at Etowah, rather than being an act of top-down coercion, might have been constructed as an act of community. They stood as a testament to the successful avoidance of large-scale violence. Of course, this did not preclude Etowah from using violence against people its elite perceived as outsiders, or otherwise exploiting neighbors to aggrandize its ruling elite. If this scenario is accurate, then the Mississippian culture of violence in use at Etowah, which probably sanctioned some forms of violence but forbade others, was a boon to the people it protected and vastly preferable to the chaotic violence of the Etowah River valley before the development of the Mississippian-style chiefdom there. The rise of Etowah did not end violence in the area completely, and by 1375 Etowah's neighbors were sufficiently fed up and powerful enough to destroy the capital. The burial record indicates that the last defenders of Etowah buried marble statues of chiefly ancestors and other sacred goods before they themselves were killed. The site was not reoccupied until just before Hernando de Soto's arrival, and his chroniclers referred to it as Itaba, a tributary of the paramount center at Coosa.[34]

A similar situation obtained at Moundville, on the Black Warrior River in Alabama. Moundville was the largest Mississippian town after Cahokia, and it consolidated quickly starting in about 1225, which archaeologists have labeled the beginning of the Moundville II phase.[35] The town was planned over the top of a previous Mississippian center and featured nearly thirty mounds, laid out in a way which attempted to establish a hierarchy of clans. All of the clans were subordinate to the chiefdom itself, whose dominance was expressed in the colossal Mound B.[36] As with Cahokia previously, people moved to Moundville and set up productive farms in its vicinity. Unlike Cahokia, Moundville featured a wall from its earliest expansion. As large as Moundville was, and as impressive as its wall might have been, its ability to enforce tributary relationships over its neighbors was limited. It could conduct small-scale wars until the offending polity performed the rituals required to make peace. No major Mississippian centers existed in the area immediately adjacent to Moundville, but other towns were present, and these appear to have functioned in a semiautonomous fashion. Thus Moundville may not have exercised direct control but may have spread its ideas through strategic acts of violence. It could have influence over neighboring polities without ever needing to directly conquer them.[37]

Thanks to the site's pillaging by looters in the 1930s, our record of the polity at Spiro, in far eastern Oklahoma, is incomplete. We will never know how many artifacts were sold off by the Pocola Mining Company between 1933 and 1935, when this disreputable organization ripped through Craig Mound, sometimes breaking apart items to sell their pieces separately. Another entire volume could be dedicated to the violence done by some citizens of the United States to Native American artifacts. What the Pocola Mining Company found and sold was probably the greatest assemblage of Mississippian warfare-related art in North America. The mound site at Spiro, which apparently converted to Cahokian-style religion and government, experiencing its peak between 1250 and 1450, was not the same kind of large chiefdom as existed at Moundville. Its relatively small population tended what some archaeologists have come to regard as primarily a ceremonial center containing hundreds of pounds of ceremonial objects in what is now called the Great Mortuary, including some of the most exquisite depictions of violence in Mississippian art. Local leaders could, and did, modify the teachings of Cahokia to their specific historical and environmental circumstances.[38]

Recent archaeological studies have improved our understanding of the Mississippian world, and the violence practiced there, dramatically. From Mississippian centers and peripheral towns and farmsteads throughout the Southeast, the picture that is emerging is a diverse one. Like their modern-era counterparts, Mississippian governments could sanction occasional acts of mass violence, engage in extremely limited raids with extremely limited goals (down to the individual level of masculinity and war prestige), and engage in a whole range of behaviors in between. One widely held assumption about chiefly violence is in need of revision. If chiefdoms were as inherently violent as the Soto expedition chroniclers would have us believe, one might expect to find widespread evidence of large-scale violence. The problem is that such evidence does not exist.

Between 1400 and 1600, two Mississippian cultures, Mouse Creek and Dallas, existed in close proximity to each other in the Tennessee River Valley. Dallas was a ranked chiefdom, with a well-defined community plan, mounds, and clear elite and common mortuary practice. Mouse Creek towns were palisaded, with open community space but with a slightly more egalitarian distribution of grave goods. Based on the assumptions that guide much of our understanding of what it meant to be Mississippian, plenty of signs of violent death should be present. One could argue that the more centralized polity should be the more violent one. Another might counter by citing the kind of chaotic violence that led to consolidation at Moundville and Etowah, noting that less organized polities might be expected to be less violent. Close analysis of skeletal remains at the sites fail to bear out either hypothesis. Without a doubt, people committed acts of violence in Mississippian eastern Tennessee. There were blunt force traumas and projectile points embedded in some skulls in the sample, as well as evidence of scalping. But, significantly, there were no multiple burials, which might indicate ambushes, massacres, or other large-scale episodes of combat. Instead, the towns engaged in small-scale raids to purposes of trophy taking, and people within each culture occasionally fought against each other.[39]

Much of the research on the Mississippian world has focused on the largest sites. To be sure, Cahokia, Moundville, Etowah, and other such places were impressive, and many retain their capacity to awe a millennium after their construction. But most people did not live in mound complexes, and intensive study of just the largest polities risks skewing our picture of how most people experienced life, and violence, during this time period. Studies from smaller sites, while they do not lend themselves to pacifist Utopian interpretations, do call into question the nature of Mississippian hierarchy and, by extension, Mississippian violence. A mound site in western Kentucky is instructive. At Annis Mound on the Green River, a clear hierarchy existed. Certain elites lived on the mounds, for instance. Yet archaeological evidence shows that these elites were engaged in many of the same activities of their less notable neighbors. The implications for violence are not well documented, but it seems to follow logically that people who interacted on a relatively egalitarian basis might have trouble ordering others into combat for prestige goods or sacrificing them for religious reasons or to increase political clout.[40]

Town Creek in North Carolina, another late Mississippian site, exhibits similar features. Town Creek features a single platform mound and thus fits the description of a small Mississippian polity. Elites were treated differently at death than commoners, and some were buried with objects connected to military struggle, such as projectile points and copper axes. Edmond Boudreaux, the site's leading interpreter, has written that in the last years of Town Creek, leadership roles appear to have fallen to younger and younger men. Even in a site where there is a clear enough connection between young men and violence, though, the people of Town Creek did not replicate the hierarchy of other Southeastern sites. There were clearly elites and commoners at Town Creek, but the elites weren't *that* elite. In this way, Town Creek may represent a more egalitarian culture of violence than is commonly assumed about Mississippians.[41]

A brief analysis of power and tribute can provide some insight into one of the ways that violence or even the threat of violence functioned in the sixteenth-century Southeast. According to anthropologist David Dye, "*Force* is direct physical action, exerted only in proportion to its availability and consumed in its application. *Power,* on the other hand, operates indirectly and is not consumed in use."[42] In the Southeast, paramount chiefdoms that could command tribute and labor from outlying towns could conserve their own local resources while still maintaining their dominant status. Often, one chiefdom would use force to establish a tributary relationship over another, but once this relationship was established, the threat of actual warfare lessened. The relationship between the chiefdoms of Coosa and Napochies, in northern Georgia and eastern Tennessee, drives this point home. In 1560, Coosa and Spanish forces combined to resubjugate

Napochies. Under the new arrangement, Napochies had to provide "game, fruits, and nuts to Coosa."[43] Warfare was not endemic to Southeastern Mississippian society, but relations between chiefdoms were often tense.

One stereotype about Mississippian chiefdoms is that these were totally hierarchical societies dominated by men. The implications for violence are pretty clear. According to this view, the men on top of the mounds could order people to do their bidding and commit acts of violence. A better understanding of the diversity of Mississippian forms indicates that not all Mississippian towns functioned in this way. Women could hold positions of influence and power, for instance. The "Lady of Cofitachequi," a female cacique from what is now upstate South Carolina, features prominently in the records of the Soto expedition. Further, the power of elites was not all-encompassing in most places in the Mississippian world. Some scholars have proposed heterarchy, a system in which power is spread horizontally among various groups according to gender, age, and other factors, as an alternative to the top-down social organization commonly associated with Mississippianism.[44] The Mississippian world is big enough for both interpretations. Relatively egalitarian social relations could have been the order of the day at smaller settlements, while strict hierarchy according to lineage might have governed the larger sites. The cultures of Mississippian violence could vary accordingly, as individual leaders at small settlements could engage in small-scale skirmishes to enhance their prestige and the leaders of larger polities could put together more elaborate campaigns of the sort that toppled the chiefdom at Etowah.

One popular theory about Mississippian warfare holds that Mississippians fought primarily for access to scarce resources, most likely in the form of arable land. According to Lewis Larson Jr., the most sought-after lands in the Mississippian Southeast were alluvial valleys near forested uplands. Chiefdoms developed in these diverse environments, and rival groups competed for the best ones. Individual chiefdoms struggled to hold on to their ideal environments by constructing defensive fortifications, and the object of most offensive Mississippian warfare was to take the town that controlled the land, thereby gaining access to it.[45] According to this model of Mississippian conflict, "warfare seems to have been essentially an adaptive mechanism whereby the pressure generated by an increasing population was relieved either by predatory expansion or a large number of deaths."[46] Written in an era before it was widely known that complex, hierarchical chiefdoms could exist outside of floodplains, Larson's argument can be forgiven some oversights. Still, it smacks of ecological determinism and fails to account for the fact that large swaths of potentially productive farmland were abandoned by the late Mississippian period, while chiefdoms continued to prosper in adjacent areas.[47]

A deeper understanding of Mississippian culture allowed for a more complex portrait of the causes of conflict between chiefdoms, and Jon L. Gibson, writing in 1974, argued for a psychological interpretation of warfare. Many Mississippian societies were ranked, and success or failure in combat was a major factor in determining a lineage's fortunes. Moreover, over generations, one's ties to major chiefs, particularly if he was not a blood relative, weakened considerably. Offensive combat could have served, in Gibson's words, "as a principal equilibrium-regulating institution through which cancellation of status deterioration . . . might have been achieved."[48] The real motivations for Mississippian combat probably fall somewhere between the ecological (materialist) and psychological (idealist) approaches put forward by Larson and Gibson, respectively. Bruce Dickson reached this compromise in a 1981 synthesis.[49] David Anderson, working on the Savannah River chiefdoms, has moved beyond this earlier debate in some significant ways. He sees warfare, or its constant threat, as part of ongoing competition among factions of rival elites. Elite rivalry over territory, tribute, and trade fed a larger "cycling" process through which some paramount chiefdoms held sway only to be usurped by others.[50]

There are a number of ethnohistorical clues as to Mississippian motivations for going to war or engaging in other, less drastic forms of intercultural violence. In Arkansas in June 1541, the longstanding rivalry between the chiefdoms Casqui and Pacaha erupted into violence and resulted in Casqui and the Soto expedition allying against Pacaha. According to one Soto account, Casqui "and his parents, grandparents, and ancestors for many centuries had war with the lord and lords of another province, called Capaha, which bordered upon his own."[51] Historical rivalries and revenge certainly played important roles in why Mississippians chose to fight. Such an explanation does not preclude the fact that some chiefdoms expanded at the expense of others. The Savannah River chiefdoms, for instance, were essentially squeezed into tributary status by the larger polities of Cofitachequi and Ocute (in Georgia).[52]

Many fragments of documentary evidence point to warfare as a method of exacting tribute from a neighboring chiefdom. The female leader at Cofitachequi, a Mississippian chiefdom in South Carolina visited by Soto's army in the spring of 1540, sent one of her subordinates to a neighboring town to "to execute justice on certain of the principal men under command of the ruler who had rebelled against her and kept the tribute."[53] At Chicaça, one chief complained to Soto that "one of his vassals had risen against him, withholding his tribute, and asked that he protect him against him, saying that he was about to go to seek him in his land and punish him as he deserved."[54]

These sorts of tributary arrangements were historically contingent, not timeless. Soto's secretary recorded an argument between the aforementioned *caciques* Pacaha and Casqui: "Pacaha told Casqui: 'You know well that I am a greater lord than you and of more honored parents and grandparents.' Casqui responded thus: 'It is true that you are a greater lord than I, and your ancestors were greater than mine. . . . Notwithstanding, you know well that I am older and more than a match for you, and I confine you in your palisade whenever I want, and you have never seen my land.'"[55] Even accounting for the bias of the source, it seems clear that shifting rivalries were a fact of life in the late Mississippian Southeast.

In another example, drawn from reminiscences of the 1559–61 Tristán de Luna y Arellaño expedition, the chiefdom of Napochies ceased paying tribute to nearby Coosa and for a time may have supplanted Coosa as a paramount center. According to Agustín Dávila Padilla's account,

> In ancient times the Napochies were tributaries of the Coza people, because this place (Coza) was always recognized as the head of the kingdom and its lord was considered to stand above the one of the Napochies. Then the people from Coza began to decrease while the Napochies were increasing until they refused to be their vassals, finding themselves strong enough to maintain their liberty which they abused. Then those of Coza took to arms to reduce the rebels to their former servitude, but the most victories were on the side of the Napochies. Those from Coza remained greatly affronted as well from seeing their ancient tribute broken off, as because they found themselves without strength to restore it.[56]

When the Spanish returned to the area under explorer Juan Pardo later in the 1560s, Coosa had regained its paramount status.[57] Power plays might begin with something as simple as the withholding of tribute and could lead to outright warfare between the two groups.

Scholars have placed great emphasis on the movement of prestige goods and the role that warfare may have played in the transfer of these goods from town to town around the Mississippian world.[58] One interpretation, which posits that chiefdoms were generally unstable, insists that warfare (an external form of competition) and factional contests for chiefly supremacy (an internal form of competition) were constantly reshaping government in Mississippian towns. As John Blitz put it, "Mound centers were created, abandoned, and reoccupied in a pattern that suggested frequent polity formation, movement, or collapse."[59] Like David Anderson and David Hally, Blitz places warfare at the center of these political changes.

Analysis of skeletal trauma has also broadened our understanding violence in the Mississippian World. At some sites, such as at Norris Farms 36 in west-central Illinois, trauma to remains indicates a long period of tension, with individuals or small groups of people suffering violent deaths. This is consistent with long-term, low-level intergroup violence.[60] We should be careful not to assume that this situation existed in every Mississippian setting, though. Mary Lucas Powell's research at Moundville indicates that elites and commoners suffered similarly low levels of trauma. Surprisingly, elite men, who might be expected to injure themselves in battle, had fewer fractures than their non-elite counterparts.[61] Someone choosing to argue that early American polities were extraordinarily violent could counter the above examples by pointing to Crow Creek. This site, in modern South Dakota, demonstrates that village-wide, all-encompassing violence was not unknown. At Crow Creek, most of a village's occupants were slaughtered by attackers, as evidenced by 486 skeletons hastily buried in a pit.[62] This kind of thoroughgoing violence was rare in the Mississippian Southeast, until it was employed by Europeans in the 1500s.

If Cahokian religion, and later Mississippian religions, connected violence and the Upper World, how did this manifest itself in Mississippian artwork? The Cahokia-inspired violent imagery outlived that chiefdom's dispersal and lasted for generations after its decline. Native southeasterners continued to produce exquisite shell gorgets, some of which portrayed scenes of great violence. Consider the gorget in figure 3, created sometime between 1250 and 1350 in the Tennessee River Valley. The figure on the gorget wields a ceremonial mace and carries a severed head. The forked-eye motif connects the figure to the falcon imagery that appears regularly in Mississippian art. There are multiple ways to interpret the scene. This image might be a reminder of the cost of disobedience in a hierarchical society. Or rather than referencing an actual beheading, this might be a representation of mythic or cosmic event. Whether this depicts an actual beheading or a mythic one, there is some connection between violence and religion etched into the shell. The figure's headdress and swastika-like pose imbue the piece with a kind of spiritual power and dynamism. Though usually shown so the figure's head is at the top, the effect is heightened when the piece is shown as it would have been worn as an insignia of rank; now the central figure is flying through the air, which lends weight to the notion that this is no ordinary form of chiefly discipline. This particular gorget was one of five discovered with a single elite burial in Tennessee.[63]

**Fig. 3.** Shell gorget from Castalian Springs site, Tennessee River Valley, 1250–1350. Courtesy of the National Museum of the American Indian, Smithsonian Institution.

Warfare-related imagery, such as the shell gorget in figure 3, is one part of a group of visual motifs sometimes referred to as the Southeastern Ceremonial Complex. Archaeologists first posited the existence of the complex in the 1930s and applied the label to a wide range of themes that were common to artifacts found in various locales throughout the Southeast. Over the intervening seven decades, scholars have expanded the core definition of the Southeastern Ceremonial Complex, and some have even argued that the concept has outlived its usefulness, having gotten too broad.[64] When trying to identify a theme like violence in Mississippian art, one could get the impression, for instance, that since warfare-themed prestige goods appear throughout the Southeast, the people of that region were particularly violent or obsessed with warfare. The archaeological evidence does not bear out that assertion. It would be safer to say that certain elites at certain Mississippian sites did connect warfare and spirituality and that elites of those sites fought against other elites in contests for these sacred items. In doing so, some Mississippians may have been attempting to reenact the events of cosmic violence that featured prominently in their art.[65] But these developments should not be perceived to be timeless. In the case of Birdman iconography at Etowah, skilled analysis has indicated that as the elites at Etowah attempted to set up a dynasty, the Birdman motif played a prominent role. Shifting political realities prompted a move away from this violent imagery.[66]

Archaeologist Vernon James Knight Jr., eschewing both the concept of the Southeastern Ceremonial Complex and the Southern Cult idea that it replaced, has proposed a new way of looking at Mississippian religion.[67] Knight's work focuses on three iconic families, or groups of sacred objects bearing similar images and meanings. The three iconic families are temple statuary, the platform mounds themselves, and, tellingly, warfare/cosmogony—the group of sacred images formerly called the Southeastern Ceremonial Complex or the Southern Cult.[68] Warfare was a part of Mississippian life and world view, and sacred art objects often depict stylized weapons of war, including axes, swords, maces, and arrowheads. These objects also point to a connection between warfare and social stratification, as they are almost always associated with the burials of elites and paramount chiefs. Mississippians apparently connected their paramount chiefs to the supernatural forces that brought success in warfare.[69]

The warfare/cosmogony cult survived in an altered form into the period of colonization. On one hand, the imagery of this cult was no longer associated exclusively with a class of warrior-chiefs; some of its motifs appear on pottery. Still, certain elements—serpents, for instance—remained tied to community elites as they had during Mississippian times. William Bartram, in his *Travels,* describes a Muskogee council house, noting that "the pillars supporting the front or piazza of the council-house of the square, were ingeniously formed in the likeness of vast speckled serpents, ascending upward."[70]

Mississippian warfare and religious belief intersected in other crucial ways, though the details of the relationship remain blurred at this great remove. Some of the major symbols of Mississippian religion, including the falcon-impersonator and the forked-eye, both of which appear as motifs on sacred objects found throughout the Southeast, have been associated with warfare, both in before and during the era of European colonization. The falcon in particular may have "served as the model for the Cherokee Tlanuwa, which killed men with their sharpened beaks."[71] The falcon was revered by Southeastern Indians above other birds; it struck quickly, attacking enemy birds in flight, no matter their size.[72]

Most of the examples in this chapter have come from what archaeologists call the Middle Mississippian period, so the question remains: what sort of cultures of violence were present in 1500, on the eve Spanish colonization? The best answer is that there were many different cultures of violence. Some were elite, wherein the drive to control high-quality items, many of which were imbued with sacred significance, drove small groups of elites and followers into conflict with one another. Others were more broad, and it was not unheard of for entire towns to participate in conflict against other towns. The object was rarely to erase other towns entirely but was more often to reduce a town to tributary status. Finally, some towns, particularly those more egalitarian places that lacked the more rigid hierarchy associated with the big Mississippian centers, did not fit neatly into either category. In these places, groups of young men could travel abroad to seek war honors and prestige in a culture of violence which would come to dominate much of the Southeast. So on the eve of European colonization in the Southeast, many different cultures of violence were on display, but all probably owed some debt to the world of the Mississippians.

The ethnohistorical technique of upstreaming (inferring the presence of certain traits because such traits exist in later groups), if applied cautiously, can give great insight into the last Mississippian cultures of violence. David Dye, noting that many modern native nations in the Southeast featured a division between Red (war) and White (peace) factions, has scoured the evidence from the late Mississippian world and determined that modern nations based their organizations on a long-established duality between peace and war. Though the Mississippians might not have used the same terminology, the archaeological evidence seems to indicate a dual sort of political organization in which younger men participated in guerrilla warfare, quick raids and strikes against enemies and the like, while older men participated in warfare-related rituals whose purpose was more diplomatic than anything else. Principal war chiefs in the Mississippian world held the kind of power necessary to orchestrate the kinds of military maneuvers on display in the resistance to Soto and other Spanish expeditions.[73] Late Mississippian societies maintained a hierarchical military structure: the chain of command was supported by war councils and the priests of the cult of war. Individual warriors reported to captains, members of the lower elite rungs, whose actions were determined by chiefs, council members, and priests.[74]

Late Mississippian warfare featured the use of bows and arrows to great effect.[75] Álvar Núñez Cabeza de Vaca noted that he had "seen the strength and skill with which they shoot them, because I myself saw an arrow in the base of a poplar tree that had entered it to the depth of a *xeme* [the distance between the tip of the thumb and the tip of the outstretched index finger]."[76] Cabeza de Vaca probably exaggerated when he claimed that "they can shoot arrows at two hundred paces with such great skill that they never miss their target," but Mississippian archers' accuracy was remarkable; during the battle at Mabila, for instance, Soto removed more than twenty arrows from Rodrigo Rangel's quilted cotton armor, and many of the wounded there had received multiple arrow wounds.[77]

Mississippian towns could field well-organized forces capable of multidirectional attacks against their adversaries. At Chicaça, Soto's army came under attack "at the quarter of the modorra [second, or sleepy, watch]." The native attackers came "in four companies, each company coming from a different direction." The element of surprise was important, but "as soon as they were perceived, they beat a drum and with loud cries rushed forward." They also set fire to half the houses of the town in which the Spanish were lodged. This particular battle, in the winter of 1540–41, cost the Spanish army dearly: eleven soldiers and fifty horses perished.[78] The following spring, Indians again attacked in squadrons, "each company coming from a different direction."[79]

Spanish accounts also provide clues about the preparation for conflict in the late Mississippian world. In the spring of 1541, Chicaça Indians positioned themselves atop a stockade to battle the Spanish. According to one chronicle, the men were "daubed over with red ochre and with their bodies, legs, and arms painted black, white, yellow, and red, in the manner of stripes which made them look as though they were in breeches and doublet. Some had feather plumes on their heads and others horns, with their faces black and the eyes ringed round in red in order to look more ferocious."[80] Rodrigo Rangel, Soto's secretary, described an earlier incident in which Soto's army came upon "twenty Indians painted red (which is a certain red ointment that the Indians put on when they go to war or wish to make a fine appearance), and they wore many plumes and carried their bows and arrows."[81] The color red, later associated with warfare among many natives of the Southeast, had deep roots.

Like the Spanish fighting men they opposed in the sixteenth century, Mississippian warriors were not technically professional soldiers. Neither society set civilian and military roles apart in a strict sense. Mississippians were farmers and hunters above all else, though they used bows and arrows for both hunting and combat. Their skill with the weapons indicates that they trained from a young age. While Mississippian men used the bow and arrow for both hunting and warfare, their other major weapon, the war club, was exclusively used in hand-to-hand combat. Several different varieties of clubs existed, and they ranged from simple hickory clubs to elaborately decorated weapons that may have been reserved for higher-status individuals. Head trauma and fractures are commonplace among victims of interpolity violence, probably as the result of being on the receiving end of a war club's blow. The war club was also a major symbol of war for Mississippians; stylized copper, stone, and mica clubs—all useless in combat—have been found at elite burials throughout the Southeast.[82] The symbolism of the war club lasted past Mississippian times into the era of English colonization. Writing around the turn of the eighteenth century, John Lawson described a dance performed in the Carolina backcountry: "Presently in came fine Men dress'd up with Feathers, their Faces being covered with Vizards made of Gourds; round their Ancles and Knees, were hung Bells of several sorts, having Wooden Falchions in their Hands, (such as Stage-Fencers commonly use;) in this Dress they danced about an Hour, shewing many strange Gestures, and brandishing their Wooden Weapons, as if they were going to fight each other."[83]

Beyond the physical aspects of combat lay the sacred considerations of intergroup violence. In Florida, European chroniclers witnessed something of the spiritual nature of sixteenth-century warfare. When one powerful leader, Saturiwa, prepared for battle in 1564, he

> turned his face toward the direction of his enemies to threaten them with death. He also looked toward the sun, praying for glorious victory over his enemies. Having done these things for at least a half hour, he sprinkled water from his hands over the heads of the chiefs. . . . Furiously he threw the rest of the water on a fire which had been made for this purpose. . . . According to one of the Indians this ceremony signified that Satouriona [Saturiwa] begged the sun to give him victory and happiness so that he could scatter the blood of his enemies as he had scattered the water at his pleasure. Moreover it besought that the chiefs who were sprinkled . . . might return with the heads of their enemies, which is the greatest and only measure of their victory.[84]

Even through the filter of European biases about Native Americans, it is clear that warfare in the sixteenth-century Southeast was not undertaken lightly and that certain rituals were to be performed to help ensure success in battle. Those rituals certainly varied from group to group, but no people in the Southeast went to war without careful ritual preparation.[85]

Earthly warfare, as a reflection of cosmic combat between order and chaos, was not undertaken carelessly. Men underwent dramatic rituals to purify themselves before fighting; these often included prolonged fasts followed by ceremonial feasts, abstinence from sex, sleep deprivation, and physical separation from the community. In addition, they took special potions and used sacred objects to prepare for combat.[86]

The rituals of combat and their associated paraphernalia have yielded a depiction of Mississippian violence that provides earthly concerns such as access to labor and surplus resources with a spiritual backdrop. The exact nature of the connection between mythic violence and actual violence remains dimly understood, but it is clear that human warriors in This World tried to emulate the actions of cosmic warriors in the Upper World.

Elaborate preparations such as the ones described above, whether performed in plazas in the center of Mississippian towns or in sex-segregated ceremonies on the outskirts of town, were not easy to keep secret. Matthew Restall has argued that a highly ritualized Mexica culture of war, with time-consuming mass ceremonies, precluded the element of surprise in that state's resistance to the Spanish invasion.[87] Though Mississippian era native communities clearly valued the ritual aspects of warfare, they valued the element of surprise as well. Thus rituals could be performed before setting out on military campaigns, such as the Timucuans did in the example above, and not interfere with the overwhelming desire to surprise one's enemies. In the case of Saturiwa, once the necessary ceremonial steps had been taken, the party arrived in its enemies' territory around sunset the night before the planned assault. By dawn, five war leaders had moved along the river and assembled outside the homes of their enemies while Saturiwa and others went "through the woods and forests as quietly as possible."[88] Achieving surprise enabled communities in the late Mississippian Southeast to gain victories without exposing themselves to what they deemed an inordinate amount of risk.

As ferocious as they might have appeared to the Spanish army that invaded their towns in the 1530s and 1540s, the people of the late Mississippian Southeast confounded Spanish expectations about violence in one key area. From the Spanish perspective, Mississippian violence didn't cause enough death. Native Americans relied on quick strikes to establish dominance and allowed their adversaries to recuperate and fight again—a telling difference in cultures of violence with long-term implications. Native peoples in the early Southeast, with few exceptions, fought to gain advantage over their enemies, not to annihilate them. If pressed, the Spanish might have argued that their entrada was an example of the same. The difference was in the level of death. Contemporary histories of the Soto expedition chastise native communities for failing to follow-up sharp attacks with death blows. Luys Hernández de Biedma, the royal factor for Soto's army, wrote concerning an engagement after Mabila that "it was a great mystery of God why, without our resisting them or doing a thing, the Indians turned to flee and left us, because if they had pursued us, not a man of all of us would have escaped."[89] Describing the same engagement, Rangel noted that "if the Indians had known how to pursue their victory, this would have been the last day in the lives of all the Christians of that army and would have put an end to the demand for the *tamemes* [burden-bearing Indians]."[90] The Spanish, reared in a culture of violence that valued total destruction, could not fathom a Mississippian culture of violence in which a complete victory might consist of a quick strike to prove one's superiority followed by a cessation of hostilities and then perhaps a gathering to assess the new terms of the relationship—who owed who tribute and how much?—and maybe even the establishment of a new trading regime.[91] The willingness of the Spanish to annihilate and the unwillingness of the Mississippians to do so cannot be explained solely by the military advantages of steel swords and horses. Having the technological ability to cause great devastation is one thing, but in early America as in the twenty-first century, human hands wield weapons, and human ideas determine when enough is enough.

The Mississippian towns of the Southeast were heirs of Cahokia to a degree, but each town appears to have exhibited a slightly different culture of violence. In future years, scholars benefiting from a larger body of archaeological evidence may be able to reach more definitive conclusions about Mississippian violence, but the work already done at some sites points toward a diversity of violent forms.

In the years after Cahokia's dispersal, Mississippian ways spread to many other parts of eastern North America. The towns bearing the most resemblance to Cahokia grew along the river systems of the Southeast. And it is in these towns that Mississippian cultures of violence took the forms that they would carry over into the sixteenth century, when Europeans arrived, bringing with them their own notions about the proper use of deadly force.

Warfare between groups was not endemic to Mississippian society in the early Southeast. But when these communities did go to war, they followed culturally specific rules about the use of violence. Despite a wide variety of styles of violence and even levels of violence, some broad outlines of the various Mississippian cultures of violence were shared. Mississippians perceived violence as one way of maintaining balance between the Upper World and the Under World, and as such it took on spiritual significance. Mississippian men prepared carefully for violence, praying and purifying themselves to assure success. Speaking of men, most, though not all, Mississippian violence was carried out by men and probably has some basis in longstanding eastern North American ideas about gender: specifically, women were associated with agriculture and the productive capacity of the earth. Women may have joined raiding groups, and certainly defended their towns against assault, as would be the case at Mabila, but female participation in combat was relatively rare. The Mississippian cultures of violence had been evolving for centuries into forms that made historical and cultural sense to the people who employed them. Mississippian cultures were not any more or less inherently violent than other human societies. They had cultures of violence, but they were not innately violent cultures. This, then, is the world into which Europeans stumbled in the sixteenth century.

# CHAPTER 2

# Spanish and Mississippian Violence

The Mississippians and Spanish who squared off against one another in the sixteenth-century Southeast inherited long-developing and distinct cultures of violence. Some Mississippian elites used violence to legitimize their power over commoners, and many Mississippian communities went to war to acquire prestige goods, for religious reasons, and to accumulate war honors and prove masculinity. The Spanish soldiers who served under Hernando de Soto were fighting in the name of their sovereigns and according to the mandates of their brand of Christianity and notions of gender, and they stood to benefit economically from a successful expedition. Soto and his soldiers used a particular culture of violence that owed much to Castilian ideas about colonization. The most notable difference between Mississippian and Spanish violence was in the amount of death each caused. The conflict between Mississippians and Spaniards, and Mississippian and Spanish cultures of violence, set the stage for the violence that was to occur in the future by speeding the dispersal of large polities throughout the Southeast. The clash between Mississippians and Spaniards showcased sophisticated cultures of violence at the moment those traditions began to adapt to the violent realities of colonization in the American Southeast. Remnants of Mississippian and Spanish ways of violence would survive into the 1700s, albeit in forms altered significantly by the arrival of the English and the coalescence of early modern native nations.

From the Christian *reconquista* of the Iberian peninsula onward, Spanish people—mainly Castilians, though others participated as well—had mounted increasingly expensive and aggressive expeditions against people they viewed as innately inferior to themselves, first in the Canary Islands, then in the Caribbean, and finally in mainland North and South America. The Spanish presence in Southeastern North America during the 1500s should be seen as a part, albeit a late and generally unsuccessful one, of the Spanish exploration and conquest of other parts of the Atlantic world.

The Spanish combined the cultural theories they had accumulated through centuries of fighting "others" on the Iberian peninsula and in the Atlantic world with the military tactics they perfected in the invasion of the

Americas as they probed the Southeast as a possible candidate for conquest and colonization.[1] By the 1540s, however, the American Southeast remained firmly under native control. Still, Spanish activities reshaped the Southeast, weakening some groups, destroying others, and accelerating the changes that may have already been taking place as autonomous villages, and, later, towns and nations replaced the chiefdoms as the principal native polities in the Southeast. In fact, the conflicts of the sixteenth century proved to be the last gasp for each of these formidable cultures of violence in the American Southeast—or at least the forms of those cultures that faced off against each other. By the time the English began their colonial forays in the interior of the region in the seventeenth century, many of the chiefdoms Soto invaded had dispersed—a result of internal and external pressures—and autonomous villages demonstrated many of the characteristics which would define early modern Native American warfare. Similarly, after their initial violent and unprofitable excursions in the Southeast, the Spanish concentrated on setting up missions and drawing labor from native villages as well as protecting the northern rim of the empire from European interlopers. Future Spanish expeditions continued to engage in violence but were more attuned to the political realities of indigenous life in the Southeast.

## Forging a Spanish Culture of Violence

By the time they reached the American Southeast in the 1500s, the Spanish had a longstanding culture of violence, and a superb military, with its roots in Iberian campaigns against Muslims and the conquests of the Canary Islands and the Caribbean. In the years before Soto's entrada, the Spanish would extend their domination over vast portions of the Americas. The two most stunning examples of this domination were achieved in Mexico's central valley in the 1520s under the leadership of Hernán Cortés and in the Andes by Francisco Pizarro in the 1530s. The Spanish did not launch this assault on the Americas simply because they could. A number of complex cultural factors and ideas prompted the Spanish to exert extraordinary effort and spend colossal amounts of money to conquer and later to colonize the Americas. Their religious beliefs, like those of the Mississippians, placed great emphasis on military success.

As Charles Hudson and others have noted, the term "Spanish" is flawed when it comes to describing the people who made the discoveries, explorations, and conquests of the fifteenth and sixteenth centuries. Like the Mississippians they met in the Southeast, their primary allegiances were local. Christian Iberians felt relatively weak ties to one of the three major Christian kingdoms: Portugal, Aragon, and Castile. In the second half of the fifteenth century, Castile and Aragon allied through marriage, and all three Christian kingdoms began a period of unrivaled prosperity and influence.[2] To complicate matters more, the armies that invaded the Americas often included African slaves and Native American allies from other parts of the growing Spanish American empire.[3]

Spain's military tradition, and culture of colonial violence, took shape during the period known as the *reconquista*.[4] Muslims from North Africa, the Moors, had ruled much of the peninsula for centuries. As Christian forces gradually won and resettled Iberia, Spanish military organization took on the form that would lead it into the Atlantic and the Americas beyond.[5] Each Christian male owed his particular king military service, the nature of which varied according to class. Nobles served as knights on horseback, and commoners served as foot soldiers. Commoners who were able to pay for and maintain their own horses could serve as a special class of villein knights (*caballeros villanos*). Knights, according to their ability to pay for their own equipment, received tax exemptions. Lesser nobles, both wealthy and poor, along with successful merchants and military men comprised the restless, fortune-seeking class of *hidalgos*—short for *hijos de algo* or "sons of something"—men of substance who would lead the Spanish into the New World.[6] J. H. Elliott described the perfect hidalgo as a "man who lived for war, who could do the impossible through sheer physical courage and a constant effort of the will, who conducted his relations with others according to a strictly regulated code of honour, and who reserved his respect for the man who had won riches by force of arms rather than by the sweat of manual labor."[7]

Hidalgos, in exchange for their assumed support for the sovereign and gratitude for their skill at arms, were granted certain privileges. Their horses and weapons could not be taken from them, even if they fell deeply in debt. They were immune from torture. Even if they received a death sentence, it was carried out in a noble fashion: they were to be beheaded instead of being put to death in some more pedestrian manner.[8]

Massive armies sponsored by monarchs were not the norm during the reconquista. Indeed, most military action in medieval Iberia was undertaken by armies that were assembled in the spring for a particular campaign.[9] Until the final assault on Granada in the 1490s, it was far more common for individual landowners to sponsor campaigns in an effort to gain booty and prestige. Successful assaults on Muslim areas usually brought the title of governor to the leader of the Christian forces. The spoils were distributed among the victorious soldiers, and these men expected to receive tribute from the defeated population.[10] When Spanish knights moved into the Americas, they often financed their own expeditions. A notable exception to the rule of self-finance was Columbus's second voyage to the Caribbean. The monarchy provided the majority of the funding, even going so far as to salary many of the colonists. Still, when the expedition landed, old habits prevailed, and the colonists set about trying to raise profits for themselves.[11]

Spanish motivations for combat during the Iberian campaigns were complex. Individuals could take sheep, cattle, slaves, and gold for their military services.[12] Religious and cultural motivation for conflict also played a significant role. Christianity bound Spanish fighters across lines of kingdom and social distinction. Spanish Christians perceived conflict against Muslims as a natural and normal state, and one scholar has even gone so far to characterize Spain during this era as "a society organized for war."[13]

Christian warriors believed they had supernatural protection in the form of Santiago (Saint James), whose image, occasionally fighting astride a white horse, was supposed to have appeared during several crucial battles against Muslim forces. Admission to the Order of Santiago was a great honor requiring multiple generations of Christian ancestry and wealth, and the Order of Santiago itself was quite powerful.[14] Soto's successful effort to join the order rested on the testimony of many witnesses who swore that he was descended from noble "old Christians," with no trace of Jewish, Muslim (even if converted), or peasant ancestry, and that he owned horses.[15]

Christian rituals accompanied Spanish soldiers on the battlefield; chaplains said mass, heard confession, and gave communion before major engagements.[16] Militant religiosity was one of the hallmarks of Castilian character in the late stages of the reconquista, as Christian forces began to succeed in their military crusade against Muslims.[17] It would not be much of an exaggeration to argue that all of Spanish society—its military bent, its religion, its politics, its concepts of manliness and honor—were forged in a crucible of frontier warfare.[18]

Spanish culture, particularly among the hidalgo class, placed heavy emphasis on an individual's honor and Christian Spain's honor, generally speaking; during times of violence, especially intercultural combat that pitted Christians against Muslims, the link between military service and Christian honor was inescapable. Rodrigo Rangel wrote after the single deadliest engagement in the Southeast that Soto's men "fought valiantly, and each Christian did his duty as a most valiant soldier."[19] This brand of Christian valor and duty had deep roots by the 1540s. Francesco Guicciardini, a Florentine diplomat in the court of Ferdinand, was generally unimpressed by Spanish cultural achievements and what he perceived as a disdain for manual labor. He wrote the following assessment of Spanish character in the opening years of the sixteenth century: "They believe no other nation can compete with them; in speech they brag and puff themselves up all they can. . . . In war they have a high regard for honor, and would rather suffer death than dishonor."[20] From its cloudy medieval origins, honor emerged during the reconquista as a "national passion, as a powerful motivating force."[21] According to Bartolomé Bennassar, honor "was the basic spring of an individual and collective heroism whose daily practice was necessary for the survival of Christian civilization, inferior on a technical level to Moslem civilization."[22] Perceived in this way, honor's trajectory ran parallel to that of the Catholic Church. These two forces drove formerly isolated Christian Spain into the outside world. Honor remained an important component of Spanish colonization, even as the process deployed the concept of honor farther away from home.

Tactics and skills perfected during the reconquista made their way into the Americas as well. By the time they began to take an interest in colonizing the Southeast, Spanish knights had extensive experience on horseback and with protracted siege warfare. Both of these skills came into play as Soto's army wound its way through the Southeast. Also, the practice of hauling off trophies from defeated Muslim enemies seems to have parallels in the Americas. In Iberia, these ranged from Muslim battle flags to the legs, arms, and heads of Muslim governors.[23]

Islamic rule and its overthrow also had a profound effect on the mentality of Spanish colonization. Beginning in the early sixteenth century, Spanish colonizers read their future adversaries one of several versions of a document known as the Requirement (*Requirimiento*). The Requirement stated that if natives resisted Spanish civil authority or Christian teachings, an all-out war, a legal war, could ensue, with disastrous results. Shouting the Requirement from ships under sail before landing or reading it to abandoned coastal villages before soldiering inland seems preposterous. As Patricia Seed put it in her *Ceremonies of Possession,* the Requirement was unique among the ceremonies employed by Europeans in their takeover of the Americas in that it took the threat of warfare a step further by blaming that warfare on natives. Still, by calling on natives to submit, the Spanish were emulating a legal form of violence, the jihad, that had been popular in Islamic Spain and fusing together political and religious conquest. Even though the Requirement proper was not widely used before the early years of the sixteenth century, Islamic thought and legal forms influenced the ways in which the Spanish conceived of violence and carried it out.[24]

The various regions of Spain went about colonization in different ways. John Kicza has identified two distinct traditions, and the combination of these two traditions shaped the Spanish colonization model. The southern coast of Spain was tied into the Mediterranean mercantile world and was home to several Genoese trading houses; merchant families often intermarried with local nobility, and both groups sent trading expeditions throughout the Mediterranean and along the coast of Africa. Christopher Columbus, himself a native of Genoa, conceived his first voyage to the East as a way to set up trading relations with the people he hoped to meet. At the same time as this far-ranging trade model was operating from Spain's Mediterranean coast, families from other parts of Spain, particularly the areas of Castile that had been resettled by Christians as Muslims lost the military struggle for Iberia, were developing what Kicza has called the "full-settlement" method of colonization. Full settlement required the subjugation of enemies, the founding of cities and recognizable political structures, and the redistribution of land among the victorious soldiers. This model eventually came to dominate New World colonization, but its place as the preeminent method for colonizing was not secured immediately. It would take the experiences of Spanish people in the Canary Islands and the Caribbean to show the efficacy of full settlement on a large scale.[25]

During the later stages of the reconquista, the Christian kingdoms of Iberia turned their attention to islands in the Atlantic and the coast of Africa. The Canary Islands served as a sort of laboratory for Spanish exploration, conquest, and subsequent colonization. Spanish dealings with the native populace of the Canary Islands offer a preview of the activities they undertook in the Americas. In the fourteenth century, the Canaries, which had been known to the people of ancient Europe, were rediscovered, first by Mediterranean sailors and later by the emerging Atlantic powers of Castile and Portugal. The earliest expeditions to the archipelago were trading voyages; early mariners raided and traded for slaves, animal hides, and materials used to make dyes. The military conquest of the islands was carried out in the midst of a larger transition in European society. The papacy arbitrated the dispute over the islands between the rising Iberian powers. National competition would become one of the hallmarks of Atlantic colonization. In a series of devastating wars for conquest and domination, the Europeans—at first Normans sponsored by the Crown of Castile, later Castilians themselves—faced off against various groups of indigenous Canary Islanders, or Guanches, with an increasing amount of aid provided by the monarchy itself.[26]

Juan de Abreu de Galindo, a Franciscan friar, recorded the history of the conquest of the Canary Islands in a 1632 manuscript. The manuscript reveals the early development of several key components of Atlantic colonization. Colonization began as a commercial venture (Abreu notes a 1385 voyage to "make descents upon and plunder the Canary Islands"), maintained an evangelical ingredient (a Spanish nobleman gained a grant to the islands provided he "would cause the Gospel to be preached among the natives"), and resulted in European institutions being transplanted across wide spans of ocean.[27] In the Canaries this process took many years and was accompanied by many of the violent trappings of later Atlantic undertakings. The first meeting between Spaniards and Canarians resulted in hostilities. When Francisco Peraza of Seville landed on Lanzarote in 1385, a group of natives gathered at the shore, only to become easy targets for Spanish arrows. Following the initial assault, the Spanish "marched to the town where the natives resided, which they sacked, and carried off a large booty of goatskins, tallow, and sheep, and one hundred and seventy of the inhabitants."[28] Plunder, slave raiding, and random killing would remain components of Spanish colonization, though they would come to be frowned upon at an official level; most of the Canary Islands were subjugated before Pope Paul III's *Sublimis Deus,* a 1537 bull in which the pontiff declared Indians to be human beings and therefore not to be enslaved.[29] On La Palma and Tenerife, the Spanish were able to play on existing ethnic rivalries as they slowly but surely gained control over the produce and people of the islands—this effective colonization tactic appeared throughout the Americas as well, most dramatically in Mexico's central valley, as Cortés entered Tenochtitlán, the Aztec capital, with thousands of native allies. In retrospect, the Canary Islands afforded Spanish colonizers an opportunity to experiment with a variety of methods of conquest and colonization.[30] It is unlikely that the people actually colonizing saw the islands as such. Fourteenth- and fifteenth-century Spanish merchants and noblemen were trained to fight against and enslave people they considered their cultural inferiors, to convert the islanders to Christianity, and to profit personally from the spoils of war. It is also not a coincidence that Christopher Columbus, upon meeting the Tainos, placed them in the same racial category as the Canary Islanders, noting that "they are the color of the Canarians, neither black nor white."[31]

The expeditions undertaken by Christopher Columbus on behalf of the recently united Spanish monarchy are some of the most important events in human history. The meeting of Europe and the Americas ignited processes of biological and cultural exchange whose shockwaves are still being felt over five centuries later. As such, much ink has been spilled pertaining to Columbus's motives, the native cultures he encountered, and the ramifications of that encounter. As far as cultures of violence are concerned, the Spanish continued to build on the knowledge they had accumulated in the Canaries as they exploited the native communities of the Caribbean.

By the time the Spanish began their exploration and conquest of the Americas, three pieces of their culture of violence stood in contrast to those they would encounter across the ocean. First, the Spanish had a built-in system for aggressive assaults that resulted in the dispossession of the victims of their land. Second, fifteenth- and sixteenth-century Spaniards were predisposed to regard racial, ethnic, or religious outsiders as appropriate targets for the violence of conquest.[32] Mississippian towns may have gone to war against one another, but rarely with the goal of conquering neighboring peoples totally, dispossessing them of their territory in the process. Finally, the Spanish style of war featured levels of death that, while not unknown in the Americas, were exceedingly rare.

Spain's entry into the American Southeast coincided roughly with that nation's invasion of the two largest American empires, one in Mexico's central valley and the other in the Andes. Spanish experiences in these regions have received scholarly attention elsewhere, though the effects of these conquests on the Spanish culture of colonial violence in the American Southeast are often overlooked. Spain's earliest activities in Florida were modeled on techniques used in the Caribbean and spurred on by the conquest of Mexico, while Hernando Soto's entrada was a direct outgrowth of Spanish enterprises in Peru. Soto even deployed some of the same maneuvers in Alabama as he did at the court of Atahualpa. The personal stories of conquistadors such as Juan Ponce de León and Hernando de Soto—two men who would appear in the violent history of the American Southeast—need to be retold with an eye to what earlier lessons they applied to their efforts in Florida. Connecting the island and mainland conquests of the 1490s through the 1540s with the comparatively tentative probings of the Southeast allows scholars to view that region's colonization in a wider context. Spanish dealings in Mexico and Peru did not filter abstractly down to the men who invaded the American Southeast. Rather, they served as concrete examples.

The sort of violence employed by the Spanish often depended on their perceptions of the native societies they encountered. Columbus's famous initial assessment of the Tainos—after noting their physical appearance and seeming ignorance of arms, the admiral mentions that "they should be good and intelligent servants"[33]—was followed by rapid enslavement, horrific violence, dislocation, and dispossession. The violence of Caribbean colonization, described by Las Casas, formed the basis for much of the Black Legend of Spanish conquest. Consider the contrast with the initial reaction of the Spanish upon entering Tenochtitlán. Through the haze of his advanced age, Bernal Díaz del Castillo remembered some Spanish soldiers questioning whether they had dreamed such a fantastic place.[34] To topple a large, complex society, the Spanish had to rely on diplomacy and hostage taking. In the Mexican case, Moctezuma was taken and eventually murdered. When violence did erupt, the Spanish expected, and received, the assistance of former Aztec tributary peoples in destroying the sacred city.[35] Soto's expedition would employ both of these tactics in the American Southeast.

## Soto's Army in the Mississippian Southeast

At least two distinct cultures of violence encountered each other for the first time in the American Southeast in the first half of the sixteenth century. These cultures of violence developed in the years before the encounter to deal with different historical contexts and then were reshaped to try to deal with the realities of contact with people who had previously been separated by the Atlantic.[36] It would be easy enough to engage in broad generalizations about the meeting of two worlds, the Old and the New, but to do so would drastically oversimplify the situation. The chiefdoms of the Southeast already had mechanisms and strategies for dealing with the sort of threat posed by the Spanish, even if they had never faced warriors on horseback armed with crossbows and steel swords. Similarly, the Spanish had developed mental, and legal, categories into which they placed people who were neither Christian, Jewish, nor Muslim.

The earliest Spanish expeditions to the Southeast can be characterized as little other than disappointments and failures to their sponsors. Juan Ponce de León's search for gold and slaves (not a mystical fountain) in the 1510s and 1520s ended with his death at the hands of the Calusas. Lúcas Vázquez de Ayllón launched an even more disastrous attempt to plant a colony in 1526, first in Winyah Bay (in present-day South Carolina) and later on Sapelo Sound (in present-day Georgia). Ayllón's colony, and Ayllón himself, fell victim to an unknown disease, and only 150 of the 600 original settlers made it back to Hispaniola, after many African and Native American slaves revolted. In the late 1520s, Pánfilo de Narváez set out to conquer the Gulf Coast of Florida. A series of misfortunes befell the expedition, whose famous survivor, Álvar Núñez Cabeza de Vaca, published an account of the interior of North America that hinted at the presence of large, wealthy cities.[37]

The Spanish men who advanced into the Southeast during the first half of the sixteenth century were not novice conquistadors. Most, like Ponce, Soto, and Narváez, were accomplished warriors who had amassed some personal wealth and prestige but desired more, perhaps a northern counterpart to the Aztec and Inca empires to subdue. Ayllón, while not as militarily minded as the others, was a nobleman, a high-ranking government official, and a prosperous Hispaniola sugar planter when he made his way to the Southeast.[38]

Juan Ponce de León, who had served as a squire in the conquest of Granada, arrived in the Americas in 1493, on Columbus's second voyage. In the early sixteenth century, he was well established on Hispaniola. Ponce's desire for gold and slaves led him east to Puerto Rico. In 1508, he led the conquest of Puerto Rico and subsequently became governor of that island, and one of its richest residents, though colonial politics convinced him to move elsewhere.[39] As in other Caribbean locations, placer gold and native slaves became scarce, so Ponce applied for and received permission to exploit resources farther to the north.[40] Ponce's 1513 landings—among the Ais on the Atlantic Coast and the Calusas on the Gulf Coast—evince none of the tentative "feeling out" period of Columbus's earlier voyages. As the Taino population in the Caribbean declined, Spanish ships began to raid neighboring islands, and probably Florida, for slaves to replace the native labor force; the Ais and Calusas knew what to expect. Both sides resorted to violence early, as Ponce took native women and men hostage and native canoes—twenty on one occasion and eighty on another—repeatedly attacked Spanish boats. Ponce took legal possession of Florida, a fact that mattered only to Europeans. He returned to Spain and received the position of *adelantado* in 1514, but the death of his wife and the desire to see his daughters married cooled his interest in colonizing ventures, until Cortés's shocking encounter with the Aztecs rekindled it.[41]

In 1521, Ponce returned to Florida's Gulf Coast, intending to establish a colony there—according to the chronicler Gonzalo Fernández de Oviedo y Valdés, since Ponce was "a good colonist," the expedition included horses, cattle, pigs, sheep, seed, and priests. However well equipped it might have been, the expedition could not stand up to a furious massed attack by the Calusas. Wounded in the leg, Ponce returned to Cuba, where he died. Oviedo found it hard to fault Ponce; he argued that it wasn't yet time for Florida to be Christianized and that God "permits the devil still to keep those Indians deceived and for his own, and the population of hell to be augmented with their souls."[42]

Lúcas Vásquez de Ayllón's Atlantic Coast colony failed just as catastrophically from a Spanish perspective. In 1523, Charles V granted Ayllón permission to explore and plant a colony. Charles's *capitulaciones* warned against poisoning relations with native peoples, particularly those living in large villages. The king reminded Ayllón of the religious directive to treat native peoples civilly—to make sure that any slaves had been acquired legally and paid for fairly, for instance. Still, in 1526, some men from the expedition imposed themselves on a local village, overstayed their welcome, and wound up dead. Even among native peoples who did not reside in large towns in the interior, mistrust of Spanish intentions seems to have been a hallmark of some of the earliest face-to-face meetings.[43] Early explorations by Ayllón and the improbable overland journey of Esteban and Cabeza de Vaca ignited rumors concerning the natural and material wealth of the Southeast.

Spurred on by inflated rumors based on such accounts, Soto led an army of approximately six hundred people on an entrada that tore through the indigenous Southeast from the time he landed near Tampa Bay in 1539 to the sinking of his body in the Mississippi River in 1542; his *maestre de campo*, Luis de Moscoso, continued the march and eventually led the survivors

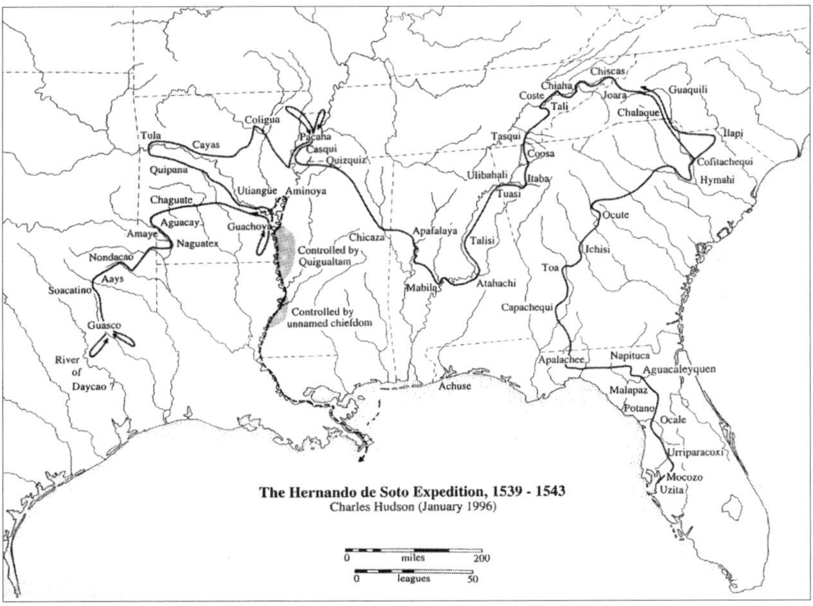


**Map 2.** The precise route that de Soto's army took through the Southeast has been the cause of some historical controversy, but Charles Hudson's proposed route is accepted by most scholars. Illustration by Charles Hudson reproduced from *The Hernando de Soto Expedition: History, Historiography, and "Discovery" in the Southeast,* edited by Patricia Galloway. Used by permission of the University of Nebraska Press. Copyright 1997 by the University of Nebraska Press. Copyright 2005 by the Board of Regents of the University of Nebraska.

to New Spain.[44] Unlike his contemporary Coronado, and his predecessor in the Southeast, Ayllón, Soto was not an administrator. He was a warrior. He arrived in the Americas as a teenager, participated in the conquest of Central America, and gained wealth and prestige by his military feats in Peru. The experience he gained battling large, sedentary native communities elsewhere in the Americas prepared him for his march through the Southeast. The wealth of the Peruvian conquest provided the means and titles required of a conquistador, but it was in Central America that Soto formed the personality that would guide his actions in the Southeast.

The Soto expedition produced remarkable descriptions of violence between Spaniards and Mississippians at the precise moments when the two peoples' sophisticated cultures of violence came into contact with each other. The sources are not without their troubles, and the specific nature of these troubles is closely intertwined with the rhetoric of violence. The major accounts of the voyage are written from European perspectives, so the usual care must be taken to avoid repeating the cultural biases of the sources. The various descriptions of Soto's entrada appear to rely on each other so heavily —the practice was common in sixteenth-century history writing—that one scholar has labeled their borrowing "incestuous."[45] The decision on which sources to use or discard is one that each individual scholar must make for her or himself, and the Biedma, Oviedo/Rangel, and Elvas accounts form the basis of my discussion of violence.

The account written by Luys Hernández de Biedma, a royal factor who accompanied the expedition, is the only one that is primary in a technical sense. Because it lacks the editorial commentary of the other accounts and does not praise or condemn Soto, Biedma's text is generally perceived as the most impartial. He writes in the matter-of-fact style of a royal functionary, concerned primarily with the problems of logistics and supply, but his account, not surprisingly, was written for a specific audience by a man who intended to advance his career. Since many of the expedition's efforts to secure treasure came up short, they do not feature prominently in Biedma's account, though the correspondence between Soto and the king made it clear that treasure was a primary concern.[46]

The 1540s account of Rodrigo Rangel exists primarily as a portion of a much longer work by Oviedo, the *Historia General de las Indias*. For the portions concerning Soto, Oviedo relied on Rangel's diary, supplemented by testimony given in Santo Domingo. Rangel's testimony and any materials related to it are long gone, so Oviedo's account is what historians have to work with. It is impossible to determine precisely where Rangel's account ends and Oviedo's commentary begins. Oviedo, for instance, had undergone a religious conversion not unlike that of the Dominican Bartolomé de Las Casas, and he condemned Soto as a murderous monster for his actions in the Southeast.[47]

The publication history of the "Account of a Gentleman of Elvas," which appeared in 1557, is as frustrating and fascinating as that of the Rangel text. For instance, if the "Gentleman of Elvas" really was a gentleman from Elvas, one of the eleven Portuguese soldiers that survived the expedition, it seems unlikely that his exploits in the Southeast would allow him to remain anonymous for more than four centuries. It appears that André de Burgos, a Spanish publisher working in Portugal, probably with access to both Oviedo and one or more Portuguese survivors, crafted a narrative that owed a great deal to both historical and literary traditions. The Elvas account keeps the same sequence of events, but it owes a great deal to literary conventions popular in Spain in the sixteenth century. For example, Burgos, or his consultant(s), added lengthy, dramatic speeches by native caciques at various points throughout his narrative. Some of these are lifted directly from other accounts, while some merely reflect trends in Iberian literature, most notably the reliance on medieval tales of chivalry.[48]

The longest, most colorful, treatment of Soto's expedition, and the least useful in reconstructing its events, is Garcilaso de la Vega's monumental *La Florida del Ynca*. Garcilaso de la Vega, sometimes referred to as El Inca Garcilaso de la Vega, was born Gómez Suárez de Figueroa in Cuzco in 1539 and was raised between Inca and Spanish worlds, though his literary career developed mainly along Spanish lines. Scholars have developed a troubling relationship with his fanciful text. Many are inclined to point out its massive shortcomings as a source for history, then proceed to rely on it implicitly and explicitly to make their points, as if once they've admitted its faults, it is permissible to use the text.[49]

Garcilaso's text represents many things. It brings to mind chivalric romances and courtesy books by establishing Soto as a romantic hero. It is a providential version of American history, since Garcilaso believed the Americas existed primarily as a theater for conversion to Christianity. It is also a strange brand of early ethnography, since Garcilaso applied the lessons of his Inca upbringing and Spanish education to the early American Southeast uncritically. The Mississippians conjured by Garcilaso are both too Spanish, in terms of their feudal institutions and courtly manners, and too Incan, from temple design to the rigid hierarchy of their societies.[50]

Garcilaso's *Florida* points up some of the difficulties facing anyone interested in Soto's entrada as a moment of cultural encounter and intercultural violence. There are two sides of a debate that seem to be talking past each other. One side, brandishing the latest archaeological evidence gathered along Soto's most likely route, seems interested in figuring out precisely what took place and corroborating the various accounts with each other and the archaeological record. The other side seems primarily interested in the textual analysis of the major accounts as important cultural artifacts in their own regard, with careful attention paid to the publication of each work, its intended audience, and intertextuality between the works. Scholars in this literary vein seem to be less concerned with what actually happened in 1539–42 than what people wrote about it. As far as the study of cultures of violence is concerned, both approaches are valuable. It is necessary and desirable to study both the physical violence committed by Spaniards and Mississippians and the colonial violence of the texts the Spanish created to justify their actions and legitimate future conquests. It is impossible to ever know exactly what took place when Mississippians fought Spaniards in the first half of the sixteenth century; it *is* possible, and crucial, to discern what violence between Mississippians and Spaniards looked like to its earliest chroniclers. From this perspective, even Spanish biases can provide useful clues as to how violence functioned in that culture. For the secretary Rodrigo Rangel, the recording of deeds from the entrada served an additional purpose: they allowed him to unburden his soul. As he put it, "Each Christian ought to do it [write down his actions regularly] in order to know how to confess and bring his sins to memory, in particular those who go to war."[51]

As the sources become more like literature and less like reportage, the descriptions of violence become more dramatic. This is particularly true in the case of Garcilaso, but neither the Elvas account nor the Oviedo/Rangel account on which it is based avoid the temptation entirely. The reasons for this vary. Garcilaso was interested in advancing his vision of the New World as part of God's plan for the expansion of Christendom; he also chose examples that illustrate the chivalric, courtly, and virtuous to impress these characteristics upon his readers. Oviedo criticizes atrocious Spanish behavior and appears to despise Soto, but he blames native depravity for many native problems. The Elvas narrative may take Rangel as its baseline, but it adds rhetorical flourish to emphasize the cunning nature of Mississippians. Whoever wrote the Elvas account also seems to have had less of a problem with the sort of violence unleashed by the Spanish.[52]

The Spanish culture of colonial violence was so ingrained that many of its characteristics were unremarkable to chroniclers such as Biedma, Rangel, and Elvas. The conventions of colonial violence appear first in the correspondence between Soto and Charles V as Soto asked and received permission to undertake his entrada. In a *capitulación* dated April 20, 1537, Charles V mentioned that Soto should "conquer, pacify, and populate" the new lands. Later in the same letter, the language changed slightly to "conquer, pacify, and hold in government," but the intent was clear. Conquest came first. Regarding colonial violence and the use of terror-inducing tactics, the king's instructions made it clear that certain conventions of colonial violence were entirely legitimate. Charles V allowed for the taking of high-ranking captives, provided the ransom was divided among Soto, the Crown, and the conquistadors. He allowed Soto to take his army into towns and to plunder and destroy food supplies. He also recognized that the ever-present treasure search might result in the desecration of native temples, graves, and sacred places.[53] Given the attention that Mississippians paid to the grave goods buried with their elites, and the high esteem in which they held chiefs and priests generally, the tactics of grave robbing and kidnapping elites would have been especially horrifying to Mississippians. Of course, that was exactly the point. The Spanish culture of violence relied heavily on shocking episodes of violence designed to ensure native submission and cooperation.

The relationship between Soto's entrada and the Requirimiento deserves some attention. The Requirimiento, with its roots in the reconquista, once read, left native communities with two choices. They could submit to papal and Spanish authority or be held responsible for the just war launched against them by the Spanish, which might result in enslavement and death for large numbers of people. The Requirimiento appears not to have been read during Soto's entrada, but its message underlay the division of native peoples into those who came in peace and those who resisted, and the Spanish were free to interpret "resistance" as they wished in their quest. In one of the chronicles of the Soto expedition, Soto puts a rather positive spin on the ideas behind the Requirement. In response to a series of questions—"Who are you? What do you want? Where are you going?"—raised by emissaries from the town of Ichisi, near present-day Macon, Georgia, Soto suggested that in terms of religion, they should "give obedience to the apostolic church of Rome," and for more worldly matters, "they should recognize as king and lord the Emperor, king of Castile." Should they submit to these religious and civil authorities, "they would treat them all well."[54] Soto didn't mention what might happen should they refuse the offer, though his army's behavior in other towns leaves little to the imagination. The fact that Charles V ordered the reading of such a document indicates that the Spanish people who planned the colonization of the Southeast assumed a state of war; the Requirimiento itself was a justification for an offensive war that was essentially a foregone conclusion.[55] In effect, the Spanish launched an offensive war and then justified that war and legitimized the level of violence required as they conducted it.

Once Soto's army arrived in the Southeast, probably at Tampa Bay, in May 1539, the tactics outlined by Charles V in the *capitulación* were used against native communities to devastating effect. Biedma's account, mainly concerned with logistics and provisions, considers the capture of hostages both normal and necessary. At Coosa, a northern Georgia chiefdom which Soto's army reached in the summer of 1540, Biedma relates the capture of a cacique in telling language: "We captured the cacique, so that he would give us Indians to carry our burdens, but he detained us several days before he gave them to us."[56] In Biedma's view, and one can assume Soto's, the hostage cacique actually detained the Spanish by refusing to hand over porters. From a Spanish factor's perspective, native people and food served a similar function. Both usually had to be taken, and both allowed Soto's army to continue its meandering march. The taking of hostages appears so often in the chronicles that it seems standard. This particular form of violence was entirely legitimate to the Spanish and needed no extra explanation. Refusal to help the Spanish "voluntarily" usually resulted in hostage taking, enslavement, or other forms of violence.

In the three accounts, several forms of violence, and ways of writing about violence, stand out. Aside from several pitched battles, including the showdown at Mabila described below, there are relatively few instances of large groups of Mississippians taking on large groups of Spaniards. Biedma, Rangel, and Elvas all mention kidnapping caciques and enslaving lower-ranking Indians as if the practice were not particularly unusual. In the Spanish culture of colonial violence, it was not. The capture and enslavement of tamemes was a constant throughout the entrada.

It would be impossible to determine the numbers of native people killed, wounded, or displaced by the practice, since all of the accounts give different numbers; Elvas, for instance, uses forms of the phrase "many Indians were captured" repeatedly. A cursory count reveals that there are at least twenty-three such incidents in Elvas, four in Biedma, and eight in Rangel. Rare were the times that Soto's army would enter into a region and *not* avail itself of whatever resources, including people, were present. Not only was Soto's army responsible for depleting food stores, burning towns, and otherwise wreaking havoc on the Mississippian Southeast, but thousands of native people were dragged around the region as tamemes to the expedition, and the Spanish had few qualms about the practice. This indicates that although the Requirimiento itself was not read during the entrada, its basic principles of just enslavement influenced Soto and subordinate officers. Since Mississippians identified primarily with their particular town and cacique, the practice must have been especially damaging.

Captured Mississippians, if they managed to survive, might find themselves many miles from their hometowns in hostile territory. Elvas recorded that "as soon as the women and young children were a hundred leagues from their land, having become unmindful, they were taken along unbound, and served in that way, and in a very short time learned the language of the Christians."[57] Not all tamemes and women that joined Soto did so because they were captured. The accounts document several instances of women and tamemes being given Soto and his soldiers as gifts. One such group, given by the cacique at Patofa, on the Oconee River in Georgia, expressed "great sorrow to him [Soto] at returning without leaving them in a village."[58] The theme of displacement also appears in the lament of the cacique of Coosa, who was "very angry and tearful because the Governor [Soto] refused to give up a sister of his that they took, and because they had brought him so far from his land."[59]

The treatment afforded tamemes and women, whether they were given or taken, was brutal. They were often dragged "along in chains with collars about their necks and they were used for carrying the baggage and grinding the maize and for other services which so fastened in the manner they could perform."[60] There is no way to achieve an accurate count, but Mississippians captured by the Spanish died in droves. In the winter of 1539–40, "most of the Indians whom they had to serve them, being naked and in chains, died because of the hard life they suffered."[61] Oviedo, who wrote the following words, had it in for Soto, so they must be read with that in mind. Oviedo related that at Coosa, "they [the Spaniards] went to round them [the people of Coosa] up and took many, whom they imprisoned in collars of iron and in chains: and in truth, as eyewitnesses testified, it was a thing of much pity to see it."[62] Oviedo could not resist adding, "But God forgets no evil thing done nor does it remain without punishment, as this history will relate."[63]

Oviedo asked Rangel why the Spanish army took so many hostages, and so many of them women who were "not old nor the most ugly." The secretary responded, and his account elucidates one way in which Spanish violence begat more Spanish violence:

> They took those burden-bearing Indians or tamemes in order to have more slaves and servants, and to carry their supplies, and whatever they stole or what they gave them; and that some died and others fled

> or weakened, and thus they had need to renew and take more; and that they wanted the women also in order to make use of them and for their lewdness and lust, and that they baptized them more for their carnal intercourse than to instruct them in the faith; and that if they detained the caciques and principal Indians, this was advisable so that the others, their subjects, would be quiet and not obstruct their thefts and prevent what they might wish to do in their land.[64]

Even serving the Spanish faithfully, and converting to Christianity, was no guarantee of humane treatment. In July 1543, Luis de Moscoso determined that the remaining Spanish soldiers should construct boats to be sailed and rowed down the Mississippi to the Gulf of Mexico and on to New Spain. As they departed from Aminoya, in present-day Arkansas, they abandoned approximately five hundred natives "male and female, among whom were many boys and girls who spoke and understood Spanish. Most of them were overcome with weeping, which was a great pity seeing that they had all readily become Christians and were now lost."[65]

Soto's army, both before and after he died in 1542, captured caciques to ensure safe passage as a matter of course. Soto himself may have recognized the prudence of such tactics, since he was present at the capture of Atahualpa during the fighting for the Inca Empire. In one case, Soto allowed the paramount chief at Coosa to return to his chiefdom the same day he heard about the prosperous chiefdom of Tascaluza.[66] The *capitulación* of Charles V mentioned the practice, and each of the accounts lists many prominent Mississippians taken by the Spanish. Mississippians were somewhat familiar with the problem, at least on a smaller scale. They had a routine they used to try to gain caciques' freedom: usually offering gifts and tribute, then threatening the use of force. Mississippian devotion to the preservation and recovery of leaders comes through again and again in the Spanish Soto accounts. Many Mississippian towns resorted to subterfuge, hoping to protect their leaders from falling into the hands of Soto's army. At Napoteca, in northern Florida, after asking Soto to free the cacique of Caliquen, which he would not, the people resorted to force. "Thirty or forty Indians were lanced" in the ensuing battle.[67] At Coosa, the Spanish uncovered a plot to free the hostage cacique, if he desired his subordinates to try to liberate him.[68]

In some cases, Spanish soldiers used more terror-inducing tactics, including throwing people to the dogs or burning and mutilating them. Spaniards under Soto, and later Moscoso, used such techniques. They understood the value of highly dramatic acts of violence. After thwarting an attempt to free the cacique of Caliquen, subduing and enslaving hundreds in the process, Soto ordered some unfortunate resisters "to be punished by being fastened to a stake in the middle of the plaza and the Indians of Paracoxi shot them with arrows."[69]

The Spanish army employed various mutilations, from the removal of noses, to the cutting off of hands and arms, as well as burnings. The point of violence like this was usually to intimidate nearby communities into assisting the Spanish. At Tulla (also spelled Tula) in western Arkansas in 1541, "some Indians were captured, six of whom the governor sent to the cacique with their right hands and noses cut off."[70] At Nilco (or Anilco) on the Mississippi River, one Spanish captain "ordered that no male Indian's life should be spared." After killing scores of Indians, the captain did indeed spare the lives of others who "were badly wounded with the lances, who were let go in order that they might strike terror into those who did not happen to be there."[71] In far southwestern Arkansas, near the town of Naguatex, Soto's successor Luis de Moscoso sent a similar message when he ordered a man's "right arm and his nostrils cut off and sent him to the cacique of Naguatex, ordering him to say that on the morrow he would be in his land to destroy him."[72] As the Spanish built boats and prepared to evacuate down the Mississippi in 1543, "thirty Indians came with fish." Moscoso, who had previously tortured a messenger until he confessed that a regional coalition was planning to attack his army, "ordered their right hands cut off, and in that condition sent them to the cacique of Guachoya to whom they belonged."[73] At Himahi, a town south of the chiefdom of Cofitachequi, a Spanish captain brought in "four or five Indians, and not one of them would make known the town of their lord nor disclose its location, although they burned one of them alive in front of the others, and all suffered that martyrdom, in order not to disclose it."[74]

War dogs, usually greyhounds or mastiffs, had been used to terrorize indigenous peoples since the beginning of the Spanish invasion of the Americas, and the Soto expedition was no exception to this rule. A guide from the town of Nondacao, in present-day east Texas, deliberately misled the Spanish army in the summer of 1542. After being tortured, the man admitted to the deceit, at which point "the governor ordered him thrown to the dogs."[75] Rangel, or perhaps Oviedo, described the process in relation to an incident near Tampa Bay in 1539: "He [Vasco Porcallo de Figueroa, one of Soto's officers] found the people gone, and he burned the town, and he set the dogs on [*aperrear*] an Indian he brought as guide. The reader must understand that to set the dogs on [an Indian] is to make the dogs eat them or kill them, tearing the Indian to pieces. The conquistadors in the

Indies always used greyhounds or fierce and valiant dogs in war." An old woman who had aided the escape of a slave was thrown to the dogs shortly thereafter.[76]

In one bizarre incident, Soto employed intracultural rather than intercultural violence to achieve his desired ends. At the eastern Tennessee town of Acoste, Soto and the local cacique had established peaceful relations. Foot soldiers, perhaps replicating behaviors from other towns on the march, ransacked the town's stores of food. Incensed Indians attacked them with clubs and found an unlikely ally in Hernando de Soto, who picked up a club himself and began beating the offending troops. This may have been a shrewd diplomatic maneuver, designed to convince the town that Soto was a fair man. It is also possible that Soto was expressing a noble's frustration with the insubordination of commoners.[77]

Apart from the community-wide resistance described above, and the regional military resistance the Spanish encountered at Mabila and as they floated down the Mississippi, individual Native Americans also committed acts of violence against individual Spaniards. Elite Mississippians struck Soto when the opportunity presented itself. Both Elvas and Rangel took notice when a cacique hit Soto, drawing blood. The "valiant man," as one of the accounts described him, was captured in fighting that erupted in northern Florida in 1539: "As soon as he saw an opportunity he seized hold of the governor, and before he got his hands about his neck, struck him so hard on the nose that it was all covered with blood."[78] Rangel details the same incident but offers more on the aftermath: "One of those caciques, as soon as they untied him, the Governor being next to him, raised his arm and gave the Governor such a great blow that it bathed his teeth in blood and made him spit out much of it, for which they tied him and the other [caciques] each to poles and they were riddled with arrows."[79] One fragmentary account of the fighting at Mabila mentions "an Indian who went looking for the most valiant and best-armed Spaniard in order to kill himself with him."[80] These bits of evidence indicate that high-status Mississippians may have recognized some parallels between their position and that of the Spanish captains and governor. Their quick, personal strikes were attempts to assert dominance over rival nobles.

Something of the Mississippian and Spanish cultures of violence can be recovered by examining the spectacular conflict at Mabila. Soto's army marched southwest from Coosa (in the northwest corner of Georgia) reaching the outskirts of Mabila (in central Alabama, perhaps near the confluence of the Alabama and Cahaba Rivers) at about nine o'clock in the morning on October 18, 1540. Awaiting the Spanish arrival were thousands of

Mississippians, brought there under the aegis of Tascaluza, a man whose power extended to several towns in the region.[81]

The rituals that ensued were crucial to both Spanish and Mississippian forces. Soto ordered his horsemen to dash back and forth in front of Tascaluza "turning them from one side to another, and at times toward the cacique," a move designed to impress a possible military adversary, and reminiscent of Soto's own behavior a few years earlier in the presence of Atahualpa.[82] For his part, Tascaluza appeared unmoved by the spectacle: "He with great gravity and unconcern from time to time raised his eyes and looked as if in disdain."[83]

Biedma's account gives the most concise treatment of the battle. For the Spanish, the origins of this conflict can be traced to Tascaluza's refusal to supply Soto's army with porters. In this instance, the paramount chief responded to Soto's demands by noting that "he was not accustomed to serving anyone, rather all had served him before."[84] The violence that ensued was not fundamentally different from other instances of Mississippian-Spanish conflict; the resistance at Mabila was more severe, and the Spanish response was more ferocious.

The defenders of Mabila were determined to surprise the Spanish. In fact, Tascaluza told the Spanish that many porters were waiting for them at Mabila and sent runners ahead, allegedly to confirm this fact. What he was probably confirming was that the thousands of people necessary to resist the Spanish were in place. Upon his arrival at the fortified town, Tascaluza joined his warriors in one of the houses. Tascaluza refused to meet with Soto, noting that "if the governor wished to go in peace, he should go immediately and should not insist on trying to take him out of his lands and dominion by force."[85] Rangel wrote that as soon as the Spanish entered the town, the inhabitants began to dance and sing; the celebration may have been intended to distract the Spanish from the war preparations going on: "Some soldiers saw them placing bundles of bows and arrows secretively in some palm leaves, and other Christians saw that the huts were filled high and low with concealed people."[86]

Though small in size, Mabila was a well-fortified town. The Spanish force had taken Tascaluza hostage to ensure their safety as they passed through hostile territory. Once inside the palisade, Tascaluza turned on his captors, leading the stiffest resistance that Soto's army faced during their expedition through the Mississippian Southeast.[87] Rodrigo Rangel described the results of the first phase of the engagement: "There was so much virtue and shame this day in all those who found themselves in this first attack and the beginning of this bad day. They fought valiantly, and each Christian did his duty as a most valiant soldier. . . . In effect, the Indians ended up with the town and all the property of the Christians and with the horses that they left tied within, which they then killed."[88] A false Spanish retreat drew the warriors of Mabila temporarily from their palisade, and Soto launched a furious counterattack: "Then, the adelantado encircled them on many sides until all the army arrived, and they entered it through three sides setting fire, first cutting through the palisade with axes; and the fire traveled so that the nine arrobas [about 225 pounds] of pearls that they brought were burned, and all the clothes and ornaments and chalices and moulds for wafers, and the wine for saying mass, and they were left like Arabs, empty-handed with great hardship."[89]

Though the Spanish eventually routed the people of Mabila and their allies from neighboring towns, the casualties were high on both sides. The Spanish lost their pearls (some of which came from the body cavities of elites buried in a temple at Cofitachequi), much of their clothing and baggage, and 22 men, including 7 notable or high-status soldiers, among them a relative of Soto. In addition, about 150 men were wounded—many of them struck by multiple arrows, and the expedition ground to a halt as they recuperated. The defenders of Mabila died in far greater numbers. Elvas estimated twenty-five hundred, while Rangel put the number over three thousand.[90] The fate of Tascaluza was unknown, though the body of his son was found. The Spanish set fire to the town and put the escaping natives to the sword and lance. Many of the defenders suffocated or burned to death. As a result of the fighting and the fire, the Spanish lost nearly all of the treasure they had, and their sacred wares as well. The aftermath of the battle was nearly as grisly as the battle itself. According to Biedma, the Spaniards used the rendered fat of dead Indians as medicine as they recovered.[91]

Soto abandoned his plans to establish a colony in the area and marched off to the northwest.[92] The fighting at Mabila between Mississippians and Spaniards showcased two cultures of violence at the exact moment before those traditions began to adapt to the violent realities of colonization in the American Southeast.

Mississippian and Spanish ways of war were intricately interwoven with each group's culture of violence. The Spanish tried to recreate forms of violence they had used to great effect in other parts of the Americas. In this sense, Soto's entrada was a style of violence that was fading from view. Soto did not seem to have any real desire to colonize, choosing to believe instead that there was a more fertile and populous lands just across the next river or just over the next mountain. There were several points when he came upon agriculturally viable lands, or usable ports, and decided to move on, seeking great riches. Even when he found riches—the pearls at Cofitachequi, for instance—he appears to have been disappointed with their quality. Soto was not alone in his disappointment. Even after he had died and the army had been weakened considerably, some soldiers voiced their intention to stay on at the same time as others grew tired of the expedition: "They hoped to find a rich land before reaching the land of the Christians, because of what Cabeza de Vaca had told the emperor. . . . They would rather have risked death in the land of Florida than to leave it poor."[93]

Subsequent meanderings through hostile territory in what is now Texas convinced Moscoso and other officers that by 1543, the time had come to construct boats and try to float down the Mississippi to the Gulf of Mexico and from there hug the coast and reach the relative safety of New Spain. The trip down the river itself demonstrated more Mississippian tactics. As the Spanish headed downriver, Indians killed eleven or twelve soldiers when they "seize[d] the canoes of the Spaniards and caused them to overturn. . . . The Christians fell into the water and because of the weight of their armor sank to the bottom. And if any, by swimming or laying hold of a canoe, were able to keep afloat, they [the Indians] struck them over the head with their paddles and the clubs they were carrying and made them sink."[94] Twenty-five more men were wounded in a subsequent canoe battle. Some of the Mississippians' water craft were truly impressive. Biedma described "forty or fifty very large and swift canoes of Indians, among which there was a canoe that carried eighty Indian warriors." The naval engagement demonstrated some of the risks involved in the Spanish culture of violence. Once the assault began, the Spanish perceived that it would be cowardly not to fight back. As a result, "twelve honorable men"—a phrase often used to describe high-ranking individuals—perished.[95]

Both cultures connected earthly violence to the spiritual realm. In Soto's case, the connection is so apparent that it rarely appears in the chronicles of his expedition. Spain's hidalgo class, especially the members of it engaged in American conquest, forged a strong connection between Christian ethics and all-consuming warfare against nonbelievers. The cult of Santiago was prevalent among the men who fought in the Americas. In fact, one image of Santiago, created in the Andes in the seventeenth century, makes the connection explicit. The Christian saint appears on horseback, brandishing a sword. A deceased Indian lies across the bottom of the page.[96] Rangel recalled that Moscoso rallied the Spanish to fight in Florida's panhandle by shouting, "Come on, men, Santiago, Santiago, and at them."[97] Mississippians used combat for many purposes, including to bring prestige and honor to one's chiefdom. Both cultures used success in battle as a way to define masculinity and to determine who could climb the ranks of society. The practice of rising in social class due to military prowess was more common among the Spanish, though.

The Spanish described their violence as legitimate and justifiable. When the Iberians sat down to write about violence in the months and years after Soto's entrada, they were writing in a colonial mode; the very act of recording the violence in a certain way served a colonial project that elevated Spanish aims and legitimated Spanish violence.[98] Even so, there are instances in the accounts when the authors demonstrate a sincere respect for the Mississippians' culture of violence and skill at arms, even if some of the compliments are underhanded—after all, what were "savages" good at if not fighting savagely?

The "Gentleman from Elvas" was impressed with Mississippian skill with bows. He noted that the people of Florida were

> so skillful with their weapons. Those people are so warlike and so quick that they make no account of foot soldiers; for if these go for them, they flee, and when their adversaries turn their backs they are immediately on them. . . . They are never quiet but always running and crossing from one side to another so that the crossbows or the arquebuses can not be aimed at them; and before a crossbowman can fire a shot, an Indian can shoot three or four arrows, and very seldom does he miss what he aims at. If the arrow does not find armor, it penetrates as deeply as a crossbow.

Moreover, Florida's Indians were clever and dangerous when it came to Spanish weaponry, too: "He who could get a lance or sword in his hand so handled himself with it as if he had used it all his life."[99] The constant harassment at Aminoya, as the Spanish built their boats and planned their escape, demonstrated that "opposed on foot, one to the other, on water or land they [the Indians] had the advantage, because they were more cunning and agile; and because of the lay of the land which suited their wishes in the manner of their warfare."[100] In a similar vein, Rangel praised native accuracy with the bow and rated his adversaries in Florida as "bellicose and indomitable and strong people."[101] Later, at Tulla, the people "fought like desperate men, with the greatest courage in the world."[102] Speaking of manliness, after an earlier episode of violence, Rangel wrote that "those Indians are so agile and such fine warriors that in any nation of the world they would be seen as men."[103]

The similarities between the two cultures of violence impressed the Spanish in some ways, even if the repeated references to the "cunning" or "warlike" nature of native peoples ring somewhat hollow and serve the Spanish need to justify their own use of violence. Mississippians were assumed to serve their caciques for the same reasons that Spanish foot soldiers were to serve their lords in the reconquest of Iberia and the conquest of the Americas. Rodrigo Rangel described the loyalty of the people of Apalache in terms that would have made sense to sixteenth-century Spaniards:

> Although the Spaniards pursued them and burned them, never did they wish to come in peace. If they cut off the hands and noses of some Indians, they did not show more feeling than if each one of them was a Mucio Scévola, the Roman. Not one of them denied being from Apalache for fear of death. And upon taking one, when they asked him where he was from, he responded with pride: "Where am I from? . . . I am an Indian of Apalache," like one who gave to understand that he took offense from whoever might think that he was of another people but Apalache.[104]

It seems the governors and captains of the expedition even recognized some parallels between their position and that of the Mississippian leaders against whom they battled. Soto's reference to both himself and Mississippian caciques as great lords (as in the presence of Casqui and Pacaha), and his successor's ham-fisted attempt to convince the people of Guachoya that Soto had not died but rather had gone to the sky, indicates at least a surface-level understanding of Mississippian society.[105]

It is difficult to tell what Mississippians thought about the Spanish culture of colonial violence. Most likely, they tried to fit Soto and his army into categories they knew: powerful leaders had overstepped their bounds before, overreaching in their grasp for tribute. Large armies in the service of one chiefdom had occasionally attacked other chiefdoms in an effort to gain prestige, as the archaeological evidence at places like Etowah demonstrates. Some of the coastal communities Soto encountered had undoubtedly had previous experience with the Spanish, as slavers, traders, or some combination of the two. This could explain the generally icy reaction Soto received in Florida. One of the histories notes that "more warlike" people lived on the coast.[106] This speaks less to the innate militarism of such societies than their specific historical circumstances. Hostility was not universal, though, as some towns recognized the power of Spanish weapons and joined the Spanish against other peoples, such as the archers from Paracoxi who executed resisters at Napoteca.

Mississippians were perplexed by one aspect of the Spanish culture of violence. Most Mississippian towns, while they may have existed in tension with other towns, appear not to automatically assumed a war footing in the same way that the Spanish army did as it snaked through the Southeast. Violent competition was only one of the ways in which the towns of the Southeast interacted with each other, but it seemed to define the relationship between Spanish intruders and indigenous communities. An incident in northeast Arkansas in the summer of 1541 demonstrates a clash of cultures. The cacique Casqui questioned the level of violence the Spanish employed, asking through interpreters, "Why do you wish to use such cruelty without us meriting it? . . . To what end, to what purpose were you moved to do or think a thing so wrongful [Soto's army had looted a nearby town, and Casqui had fled in response] against people without guilt and friends of the cross and yours?" According to his secretary, Soto responded tearfully that "we do not come to destroy you, but rather to make you know and understand the cross and our God. . . . Since you went away without my permission, I thought that you held little regard for the doctrine that we had given you; and for the contempt that you had for it, I wished to destroy you." Soto's words had the desired effect, and Casqui, along with his rival Pacaha, sat down to eat with the conquistador.[107]

There are reasons to doubt that this encounter took place precisely as Rangel rendered it. Rangel's account was edited by Oviedo, who believed that the Spanish had behaved too cruelly in their invasion of the Southeast. Moreover, Casqui's speech, in order to be understood by the Spanish, had to go through at least one interpreter. Accompanying Soto's army was a man named Juan Ortiz, who had been held captive in Florida for years and managed to learn a language that was spoken in the vicinity of Tampa Bay. Other interpreters, some of them Mississippians enslaved by Soto, worked with Ortiz to break down the substantial linguistic barriers present in the Southeast. These factors make it unlikely that Casqui and Soto understood each other on the level posited by Rangel. Still, it is obvious from archaeological and historical evidence that the Spanish did introduce levels of violence and death that were rare in, if not alien to, the late Mississippian world. So even if Casqui did not utter these exact phrases, it is not difficult to imagine that such questions were on the minds of people throughout the Southeast.

The overall impact and long-term legacy of the Soto expedition are difficult to gauge. The entrada did not result in the planting of prosperous Spanish colonies or the subjugation of a wealthy inland empire, so from a Spanish perspective, it would seem to have failed like its predecessors. It did not result in the annihilation of the region's native populace. It caused a great deal of destruction, and introduced the people of the Southeast to

European disease, but the region remained firmly in native hands. It inaugurated a period of population decline at the same time as it accelerated the dispersal of Mississippian era polities into the towns and villages of the early modern Southeast. Soto's march gave the Spanish a leg up in the colonization of the Southeast; later expeditions would draw heavily on the experiences of Soto's army, relying on its accounts as they struggled to establish a permanent foothold in the region. From a European perspective, Soto's entrada made a significant legal claim. French and English explorers who came to the American Southeast would be trespassing on Spanish territory, no matter how shaky that territorial claim actually was.

In the second half of the sixteenth century, Spanish, Native American, French, and English people would turn the American Southeast into a battleground in the developing global struggle for empire. Northern Florida, Georgia, and South Carolina would soon witness vicious fighting between competing groups of Europeans. The region's native peoples continued to spin off in groups from paramount chiefdoms. When European armies reached the interior Southeast again in the 1550s and 1560s, and certainly by the time English explorers visited the region beginning in the 1650s, it looked remarkably different.

The earliest meetings between native and European cultures of violence in the Southeast occurred as some crucial changes were taking place, though these changes would become more pronounced in later decades; Mississippian and Spanish cultures of violence adapted and changed. Subsequent entradas took more careful stock of the political situation of the Southeast; both Pardo and Luna's expeditions traded more extensively than Soto with the chiefdoms they encountered, and were more accommodating to their native hosts' desires.[108] Spanish goals in the northern reaches of their American empire changed as well. It became more important to hold outposts like Santa Fe and St. Augustine, using them to gain converts and protect valuable colonies and treasure ships from European interlopers, than to control large swaths of native land, at which the Spanish had not proven successful in any event.

The Spanish soldiers who returned to the Southeast just twenty years later would discover a different world than the one they failed to conquer in the 1530s and 1540s. The native people of the Southeast, though still reeling from the effects of Soto's entrada and continuing the long trajectory of chiefdom dispersal, would face a different kind of threat from the Spanish, who had altered their culture of colonial violence in the interim. There was not much in the way of cultural borrowing—along the lines of the situation described for New England by Patrick Malone in his *Skulking Way of*

*War*—but the first half of the sixteenth century was more of a showcase for two cultures of violence.

Mississippian and Spanish styles of violence were shifting slowly. Their meeting in the Southeast represented a high-water mark for each. Spanish colonial violence was changing, and in the 1542 New Laws and 1573 Orders for New Discoveries, Spain's official policy placed missionary activities ahead of outright conquest in terms of colonial goals; of course, the policies were still oppressive and colonial by their very nature, and colonial violence did not stop.[109] Though the word was friendlier, "pacification" could be just as violent as "conquest." Mississippian cultures of violence lived on in the colonial Southeast, but they were no longer attached to specific chiefdoms. As identity became town-based and later national, so did cultures of violence. Mississippian thinking about the appropriateness of violence, and its role in society, continued to influence the thinking of Southeastern people long after Mississippian social organization had disappeared.

In a way, the Spanish march through the Southeast in the 1540s paralleled the English establishment of plantations in the late seventeenth and early eighteenth centuries. When chiefdoms went to war, they did so with the goal of setting up a long-term relationship, such as tribute in the form of food or exotic luxury goods, thereby exchanging the "hard power" of military force for a "softer" form of power. The Spanish culture of violence which Soto represented saw little benefit to this sort of relationship. The Spanish culture of violence sought to dominate Native Americans and subject them to Spanish civil authority. For the Spanish, violence was not a means of mediating between various groups and authorities. Especially as it was conceived in the 1530s and 1540s, it was a way of bringing Indians into line with Spanish religious, social and political order from above.[110] The Spanish would not argue that they were peaceful. How could they, when their own colonial accounts were rife with episodes of violence? Since they could not juxtapose Spanish peacefulness with native violence, they strove to separate their "civilized" violence, with its insistence on the benefits of papal and Spanish authority, from the chaotic, supposedly primitive violence of the innately "warlike" late Mississippian world. The English culture of violence, though it would not appear in the Southeast for more than a century, had a similar take on native violence.

## CHAPTER 3

# The Fight for Florida

The American Southeast existed "beyond the line" that divided Europe from the rest of the world in the mind of many European theorists. In this area, rules governing violence, which had just begun to exercise some influence in Europe in the sixteenth century, did not apply. Piracy, smuggling, and violent conflict, even between nations which were at peace in Europe, were all standard practices. As a result, early Florida erupted in violence in the second half of the sixteenth century as the French and Spanish staked imperial claims, albeit tenuous ones, to the Atlantic Coast. These Europeans, of course, were not operating in isolation. Both groups of Europeans engaged the region's indigenous communities, at some points in a spirit of peace and cooperation, but at others in violent clashes.

In terms of northern Florida's history tourism industry, Fort Matanzas National Monument, on the Matanzas Inlet, is destined to play a subsidiary role to the attractions at St. Augustine, about fifteen miles to the north. St. Augustine boasts the spectacular Castillo de San Marcos, along with an entire historical district, not to mention the first Ripley's Believe It Or Not! museum. Visitors to St. Augustine can join a crowded procession through the fortress then emerge to buy things. There are a handful of historical reenactors, eager to discuss the Castillo's glory days. Judging from the amount of money changing hands in and around the major attractions, one could make the case that St. Augustine never had it so good. At the Matanzas site, the pace is markedly slower. On the day I visited, one lone park ranger staffed the visitor center, and one more took visitors on the free ferry ride across the inlet to the fort, a small masonry watchtower dating to the 1740s. Unfortunately, an anticipated storm kept the ferry from crossing when I was there. In any event, St. Augustine's historic downtown has overshadowed Matanzas for a very long time.

In the study of colonial violence, however, Matanzas is the main attraction, predating Sir Francis Drake's 1586 attack on St. Augustine and the construction of the massive Castillo de San Marcos, begun in 1672. At Matanzas in 1565, Pedro Menéndez de Avilés exterminated hundreds of French Huguenots, many of whom had asked for quarter.[1] In the dunes along Florida's Atlantic Coast, the surrendering French troops were led away in small groups and put to the sword. Menéndez's motivations and actions, as well as those of the French commanders Jean Ribaut and René Goulaine de Laudonnière, call into question many assumptions about colonial violence. One of the longest-standing images of European colonization in the Americas is that of European colonizers squaring off against a mass of native colonized. This dichotomy places all Europeans on one side of a gaping cultural divide that is more reminiscent of the film *Zulu* than any episode of fifteenth- or sixteenth-century colonization. In the sixteenth century, there were also wide differences between Protestantism and Catholicism, which must also factor into discussions of early American colonization. For instance, Menéndez believed that Protestants and Indians had similar sets of beliefs and laws, both of which were misguided and dangerous, and this assumption probably informed his slaughter of the French. The Matanzas incident also demonstrates some serious divisions between French and Spanish cultures of violence. The Spanish soldiers involved made little effort to cover up their actions, which they perceived to be legitimate. Menéndez's letters to Philip II and other Spanish contemporary accounts are written in a frank, open tone.[2] Spanish sources explain who was killed, who was spared, and why. French sources, which appeared rapidly in English, highlighted and exaggerated Spanish excess and cruelty. Once reprinted in influential volumes like those compiled by Richard Hakluyt, accounts of the fight for Florida helped to secure Spain's international reputation for colonial violence, the Black Legend, and motivated ever more aggressive raids by Protestants sailing for England, France, and eventually the Netherlands.[3] The reputation may be deserved, but the French and English committed similar acts for similar reasons. The Spanish held no monopoly on colonial violence.

In the second half of the sixteenth century, the Atlantic Coast of Florida, Georgia, and South Carolina made up one small, violent corner of the developing global struggle for empire among the nations of Europe. In this region, Europeans resorted to tactics that were frowned upon though not yet entirely eradicated in Europe, indicating that cultures of colonial violence were special subcategories of larger sets of ideas concerning the appropriate use of violence.[4] The northern coast of Florida was the site of a particularly violent struggle for two main reasons. First, it existed "beyond the line," so the rules of intercultural violence that were forming in Europe were significantly weaker in the American Southeast. Second, the Spanish had staked their empire's success on the safe transport of precious metals from New Spain to Seville and regular treasure fleets sailed up the Atlantic Coast of North America before catching favorable winds to carry their riches to Europe. Other European nations could, and did, profit by attacking Spanish shipping. A foothold in Florida was vitally important to the safety of Spanish shipping lanes.[5] The intercultural violence of the fight for Florida is reminiscent of other fighting around the Caribbean.

In European legal terms, the Spanish had a long-established claim to North American territory dating back to the days of Juan Ponce de León and Lúcas Vázquez de Ayllón and earlier.[6] French colonists were aware of these claims and rejected them. French claims to the Southeast were legally based on the 1524 voyage of Giovanni Verrazano. In more practical terms, French colonizing schemes banked on Spain's inability to control such lengthy stretches of coastline. Some tension existed between French officials, who desired American possessions but did not want war with Spain, and French corsairs, who wanted to get as close to the riches of New Spain as possible. Despite Spanish, French, and English incursions, the Southeast remained firmly in native hands throughout the sixteenth century. Native peoples in the Southeast could fight with against various groups of Europeans as they saw fit. Florida's Indians certainly expressed their displeasure with the establishment of missions in their territory, most notably at Guale in 1597.

## "Limiting" Warfare in Europe

European cultures of violence were beginning to undergo slow but significant transformations during the sixteenth century. Many of these shifts did not make the journey across the Atlantic, and were rarely—if ever—applied to violence between Europeans and non-Europeans, but a brief discussion of European cultures of violence may throw American cultures of violence into deeper relief. Europeans were continuing to rework conventions that would ideally spare noncombatants from the horrors of war, as part of a larger project of making warfare—something uncivil and disorderly—civil and orderly. By 1700, certain limitations were in place. Surrenders were usually honored, wounded combatants were usually spared, and flags of truce were respected, for the most part. In the 1500s and 1600s, the theory of war was changing, and, slowly, the practice of war was following suit. French accounts of Spanish atrocities in the Americas hoped to impress upon their European audiences the illegality of such actions, since the nations were not technically "at war" when they were committed.[7]

There are two areas of legal theory that Europeans applied to the conduct of violence between cultures. The first, *jus ad bellum,* dealt primarily with the legitimacy of a given war; the second, *jus in bello,* focused on the conduct of war once it had begun. *Jus ad bellum* theory came out of the Middle Ages as a highly religious concept, while *jus in bello* was largely a secular concern. Theologians pondered whether a certain conflict might be deemed legitimate in the eyes of God, but the rulers of Spain, France, and England did not need much prodding to go to war. When the war was against non-Europeans, a special subcategory, *bellum Romanum,* "governed" its conduct. *Bellum Romanum* allowed for the annihilation of non-Christians wherever they might exist.[8]

In the sixteenth century, Europeans could justify almost any sort of armed conflict. According to a 1582 treatise by Balthasar Ayala, war was legitimate when its purpose was to defend oneself or one's allies, to regain something taken unjustly by force, to take vengeance for an unjustifiable wrong, to assert an army's right to pass through a neighboring territory peacefully, and to "repress heresy and rebellion." Ayala's vision of holy war was based on chapter 20 of Deuteronomy, in which God lays out the rules of war against enemies of Israel: "Thou shalt save alive nothing that breatheth."[9] Some sources refer to this type of conflict as a "war of fire and blood."[10] Loosely constructed, the repression of heresy could motivate wide-ranging, aggressive military action, as occurred on Florida's northern coast in the 1560s. Menéndez believed he was striking a blow against heresy, for instance, when he executed unarmed French Huguenots in 1565. Ayala wrote to justify a practice that was ongoing—he wrote in the midst of Philip II's attempts to suppress a Protestant revolt in the Netherlands; his ideas would slowly be replaced by more secular thought governing the initiation of war. Francis Bacon, among others, argued that violent conflict between Christians was illegitimate. In practice, though, Europeans would continue to use holy war justifications and tactics, particularly in conflicts with non-Europeans.[11]

The period between 1550 and 1700 also witnessed the rise of intercultural violence for reasons beyond religion. Religion could be used as an excuse to fight a war with mainly commercial goals, for example. In fact, by the time of the Glorious Revolution in England, commerce and empire, usually intertwined, had become the primary motivations for fighting between European nations. The fight for Florida in the second half of the sixteenth century demonstrates that commercial, religious, and imperial interests are difficult, if not impossible, to separate from one another in the early modern Atlantic world.

*Jus in bello,* the section of the law covering the conduct of war, underwent slight but perceptible modifications in the sixteenth century, though the religious wars that wracked Europe constantly between the 1550s and

1700 serve as reminders that these modifications were comparatively infinitesimal.[12] Warfare between Protestants and Catholics, whether across international boundaries or within nations themselves, was a fact of European life at this time. The fight over the Netherlands provides examples of the extent and limitations of religious warfare in the latter half of the sixteenth century. In 1576, a Spanish army, upset at having served two years without pay, sacked the city of Antwerp, killing more than eight thousand of its inhabitants. An inquiry was held later to determine who had been responsible, indicating that such behavior was officially frowned upon, even if said frowning didn't stop the sack of Antwerp.[13] Two years earlier, in 1574, Philip II had dismissed a proposal to break a series of dikes and flood the entire region, noting that it would "earn for us a reputation of cruelty which would be better avoided, especially against our vassals, even though their guilt is notorious and the punishment justified."[14] The Duke of Alba divided Dutch towns into several categories depending on the amount of resistance they offered, and punished the towns accordingly. Alba himself came under official scrutiny for the tactics he employed in the suppression of the Dutch revolt. He emerged unscathed, but some of his officers were sent away from court.[15]

Warfare, especially of a religious nature, was a central feature of European life in the sixteenth century. The application of the prevailing European theories and practices concerning intercultural violence to Florida's Atlantic Coast highlights the fact that colonial violence flourished outside of even the loose confines of legitimate violence in Europe. Even as slight constraints began to change European cultures of violence, representatives of Spain, France, and England, battled without rules "beyond the line." The fight for Florida is one small, violent chapter of this burgeoning fight for empire in the Atlantic world.

## French Interest in Florida's Atlantic Coast

French involvement in the Americas began with Francis I's sponsorship of the voyage of Giovanni da Verrazano, who explored North America's Atlantic Coast in the 1520s. After this initial reconnaissance, France established frail colonial outposts: in Canada in the 1530s and Brazil in the 1550s.[16] French mariners became heavily involved in the lucrative fishing business developing off of North America's northern Atlantic Coast. The French also began to harass Spanish shipping through a series of devastating raids. These raids were carried out whether Spain and France were at war or peace. The men responsible sometimes bore "letters of marque," which gave them some diplomatic protection in the event of their capture.[17]

Whether or not the corsairs had the official sanction of a letter of marque, they generally operated outside the purview of the French state. Nobles or merchants sponsored their own raiding and trading voyages. This practice stands in contrast to the Spanish model: the Spanish relied on individual nobles to finance exploration and colonization, but they were selective about who could undertake such missions and retained greater control. This is not surprising considering the high stakes involved in the extraction and transport of huge amounts of precious metals.[18]

Ocean currents and unpredictable weather made the Caribbean Sea a difficult place to navigate under sail. For vessels leaving Havana, it was much easier to sail north out of the sea then strike out across the Atlantic at a more favorable latitude. An added benefit of this route was the opportunity to resupply in the Azores and pick up more protection if necessary. In the 1550s and 1560s, Spain regularized the passage of an armed fleet twice yearly across the Atlantic. Armed merchant ships—the Spanish Crown felt that a professional navy was not cost-effective—from Cartagena and Veracruz would converge at Havana and make the crossing together.[19] In the sixteenth century, Spain, France, and England engaged in sporadic fighting in the Caribbean; the legal categories of "peace" and "war" were all but irrelevant. French corsairs were emboldened to take their search for Spanish treasure "beyond the line," while the English harassed Spanish shipping and settlements. The fight for Florida must be understood in this Caribbean context.[20]

Two raids on Cuba in the 1550s merit closer examination as models for the type of violence that would occur in Florida in the 1560s. In 1554, French privateer François le Clerc—also known as "Jambe de Bois," or "Leg of Wood"—attacked Santiago de Cuba, all but destroying that settlement. The next year, Jacques de Sores, a French Protestant, took Havana with a force of two hundred armed men. After the Spanish governor broke a truce and tried to retake the town, Sores sacked Havana, killing African slaves and Spanish captives. Sores's army tormented the town for more than a month, and upon leaving, his crew burned the settlement and all the ships remaining in the harbor. Sores also made his religious leanings apparent when he ordered the desecration of the church and redistributed the priests' vestments to his soldiers. Throughout the sixteenth century, French corsairs—actually, corsairs of several nationalities—drained precious resources from Spain's overseas empire. "Raid" seems too weak a word to convey the havoc wreaked by French corsairs on Spanish holdings in the Caribbean. Corsairs killed Spaniards and their slaves, destroyed whole towns, and severely curtailed any efforts at agricultural production. Precious metals were not the only target of privateers. Incidentally, Pedro Menéndez de Avilés, who would later punish Huguenot heretics south of St. Augustine, was captured by French corsairs in 1552 and held for fifteen days, until he negotiated his ransom.[21]

Like most colonial ventures, religious, national, and economic motives all played roles in the establishment of the French colony in Florida. Discerning which was the most powerful is not an easy task, nor would this revelation go very far toward explaining the type of violence that the French and Spanish inflicted upon each other in the Americas, since each motive could easily lead to bloodshed. It is true that Protestants explored the coast and established the colony and Protestant merchants and nobles financed them and backed them at court, but the colony itself was not envisioned as an exclusively Huguenot undertaking. Many French Protestants lived in Normandy and worked in the cloth trade. In the same way that parts of England, certain regions of Spain, and much of Portugal became oriented to the Atlantic, so did Normandy.[22]

Three men, Jean Ribaut, Admiral Gaspard Coligny, and René Laudonnière, were largely responsible for the establishment of the French colony of Florida in the 1560s. Their stories can shed some light on the motives for French colonization and its connection to the rise of French Protestantism. Jean Ribaut was from the gentry class of Dieppe, Normandy, and had raided and traded under the tutelage of Jean d'Ango. He also trained in England in the 1540s and 1550s with Sebastian Cabot. Ribaut's background gave the young captain access to rare seafaring and geographical knowledge, and exposed him to Protestantism of the Calvinist variety.[23]

Colonizers and Huguenots had a powerful ally at court in the person of Gaspard de Coligny, admiral of France. Coligny, who was attending Protestant services openly by 1561, advocated for religious tolerance and the speedy entry of France into Florida. Coligny made a career out of continually rising above the religious turmoil that threatened to divide France. He was a friend and advisor to Catherine of Medici, who became regent upon Francis II's death. Political savvy allowed Coligny to take a leading role in determining France's colonial policy, and he steered that policy toward Florida's Atlantic Coast.[24]

Laudonnière served as Ribaut's second-in-command during the 1562 voyage and commanded the 1564 voyage that would result in the founding of Fort Caroline. He probably was raised in Dieppe as a Huguenot. He may have also been related to Admiral Coligny. One thing that is clear about René Laudonnière's background is that by the 1560s, he was a respected and able commander who had grown wealthy in a short career at sea.[25] In the documentary record, Coligny, Ribaut, and Laudonnière all appear eager to serve France, not simply their particular religious affiliation. One recent interpretation has suggested that one of the reasons French Protestants were so heavily involved in colonization was to prove their worth as French people.[26] Those actually doing the colonizing rarely wrote about colonization as a way to establish a safe haven for Protestants, and the colonists of French Florida were not refugees. The expedition's leaders viewed themselves as the leading edge of a blade that would cut through Spanish America.

One of the main players in the fight for Florida, Jean Ribaut, hardly mentions religion in his recounting of a 1562 mission that led to the establishment of Charlesfort on Parris Island, South Carolina, *The Whole and True Discoverye of Terra Florida.*[27] When he does treat the subject, he doesn't write about the divide between Protestantism and Catholicism, he draws distinctions between the French and Native Americans, writing of a "hope and desire" on the part of the king "that a numbre of brutishe people and ignoraunt of Jesus Christ, may by his grace come to some knowledge of his holly lawes and ordynaunces." Ribaut comes to religion late. His account prioritizes "knowledg of strange conteries," "riche and inestimable comodities," and the "honnour and praise of theire Kings and prynces" before spreading the faith.[28]

French interest in northern Florida reached its peak in the 1560s under the leadership of Ribaut, Coligny, and Laudonnière. The French forces that reconnoitered Florida's Atlantic Coast and planted small outposts there—the aforementioned Charlesfort and Fort Caroline on the St. John's River in northern Florida in 1564—were not simply looking to establish bases to aid in French attacks on Spanish shipping. A look at the extant documents reveals that early French desires for the establishment and development of American colonies were not all that dramatically different than early Spanish or English desires.

The French who arrived in the American Southeast were not painting on a blank canvas, though. They entered into a native Southeast that had witnessed several Spanish encroachments: Juan Ponce de León in the 1510s, Lúcas Vázquez de Ayllón in the 1520s, Hernando de Soto in the 1530s and 1540s, and Tristán de Luna y Arellaño in the 1550s as well as numerous slaving and trading expeditions. Each of these exploratory missions took its toll on the region's native communities, though some were clearly more damaging than others. One might expect the appearance of armed French people to provoke distrust and lead to violence. It did not, at least at first. The situation in northern Florida helps explain the warm welcome the French initially received.

Native peoples in Florida shared some aspects of Mississippian life, but not all of them. Platform mounds, one of the defining characteristics of Mississippian culture in other areas, are all but absent from northern Florida. Environmental conditions prevented the accumulation of corn that drove larger interior population centers.[29] Timucuan speakers of Florida did, however, organize into chiefdoms, with complex kinship and diplomatic ties to one another. French sources have Saturiwa using the categories of vassalage and brotherhood to delineate which chiefs were allied with him: he "had thirty vassal chiefs under him, of whom ten were his brothers."[30]

Towns in the late Mississippian era had their own cultures of violence. Timucuans participated in elaborate rituals as they prepared to go to war. French accounts describe the leader Outina seeking guidance from religious leaders and Saturiwa praying to the sun and sprinkling water on himself and his warriors in preparation for combat (see chapter 1).[31] Women participated before and after combat, mourning the dead and celebrating victories; such practices were in keeping with women's roles in intercultural violence in many parts of Native North America. Tactically speaking, Timucuan warfare appears to have been a scaled-down version of Mississippian warfare. The violence of Mississippian and Timucuan warfare was not usually linked to the conquest of territory. Rather, violence between chiefly lineages established and reinforced tributary relationships, and served a spiritual purpose. It is possible that Timucuan chiefdoms engaging in conflict viewed themselves as performing a necessary service to maintain balance between worlds.[32] Two major chiefs, Saturiwa and Outina, both imbued violence with a religious significance. The Feast of Toya, as observed by French colonists, incorporated ritual violence as well. Relatives of the chief reenacted previous victories over neighboring "Thymogona," or other groups of Timucuan speakers. In what Laudonnière referred to as "strange ceremonies," Timucuans commenced "dancing and singing in doleful tones" and "ran like unbridled horses into the midst of the thickest woods." In one climactic moment, "they grabbed the arms of young girls in a fury, and cut them so cruelly with sharp clam shells that the blood flowed."[33]

The first French visitors to Florida praised the land as abundant and assumed there was plenty of food and good farmland to support both native and French settlements. Ribaut, selling—probably overselling—the region's virtues, called Florida "one of the goodlyest, best, and frutfullest cunteres that ever was sene."[34] The relationship between the Timucuans and their land was much more complex and tenuous. Northern Florida's soils could not produce large agricultural surpluses. The political situation in Florida was already shifting rapidly. Outina, one of the most powerful leaders in the region, had recently come under attack from Saturiwa and his allies.[35] Jerald Milanich has argued, convincingly, that the Timucuans owed their very political organization to violent competition. Timucuans lived outside of the Mississippian heartland, but their territory adjoined Mississippian lands and they adopted some aspects of Mississippian life in response to violent incursions.[36] Having some experience with European firepower and trade goods, groups of Timucuans sought the French as allies and trading partners as they tried to incorporate the newcomers into their own systems of alliance and diplomacy.

## French Settlement and Violence

French–Native American conflict during the 1560s was minimal, especially on the 1562 voyage that resulted in the establishment of Charlesfort, and especially when compared with the deep wounds left by Soto's expedition.[37] According to Patricia Seed, the leading authority on the subject, the French rituals of taking possession of new lands differed significantly from the threatening Requirimiento favored by the Spanish and the encroachment of the house, garden, and fence preferred by the English. French ceremonies of possession usually involved a parade and speeches stressing the need for native consent and alliance between native leaders and the French monarch.[38] The peaceful establishment of the French in Florida supports Seed's version. In 1562, a Timucuan noble showed Jean Ribaut the easiest place to land his boats; a lively trading session followed, and Ribaut presented the chief and his kin with blue robes bearing yellow fleurs-de-lis.[39]

The records of the 1562 Charlesfort voyage, the major accounts being those left behind by Ribaut and Laudonnière, do not mention conflict between their group and local Indians. French documents do mention native warfare, but only as observed by the French. An artist, Jacques Le Moyne de Morgue, accompanied the 1564 expedition, and his exquisitely rendered drawings, later engraved by Theodore de Bry, provide a wealth of information concerning native violence and the rituals surrounding it (see figure 4).[40] Unfortunately, it is unclear how ethnographically sound these drawings are, since De Bry is known to have embellished the scenes substantially.[41]

Ribaut's arrival at the River of May (the St. John's River) in May 1562, along with one hundred soldiers and fifty sailors, was a peaceful affair. The earliest encounters between French and Timucuans featured trading, prayer, "alyance," and "amytie."[42] When a neighboring people appeared across the river in an aggressive stance, Ribaut defused the situation by trading with them as well. Like Columbus in the previous century, Ribaut was careful to

XII.

Wie der König Vtina/ wann er sein Heer wi-
der den Feind außführt/ein Zauberer rahtfragt.

R. Holata Outina.

12.

ALs der Herr Laudonniere etliche Vnterthanen deß Königs Holata Vtina oder Outina, so ohngefähr 40. Meil vom Schloß der Frantzosen/gegē Mittag/wohnt/vffgenom̃en hatt/welche im vorigē Krieg von Saturioua, seinem Feind gefangen worden/schickt er sie jhrem König wider zu: Welche/nach dem sie einen Bundt mit jhm gemacht/auch zusagten/daß sie gute Freunde bleiben wolten. Dieser Bundt aber ward darumb auffgericht/weil durch diß Königs Gebiet/allein zu Land/vnd das Wasser vffwarts/man den Paß zum Gebürg Apalatcy, darin̄ viel Golt/Silber vnd Ertz wechst/haben köndt/auff daß die Frantzosen/wegen diß Königs Freundtschafft (welche kaum ein jar währt) desto sicherer zu diesem Gebirg kom̃en möchten. Als diese Freundschafft noch währt/begert er vom Herrn Laudonniere etliche Hackenschützen/sintemal er ein Krieg wider sein Feind fürzunem̃en gesinnet: Darauff jm der Herr Laudonniere durch Herrn Ottigni, seinen Leutenampt 25. zugeschickt. Da die ankom̃en/hat sie der König mit freuden empfangen/der gäntzlichen zuuersicht/daß er nun den Sieg wider seine Feinde erhalten würde: Sintemal im gantzen Land von den Büchsen ein solch Geschrey erschollen/daß sie darob sehr erschrocken waren. Da nun der König gantz zum Anzug fertig/zogen sie fort/vnd haben den ersten Tag ein guten Weg gehabt/den andern aber/wegen der sümpffigen örter/so voll Dörner vnd Gesträuch waren/ein gar mühseligen Weg/deßwegen die Indianer die Frantzosen tragen musten/daß jnen denn/wegen grosser Hitz/sehr wol bekam/sind also endtlich an der Feinde Gräntze kom̃en. Alda der König/als er seim Heer still zuhalten befohlen/ein Zauberer/vber die 120. Jar alt/zu sich beruffen/vnnd jhm befohlen/daß er jm der Feinde Gelegenheit anzeygte: Darauff der Zauberer in mitten deß Heers jm ein Platz gemacht/in dem er den Schilt deß Herrn Ottigni, den sein Schiltjung trug/ersehen/begert er/daß man jm den geben wolt/so bald er jn bekame/legt er jn auff die Erden/machte vmb den ein Circkel/fünff Schuch weit/vnd neben herumb etliche Buchstaben vnd Zeichen/darnach kniet er vff den Schilt/vnd saß vff seine Fersen nider/also/daß er das Erdrich niergend berührt/vnd weiß nicht was prumlet/treib mancherley Geberde/als ob er ein gantz ernstliches Gebet thet: Welcher/als ers einer viertheil stund lang angetrieben/erschröcklich anzusehen ward/daß er keim Menschen mehr gleichte/Dann er all seine Glieder dermassen wandte/daß man frey hörte/wie die Knochen auß ein ander giengen. Jnn sum̃a er thet viel vnnatürlichs. Da diß vollbracht/ward er wider wie vor/doch gantz matt/vnd als erschrocken: Darauff er auß dem Circkel gangen/den König gegrüsset/vnd jm angezeygt/wie starck die Feinde/vnd an welchem Ort sie seiner warteten.

D ij Wie der

**FIG. 4.** In this engraving by Theodor de Bry, Outina consults a man whom the French described as a "sorcerer," a holy man known as a *jarua* (or *joara*). He sits in a borrowed French shield, draws patterns on the ground, and divines that there are two thousand enemies awaiting the army's arrival. This intelligence gave Outina pause, but a French captain insisted on carrying out the attack anyway. From *Der Newlich Erfundenen Landschafft Americae* (Frankfurt, 1603), Library of Congress.

point out that the native people he met would "obaye, ye, be content to serve those that shall with gentilnes and humanytie go aboute to alure them."[43] Rude behavior would only result in delays in acquiring riches. The French did not altogether avoid violent tactics. For instance, they detained two Timucuans as prisoners until their escape. In early June, Ribaut sailed for France, leaving behind a small garrison—the numbers vary slightly from account to account, but certainly less than thirty soldiers—and intending to return with a much larger force including ordinary colonists and workers. His return was delayed by the onset of religious war in France.[44]

After Ribaut's departure, violence among the French crept into the picture. Albert de la Pierria, who had been left in charge of the Charlesfort garrison, began his tenure by inaugurating peaceful relations with several chiefdoms, making a tour of their lands. Timucuans invited the French to observe one of their feasts (Toya), and the French obliged. This rosy scenario deteriorated when the French ran short of food—a situation that led them to pressure their neighbors and become involved in conflict between villages. Internal violence also struck the garrison. According to Laudonnière's report, trouble began when a drummer named Guernache was mistreated by the captain over a small matter, outraging several soldiers and leading to the execution of one soldier and the exile of another, Lachère. Captain Albert inflamed the situation through his use of harsh language, saying that "he would be glad to hear of his [Lachère's] death."[45] For this and other cruelties, the garrison rose against its captain and killed him.[46] Shortly thereafter, and facing starvation, the French abandoned Charlesfort and set sail for home. The return voyage itself turned violent, when, after subsisting on meager corn rations, leather shoes and vests, sea water, and their own urine, the French decided to kill and eat Lachère.[47] Military discipline and life at sea were both violent undertakings in the sixteenth century.

The 1564 voyage, helmed by Laudonnière, featured more tense moments, as well as outright conflict between French soldiers and native warriors. Civil war in France delayed the undertaking, and Laudonnière's ships did not leave France until April 1564. The rescue mission got off to an inauspicious start in the Caribbean. On Dominica, Caribs begged Laudonnière's men not to approach their homes. Some French soldiers ignored this request and went looking for pineapples where they should not have; as a result, one man was lost and Laudonnière's ships left Dominica in a hail of arrows. Caribs exposed to repeated Spanish depredations had little tolerance for French plundering either.[48]

Florida, just a year from becoming the site of gruesome imperial and religious violence, was relatively calm when Laudonnière's soldiers and colonists arrived. Saturiwa and Laudonnière recognized each other and engaged in friendly banter. When the subject of weaponry came up, as it might among military-minded people, Saturiwa had a target set up to compare the effectiveness of French guns with Timucuan arrows. The French seemed determined to impress Saturiwa. Besides the target-shooting contest, Saturiwa also got a tour of the recently constructed Fort Caroline, complete with cannon fire and trumpets.[49] The Timucuans and the French both used ceremonies and music to prepare for battle. In this case, the effort was purely ceremonial. Saturiwa admired the French display and looked forward to using French guns against Outina.

Some other early incidents showcase French uses of theatrical violence as it relates to the Timucuans. The French fabricated a battle in order to impress Saturiwa. Laudonnière also took advantage of a series of fires of unknown origin, telling Saturiwa, "I had been content to fire just halfway down the course [to his house] to let him know of my power. I assured him that if he continued in his good behavior, my men would not be shooting at him in the future and I would be his loyal defender against his greatest enemies."[50] In fact, Laudonnière and his officers had not decided whether to ally themselves with Saturiwa or Outina in their ongoing power struggle. Some conflict had arisen previously over the terms of the alliance between Saturiwa and Laudonnière, since Laudonnière had declined to send any men against Outina, to "purchase the friendship of one by the hatred of another," as he put it later.[51] The French rejection of native concepts of alliance might have developed into a serious problem if the Spanish had not removed the French from the picture entirely.

Internal strife among the French reappeared in late 1564, and the resulting violence had ramifications throughout the Caribbean. Laudonnière's official history, which may have been written in part to exonerate him, focuses instead on the treacherous behavior of those serving under him, especially Roquette and Genre.[52] Class divisions could lead to mistrust and even violence among small numbers of colonists. After the mutineers had made their choice to rebel, their story took an interesting turn. Sensing that Florida's coast would not provide them with the riches they sought, the mutineers took off for New Spain and attacked Spanish towns and ships in the Caribbean. Some were captured by the Spanish, and a few returned to Fort Caroline. Laudonnière pardoned most of the participants, but desired to hang the ringleaders as an example. Such punishment would not have been at all uncommon for such a serious breach of military discipline. After some brief negotiations, it was determined that Laudonnière would have the ringleaders killed and display their corpses.[53] One unfortunate side effect of the mutiny, from a French perspective, was that the resulting Caribbean raids alerted the Spanish to a French presence on the coast of North America.

The fact that there was so much infighting among the French on the first two voyages needs further exploration. Most of the French soldiers and colonists were Huguenots, so religious tensions would not appear to have spawned mutinous violence. Conflict erupted over the goals of the colonizing missions, and, perhaps, being "beyond the line" and so far from France led ordinary people to question the policies of their leaders, even to the point of threatening and deploying violence. Such violence serves as a reminder that categories like "colonizer" and "colonized" can sometimes gloss over wide differences.[54] In the closing weeks of the Soto expedition, after Soto's death and despite fatigue, casualties, and disease, some soldiers argued for a chance to stay in the Southeast and seek treasure and enhance their reputations, preferring to risk death in pursuit of treasure over the relative safety of New Spain. Among the Spanish, this situation appears not to have turned violent.

The French finally joined with Outina in a military campaign in late 1564, and the effort demonstrates some key differences between the Timucuan and French cultures of violence. Outina requested that several French *harquebusiers,* or musketeers, accompany him in an assault on Potano, another powerful Timucuan chiefdom located in present-day Alachua County. Laudonnière assigned thirty men under the leadership of Lord d'Ottigni to the mission.[55] After the force lost the element of surprise—crucial in Timucuan warfare—Outina "begged the advice of his jarua, as they call their magician, as to whether it would be wise to go on. This sorcerer made some hideous and terrible signs and used certain ritual words, and when this was ended told the king that it was best not to go on any farther and that Potavou [Potano], supported by at least two thousand Indians, was waiting for him. Besides this, he said that all the Indians were furnished with cords to bind up the prisoners whom they would assuredly take."[56]

To turn back from a fight after an arduous journey was not to d'Ottigni's liking. His response to Outina's perceived cowardice illuminates a crucial difference between French and Timucuan uses of violence. D'Ottigni wanted to deal Potano a crushing blow. He "was furious because of going through so much trouble without doing anything of importance."[57] D'Ottigni devised a new battle plan and told Outina that "he would never have a good opinion of him nor of his men if they would not take the risk; and that if the king did not wish to take it, at least he should be given a guide so that he and his small group could go on to the enemy camp. Outina was ashamed, and because of his high regard for Lord d'Ottigni decided to go forward."[58] Though the sources do not mention it, one wonders if d'Ottigni called Outina's manhood into question. Such critiques carried weight in both European and many Native American cultures of violence. No matter what d'Ottigni said to shame Outina, it had the desired effect and Outina marched on his enemies. In the battle that ensued, a combined French-Outina force wreaked havoc on the assembled Potano warriors. Laudonnière claims that Outina would have lost the battle save for the assistance of the French harquebusiers, but it does not seem at all likely that the French and Outina shared the same definition of victory. After Potano's warriors fled from the fighting, Outina began to go home, clearly satisfied that his army had demonstrated its superiority and humiliated Potano. D'Ottigni saw only retreat and an unwillingness to pursue the enemy force and annihilate it. Outina's behavior "greatly disgusted Lord d'Ottigny, who wanted nothing more than going on to complete victory."[59] There is no doubt that Outina considered his victory complete. What d'Ottigni's, and the French's, vision of complete victory would entail is left up to the reader's imagination, but one might expect it to be more bloody, given d'Ottigni's reaction. Outina commemorated his army's triumph by sending runners to "eighteen or twenty villages of other kings," gathering them "feasts and dances by which he intended to celebrate the victory."[60] The notion of "complete" victory, as the French saw it, was not part of the Timucuan culture of violence.[61]

Relations between the French and their native neighbors soured when food ran short. Each side accused the other of treachery, and violence was the result. Despite the friendly ceremonies that set initial French-Timucuan encounters apart, prolonged contact brought violence of a sort that is familiar to students of colonial history. The French took high-status captives to ensure the payment of tribute in food and the safety of their fledgling colony. Soto had seized caciques to ease his passage through the native Southeast, and half a century later the English at Jamestown would seize Pocahontas, the daughter of the prominent leader Powhatan. In Florida, Laudonnière took hold of Outina.

The seizure of Outina, while not the first capture of its kind by the French in Florida, certainly changed the nature of the conflict between the French and their Timucuan neighbors. It also provides some insight into intergroup politics and the tense situation that remained between Laudonnière and his French soldiers. Timucuans, growing tired of the French presence on their lands and sensing the impending French famine, began to sell their food to the French at inflated prices. If the French found the prices unfair and complained, too bad. One derisive response was "If you value your merchandise so greatly, eat it, and we will eat our fish."[62]

Laudonnière saw the situation clearly; Outina "had begun to treat us like other Indians."[63] Laudonnière did not see himself as one of Outina's vassals and proved it by taking the chief hostage.

Among Outina's allies and enemies, the effect of his capture was striking. In the chief's home village, Laudonnière reported that one of Outina's children was chosen in a controversial election as his successor.[64] This might have happened, but it is more likely that Outina's eldest nephew by his eldest sister would have acceded to his position.[65] Outina's enemies were quick to try to turn his capture to their advantage. Several opposing chiefs lavished food on the French in an effort to convince Laudonnière to put Outina to death.[66] Not surprisingly, many French soldiers thought this was a great idea, and Laudonnière's refusal to execute the chief further upset an already volatile bunch. Despite continued small food gifts from local native communities, and some much-needed supplies acquired from the visiting ships of English mariner and slaver John Hawkins, Laudonnière made the decision to pull up stakes and head back to France. Shortly thereafter, Jean Ribaut appeared with reinforcements.[67]

Ribaut's arrival in Florida in August 1565 capped a remarkable race across the Atlantic by Spanish and French fleets. In Europe both Ribaut and Pedro Menéndez rushed to prepare expeditions back to Florida's coast. In Menéndez's case, this required a formal contract, or *asiento,* be drawn up between himself and representatives of Philip II.[68] Like most asientos, this particular agreement required certain tasks be accomplished and conferred privileges on the holder. Menéndez's contract does not refer specifically to the French at Ft. Caroline, but it does give him the authority to remove any corsairs or intruders between the Gulf of Mexico and Newfoundland, using whatever means he thinks would be best.[69] The use of force is more explicit in other correspondence from the summer of 1565. One letter from Menéndez states that he will not offer quarter to any French corsairs. Menéndez also noted that whether the intruders were English or French, their status as "luteranos," or Lutherans, could facilitate friendly relations with local Indians, since Protestants and Indians were "almost of one law."[70] Menéndez seems to have viewed Native Americans and Protestants as misguided and degenerate. As such, both could be subjected to almost unlimited violence. There were economic considerations as well.

From a base in Florida, corsairs could effectively halt the lucrative shipping route between the West Indies and Spain. For Jean Ribaut's part, he spent the spring of 1565 assembling ships and men to go to Florida. Upon learning of Menéndez's plan to retake Florida, the nature of the French mission switched from resupply and reinforcement to something more aggressive. Two additional ships were outfitted, and a large contingent of soldiers joined the expedition. French and Spanish rulers and the captains who served them understood why they were going to Florida and recognized that violence between the two groups was possible, even likely. The stage was set for a contest between European nations in Florida.

## Massacres, 1565

What happened on the Florida coast in the fall of 1565 depends on which sources one believes. French and Spanish reporting of the same set of events varies so widely that John McGrath, the leading scholar on French Florida, has argued that "one cannot even attempt a synthesis."[71] It is not possible to determine, outside of a few broad generalities, precisely what took place at Matanzas, but it is possible to examine what the participants wrote about it. What the Spanish and French recorded in the aftermath of the fight for Florida can be useful for determining the contours of each group's culture of colonial violence.

Ribaut's fleet departed the Isle of Wight on June 14, reached Florida's coast on August 13, and landed with reinforcements near Fort Caroline on August 28. Menéndez's ships left Cadiz on June 29 and made Puerto Rico by August 9; after discovering the location of the French fort, Menéndez sailed down the coast a ways, taking possession of the country and founding St. Augustine—where he left his noncombatants. Bad weather hindered both Spanish and French crossings. At Fort Caroline, Ribaut and Laudonnière disagreed about the best way to proceed. Ribaut wanted to catch the Spanish at sea, where he felt the French had an advantage. He left Laudonnière and the colonists, with minimal protection, behind at Fort Caroline and took the larger part of the force out to sea, where several ships were promptly destroyed by a ferocious storm.

Menéndez, experiencing the same storm a few miles to the south, consulted his captains and decided on an overland assault on the weakened fort. On September 20, Menéndez's well-armed force (three hundred musketeers and two hundred pikemen) approached the fort. After a prayer to God and the Virgin for victory over "estos luteranos," as Menéndez called the French, the Spanish overran the fort completely, killing more than 130 men.[72] A handful, including Laudonnière, were captured but escaped into the woods. Le Challeux, a carpenter, and Le Moyne, the artist upon whose paintings the well-known De Bry engravings would be based, both managed to escape, and each would eventually publish a narrative. In a letter to Philip II describing the assault, Menéndez noted that he found "among women, creatures, and children of less than fifteen years of age, about fifty people." He did not want to keep them alive, fearing the influence of their "evil sect," but he feared God's punishment should the prisoners meet with cruelty.[73] The carnage was awful, but not complete. Two ships at anchor near the fort managed to carry about one hundred survivors back to France. The *Pearl* and *Levrière* left America on September 25 and arrived in England in November. When these ships sailed, no one knew the fate of Jean Ribaut and his force.

At least two distinct waves of French soldiers survived the storm that destroyed Ribaut's fleet. Menéndez, guided by Timucuans, found the first on September 29. It consisted of more than one hundred bedraggled Frenchmen, who tried to negotiate for their lives and safe passage back to Fort Caroline since France was not currently at war with Spain.[74] Of course, Fort Caroline had been captured, many of its guardians killed, and it currently housed a large number of Spanish soldiers. Menéndez explained the situation in no uncertain terms: "I responded to them that their fort had been taken and those who had been inside had their throats slit, because they were there without the permission of Your Majesty [Philip II] and because they were sowing their evil Lutheran sect in these provinces of Your Majesty I made war with fire and blood as governor and captain-general of these provinces."[75]

According to Menéndez, his brother-in-law, who wrote a lengthy account of the conquest of Florida, and other Spaniards present, Menéndez made no promise to spare the lives of the French should they surrender. He did promise that they could ask for mercy and he would deal with them according to God's will. Faced with starvation, the French decided to surrender, and all but a handful—some Catholics and carpenters—were bound, led behind the dunes, and put to death. The Spanish chaplain, Francisco Lopez de Mendoza Grajales, referred to the incident in his memoirs as "the happy result."[76]

On October 10, Timucuans reported that another contingent of starving French shipwreck victims had arrived at Matanzas, not far from where the first party had washed up. This group, consisting of about two hundred Frenchmen, was led by Jean Ribaut, whom Menéndez considered extraordinarily skillful and too dangerous to be left alive. Events proceeded much like they had at the first mass execution, though this time around fewer than half of the French decided to surrender; the majority fled into the woods. Of those who remained on the beach, Menéndez spared a handful of young men and musicians. Of Ribaut's execution, he remarked that he assumed such an action would be in accordance with the king's wishes "since the king of

France could do more with him and one hundred thousand ducats than with others and five hundred thousand, and he could do more in one year than others in ten, because he was the most practical mariner and corsair known, and very skillful in the navigation of the Indies and the coast of Florida."[77]

Ribaut's Protestantism, and the Protestantism of the other French in Florida, was not the only reason Menéndez applied the "war of fire and blood" to those unfortunates. The French and Spanish in Florida were of separate nations as well as separate faiths. And each nation had sent armed men across the Atlantic to defend its interests. The decision to undertake expensive and violent colonizing ventures was a feature of both French and Spanish, as well as Protestant and Catholic, cultures of violence. Militant, crusading religion exists in the surviving documents alongside concerns like nation and profit as a justification for bloodshed.

Beyond the line, no rules of war applied. The developing fight for empire outside of Europe was too important to all parties to be limited by contrivances like the rules of war, even as those rules began to be codified in Europe. The French who were being killed, and those who survived, used the Matanzas killings and Fort Caroline as an example of what could go wrong when the rules of war were not followed. Le Challeux accused the Spanish of all manner of atrocities. When they entered Fort Caroline, "they made a most horrible and dolefull slaughter of our men, such a rage and crueltie they had conceyved against our nation."[78] A 1582 treatise on geography written by Henri Lancelot Voisin describes an incident in which a Spanish officer assures the French that "it was the custom of the Spanish, even toward the French, always to recognize the courtesies of gentlemanly warfare."[79] According to Voisin, the Spanish immediately broke their word, and slashed the French to death, "earning for themselves the badge of dishonor and perfidy."[80] As if all this slaughter was insufficient, Voisin goes further, claiming that the Spanish burned the bodies of men, women, and children and cut off Ribaut's beard and facial features for display in Peru. Le Challeux, perhaps confused in the heat of the battle at Fort Caroline, describes all sorts of atrocities for which there is no other evidence. Le Moyne's account is somewhat calmer; though he mentions a dismembering, he was aware enough on the night of the attack to realize that the Spanish had sought out the soldiers among the French to bear the brunt of their violence. It might not be a coincidence that the one woman mentioned specifically in the French sources—Laudonnière's maid—survived, as did the carpenter Le Challeux and the artist Le Moyne. The French sources mention all kinds of atrocities: dismemberments, roastings, eyes being plucked out of corpses' sockets and thrown into rivers, and the like.[81]

French complaints about Spanish brutality ring hollow in light of French activities in the Caribbean in the years before the fight for Florida. Menéndez was following orders from Phillip II, and felt that the importance of keeping France out of the Southeast trumped any such legalistic concerns. It bears mentioning that in the wake of the failed Luna expedition, Spain had officially quit trying to colonize the Southeast until the construction of Charlesfort and Fort Caroline. Afterward, Menéndez launched a wide-ranging plan of colonization for the entire region. Menéndez's efforts would eventually result in the founding of missions throughout Florida and as far north as Chesapeake Bay.

There is another point of serious contention between French and Spanish retellings of the Matanzas executions. Le Challeux and Le Moyne mention one massacre of shipwrecked French colonists, when the Spanish sources mention two. It is likely that French inflated Spanish violence, combining two smaller sets of executions into one larger massacre for dramatic effect. In other instances, the French seemed to have little difficulty twisting events to make the Spanish seem excessively cruel. Also, while the French sources made the case for Menéndez's conduct being reprehensible and cowardly, he reported the incidents in such a cool, detached way, it is clear he anticipated little or no rebuke for his actions.

The differing reactions to the killings at Fort Matanzas indicate crucial differences between Spanish and French cultures of violence. Spanish officials felt no need to defend their actions against possible criticism because they thought that French intrusions into territory they perceived as Spanish were a threat to Spanish interests. The fact that the trespassers were "luteranos" was a bonus; losing so many possible native converts to a misguided sect only raised the stakes. French and English reactions, on the other hand, stressed the cruelty and illegality of the assaults, even though people from England and France had engaged, and would continue to engage, in similar forms of violence, usually on a smaller scale. English colonial promoters were eager to portray Spanish colonization in the least favorable light, and English audiences had access to the accounts of the fight for Florida. Many of the French sources, complete with exaggerations of the quality and quantity of violence enacted by the Spanish, made their way rapidly into English translation. Some found their way into Richard Hakluyt's *Diverse Voyages*, *Principle Navigations*, and other influential publications, continuing the Black Legend of Spanish colonization in the Americas.

## French, English, and Guale Challenges

As payback for the destruction of the Fort Caroline garrison and the killings at Matanzas, France struck Spanish Florida hard in April 1568. Dominique de Gourgues, probably a Catholic, undertook a mission of retribution on behalf of the Protestant victims of Menéndez's violence.[82] His fleet, with around two hundred soldiers, arrived in Florida in April 1568. He departed on May 3, having destroyed three separate Spanish forts, including San Mateo. At San Mateo, Gourgues burned the structure to the ground and executed the garrison. He left the bodies of several Spanish soldiers hanging, under the epitaph "I do not this as unto Spaniards, nor as unto Mariners, but as unto Traitors, Robbers, and Murderers." This was in response to a carving allegedly left by Menéndez: "I do not this as unto French men but as unto Lutherans."[83] It is not clear that Menéndez ever wrote that phrase; his letters do imply that Protestantism was akin to native heresy in his mind, but his actions betray a more practical approach. He spared Protestants he found useful, and as he ordered the execution of the French, he claimed to do so because they had violated the territory of Philip II of Spain as well as Roman Catholicism. Upon his return to Bordeaux in June, Gourgues was given a hero's welcome, despite the fact that Philip II had placed a price on his head and sent several ships after him. Local Catholics and Protestants refused to turn over a man they believed had won a great victory for France.[84]

The English entered the fight for Florida in the late sixteenth century, but would play only a minor role until they established Charles Town in 1670. Unlike the Spanish and the French whom they ejected, the English who came to Florida's Atlantic Coast in the 1580s had no interest in staying. They simply wished to wreak as much havoc on Spanish colonizing efforts as they could. In this, the English were remarkably successful, though they were never able to take the fortress in which many of the Spanish residents of St. Augustine took refuge. Francis Drake's 1586 raid on St. Augustine is a prime example of the sort of fighting that Europeans engaged in beyond the line, and is of a piece with the back-and-forth Spanish and French raids in Florida and the Caribbean discussed above. The goal was never to settle, only to ruin Spanish settlements. One could even make the case that Drake's attack accomplished exactly the opposite by removing English colonists from North America. After sacking St. Augustine, Drake continued up the coast where he rescued the beleaguered Roanoke colonists. Drake's use of violence continued a tradition of piracy and raiding that was widespread in the Atlantic. The sort of violence that Drake's force employed merits some consideration. While English and French critics were quick to pick up on any aspects of Spanish colonization they perceived as excessively or brutally violent, English and French colonizers engaged in the same sorts of behaviors writers condemned. Drake's destruction of St. Augustine was nearly perfect, and it followed on the heels of the sack of Santo Domingo and Cartagena.[85]

Drake sailed to St. Augustine with a huge fleet: twenty-three large ships and nineteen smaller ones. Drake's fleet transported about two thousand fighting men. As a point of comparison, Soto's army topped out at six hundred soldiers. Drake and his men were relentless. On May 28, 1586, "wee tooke ordinawnce on shore to batter the Bastle which stoode on the one side of the river . . . wee had shot ii pieces at them, like fainte harted Cowardes they ranne awaie."[86] At this point, native allies of the Spanish entered the fray: "The savages & others came owte of the woodes & with a verie strawnge crie, assawlted our men. But they weare soon driven backe."[87]

Drake's force assaulted the town, and his soldiers carried off as much of the town's property as they could, cut down the fruit trees, and burned the crops in the fields and the town in general: "There was abowte 250 howses in this Towne, but wee left not one of them standinge."[88] Spain and England were not technically "at war," but Drake's actions were part of the wide-ranging naval conflict between the two nations.[89] The English would harass Spanish Florida off and on for decades until the establishment of a permanent English presence at Charles Town—"in the very chaps of the Spaniard," as one settler felicitously phrased it.[90]

All of this attention paid to fighting between Europeans in and around Florida threatens to overshadow the fact that the American Southeast remained fundamentally native land throughout the sixteenth century and beyond. At several locations throughout the province of Florida in the second half of the sixteenth century, native peoples made that clear by killing the Franciscan missionaries who had settled among them. Spanish colonizers described these as revolts and portrayed the Franciscan victims as martyrs. When they treat the upheaval at all, historians usually refer to it as the Guale Rebellion.

The main chronicle of the Guale Rebellion of 1597 was recorded by a Franciscan friar, Luís de Gerónimo de Oré, based upon interviews he conducted with his peers in the second decade of the seventeenth century. The revolt broke out when a Franciscan tried to prevent a young native elite in the town of Tolomato, known as Juanillo, from taking multiple wives. The young man and his confederates left the mission, but returned some days later, "with many other pagan Indians, painted and smeared with red paste, and with feathers on their heads. This among them is a sign of cruelty and slaughter."[91] Although what constituted "cruelty and slaughter" varied from culture to culture throughout the Southeast, Oré was correct about the general symbolism of the color red. From Mississippian times through the nineteenth century (and beyond), Native Americans in the Southeast used red to represent violence or to signal hostile intent.[92]

The people of Guale, a mission province on Georgia's coast, and Tama, farther inland, were upset with Spanish assaults on indigenous marriage, but they also sensed an opportunity to renew trade with the French. According to Oré, Father Corpa was felled by a stone axe and had his head cut off and put on public display.[93] The public display of the body parts of defeated enemies was another symbol that crossed cultural lines in the Southeast, as multiple cultures engaged in the process. A wide-ranging rebellion against mission life ensued. Four missions were attacked, five friars were killed, and another was captured (his captors tried to force him to teach them to make powder and shot for their muskets). From the start of the conflict, it was clear that native loyalties were split between the Christians and Juanillo. In one engagement, Christian Indians from one of the missions turned backed a furious canoe-borne assault. The cacique of Guale warned the Spanish and tried to keep them out of harm's way.[94] Violence flared sporadically in the late 1590s and early 1600s. Occasionally French ships would show up with trade goods, perhaps kindling hopes for an alliance against the Spanish.

The Spanish responded by reasserting their authority in brutal fashion, bringing state-sponsored violence to bear on behalf of the church. In late 1597, Spanish soldiers and their Indian allies burned towns in Guale (present-day Georgia). Spanish soldiers would reappear in Guale villages periodically to burn houses and crops. According to Oré, "Since all the Indians were hidden in the woods, the governor could neither punish them nor get in touch with them. They burned the maize fields and foodstuffs of the Indians. . . . On this account and due to what followed, during the subsequent years they had no maize harvest. . . . Though the Indians sowed, it was little, while the Spanish destroyed it every year, by which they understood that it was a punishment of God for having killed the fathers."[95]

Facing starvation, most Guale towns welcomed Franciscan missionaries in the early 1600s. Jerald Milanich, a leading scholar of Florida Indians, has written that "the sixteenth-century uprisings in Guale provided the Spanish military government with ample justification for forcing the Guale Indians into the colonial system."[96] Accepting Spanish colonial rule meant giving up certain indigenous concepts of violence. At the same time, the Spanish culture of violence in the Southeast continued to shift from the treasure-seeking entradas of the 1530s through the 1550s to the state-endorsed violence of Catholic discipline.

CHAPTER 4

# Violence after the Entrada

The question of how much influence Mississippian world views had on later native communities is not without some contention. In a 2004 *New York Times* review of an exhibit at Chicago's Art Institute, critic Edward Rothstein accused the Art Institute of pandering by asserting a connection between the art of America's ancient peoples and modern native nations. Though "Hero, Hawk, and Open Hand" did not tread in the territory of the National Museum of the American Indian—"homogenized pap," as Rothstein put it—it did blur a line between America's distant, unwritten past and a more thoroughly documented, more recent past. The conceptual leap made Rothstein uncomfortable.[1]

In the Southeast, the leap from Mississippian to early modern life was substantial. But it is not beyond comprehension. Some of the most rewarding recent work in Southeastern history and archaeology has connected early modern peoples to their Mississippian antecedents.[2] Many aspects of Mississippian life were altered significantly; most obvious from an archaeological perspective was the abandonment of large temple mounds in favor of central plazas. Some aspects survived the transition: the Busk, pole ceremonialism, and some general ideas about violence, including the religious and gender significance attached to intercultural violence. Charles Hudson has described the process as a storm which destroys the top story of a house, leaving the first floor (and one assumes the foundation) untouched. James Carson, following Hudson, has suggested that the story of how the modern nations of the Southeast came into being is the story of how each group decided to build back the second floor of its house.[3]

Mississippian violence reflected the contours of Mississippian society. Chiefs undertook war as part of an ongoing competition over prestige and its associated goods, and when chiefdoms fought, their methods underscored the hierarchical nature of the Mississippian world, especially in the places most thoroughly transformed by Mississippian ways (fringe areas, or smaller communities had their own notions about violence). Chiefs and priests determined when to send their highly organized forces into battle, whether the size of the force was a handful of raiders or an army of hundreds. Once the battle began, warriors operated according to a strict chain of command. It is difficult to tell if warfare was an essential part of Mississippian religion or if religion was a part of warfare, but the two were linked. Priests played significant roles in advising chiefs, and violent themes appear regularly in Mississippian art. Warfare among Southeastern chiefdoms had cultural as well as political imperatives.

With the exception of the Natchez, chiefdoms no longer dominated most of the Southeast when the English arrived in the second half of the seventeenth century. How and why decentralization occurred is not really resolved. Spanish entradas, but more important, the birth of St. Augustine and the mission system, introduced the native Southeast to European disease. Disease wreaked havoc on Southeastern populations, and chiefdoms fell apart. At least according to the traditional narrative.[4] It is true that very few chiefdoms survived into the era of English colonization as polities. Yet their cultural influence, and a worldview reminiscent of theirs, was still felt throughout the Southeast. By the second half of the seventeenth century, Native Americans in the Southeast were making new political arrangements with pieces of their former identities. Some of the new polities proved well suited to deal with the realities of the colonial Southeast. This story can be a story of decline and destruction, but it can also be told in a more positive way: Native Americans forged new identities (or refashioned old identities) in ways which made sense given their new circumstances. These new identities could aid in the resistance to colonialism.[5]

Smaller polities emerged as chiefdoms dispersed or lost power. Among Muskogean and Iroquoian peoples, for instance, identities were rooted to specific towns. Each town had its own oral traditions and history. While these traditions and histories did follow some broader patterns (linguistic ones, for instance), the fact that each town was distinct should not be forgotten. For the time period between the 1540s and the 1650s or 1660s, it would be extremely difficult to dig as deeply as Joshua Piker has done in his masterful *Okfuskee,* for example.[6] But to not attempt to reconstruct the native Southeast during this crucial time period is to surrender to Euro-centric (especially Anglo-centric) history. Since there are few Europeans to record what happened after Hernando de Soto and before the English, apart from the Spanish, this time period is less important than others. At least that's what many American history textbooks assume. Charles Hudson and Carmen Chavez Tesser labeled these years "the forgotten centuries" in an edited collection of the same name. When attempting to piece together cultures of violence over a wide chronological span, ignoring this time period is unsatisfying in the extreme, since the well-documented cultures of violence of the 1540s and those dating to the 1670s are different in many ways.

The dispersal of chiefdoms as political units and the emergence of smaller polities altered violence in the Southeast, but not as fundamentally as one might think. Large, pitched battles were a thing of the past, but towns and villages went to war for similar reasons, and with similar ceremonial preparations, as they had during the Mississippian era. Warfare remained intimately tied to the construction of gender as well. Mississippian art suggests a strong connection between masculinity and success in warfare that would continue into the colonial period.

## Mississippian Twilight

The expedition led by Tristán de Luna y Arellaño, which explored the Southeast from 1559 to 1561, was a miserable failure from its sponsors' perspective, but the documentary evidence it left behind hints at the kinds of changes going on in the interior Southeast and offers some clues regarding Southeastern cultures of violence, both Spanish and Late Mississippian. Just sixteen years after the survivors of the Soto expedition limped into New Spain, a new Spanish army appeared in Florida. The five hundred soldiers and thousand or so camp followers had been sent, with typically grand goals and high expectations, to secure a foothold on the Gulf Coast then march overland to plant a colony at Santa Elena, hundreds of miles away on the Atlantic Coast. Luna himself was a veteran colonizer, having joined Coronado on his journey through Pueblo Country and onto the Plains in the 1530s and 1540s. Some of the younger colonists undoubtedly wished to strike it rich.[7]

The towns of the Southeast responded coolly to the Luna party's presence in most cases, perhaps reflecting the level of damage done by the Soto expedition. Immediately, the Spaniards' lack of food became an issue, as Luis de Velasco, viceroy of New Spain, had predicted it might. He had warned: "Your army must not perish from hunger because the Indians do not want to give it food. Thus in case of necessity, such as exists, you may take it from them, leaving them what is necessary for their sustenance. Moreover you may act on the defensive and offensive against those who take up arms against the army and impede the preaching of the holy gospel."[8] Luna's soldiers and colonists laid out a town on Pensacola Bay, which they later had to abandon because they couldn't find enough to eat. Most of the party relocated to a native community north of Mobile Bay, Nanicapana, where the inhabitants acted quickly to deny the Spanish provisions. They also traced the roots of their recent hardship to Spanish depredations. Spanish soldiers later testified that the Indians had "revolted" and denied them corn.[9] The use of "revolt" is interesting in this context, since that term assumes that the people of Nanicapana were under Spanish dominion in the first place. In 1560, this was more a Spanish legal fantasy than an American reality.

Some soldiers in the Luna expedition headed to Coosa, hoping to find an abundant land and a warmer welcome. Things were less tense, and the Spanish even joined a military campaign to reduce nearby Napochies to its prior tributary status. This, combined with the fact that some Spanish attempted to purchase corn and negotiate, indicates that the "smash-and-grab" method of colonization preferred by Soto was going out of style.[10] Franciscan friars also played a larger role in the Luna expedition than they had in Soto's, indicating that while the Spanish still intended to dominate the Southeast and protect it from European rivals, brute force was not the only tool at their disposal. A letter from Fray Pedro de Feria stressed the importance of distancing the expedition from its predecessors: "If the Indians see that those who go now do the same thing as those who have gone before, they will rightly think that they go for the same reasons which the others went." The result would be justifiable native violence against the Spanish, as "they will most properly endeavor to drive them out of their lands and entirely close the door to the conversion of those people, which is the purpose for which we are going and the intention of the king, our Lord."[11] Of course, conversion was only one of the reasons that Luna's army had shoved its way into the interior Southeast.

It was clear by the late summer of 1560 that Coosa's goodwill was not permanent, in spite of a tenuous alliance with the Spanish.[12] More perceptive Spaniards recognized that "it is to be feared that the natives may revolt when they collect their corn from the fields, and the Spaniards take it from them as they will have to do to maintain themselves. Even now the Indians think that they [Spanish] are only passing through, and give them carriers and everything they ask merely to get them out of the country." Indeed, some episodes of violence had broken out, and the Spanish were unable to counter when "they appeared and shot a few arrows at us" because "when we sought them not an Indian could be seen, nor could any be found because of the dense undergrowth of the country."[13]

In the middle of all of this, international affairs intruded when the Spanish received intelligence that the French had plans for a colony on the Atlantic Coast. Velasco ordered Luna to move fast, but the expedition was paralyzed by the lack of food, discipline, and Luna's own declining mental state. Native Mexicans and married soldiers had asked to be sent back to New Spain, citing the lack of food.[14] Luna's captains questioned the wisdom of splitting the Spanish force between Nanicapana and Coosa, arguing that to do so "would cause the Indians, they being hostile, as they are, to destroy us by availing themselves, as they have hitherto done, of the opportunity to lie in wait for us at certain places where they could attack us while we, not knowing the country or the roads, could not oppose them."[15] Velasco recalled Luna in 1561; his successor also failed to plant a colony on the Atlantic Coast.[16]

The native Southeast that confronted the Luna expedition was unable to field large enough armies that might have sent the Spanish packing. It is difficult to imagine, for instance, that had the thousands of people who fought to the death at Mabila come upon Luna's hungry, pathetic corps they wouldn't have driven them off. Native resistance to Spanish encroachment continued, but the style of violence that prevailed in the native Southeast was more skirmish-oriented. It was low-risk, limited warfare. The decreased size of polities was even more noticeable to the next Spanish army that invaded the Southeast. Following the French challenge of the early 1560s and the explosive Spanish response, a permanent Spanish presence became even more imperative. Of course, the relatively meager attempt failed to live up to the grand scheme. In the case of Juan Pardo's expeditions of the late 1560s, the plan was to establish a beachhead at Santa Elena to solidify the Spanish hold on the Atlantic Coast, then to plant forts and missions along a road all the way to the silver mines of Zacatecas, well over a thousand miles to the southwest. Pardo's soldiers made one brief foray out of Santa Elena in the winter of 1566–67 and another, longer incursion in the winter of 1567–68.

The instructions given to Pardo stressed the need for friendly relations. The captain was to "make all friendship with the caciques" and in towns which had a "principal cacique," Pardo was to erect a cross and leave people behind to instruct Indians in the basics of Christianity.[17] The first trip passed without incident, but in October 1567, Pardo began to suspect that a regional conspiracy was afoot. At the town of Satapo (presumably the submerged Citico archaeological site in eastern Tennessee), a midnight visitor informed Pardo's interpreter, Guillermo Rufín, that "Cosa, who had arrived there that night with many Indians, his vassals, and Olameco, and Uchi, and Casque, caciques, with all the Indians whom they had there, and the cacique of that place, with all his Indians, were accustomed to kill many Spaniards who before now had come through those parts and that they would have discussed no less and agreed among themselves to make three ambushes and put them in a spot where the captain and his company had to pass on their way to Cosa."[18] The informant pointed out that the Indians in the region would no longer be providing food to Spaniards unless they were willing to pay for it.[19] Although Pardo seemed generally disinclined to change course—he stated, "I determined to continue in my road"—in this instance he called his officers together and decided to head back to Santa Elena.[20]

What is meant by the statement that Coosa was "accustomed to kill many Spaniards"? Charles Hudson speculates that this may indicate that people from Coosa had participated at the battle of Mabila in 1540 or that the story might even have originated in Coosa. It would work to Coosa's advantage in relation to the Spanish if its leaders could convince Spaniards that the chiefdom had taken on their countrymen and won (and given the holes in the Soto accounts, this may reference an actual event). If the man who delivered the intelligence to Rufín was not from Coosa but from a nearby or subsidiary town, the story gets even more interesting. What if Coosa sought to maintain its tributary towns by referencing a violent past in which Coosa had taken on mounted enemies with firearms and defeated them? Perhaps a mythical victory over the Spanish helped burnish the military reputation of Coosa.[21]

Along the road to Zacatecas, Pardo ordered the construction of houses in some Indian towns, mainly as repositories for tributary corn to be set aside for Spanish use. He also left small garrisons to guard hastily constructed fortifications at Olamico, Cauchi, Joara, Guatari, Cofitachequi, and Orista.[22] Coosa, its tributaries, and other towns may have not been able to mount a concerted assault against Pardo's army or didn't want to risk the level of casualties they might have incurred. But once the army was broken into tiny pieces and isolated in Indian communities, warriors destroyed every single one of the installations and killed nearly all of their Spanish defenders. The historical record offers two explanations for this violence, the appropriation of native food stores and the abuse of native women. Either one could easily explain the destruction of the forts and their garrisons.[23]

There is recently uncovered archaeological evidence in North Carolina that has already revealed a great deal about the Pardo fort at Joara, Fort San Juan, and ongoing digs may provide more clues about the fort's demise. Since 2001, students under the supervision of David Moore, Robin Beck, and Christopher Rodning have participated in summer field schools put on by Warren Wilson College and Western Piedmont Community College. These excavations, combined with work at the site from the 1980s and before have enhanced our understanding of native-Spanish interaction. "Structure 1," as the archaeologists labeled it, was built in a native style but with some clear European influences (nails, for instance) that indicate at least some back-and-forth between the two groups. After all, Joara and Spanish people lived next door to each other for a year and a half at the site. The structure may also reveal more clues about the last days of the fort, since some of its features appear to be undisturbed since that violent time.[24] Important archaeological work continues to be done at this site, as well as others, around the northern edges of Spain's American empire.

Native American resistance in the interior combined with continuing pressure on the Atlantic Coast from Fort Caroline to Drake's raid to force the Spanish to consolidate their power at St. Augustine. Mission activities would, of course, continue, but grand schemes of North American domination were shelved in favor of more pragmatic plans. Decades of Spanish intrusions into the interior and the permanent coastal presence of Europeans after 1565 took a fearsome toll, though. Europeans introduced new pathogens and animals and dislocated populations by enslaving and moving large numbers of people.

Smallpox was probably not the culprit, as recent work by Paul Kelton has shown, but the native population of the Southeast was dropping precipitously in the decades after Soto's entrada, perhaps as the result of other epidemics, though the evidence is more anecdotal than anything.[25] At Cofitachequi, the people told Soto that their town had been stricken in 1537, though it's not clear by what.[26] Still, by the time Pardo's army arrived in the same area, there was no one as powerful as the "Lady of Cofitachequi" who had greeted Soto. The fastidious record keeper of the expedition noted the presence of Canos Orata (an *orata* being a low-level leader) but did not mention a *mico* (a slightly higher-up official) or a *cacique grande* (a paramount or very powerful leader).[27]

Population estimates for the chiefdom of Coosa tell a similar story of decline. Coosa was a paramount chiefdom with a population of thirty to fifty thousand about the time Europeans arrived. Nearly twelve thousand lived in the Coosa heartland in northeast Georgia. By 1715, this population was estimated to be about seventeen hundred.[28] To be sure, this decline may not be solely attributable to disease. In the early modern Southeastern, large numbers of people migrated for a variety of reasons.

Numbers do not tell the whole story, of course. When disease and violence moved into the Mississippian Southeast, they began to unmake those societies and to unravel those ways of looking at the world. The descendants of the Mississippians no longer created monumental architecture in the form of earthen platform mounds, for instance. Not every settlement had a platform mound, but most sizable towns had at least one, and they remain one of the signature features of Mississippian era Native American life.

Violence also played a role in the rearrangement of societies. Mississippian polities like Tascaluza's, which had been the site of shocking violence in 1540, were essentially wiped off the map. Most towns did not face this kind of all-consuming violence. News did travel, though, and even places that didn't experience Spanish violence directly were aware of it. Documentary evidence is hard to come by, so what follows is speculative. But what might the people of subordinate Mississippian towns have thought when they saw Spanish armies run roughshod through mound complexes? Might it have emboldened local leaders to challenge established hierarchies? The leaders of Napochies sensed Coosa's decline in the years after Soto and stopped their tribute until Luna's Spanish army tilted the balance in favor of their former rulers. The point is that there may be biological explanations for the decline of populations, but we should not discount the human component either. History needs both the stage set by environmental factors and the drama provided by people.

## Coalescent Societies, Violence, and Gender

The trouble with trying to discern how autonomous towns understood violence and its proper deployment is that identity was in flux during the era between Soto's entrada and the establishment of Charles Town. Of course, when is identity not in flux? To search for a pure, unaltered Muskogean or Iroquoian culture of violence in the Southeast would likely be fruitless. Having said this, a closer look at the coalescent societies of the Southeast illustrates some of the key features of the emergent early modern cultures of violence.[29]

In the 1400s and 1500s, at the peak of their dominance, chiefdoms went to war for chiefly reasons. Individual chiefs and their lineages fought to legitimate their authority, to obtain prestige goods and other important resources, and to resolve grudges. Once the power of individual chiefs was curtailed as chiefdoms dispersed, these motivations shifted. In many Southeastern villages, the office of the chief was split between a war chief and civil chief. War chiefs' powers expanded before and during the era of English colonial expansion.[30] Grudges between chiefs developed into the kin-based patterns of intergroup violence familiar to students of the early modern Southeast. The addition of firearms and other European imports, including disease, to this already volatile situation increased the stakes for many communities, who aligned themselves with Europeans to partake in the new economy. Population declines brought on by disease could be made up quickly by increased captive taking, as Daniel Richter as shown for the people of the Iroquois League.[31]

Following the widespread social changes of the period prior to English colonization, war parties became increasingly informal. They were not as organized as Mississippian armies, and their aims were altered. Despite the marked shifts from Mississippian to later societies, and despite the changes in tactics and motivation brought about by firearms, pieces of the Mississippian culture of violence informed the emerging polities of the native Southeast. Native war parties continued to be hierarchical, and the hierarchy was determined by previous success in battle. Young men entered the hierarchy when they took their first scalp. Higher classes of warriors included those who had taken multiple scalps and earned the respect of their peers through skill in battle. At the top of the scale for many Muskogean communities was a town's *tastanagi thlucco,* or "big warrior." When Thomas Nairne visited the "Ochessees"—a Muskogean town located on the Ocmulgee River in the shadow of the mound complex and Mississippian fields[32]—a brief aside in his journal gave some indication of how seriously those people took military rank: "The Ochessees and other warriors use these small white featherd arrows likewise [to show their position in the military hierarchy]. No man ever presumes to wear one unless thus publickly given, he would be a comon redicule the same as if a tradsman in England should wear a star or Garter."[33]

For Choctaws, and their Western Muskogean ancestors who had built Moundville, military prowess was an indicator of masculinity and honor as well, and failure was costly. Jean-Bernard Bossu, who traveled to Choctaw country in the 1750s and 1760s, wrote that a chief who did not succeed at war "loses all his credit; nobody has any trust in his command, and he is obliged to come down to the rank of a mere warrior."[34]

Some remnants of Mississippian political organization survived the disappearance of the chiefdoms as political entities. As Steven Hahn put it in his *Invention of the Creek Nation,* "As the hierarchical superstructure of the chiefdoms became impossible to maintain, the emergent Creeks came to rely more on the social substructure of the Mississippian culture."[35] These "emergent Creeks," who inhabited the autonomous towns of Georgia and Alabama, played down formerly sacred chief's roles and "emphasized the balance and harmony of the group."[36] Thomas Nairne's journal is instructive in this regard. He visited the "Ochessees and Talapoosies [Tallapoosas, another Muskogean town with Mississippian roots]" in 1708 and noted that "the Government of this people such as it is, seems to be the shadow of an Aristocracy, nothing can be further from absolute monarchy."[37] Nairne elaborated: "They seldom use any Coercion, only harangue, if by that they can persuade it's well."[38] A consensus-building style of civil leadership began to emerge at the same time as the towns of the Southeast were coalescing to become the region's early modern Native American nations.[39]

The Iroquoian-speaking towns which dotted the valleys of the Appalachian mountain range had an interesting relationship with the Muskogean towns farther to the south and Catawban towns to the southeast. Their Iroquoian-based language indicates northern origins at some point in the distant past (thousands, not hundreds of years), but their long residence in the Southeast brought them into contact with different ways of looking at the world: some of the town names are decidedly Muskogean, while others are Iroquoian, for instance. Iroquoian towns in the sixteenth-century Southeast often featured platform mounds. Even if Iroquoian speakers did not construct mounds in some places, it was a fateful choice to plant towns on or near sites that had so clearly meant a great deal to their previous inhabitants. Archaeologist Christopher Rodning believes that this practice "laid claims to places that had symbolic significance to native people in the region."[40]

Among these towns, the inhabitants of which the English would call "Cherokee," the process of coalescence seems to have happened slightly later than among the Muskogean towns, but along broadly similar lines.[41] Emergent Cherokee towns were more egalitarian than their Mississippian predecessors, and Raymond Fogelson attributes this to a deep-seated notion that no individual should have too much power. Iroquoian towns, after all, favored consensus building over coercion.[42] This is one of the main differences between Iroquoian and Muskogean political organization in the early Southeast. Both had chiefly traditions, but individual leaders held power in somewhat different fashions. Not that Muskogean leaders were terribly coercive, but Iroquoian, and later Cherokee, leaders were likely to view themselves as spokesmen for their towns. On a town level, the power of Cherokee men was balanced by the power of Cherokee women. Most clan leaders were women, as they were in Iroquois country (present-day upstate New York and Ontario), which elevated women's status within Cherokee towns as a whole.[43] Violence between Cherokee towns and other polities was exclusively the province of men, but even though women rarely participated in combat, they advised men on matters of war and peace.[44] They also determined the fate of captives taken in warfare. Men brought captives into Cherokee towns, but it was often women who performed the ritual acts of torture. Men brought back scalps of defeated enemies, but it was women who led the Scalp Dance and imitated the gestures that men performed in combat in a kind of theatrical violence.[45] Theda Perdue argued in *Cherokee Women* that during times of hunting, warfare, menstruation, and childbirth, Cherokee society was most strictly divided between men and women. These were points at which "women were most female and men were most male."[46] This proscription did not prohibit a handful of eighteenth-century Cherokee women from participating in battles and garnering honor as "War Women."[47]

Cherokee military rankings appear to have been less rigid than their Creek counterparts, but Cherokee manhood itself depended on skill at the hunt and in battle. Alexander Longe, one of the earliest English visitors to Cherokee country, described the process through which young Cherokee men received war honors: "The king calls the head Senator that has the public store which consists only of beads and dressed deerskins. He brings to the King some of each sort. The king stands up if it be a great warrior and gives each of them a war name and a present."[48] In 1751, Satchetche, a Cherokee headman, addressed Governor Glen of South Carolina: "I am head Man of Tucosigia, and of several Upper Towns, and though I am but a young Man I have been at War."[49]

Nearly a century before, and far from Cherokee country, a Timucua man expressed a similar sentiment regarding the connection between masculinity and violence. During a 1656 Timucuan uprising, an Indian man, who had been previously kicked and called a dog by a Spanish captain, Agustín Pérez, killed the offending officer and scalped him. When questioned at trial, he "confessed that he had known he would have to pay for what he had done sooner or later, but that he was satisfied because until then '*he had not been a man,* and with that action he was a *noroco* of God and the King, and he was very content.'"[50]

The Choctaws, a nation coalesced from the remnants of several Mississippian chiefdoms, including Moundville and Bottle Creek, followed a similar transition as those laid out for the Creeks and Cherokees.[51] According to James Carson, a leading chronicler of Choctaw history, early modern Choctaws "shared a common baseline of Mississippian culture that consisted of four 'deep' structures: chiefly political organization, matrilineal kinship, a gendered division of labor, and a complex cosmological system based on the sanctity of the sacred circle and the rules and rites necessary to prevent it from foreign invasion."[52] The implications for a Choctaw culture of violence are not precisely clear, but in later descriptions of Choctaw society, a special category of manhood was reserved for men who had not participated in war or who had killed only women or children.[53] It is also possible that Choctaw moieties, red for war and white for peace, are related to the prevalence of red and white in Mississippian artwork.[54]

The Catawban speakers of the Piedmont, who would become quite powerful in the eighteenth century, suffered tremendously in the aftermath of Soto's entrada. The region had been the heart of the powerful Cofitachequi chiefdom. In Soto's time, it collected tribute from a number of subsidiary towns and featured an elaborate social hierarchy: the Lady of Cofitachequi who greeted Soto was borne on a litter and had an ornate canoe with awnings and cushions. As mentioned above, by the time of the Pardo expedition, its population and power had declined precipitously. Its mounds and central location made it a meeting place (a handful of caciques came to hear Pardo's speech there, for instance), but it was a shadow of its former self, and polities on its fringe, Joara (Xualla) and Guatari, had grown in stature. Thirty caciques greeted Pardo at Guatari. Pardo decided to plant a fort in Joara and leave thirty soldiers behind. The next European visitor to the region, a German physician named John Lederer, arrived in the 1670s and found the former chiefly towns all but depopulated. New centers were forming, though, perhaps in response to the predations of slaving groups such as the Occaneechis and Westos. Before either of these groups could attack the coalescing towns in earnest, the former slavers were weakened by conflict with the English and allied Indians. A new Piedmont economy, based on trade with the English, and a shared Mississippian past allowed Catawban speakers to build the Catawba nation in the early 1700s.[55]

Spanish and French colonizers in the Southeast both noticed men who did not go to war. European bias in this area is hard to get around. Spanish and French men were raised in a culture that equated biological maleness with masculinity and biological femaleness with femininity and generally did not look favorably on individuals who blurred the distinction between the two. Many Native American groups, including those in the Southeast, had more complex understandings of gender. In Cauchi, a town in western North Carolina, Juan Pardo's expedition came upon a man dressed as a woman, and the captain was fascinated. Pardo insisted that the notary Bandera take down exactly what transpired: "Pardo told them to ask why that Indian went among the Indian women, wearing an apron as they did. The interpreters asked the above mentioned of the cacique of the place and the cacique replied through the interpreters that the Indian was his brother and that because he was not a man for war nor carrying on the business of a man, he went about in that manner like a woman and he did all that is given to a woman to do." Pardo insisted that all of this be recorded "in order that it may be known and understood how warlike are the Indians of these provinces of Florida."[56] This role seems similar to other gender categories around native North America, such as the two-spirit or *berdache*.[57] One of Le Moyne's paintings engraved by De Bry depicts a similar phenomenon among Timucuans: men dressed as women assisting women with agricultural labor (see figure 5).[58] The connection between the "warlike" nature of Cauchi and the chief's brother taking on a feminine role is not readily

**FIG. 5.** In this de Bry engraving, men fulfill a feminine role. Women load the baskets of food, then men dressed in women's clothing carry them away. From *Der Newlich Erfundenen Landschafft Americae* (Frankfurt, 1603), Library of Congress.

apparent. Was he being shamed for not going to war? While it is impossible to say with certainty, this seems highly unlikely, given his brother's obvious lack of shame regarding the situation. Perhaps Pardo thought it "warlike" because he believed that some men were not deemed masculine enough to bear arms, with only the most skilled at combat earning the right to be perceived as men, and found the situation confusing.

Violence in the Southeast continued to have religious significance. Though James Adair spent much of his monumental *History of the American Indians* trying to prove the connection between Southeastern Indians and the ancient Hebrews, the work remains valuable to ethnographers and historians. Adair's description of war preparation gives some idea of its spiritual significance. "Before the Indians go to War," according to Adair, "they have many preparatory ceremonies of *purification* and *fasting*, like what is recorded of the Israelites."[59] The account goes on to describe the taking of black drink and the use of medicine bundles, or "Indian arks," as Adair terms them. Many Southeastern peoples continued to use medicine bundles to prepare for war. Among Cherokees, medicine bundles often contained coals from a scared fire. Vernon James Knight Jr. has posited a link between an eighteenth-century Chickasaw bundle and Mississippian religion.[60] Among Choctaws, stuffed animal skins provided divine guidance for war parties. If the skins touched the ground or were otherwise upset, it bode poorly for the expedition.[61]

Apart from the Chickasaws' "sacred ark," a box containing ceremonial objects carried near sites of battle, other evidence exists for a connection between Mississippian and colonial era sacred objects related to warfare. Stylized war clubs, worthless in actual combat, continued to be carried by native southeasterners, particularly Muskogeans. At Tuckabatchee, a Creek town in present-day Alabama, Adair spoke with Old Bracket, an elderly warrior whose official title was Ispokogi Mico, concerning several brass and copper plates. These plates, really ceremonial representations of celts or war axes, were only to be brought out at certain prescribed times and then only handled by "particular people, and those fasting; and no unclean woman must be suffered to come near them," according to Old Bracket.[62] Some vestiges of a Mississippian culture of violence persisted into the late eighteenth century.

The major difference between Mississippian and coalescent cultures of violence lies in how societies were organized and what these new political arrangements meant for the ways in which those societies carried out intercultural violence. In Mississippian societies, sacred objects related to warfare and the decision to go to war were usually in the hands of paramount chiefs, high priests, and their lineages. Outside of this small handful of individuals, commoners were forbidden from taking part in discussions about violence or handling sacred objects associated with war. Once chiefdoms declined and autonomous towns became the dominant polities of the native Southeast, decisions to go to war were spread out among a larger number of people and could even devolve to the clan level. Once few extraordinarily powerful leaders ruled in the Southeast, one of the reasons for warfare between Mississippian groups—to legitimize ruling lineages and chiefs' power—was taken out of the equation. While Mississippian polities could mass large forces or engage in small-scale fighting, coalescent societies were much more likely to eschew large, high-risk battles, instead opting for quick strikes. Depopulation associated with disease and violence heightened the need to take captives alive, though adult men were usually killed. Conversely, though Mississippian leaders would have preferred not to lose warriors in battle, the desire to avoid high-casualty affairs was imperative since one defeat could be catastrophic. Intensive contact with Europeans altered Native American cultures of violence in significant ways.[63]

While searching for a better word than "massacre" or "uprising" to describe the 1622 Powhatan attack on the English settlements outside the colony at Jamestown, anthropologist Frederic Gleach hit upon "coup," from *coup de main,* a "stroke of the hand." Gleach uses the word to refer to a swift, acute attack. This avoids the Anglo-centrism of "massacre" and eschews the notion that Powhatans were under English rule and therefore could rise up against it. More important, though, it most closely approaches how the native peoples of the post-Mississippian world conceived of violence. They preferred surprising, sharp blows designed to demonstrate mastery or to punish misbehavior while not risking high casualties. There were, of course, no universal ways of violence among the hundreds of distinct Native American communities, but coup-style violence was prevalent in many parts of eastern North America.[64]

The difficulties in pinning down cultures of violence of Southeastern peoples in the period between Soto's entrada and the establishment of English Carolina attest to the flexibility of cultures of violence in general. Even among one nation, the Creeks, for instance, violence in 1700 was different from violence in the 1750s or during the era of removal. Still, showing how cultures of violence interact and evolve over time is a useful exercise that sheds new light on the English conquest of the region from all of its complex sides. Chapter 5 explores the deep historical roots of English ideas about violence and its proper role in colonizing near and distant lands, and chapter 6 will demonstrate the impossibility of separating early modern Southeastern cultures of violence from the arrival of English traders and goods on the scene. If Creek and Cherokee people began to see themselves as nations in response to English colonization, or that process pushed them along an already-determined road toward national identity, then it follows logically that their cultures of violence would be reshaped by contact with the English. The cultures of violence that developed among colonial era Native Americans were profoundly influenced by those peoples' interactions with Europeans.[65]

# CHAPTER 5

# Creating English Conquest

Wingina, who had recently taken the name Pemisapan, leader of a small Algonquian community in present-day North Carolina, had reason to fear for his life in the spring of 1586. He had been confronted by a band of outsiders whose demands were becoming increasingly outrageous. Wingina's people had already cleared fields and planted crops for their overbearing neighbors. They had even gone so far as to construct weirs in nearby rivers to assist the intruders in catching fish before moving into the interior and leaving their unwelcome guests to their own devices. Following a series of purported intrigues, the English newcomers launched a preemptive assault against Wingina's people. Wingina, along with several other Algonquians, were shot and beheaded during the assault. Though it was Edward Nugent who committed the act, his governor, Ralph Lane, who like Nugent was a veteran warrior of Irish campaigns, approved heartily and put the trophy head on display.[1]

Why did the English cut off Wingina's head? They had certain ideas about which sorts of violence were appropriate for any given situation. These ideas were not of Lane's or Nugent's invention; they place these men firmly within the longstanding tradition of violent English colonization. They probably should be credited with being the first English men to deploy these ideas in North America. The incident between the English and Algonquians points up some crucial characteristics of the English culture of colonial violence, before it went on to transform Southeastern North America. Small but increasing numbers of English men and women began to arrive in the American Southeast in the second half of the seventeenth century. They brought with them the tools to build settlements, goods to trade with local populations, African slaves, and animals for food and work. English people, wherever they went in the Atlantic world, also carried with them ideas about violence and its proper use in a colonial setting. In 1670, the English overseas empire may have been a relatively recent creation, but English ideas about violence had a long history.

The Indian trade and plantation agriculture made Carolina economically viable at the same time as they brought about violence between the people of the Southeast. These institutions also altered English, African, and Native American cultures of violence. The violence of English planting and trade reached its most recognizable form in the Americas in the seventeenth and eighteenth centuries, but it had deep roots in the historical experiences of the English people before they arrived. England, Ireland, the Caribbean, New England, and Virginia all played some role in the development of an English culture of violence as it related to conquest and colonization in Carolina. The English entrance into the American Southeast marked a significant turning point in the region's history of violence. This entrance would not occur until the second half of the seventeenth century. By that time, English men and women had been involved in many violent colonial situations at home and abroad.

## Roots of English Colonial Violence

English identity was formed in the violence of conquest. This fact is not only apparent to historians looking back, but English people understood it quite well in the sixteenth and seventeenth centuries. Queen Elizabeth's secretary, Sir Thomas Smith, looked to Roman and Anglo-Norman precedents as he planned the "Enterprise of Ulster" in the sixteenth century.[2] William Strachey was even more specific. In *Historie of Travaile into Virginia Britania,* Strachey wrote that England owed its virtues, specifically "the powerfull discourse of divine reason," to its conquest by Romans. The Romans had "reduced the conquered partes of our barbarous iland into provinces, and established in them colonies of old souldiers," saving the English from living as "overgrowen satyrs, rude and untutred."[3]

From the arrival and subsequent evacuation of the Romans, through Jute, Angle, Saxon, Viking, and Norman invasions, England itself was the site of bloody wars of colonization and conquest. The people of the British Isles, whether they were doing the colonizing or being colonized, were familiar with intercultural violence as a way of life from a very early date. Their experiences shaped the way they conceived of the Americas, Native Americans, and colonization in general. Colonial violence in the British Isles began long before the so-called Age of Discovery and continued to be significant even as colonies developed on North America's eastern seaboard and in the Caribbean. Only a small number of colonial promoters, merchants, and settlers were interested in trans-Atlantic colonization, at least in its early stages. Most colonizing took place closer to home.[4]

Colonization, trade (often armed), civilization, warfare, and religious conversion were all linked in the English mind of the sixteenth century.[5] All fell within the notion of dominion. Dominion as an idea and domination as policy run through several centuries of English colonization and appear in both Europe and America. Dominion, as learned Europeans understood it in the fifteenth century, was a blend of Roman imperial and Christian ideologies; Romans tried to civilize the world, and Christian monarchs equated civilization with Christianity.[6] All European colonizers subscribed to the concept of dominion, but each emphasized different aspects of it and used different goals to achieve it.[7] By the time they got to Carolina, the English had refined what they meant by dominion, emphasizing the benefits of English agricultural production and profitable trade and deemphasizing warfare and religious conversion. English planters and traders did not perceive their work as extraordinarily violent. Or, more accurately, they recognized that their brand of colonization was violent but they legitimized this violence by referencing its civilizing effects. This sort of conquest dovetails with the founding myth of the United States, which emphasizes the organic spread of English-speaking people across North America.

While the Christian kingdoms of Iberia were refining their identities against Muslim occupiers, English identity was coming into focus throughout the British Isles, often accompanied by colonial violence. Ireland proves an interesting comparison to the colonization of the North American Southeast.[8] Both experienced successive waves of English interest, in Elizabeth's time and then again during the mid- to late seventeenth century during Cromwell's time and after the Restoration. Roanoke and Jamestown date to the early period, and Carolina was founded in the immediate aftermath of Charles II's return to the monarchy. The same set of English colonial ideas prompted efforts to colonize in both regions. Similar English ideas about violence underlay military campaigns in Ireland and at Roanoke. The main difference between the two in the late sixteenth century was scale. England mustered large armies to inflict punishing blows on Ireland, a densely populated land close to home. One scholar estimates that to fight against the Irish during what came to be known as the Nine Years' War, the English called on the services of more than thirty thousand soldiers.[9] Elizabeth's army killed thousands—twelve hundred in two hours at Kinsale in 1602. Ulster's civilian population suffered tremendously, as English lords took steps to starve it into submission while also killing Irish peasants at an alarming rate.[10] The geopolitical situation in the American Southeast was somewhat different. The English were very far from home, and their resources were stretched to the breaking point. Though Powhatan's land, Tsenacommacah, may have been well peopled, the coastal Algonquian settlements near Roanoke appear to have been less so. The English intent may have been similar—to subjugate "unruly" natives and to impose English plantations and "civilization" through force—but the scale at which they could operate was much reduced.

The history of English involvement in Ireland is long and ugly. It began in the late twelfth century, when several Irish kings pledged their loyalty to Henry II and began to pay tribute to him. The English (or Anglo-French) established dominion over some of the island through conquest and set about Anglicizing Ireland. English zeal for colonization waxed and waned over the next two centuries, but the process itself slowed as native Irish leaders began to resist violently and English settlers moved away from border areas. By the sixteenth century, Ireland outside the Pale fell under the control of a mix of Gaelic lords and Old English lords. From Dublin and London, English leaders perceived Ireland as degenerate and savage. The religious upheavals of the 1530s and 1540s gave colonizers' arguments a religious tint, and the stage was set for a massive reconquest of Ireland.[11]

The connections between English activities in Ireland and the Americas are often misunderstood, according to Nicholas Canny.[12] The connections between English violence in Ireland and the Americas are clearer. This is true not only in terms of tactics employed but the ideas underlying the various colonizing missions and the rhetorical justifications of colonial violence. The colonization advocates that surrounded Elizabeth I had experience with colonial violence in Ireland, and their ideas influenced future generations of colonizers in the Americas.

Elizabeth's reign coincided with renewed English interest in colonization in Ireland and to a lesser extent America, a flowering of culture, and a virulent strain of Protestantism. A particular understanding of England's place in the world and England's history of involvement in Ireland fueled late-sixteenth-century colonization. Pamphleteer Thomas Churchyard described Flanders, France, Portugal, Ireland, and Scotland as "the shell of a precious Nutte, the sweet Kirnell whereof is the blessed state of ENGLANDE. And though with worldly wickednesse, and troubles of our tyme, the goodly shell is somewhat wormeaten and cracked, the Kirnell shewes itself so sounde, that Gods greate goodnesse & glorie is partly or altogether therein expressed."[13] Similar ideas propelled small numbers of English people into the wider Atlantic world at the end of the sixteenth century.

In Ireland, the English used martial law in combination with tactics designed to frighten and humiliate native lords and commoners who opposed their rule.[14] The threat of beheading and the display of trophy heads accompanied English government in Ireland, and mass killings were not unheard of. During the Kildare rebellion in 1534, Henry VIII had every male member of the FitzGerald family put to death and confiscated their lands.[15] Not all Anglo-Irish conflicts were so one-sided; when Sir Edmund Butler led an assault against English colonists in 1569, he "would cause English dead men's bodies to be stripped out of their English garments, and their hose and dubletts (being stuffed and trussed) he would sett up as markes for his kerns [soldiers] to throw their darts at."[16] For Edmund Butler, it was militarily crucial to kill the English who were colonizing his homeland. Stripping the bodies added to the humiliation, and stuffing the clothes—markers of their Englishness—and assaulting them completed the triumph by adding symbolic weight. Mutilating bodies and enacting theatrical violence using objects or animals was intended to send a message across cultural lines. Hernando de Soto had employed this tactic when he cut off arms and noses in the Southeast, and Powhatans would do the same when they assaulted English planters with farm tools in 1622.

Sir Humphrey Gilbert, who along with Walter Raleigh was one of the leading advocates of English colonization in Ireland and the Americas, sent violent messages of his own. In Munster, Gilbert gained notoriety by extending his military campaign to noncombatants—"manne, woman and child"—so that "the name of an Inglysh man was made more teryble now to them than the syght of an hundyth was before." Gilbert also ordered that the heads of Gaelic rebels

> which were killed in the daie, should be cutte of from their bodies and brought to the place where he incamped at night, and should there bee laied on the ground by eche side of the waie ledying into his owne Tente so that none could come into his Tente for any cause but commonly he muste passe through a lane of heddes which he used *ad terrorem*, the dedde feelying nothyng the more paines thereby: and yet did it bring greate terrour to the people when thei sawe the heddes of their dedde fathers, brothers, children, kinsfolke and freindes, lye on the grounde before their faces, as thei came to speake with the said Collonell.[17]

Gilbert's tactics were justified, in the words of Thomas Churchyard, because "the stiffe necked must be made to stoupe."[18] *Ad terrorem* violence was a part of the English conquest of the American Southeast as well.

The English drew support for the reconquest of Ireland from a wide range of sources. The most famous is Edmund Spenser's *View of the Present State of Ireland,* but this was not the only justification given.[19] Others included Richard Beacon's *Solon His Folie* and John Derricke's verse-and-woodcut *Image of Irelande.* Spenser, who lived in Munster from 1590 until 1598, concluded that civilization in Ireland would occur only after Irish

**Fig. 6.** This woodcut, from John Derricke's *Image of Ireland* (London, 1581), shows a victorious English army taking trophy heads as it returns from campaign. Courtesy of the University of Edinburgh Library.

society had been broken apart and put back together after the bad parts had been excised. This would obviously require military action.[20] Beacon's *Solon His Folie* took a slightly different approach. He didn't demonize the Irish and tried to plot a "middle course" between military action and the establishment of the common law.[21] Derricke's text appeared in 1581 and is notable for its woodcuts depicting the debased conditions of life in Ireland.[22] Two of the woodcuts depict the taking of trophy heads by English forces. The first depicts a triumphant English army returning from the field (see figure 6). At the front of the procession are two soldiers carrying heads on the points of their swords and one displaying his trophy in his hand. At the rear, another Irish rebel is about to lose his head.

The second woodcut is a scene of Sir Henry Sidney leaving Dublin castle on a campaign. Severed heads on pikes jut out from the ramparts. A warning verse accompanies the artwork: "These trunckles heddes do playnly showe, eache rebeles fatall end / And what a haynous crime it is, the Queene for to offend."[23]

Common themes run through all of these texts: the English are civilized, the Irish are savage and in some cases unable to reform, and as such, they will only respond to extraordinary violence. Common sense held that such atrocities could not be committed against Christians; English theorists argued that the Irish lived in paganism covered by a veneer of Catholicism.[24] English and Irish people had not always gotten along—far from it—but the sorts of violence brought to bear on the conflict in the sixteenth century were new.

Ralph Lane committed acts of colonial violence on both sides of the Atlantic Ocean. In February 1584, Lane petitioned for land in Munster. Lane hoped to conduct the O'Moores there. Doing so, he reasoned, would protect the English Pale. In March 1584, his petition became a demand. Lane wanted to be colonel, complete with a military force and confiscated estates. He reasoned that his service to the queen entitled him to as much. His demand was eventually approved, but he was not around to receive it; he had sailed for America, where he would engage in preemptive violence and approve the beheading of native lords who "resisted" English dominion.[25]

The English expected to have to use widespread, terror-inducing violence in their renewed assault on Ireland. In the Americas, a world known only from the accounts of Spanish and French settlers and English mariners, the case for preemptive violence was murky. Colonization advocates were convinced that the Spanish had colonized in a wrongheaded, brutal manner and subscribed wholeheartedly to the Black Legend. The late sixteenth century witnessed an increase in anti-Spanish and anti-Catholic feeling in England. The 1583 appearance in English of *The Spanish Colonie,* a translation of Bartolomé de Las Casas's *Brevissima Relación de la Destrucción de las Indias* fanned flames that were already burning.[26]

Las Casas, and the case of the Americas in general, sometimes gets too much credit for the creation of the Black Legend. English attitudes toward the Spanish were tied up in the desire to aid the Dutch in their fight for freedom, frustration at the Inquisition, the development of English piracy and the defeat of the Armada. The Black Legend had a habit of gaining traction whenever England's government needed to inflame public opinion against Spain. Two such moments were the late sixteenth century and Cromwell's time.[27] Whenever the English were engaged in violence, they sought to prove they were not as violent as other peoples—in this case, the Spanish. To counter alleged depravity, promoters touted a version of Englishness that stressed commercial development, civilization, weakening the Spanish, and solving England's social ills as reasons for colonization.

Richard Hakluyt the Younger was one of a number of promoters who advocated a particularly English version of colonization. In *Discourse of Western Planting,* the first reason given for a voyage is "thinlargemente of the Gospell of Christ." As to whether the Protestant or Catholic brand of Christianity would serve Americans better, Hakluyt noted that Spanish colonies were built on "filthie lucre" and "vaine ostentation" but that English colonies could spread true religion and capture "the soules of millions of those wretched people," moving them "from falsehoodde to truthe, from dombe Idolls to the lyvinge God, from the depe pitt of hell to the highest heavens."[28]

Hakluyt thought that memories of Spanish violence—"moste outragious and more then Turkishe cruelties"—would drive Americans, and their commodities, into the waiting arms of English colonizers. He repeated the charges of Bartolomé de Las Casas regarding Spanish activities in the Caribbean: the Spanish had indiscriminately slaughtered more people than could be counted, they massacred women and children, nobles and commoners alike, and they used dogs to tear apart the Indians. If his choice of sources didn't make it clear, Hakluyt let his readers know exactly how he felt about Spanish violence. The men who committed these acts were "without manhodde, emptie of all pitie, behavinge themselves as savage beastes, the slaughterers and murderers of mankind."[29] If Hakluyt viewed Spanish violence as uncivilized, unmanly, unfair, and unholy, his vision of English colonization veered to the other extreme. Hakluyt's *Discourse* contains almost no mention of the sorts of violence the English would have to undertake in order to wrest areas away from native or Spanish control. His ideas were simple: planting a couple of successful colonies in North America would convince native peoples of the purity of English intentions, and they would become Anglicans and anti-Spanish warriors.

Among Hakluyt's lists of supplies needed for colonization, there is an inventory of "Provisions tendinge to force." It includes "Captaines of longe and greate experience," "Souldiers well trayned in Flaunders to joyne with the younger," and "Harqubusshers of skill." Hakluyt also wanted the colonists to prepare specifically for combat with Native Americans; he suggested "Targett makers of harnes defensive againste Savages" and ships able to "passe to & froe offensive and defensive againste savages."[30]

Besides the obvious critique that can be leveled at most of Hakluyt's writings—that his work is naïve about actual conditions in the Americas, and that Elizabeth was unlikely to finance such an extravagant expedition—the list demonstrates some crucial considerations about early English colonization. Hakluyt was certain that Indians would join the English against the Spanish, but that certainty should not prevent the English from preparing to fight both Spanish and native enemies. Second, Hakluyt viewed colonization as, more than anything else, an enterprise that would increase the prestige of the English at the expense of the Spanish; they were the main enemies. In the list, and elsewhere in the *Discourse,* Hakluyt recommends the use of veterans from France and Flanders to man colonizing missions, reinforcing the connection between English military activities in Europe and the Atlantic.[31]

In the realm of ideas, at least, the English sought to avoid the type of conflict engendered by Spanish conquest. The violence of the English invasion betrayed even this low standard of behavior. The first English forays into the Americas were expansionist and aggressive, essentially combining militarism and trade. The leaders of some expeditions intentionally provoked native leaders, and even if English colonizers did not specifically set out to endanger native communities, their methods of claiming land, establishing dominion, and pressuring their neighbors for food ran afoul of existing native polities, with violent results.

## New Dominions: English Violence Crosses the Atlantic

Early English forays into the Americas by Martin Frobisher, Francis Drake, and John Hawkins combined interests in precious metals, the search for a passage to the East, and slaving with a culture of privateering that dominated the Atlantic world. The planting of colonies was a different sort of enterprise, because violent acts against indigenous peoples in their own territories rested on shaky legal ground. Early colonial charters soothed the consciences of colonizers, noting that the land they were moving to was underpopulated and underused. This was only one of the functions of the documents, though. In a legal sense, they began the process of turning American land into English land, which needed to be defined and developed along English lines. English imperialists did not perceive to be a violent project. However much they might argue to the contrary, though, English colonizers' documents committed the very violence they claimed to be avoiding. Maps in some American history textbooks replicate these colonial fantasies, as brightly colored bands, separated by thin black lines, slice cleanly across native America from Atlantic to Pacific. English charters set the stage for innumerable conflicts between native communities and English invaders in eastern North America. Trickiest of all, the story of the English conquest of America could be written as a tale of migration and settlement.[32]

Before 1670, when Carolina was founded, there were three main theaters of Anglo-American violence: the Chesapeake, New England, and the Caribbean. The most relevant to the current discussion are the Chesapeake and the Caribbean, on the edges of the native Southeast described in previous chapters. In the Chesapeake, English colonists and adventurers met and fought Algonquians for the first time. In both the Chesapeake and the Caribbean, the English established a labor system that relied increasingly on African slavery and the threat of violence. The connections between English American colonies have yet to be fully understood or appreciated.[33]

The men planning and financing colonial ventures drew upon the past for positive and negative models. Those colonizing Ireland during the Renaissance looked to classical times—their texts mention Alexander, the Greeks, and the Romans. Virginia's colonizers looked to the classics and Ireland as well as a growing body of Spanish, Portuguese, and French accounts of the Americas. New England's founders drew on their interpretation of scripture, but they also looked to the Chesapeake. Barbados' influences are not as clear. Settlers on Barbados drew upon earlier colonial models, mostly Dutch, and inherited a tradition of privateering. Barbados' brand of colonization was also monitored closely from London, since it was becoming fantastically wealthy.

Not every English settler had read the classics, had access to court correspondence between Hakluyt, Raleigh, and Elizabeth, or knew what was going on in other colonies. The people engaged in colonization were, however, part of a widening English Atlantic world that included Ireland and the Americas. Some had experience at sea, and some, like Ralph Lane, were veterans of military campaigns in Europe. Even those who were novices carried with them ideas about violence that were bound up in English history and identity.

It may seem at first that Lane and the other colonists were not prepared to deal with the local Algonquians, led by Wingina. They got over the wide cultural divide by treating the Algonquians much the same as they would Irish rebels, never mind the fact that the coastal Algonquians weren't technically rebelling. The English were not ready for the winter and expected their hosts to provide for them, and, in fact, Wingina's people built fish weirs, cleared fields, and planted crops in the vicinity of the English, but then moved quietly away.[34] Acting on rumors of an impending surprise attack, Lane took decisive preemptive action against Wingina, who had reluctantly come to Roanoke.[35] Lane's troops seized as many canoes as they could—beheading two Indians in the process—to prevent anybody from escaping and warning neighboring communities. Lane signaled his men with the phrase "Christ our victory"—eerily reminiscent of Moscoso's cry of "Santiago" several decades prior—and the rout was on. According to Lane, the assembled leaders, or werowances, "had by the mercie of God for our deliverance, that which they had purposed for us." Some English labored "that none of the rest should escape." Wingina, who had survived a first shot, fled to the woods, where he too lost his head.[36]

The English took trophy heads in Ireland as a means of terrorizing their enemies, and Lane was the first English commander to deploy the same tactic against Wingina and other Algonquians. Some aspects of the violence Lane used would make sense to Algonquians. The element of surprise, for instance, figured prominently in Native American warfare. So too did religion. The thoroughness of the English victory, "that none of the rest should escape," the desire to eradicate a people's leadership, and the wholesale slaughter, however, were alien to many Native American communities along the eastern seaboard.

English reporting of the event points to some of the tensions inherent in colonization itself. The expedition to Roanoke, in addition to introducing English violence to the inhabitants of the Chesapeake, also produced a celebratory tract by Thomas Hariot. Hariot's *Brief and True Report of the New Found Land of Virginia* spends its first pages describing natural commodities. When he does treat the region's native communities, the treatment is brief and dismissive: "In respect of troubling our inhabiting and planting, [they] are not to be feared; but they shall have cause both to fear and love us."[37] Nor did the English have to be present to kill. Thanks to the miracle of disease, they "might kil and slai whom wee would without weapons and not come neere them."[38] Hariot's omissions are telling; he hints that some English soldiers may have "been too fierce" but glosses over the beheading of Wingina and the ultimate failure of the colony.[39]

After Roanoke, Jamestown provided the next test case for English colonization. Within two years of the colony's founding, war had broken out between Powhatan's chiefdom and the English. The roots of this conflict can be traced to differences in world view and the English settlers' self-identified superiority. As in Roanoke, violence was largely absent from the planning and recruitment phase of the operation. Two texts from the first decade of the seventeenth century echo Hakluyt's reasons for colonization and hearken back to biblical, classical, and Spanish examples. William Crashaw, preacher to the Inner and Middle Temples of London, delivered the first, and Robert Johnson, a promoter of the Virginia colony, penned the second.[40]

The occasion for William Crashaw's sermon was Lord De La Warr's leaving for Virginia in 1609. Crashaw noted that the English, like Indians, had been pagans and devil worshippers until they were civilized by the Romans, Christianized by the apostles and disciples, and finally led away from popery during the Reformation. Virginia, he argued, should follow the same trajectory: civilization first, then Christianity. As for the enemies that stood in the way, there were only three, and not the Spanish, French, and natives one might expect. The only enemies were "the Divell, Papists, and Players."[41] On native resistance to colonization, Crashaw wrote that the English could expect none: "The savages? Nay, they invite us, and use us well: & if they were, a small matter, as long as they are their owne enemies.

But when they are converted and love their owne soules, then they will love us also, and eternize their names who brought the Gospell to them. Thus no enemies are yet found."[42] Crashaw compared Virginia to Canaan, which had been colonized by the Jews in much the same way the English were to colonize Virginia.[43]

Robert Johnson's tract, which also dates to 1609, stressed the benefits of colonization for native people and the example provided by the Romans. Johnson was willing to provide some outline for the treatment of native people that went against their best interest by opposing the English. He wrote that native people who "obstinatly refuse to unite themselves unto us, or shall maligne or disturbe our plantation, our chattel, or whatsoever belonging to us: they shall be held and reputed recusant, withstanding their owne good: and shall bee dealt with as enemies of the Common-wealth of their countrie."[44] Johnson's words betray the extent to which Virginia had already become English in the English mind. On one level, he recognizes it is "their countrie"; still, native people are no longer in control of their own destiny in Johnson's formulation. There was justification for treating natives like rebels as well. Irish lords who refused to submit to the English were labeled "recusant" and subjected to a wide array of punishments. Johnson does not advocate conquering Native Americans, as the Spanish had done in the West Indies with "rapiers point and Musket shot, murdering so many millions of naked Indians." The English could convert by "faire and loving meanes, suting to our English natures."[45]

The English at Jamestown were in no position to effect outright conquest of their native neighbors or even survive without native assistance. The initial colony was small, sickly, and exclusively male. Their weak status does mean that the English relied on "faire and loving meanes," however. English settlers at Jamestown took preemptive violent action against Virginia's Algonquians whenever they could. Tactics included the taking of hostages—who may or may not survive the ordeal—and beheadings. One August 1610 incident, related by George Percy, included both. After setting up an attack that "besett the salvages howses so thatt noene mighte escape," Percy's men "fell in upon them putt some fiftene or sixtene to the Sworde, and almoste all the reste to flyghte." One man's head was cut off, and the town's "Quene and her Children"[46] were taken prisoner. The English troops were apparently upset that anybody had been spared, and Percy gave in to their demands: "Itt was agreed upon to putt the children to deathe the w[hi]ch was effected by Throweinge them overboard and shoteinge owtt their Braynes in the water."[47] As for the "Quene," she would eventually be put to death as well, though the method was up for debate. Lord De La Warr wanted her burned alive, but Percy, "haveinge seene so mutche Blood shedd thatt day," ordered one of his subordinates to stab the woman to death instead.[48]

Attacks like Percy's went a long way to precluding any kind of peaceful relations between native communities and the English. Peace would obviously never be easy to maintain, given the nature of English colonization and the vast differences between English and Powhatan world views. The English continually expanded beyond the territory granted to them by Powhatan, planting settlements near the falls of the James River. April 1613 saw the betrayal and capture of Pocahontas. Her death in England in 1617 combined with Powhatan's death and the accession of Opechancanough to permanently poison relations between the two peoples.

Intercultural tensions that had simmered for more than a decade exploded in March 1622. There is some dispute about what to call this particular episode. It has been a "massacre," a "great massacre," an "uprising," and in the best recent interpretation, a "coup." In a well-placed blow, several groups of Algonquians attempted to force the English back into lands they had been given in Jamestown. The action left between three hundred and four hundred English settlers dead, many of them killed with farming implements. The symbolism is hard to miss. Written in the aftermath of

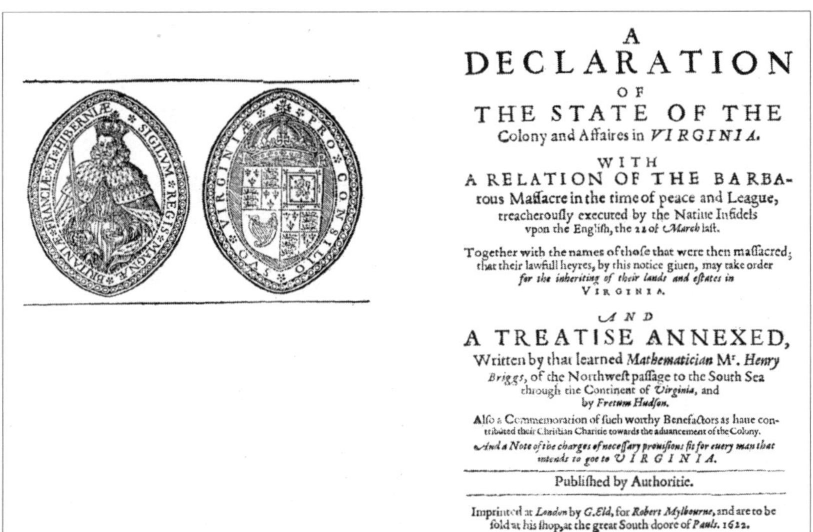

A
DECLARATION
OF
THE STATE OF THE
Colony and Affaires in *VIRGINIA*.
WITH
A RELATION OF THE BARBArous Massacre in the time of peace and League, treacherously executed by the Natiue Infidels vpon the English, the 22 of *March* last.

Together with the names of those that were then massacred; that their lawfull heyres, by this notice giuen, may take order *for the inheriting of their lands and estates in* VIRGINIA.

*AND*
A TREATISE ANNEXED,
Written by that learned *Mathematician* M^r^. *Henry Briggs*, of the Northwest passage to the South Sea through the Continent of *Virginia*, and by *Fretum Hudson*.

Also a Commemoration of such worthy Benefactors as haue contributed their Christian Charitie towards the aduancement of the Colony.

*And a Note of the charges of necessary prouisions fit for euery man that intends to goe to* VIRGINIA.

Published by Authoritie.

Imprinted at *London* by *G.Eld*, for *Robert Mylbourne*, and are to be sold at his shop, at the great South doore of *Pauls*. 1622.

**Fig. 7.** Title page of Edward Waterhouse's *the Declaration of the State of Colony and Affaires in Virginia* (London, 1622). The work condemned Native American violence as a "Barbarous Massacre" at the same time as it called for increasing amounts of violence toward the goal of consolidating English control over Native American lands.

the attack, Edward Waterhouse's oft-cited account noted that the English could now use any means at their disposal in an all-out attack against the Powhatans.[49]

In Waterhouse's reasoning, English "hands, which before were tied with gentlenesse and faire usage, are now set at liberty by the treacherous violence of the Savages."[50] The main problem with accepting Waterhouse's account at face value is that the English had never really played by the rules established by Powhatan in the first place, and they were anything but gentle in their dealings with the local Algonquians. By the middle of the seventeenth century, the English had conquered the Tidewater region of Virginia. They achieved this by planting an aggressively expanding agricultural colony. The earliest incarnation of Virginia was highly militarized as well. These factors compounded the effects of the cultural divide between English and Algonquian.

Even as the English drew hard racial and territorial lines dividing themselves from their Indian neighbors, they often compared Indian and English civilizations in terms of their approaches to warfare. In addition to disposing of their enemies, Edward Nugent, Ralph Lane, and others who beheaded native leaders were trying to communicate with bloody icons across a cultural divide that sometimes seemed very wide. Joyce Chaplin has argued that "the cultural interface between natives and English in North America almost always involved war, and war provided the main opportunity for ethnographic observation."[51] One of the most telling of these ethnographic observations, and one of the main points of intersection between English and Native American cultures of violence, was the relationship between gender and intercultural violence. English and Indian warriors by and large agreed that warfare and masculinity were connected, and each side would occasionally taunt the other by questioning the other's masculinity. As Chaplin put it, "The one thing Indians and English agreed on was that they could insult each other's soldiers most woundingly by calling them women."[52]

Over the course of the seventeenth and eighteenth centuries, European colonists claimed much of North America. The process of actually dispossessing the land of its indigenous owners took much longer, and its effects are still being felt centuries later. Where did English notions about territory and colonization come from? How were these notions imprinted on the American landscape? The answers to these questions help explain the manner in which the English conquered North America in general and the Southeast in particular. Patricia Seed has rightly commented on the "remarkable ordinariness of English possession."[53] In sharp contrast to the Requirimiento-style legal machinations of the Spanish and the ceremonies and columns of the French, English territorial claims were made by houses, fences, gardens, and other markers of what the English thought it meant to be civilized. Houses, fences, and gardens made land English, but they do not fully explain how English people imposed their ideas about landownership in colonial settings or how they conquered the American Southeast.

One of the earliest manifestations of English colonial territory was "the Pale." The term "pale" refers to a sharpened stick pointing up out of the ground, the distant ancestor to the picket fence of American dreams.[54] In Ireland, the Pale was the area most heavily under English influence. The difference between the Irish Pale and England's overseas colonies was that—at least in the beginning—the English did not dispossess native Irish with anywhere near the same intensity as they did Native Americans. England's colonies quickly became "essentially colonies of white settlement populated by European immigrants . . . or colonies under white management which relied on African slaves for a labour force," according to Nicholas Canny.[55] The ideas that supported the Pale in Ireland translated reasonably well to English activities in North America. Early colonizers and their backers spoke of bringing the benefits of Christianity and English civilization to benighted peoples.

When significant numbers of English people arrived in North America, their behavior betrayed any high-minded principles they held. One of the foundations of English colonization, and perhaps the most important for American history, was to transfer as much land as possible from native to English ownership. The traditional narrative of how the transfer occurred has been a litany of white duplicity, theft, and conquest. Recently, Stuart Banner has argued that the story was much more complex. Unlike colonial theorists in England, most colonizers in America recognized Indian land rights, for instance, and recognized the expedience and necessity of purchasing land from its prior owners.[56] English territorial expansion in the Southeast, combined with the expansion of an aggressive English trading regime in the region, remade the Southeast along violent lines around the turn of the eighteenth century. There were complex reasons for the violence that rocked Virginia, but English land acquisition was a key factor. The English at Jamestown overran the boundary set for them by Powhatan, and violence was the result.

Trade with Native Americans was a comparatively small part of the English empire's economy, the colonial portion of which was dominated by agricultural exports. In North America, however, trade with local indigenous communities was crucial to a colony's success, and in some cases survival. In some instances, such as that of William Berkeley of Virginia, it added to individual wealth. For the native communities involved, trading with Europeans was a mixed blessing. It could expand some aspects of Indian experience at the same time as it narrowed options for people who attached themselves to the developing Atlantic economy. Trade, like violence, is a useful lens through which to examine intercultural relations. Native Americans and Europeans engaged in both trade and warfare before they met each other, and each group sought to teach the other the proper protocols for interaction in these fields.

In the English colonization of North America, trade and violence were linked in ways that foreshadow the violent transformation of the Southeast. The Jamestown colony, for instance, was woefully short on food and needed to trade with Powhatan for its very survival. The terms of such a trade were reasonably clear, but the terms meant different things to each of the parties involved. John Smith and the English needed corn. Powhatan needed items that would enhance his prestige. English trade followed a model that demanded the most benefit for the least cost. Powhatan trade was based on reciprocity and generosity. In several instances, English misperceptions of Powhatan trade led to violence. It is even possible to read the 1622 attack as an example of trade turned violent. Powhatan, by granting—or trading—the English the land in and around and Jamestown, understood that he had established the English colony as a subsidiary to his chiefdom. English farmers broke the deal by expanding into prohibited areas, and the result was violence. Virginia's colonial leadership recognized the violent potential of trade and acted repeatedly to restrict or prohibit the Indian trade. In 1624, trade with Powhatans for corn was prohibited. In 1626, a Captain John Stone received a commission to trade with Eastern Shore communities—apparently their distance was a safe one for trade. Individual traders still struck out on their own, sometimes violently, sometimes at cross-purposes with the government.[57] As Virginia became increasingly self-sufficient, and the Powhatan chiefdom was defeated militarily and constricted by English expansion and other groups, Powhatans became increasingly dependent upon trade with the English. The English operating out of Jamestown used their new power to great advantage by dispossessing Indian communities of ever more land.[58]

In Virginia, and later in Carolina, trade spawned violence. It could put both natives and English in direct competition for resources in some instances. Indians who fell into debt to English traders could be pressed to sell land, which in itself could lead to violence as English settlements expanded. It also exposed key differences in the way each group perceived what sorts of trades were fair and which were unfair. Indian perceptions of unfair English trading practices led repeatedly to violent confrontations and would be one of the main causes of the Yamasee War in South Carolina.[59]

## Slavery and Violence before Carolina

On Barbados, beginning in the 1620s, English colonizers did not have to displace native peoples in order to set up their plantations. The fact that no native peoples were dispossessed did not lessen violence; it shifted the framework within which violence took place. Barbados and the Chesapeake came to rely increasingly on slave labor performed by Africans over the course of the seventeenth century. The large-scale shift away from indentured servitude toward racial slavery began in the Caribbean and was mimicked on the mainland. The "Sugar Revolution" of the 1640s and 1650s drove the demand for labor beyond the capacity of the British Isles to supply it. Negative perceptions of Africans, and the fact they had already been forced to labor by other Europeans, all but assured that English sugar would be produced by slave labor.[60]

Violence against slaves was a part of everyday life on Barbados. Planters and militia cracked down on the island's labor force. If they didn't use actual, physical violence, they found other ways to maintain their hold on power. Barbadian planters separated slaves from the same regions and outlawed African religious practice. The 1661 slave code described slaves as "heathenish," "brutish," and "dangerous."[61] Richard S. Dunn put it best: "The slave laws legitimized a state of war between blacks and whites, sanctified rigid segregation, and institutionalized an early warning system against slave revolts. After all, the price of tyranny is eternal vigilance."[62] Richard Ligon, an early chronicler of Barbados, had his own ideas as to why Africans did not rise up, "enfranchise themselves, and thereby become Masters of the Iland." He gave three reasons: "they are not suffered to touch or handle any weapons," "they are held in such awe and slavery," and "they are fetch'd from severall parts of Africa."[63] All of these factors are the result of English actions, customs, and laws, and have nothing to do with supposed African inferiority or enfeeblement.

Henry Drax, one of the wealthiest sugar planters on Barbados, explained when and why to use violence to discipline slaves in instructions to his overseer. Punishment was to "reclaim the malefactor or to terrify others from committing the like fault," never "to satisfy your own anger or passion." Slaves could be excused for stealing to feed themselves, but if they took "sugar molasses or rum, which is our money . . . they must be severely handled." This illuminates a clear connection between commercial success and violence and adds another wrinkle to the English culture of colonial violence. Physical coercion could be used to make slaves work but also could be used to discipline slaves whose actions diminished English profits. Punishments were to be meted out as soon as the overseer was aware of an infraction. Gary Puckrein, author of *Little England: Plantation Society and Anglo-Barbadian Politics,* concluded that "in all probability [violence] was not a daily occurrence. Capricious terror would have been self-defeating. . . . Planters had other means by which to regulate their slaves' behavior."[64] Capriciousness is in the eye of the beholder, of course. English planters viewed violence, or the threat of violence, as legitimate and eminently justifiable.

David Eltis outlined Barbados's transition from tobacco to sugar and indentured servitude to slavery in his *Rise of African Slavery in the Americas.*[65] A similar process obtained along the rivers of the Carolina Lowcountry, with three important differences. Carolina's reliance on plantation slavery developed more quickly than on Barbados, but Carolina's colonial society was not quite as stratified as that on Barbados. Finally, English and African settlers in Carolina inserted themselves into a dynamic world made by native peoples in their attempts to recover from the demographic havoc wreaked by Spanish colonization and the collapse of Mississippian chiefdoms.[66]

Inherent within the system of Caribbean slavery, and its Carolinian descendant, was a serious contradiction. Force was a constant, but open displays of aggression and violence were bad for business. English slavery in the Caribbean also required incentives to reach maximum production and profit.[67] In regions of the English overseas empire where the crops were not as profitable as sugar—that is, everywhere else—this was even more the case. Such an assertion is not meant to downplay the brutality of slavery, which had coercion, violence, and the commodification of people at its very core.[68]

Virginia's English planters used violence to maintain discipline among their slaves. But slavery was not the prevailing labor system in that colony's earliest years. The "tobacco revolution," as Ira Berlin has styled it, brought Virginia closer to conformity with the plantation system first elaborated in the Caribbean. As Virginia and American slavery developed together, the state threw its weight behind the right of planters to discipline their slaves as they saw fit. A 1669 statute repealed an earlier act that made killing a slave during "correction" a felony. By 1707, Robert "King" Carter could petition for, and receive, "full power to dismember" particularly troublesome slaves by cutting off their toes.[69] Such violence fits into a long tradition of maiming or otherwise physically marking or scarring those perceived as dangers to society.

The violence of slavery in early Carolina, as described in chapter 6, often operated behind the scenes. In Carolina, the physical abuse of slaves gradually moved away from the public sphere and into the realm of domestic relations. Over time, particularly gruesome punishments like maiming and castration were cast aside and corporal punishment itself moved into the household, which became a site of intercultural violence.

## Ordinary People, Violence, and the Plan for Carolina

When English men and women arrived in seventeenth-century North America, they carried the ideas about violence and violent practices described above. They also carried their particular experiences of violence. English men, for instance, were likely to have served at one point in their lives as members of a local militia. These institutions had been around for centuries, at least since the reign of Alfred (871–899), but were waning in importance over the course of the 1600s.[70]

The militia tradition was revived and expanded in the early years of English colonization in North America. In fact, for most of the seventeenth century, the piece of England's military culture that was most applicable to the American experience was the militia tradition. In the grand narrative of military history, the seventeenth century is the era of Oliver Cromwell's New Model Army, a large, well-equipped, and well-financed force capable of extending English power throughout the British Isles and beyond.[71]

In England itself, local militia were primarily defensive. Theoretically, any able-bodied man between sixteen and sixty years old had to serve. More skilled groups, the "trained bands," were selected from the wider militia. By the turn of the seventeenth century, England was home to a large number of well-trained farmer-soldiers, and in the 1640s these groups turned against each other in the sectarian violence of the Civil War; one estimate has about one in ten English men taking part in combat.[72] Strangely, few studies have engaged the violence of the English Civil War or tried to connect it in a meaningful way to English colonization.[73] Carolina was founded in the aftermath of the war; the territory itself was a gift from Charles II to a handful of prominent men who had supported his efforts to regain the throne (or claimed to once he had regained it).

In English America, the militia was a multipurpose force. It drilled regularly, though with varying degrees of seriousness—after spending mornings training, militia members could expect to be treated to afternoons drinking and eating at the expense of great planters.[74] Virginia's militia, in the words of historian Rhys Isaac, "did provide both an important means of formalizing authority in society and assemblies at which the male fraternity of warriors might get drunk together."[75] The militia could be called to deal with slave rebellions, and it could work in a primarily defensive mode, as in the Yamasee War. South Carolina's militia could also form a central part of an offensive force, such as the one that destroyed the missions of Spanish Florida in the first decade of the eighteenth century. Sally Hadden, author of *Slave Patrols,* has traced the origins of southern slave patrols back to the institution of the militia. On Barbados, and eventually in South Carolina, one of the militia's primary duties was to police the slave labor force. A Barbadian statute dating to 1661 had the effect of putting the white community as a whole, not just slave owners and overseers, into the role of slave catcher. A 1688 revision stipulated that "all Masters, Overseers, and other Persons whatsoever" must whip and detain any slaves abroad without express written consent.[76]

To this point, the discussion has focused on English ideas and cultural imperatives about violence before the founding of Carolina. Some comments on English military culture are appropriate. England's distinctive military culture was rooted in "fluidity, adaptability, eclecticism, and the ability to synthesise a manner of fighting that fit tactical reality."[77] At the same time as English soldiers and militia were engaged in conflicts around the Atlantic world, English military culture was undergoing a profound shift, its own version of the "Military Revolution" that swept through Europe. One aspect of the transformation of English military culture, with ramifications for the invasion of America, was the replacement of the longbow—England's "national weapon"—with firearms over the course of the sixteenth century. By the time they got to Virginia and fought a style of war that would have favored bows and arrows, few English soldiers were trained as archers. In the broadest terms, regardless of the number of soldiers involved, "the effort was to maintain one's massed unit, for the greatest concentration of power, and to entice the enemy into a position where parts of their unit could be cut off and subjected to the full force of one's army."[78] This proved nearly impossible in the conquest of the Southeast.

The planners and backers of Carolina were not creating a colony out of thin air. They were plugged into a widening Atlantic world and took an interest in colonies other than their own, examining what had worked and failed in New England, Virginia, and the Caribbean. They noted how violence had plagued the Virginia colony, whose settlements were stretched thinly along the rivers of the Chesapeake watershed. The people doing the actual settling, many of whom were from Barbados, also imported a labor system—plantation slavery—that required violence or the threat of violence to keep it in place. Violence provides a new perspective on the "tension between the dreams of colonial planners and colonial realities" warhorse.

In Carolina, the Lords Proprietors sought to eliminate intercultural violence; they perceived it as backwards and debilitating. Like their predecessors from Hakluyt forward, they viewed colonization as a positive good for everybody involved. Anthony Ashley Cooper and others discounted conquest and religious conversion as part of the colonial project and touted English agriculture and trade as avenues to wealth and social stability. There are two main problems with this point of view. First, the settlers of Carolina did not share the enlightened perspective of the proprietors. Second, trading and plantation agriculture were rarely peaceful undertakings in the charged atmosphere of the Southeast. The type of agriculture that developed in Carolina relied on violence against Africans, and its expansion put pressure on native communities. The type of trade—in firearms, alcohol, slaves, and deerskins—that spread out from Charles Town throughout the region could easily spark violence between native peoples and the English. Metropolitan dreams of peace and trade conflicted not only with the ideas of the settlers, but the proprietors' vision was also at odds with itself when it apportioned land to English people that was still populated by native communities.

The planting of the English colony at Charles Town in 1670 is a significant turning point in the history of violence in the Southeast. From there, plantations, worked by increasing numbers of African slaves, spread along the rivers named for Lord Shaftesbury (Anthony Ashley Cooper) and throughout the Lowcountry. From there, licensed and unlicensed Indian traders would fan out into the interior. The plantation and trading house, two hallmarks of English colonizing in the Southeast, employed and produced new sorts of violence that would reshape the region. Together, trade, expansion, and slavery forged an Anglo-American culture of violence with far-reaching implications for early American history.

The communities that would face the English invasion were different from those that had faced the Spanish invasion of the previous century. The stratified Mississippian world, in which paramount chiefdoms vied for chiefly glory and luxury goods, had faded from view, if not from memory. By 1670, most chiefdoms had dispersed into smaller, autonomous groups that were becoming the towns and nations of the early modern Southeast. Even as the central plaza replaced the platform mound as the focus of community life, elements of Mississippian culture lived on. These would shape native responses to the new threat posed by the arrival of the English.

# CHAPTER 6

# Violence and the Founding of English Carolina

The English who came into the Southeast were the heirs of the culture of violence described in the previous chapter. When they first arrived in the Southeast in numbers, in the second half of the seventeenth century, they came to a land that was already scarred by violence. The peoples of the coast, living in small communities that had been reshaped by disease and conflict with Guale, Spanish, and new slaving societies that had moved into the region, were unlikely to offer much in the way of military resistance; in fact, most welcomed English protection. Beyond the coastal communities, the people of the Southeast were migrating and adapting to life in the land between the Virginia traders and the Spanish missions; for groups like the Westos and Yamasees this entailed slave raids and violent assaults on Spanish missions. Farther inland, large nations—the Creeks, Cherokees, Catawbas, Choctaws, and Chickasaws—were coalescing from the remnants of Mississippian chiefdoms. These large polities were not likely to perceive the English as a military threat, but they would eventually get tangled up in the violence that emanated from the English settlement at Charles Town. Occasionally in the late seventeenth century, an interior nation might sign a treaty, accept a trader, or send emissaries to the fledgling colony, but most towns in most nations adopted a wary "wait-and-see" attitude in an effort to see what could be gained, or lost, by the English presence. The cultures of violence which preceded the English arrival prefigured the ways in which the people of the region would be able to resist English encroachment, even though English violence began to remake violence in the Southeast for all of the region's peoples from 1670 to the 1710s. Early English settlements and trade were tied to violence. Successive groups—Westos, Savannahs, and Yamasees—moved closer to Carolina to reap the benefits of alliance with this violent regime. The behavior of the English at Carolina, indicative of the English culture of violence, would lead to major regional wars in the second decade of the eighteenth century.

The division between South Carolina as a trading post and South Carolina as a network of plantations and an outpost of empire is not very stark; it is almost impossible to note a specific date for the shift from Indian trade to agriculture and forest produce as the main road to profit. English people were engaged in both from their earliest permanent settlement in the region. Still, sometime in the early eighteenth century, English South Carolina began to profit more from rice and less from trade with Native Americans. Each of these developments brought new forms of violence to the region's native inhabitants at the same time as they shaped the particular brand of English conquest that marked the Southeast.

The arrival of English men and women in the Southeast heralded a fundamental shift in the way violence was deployed in the region. As the English fanned out along the rivers of the Southeast, their violent institutions, the plantation and the Indian trading house, came to dominate the country. The English did not view their brand of colonization as particularly violent; to them, the Spanish had cornered the market on colonial violence. Scholars have picked up on this line of reasoning. One could even argue that subsequent generations of Anglo-Americans have excused or ignored English violence because they like to perceive their history as one of settlement and progress rather than conquest and empire.

A history of violent ideas and violent practices fed into the English culture of violence that would dominate the Southeast. English ways of claiming territory, English ways of making land profitable, and English trade were not new ideas. It is not even that innovative to suggest that each of these alone could produce violence. What makes the example of the Southeast so powerful is that English violence conquered the Southeast so quickly and that multiple factors, which the English did not perceive as particularly violent, worked in concert to promote violence and change cultures of violence in the Southeast. English ideas about violence were changing, too. The growing rift between the planners of Carolina and the people actually building the colony demonstrates this fact. The English culture of violence evolved as its carriers came into contact with new political realities and diverse Native American communities throughout the Southeast. Unfortunately for the region's first peoples, English violence evolved in ways that would lead to the subjugation and annihilation of communities nearest the colony and would make it much more difficult for nations farther inland to determine their own futures. Anglo-American violence posed a region-wide threat to Native Americans.

A permanent English presence on the Atlantic Coast north of the mission province of Guale was just what Cusabo communities needed.[1] Their ancestors had greeted Jean Ribaut's colony in the 1560s, and the meeting was tentative at first but eventually friendly. René Laudonnière listed the gifts the Cusabos bestowed: "deerskins, . . . little baskets, and a few presented pearls to them, but not in large quantities." The French responded by taking two Indians to train as translators; the pair later escaped. Things went a little more smoothly with Audusta (Edisto) and other settlements.[2] The French did not remain on the Atlantic Coast for long, and the Cusabos' world became more violent. They raided Guale, a Spanish mission province on the Georgia coast, and after the Spanish brokered a peace, they and the Guales raided the Spanish. Then they raided Guale again. The arrival of the Westos, armed by Virginia traders, posed a serious threat, and the Cusabos were in dire straits when the English arrived. They welcomed the Carolina colonists warmly, signing treaties and ceding territory.[3]

## Migration and Violence in the Southeast

The seventeenth-century Southeast was the site of several notable migrations, each of which contained the seeds of intercultural conflict. Beginning in 1670, a handful of Barbadian planters made their way to the confluence of the Ashley and Cooper Rivers, bringing with them the first of thousands of African slaves. During the 1680s, Scots under Lord Cardross migrated from Glasgow to Port Royal and established Stuart's Town. The Spanish mission system crept northward up the coast, then retreated under pressure from English and Westo raids. But the various English, Scottish, and Spanish colonial projects were not painting on a blank canvas. In fact, native people had their own long history of migration, as the communities spun off from Mississippian chiefdoms continued along their paths of coalescence.[4] Native groups like the Westos and Savannahs moved closer to Charles Town and played significant roles in the Indian slave trade. The Yamasees, refugees from raids themselves, moved from the interior toward the Spanish missions and from the vicinity of the missions toward the English. Beginning in the 1680s, the Yamasees were Charles Town's staunchest native allies. It was not until 1715 that they would become English Carolina's most deadly enemy. The three decades of Yamasee-English cooperation deserve intense scholarly scrutiny on their own terms; they may yet have much to offer to the broad-brushed portrait of colonial life in the Southeast.

Though the indigenous communities of the Lowcountry, collectively referred to as Cusabos, generally welcomed the English presence, there was a significant exception to the warm welcome. The Kussoes became the focus of some consternation on the part of the Grand Council in late 1671. They were accused of "stealing 'a great quantity of Corn'" and, more threateningly, of working with the Spanish "to cut off the English people in this place." The English declared war in October. There is not much evidence to indicate how the war was prosecuted, but in 1675 the "great and the lesser Cassoe" ceded their land and relocated, though not very far. Both the Kussah ("lesser Cassoe") and Kussoe ("great . . . Cassoe") peoples came to be known as "settlement Indians." The settlement Indians maintained close ties to the Carolina colony well into the eighteenth century, providing an early warning system for—and buffer against—attacks. They also joined Carolina's military expeditions against the Spanish, Tuscaroras, and Yamasees.[5] As a symbol of the unequal relationship between the Kussoes and Carolina, the former were required to bring a single to deerskin to Charles Town each year to pay tribute.

The first English people to settle in Carolina entered a world that was in the process of being remade through violence, though the first white Carolinians were probably only dimly aware of this fact. Nicholas Carteret, one of the first white settlers of Carolina, noted the coastal peoples' willingness to entertain the English and invite them to settle. According to Carteret, they were greeted with cries of "Hiddy doddy Comorado Angles Westoe Skorrye (which is as much as to say) English very good friends Westoes are nought, they hoped by our Arrivall to be protected from ye Westoes."[6] The warm welcome and invitation might seem at first to be a figment of the colonists' imagination. Plantation and colonization would go so much more smoothly if the neighbors were complicit in the project from the beginning. However, tracing the Westos' story through eastern North America adds weight to the colonists' claims about being invited and welcomed.

The contours of Westo experience prior to encountering the Carolina colonists are becoming clearer. Their origins can be traced to Iroquoian peoples—specifically Erie peoples—in western Pennsylvania and New York. In the wake of increased Five Nations Iroquois attacks, one community of Eries, known as the Riquerhonnons, moved to the falls of the James River by 1656. The English at Virginia called them "Rickahockans" or "Richahecrians" and, after an initial confrontation, engaged in a profitable trade with the newcomers.[7]

Within a couple of years, the Richahecrians were undertaking long-distance journeys for slaves and furs that brought them to the outskirts of Florida's missions; the Spanish called them "Chichimecos," a blanket term applied to any number of groups that lived outside of the Spanish sphere of influence. Westos wreaked havoc in Guale in 1661, forcing colonial officials to rethink their policies and previewing the English-sponsored raids of the early eighteenth century. The motivation for the 1661 violence is not clear, but it was devastating. The Westos struck the mission churches and killed

Christian Indians, but it's unclear if they took captives. They then withdrew to the interior province of Tama. This "coup" may have been designed to send a message, but that message is difficult to discern. Was this an anti-Christian statement? An anti-Spanish assertion designed to curry favor with the Virginia traders? Or a none-too-subtle claim to dominance by the region's only group equipped with firearms? Perhaps a combination of the three? The Spanish responded by consolidating mission settlements to make them more defensible. They added garrisons to the missions as well. The Westo strike helped Franciscans overcome their longstanding unease with Spanish soldiers in the presence of their native charges.[8]

The Westos combined the mentality of the mourning war with the mindset of the market to great effect. The mourning war was a defining feature of Iroquoian life before the arrival of European people, diseases, and trade goods.[9] As disease took a toll on the native Northeast, and as native people sought European goods, mourning wars increased in size and expanded in meaning to include economic motives. The introduction of firearms only increased the devastation. The Eries were on the receiving end of Five Nations aggression in the early 1650s, in spite of the fact that they could respond to Iroquois assaults with firearms.[10] When they arrived in Virginia, the Richahecrians were armed and well aware of the skills necessary to thrive in the world between the native interior and the colonial market. They came to dominate Virginia's southern trade. It follows that their Virginia experience prepared the Westos to become the premier Indian slavers of the Southeast.[11]

As elite white Virginians struggled to develop a plantation economy, they were plagued by a perennial labor shortage. To satisfy the demand for labor, wealthy planters increasingly turned toward chattel slavery. The limited and sporadic availability of African slaves in seventeenth-century North America made Native American slavery attractive. Carolina's planners envisioned it as a plantation colony from the outset, and its chronic labor shortage was much more severe than Virginia's.[12] When white planters spread out from Charles Town in the 1670s, they came into contact and conflict with the Westos, who were already engaged in the Indian slave trade and were eager to gain greater access to English goods. Authorities in Carolina recognized the importance of maintaining cordial relations with the Westos, and the Westos recognized the threat and opportunity of the new English arrivals.

In October 1674, Dr. Henry Woodward embarked on what he called his *Westoe Voiage;* his narrative offers a rare glimpse into Westo involvement in the slave trade. Woodward did not understand the Westos' language, but he divined from a series of drawings—"of a bever, a man, on horseback and guns"—that the Westos desired to open some sort of "comerse."[13] Woodward was treated well and came to understand certain things about the Westos. They traded "drest deare skins furrs and young Indian Slaves" for "arms, ammunition [and] trading cloath . . . from the northward [Virginia]."[14] In fact, as Woodward prepared to leave, the Westos presented him with a boy as a gift. Woodward also noted that the Westos were "at continuall wars" with other western peoples, notably Muskogees and Cherokees.[15] Upon his return to Lord Shaftesbury's plantation, Woodward expected that the Westos would come back in the spring of 1675 with "deare skins, furrs and younge slaves."[16] Woodward's Westo voyage inaugurated a short-lived but profitable trade between the Westos and Carolina, with serious consequences for native people in the region.

The Westos' skill at raiding coastal and interior communities was enhanced by the fact that they were the only firearm-equipped indigenous group in the area. Stephen Bull, Anthony Ashley Cooper's deputy, reported back to his boss regarding the Westos. They were "another sorte of Indians that live backwards in an intier body & war agt all Indians they are called Westoes & doe strike a great feare in these Indians havinge gunns & powder & shott & doe come upon these Indians heere in the tyme of their cropp & destroy all by killinge Caryinge away their Corne & Children & eat them."[17] It didn't hurt that the Westos had developed a reputation as cannibals. This may or may not have been the case, but the Westos were already terrifying enough by 1670 for coastal peoples to welcome Carolina's first English settlement.[18]

In the years after 1670, the Westos sold their captives exclusively to the English at Charles Town. This shift reoriented the entire Indian slave trade to Carolina. The type of violence unleashed by the Westos could only have existed within the specific historical circumstances that obtained in the shattered world of the early Southeast.[19] The Westos' exploitation of the prevailing conditions may have served as an example to other groups in the region, specifically Shawnees (known to white Carolinians as Savannahs) and the Yamasees.

Almost as soon as they arrived, the English began to remake the landscape in ways that made violence all but inevitable. Their alliance and trading relationship with the Westos was only the first in a series of moves designed to enrich Carolina's landowners at the expense of the proprietors, who intended a monopoly on the Indian trade for themselves. The proprietors sought to enhance their colony's profits and avoid violence. In the Southeast, however, profit and violence were inextricably linked. The planters realized this, but the colony's planners did not. The encouragement of the Indian slave trade also indicates a change in the English culture of violence. The English had, of course, dealt in slaves previously, but buying and selling slaves through African or European middlemen is not quite the same as arming Native American groups, and sending them into the hinterland of one's own colony to raid for slaves.

The English relationship with the Savannahs is less widely known and thoroughly studied than that with the Westos and Yamasees, but it provides some important clues as to how English violence was beginning to transform the Southeast. The story of the Savannahs before they migrated to the fringe of the Carolina colony is not too well known. The specific Shawnee community that became the Savannahs probably had roots in the Ohio and Cumberland valleys in the seventeenth century. Iroquois pressure on the Shawnees began around this time, and violence intensified throughout the 1660s and 1670s. Shawnees responded to Iroquois raids by abandoning the Ohio and Cumberland country. Hundreds of Shawnees ended up at Fort St. Louis in central Illinois, while others moved into the Southeast—Kispokothas in or near Creek towns and Thawekilas farther to the east.[20] At least one community of Shawnees settled on the Savannah River. It is almost inconceivable that the Shawnees had no experience as captive takers before their involvement in the slave trade, since most indigenous peoples in eastern North America engaged in the practice on some level.[21] Like the Westos before them, it is also highly unlikely that the Savannahs moved accidentally into the English sphere of influence. The Savannah migration to Carolina's backcountry indicates a desire for trade. In the parlance of immigration studies, Carolina's potential for trade was a "pull factor" that attracted Native Americans from surrounding regions.

Dr. Henry Woodward witnessed an early Savannah appearance on the fringe of Carolina. Woodward recorded a critical early meeting between Savannahs and Westos near the close of his *Westoe Voiage*. Eric Bowne suggests that this was an advance party of Shawnees looking for potential settlement sites near sources of English trade.[22] Woodward's description of the meeting is as spare as his treatment of the Westos in general, but it does provide some clues about Shawnee motives and the extent of Shawnee migrations. The Shawnees, or Savannahs, were returning from trading with the Spanish at Florida, though the travelers were apparently disappointed with Spanish unwillingness to provide them with guns. They passed along a rumor of an impending attack on the Westos, perhaps in an effort to curry favor with the powerful Westos.[23]

Ten years after the founding of the colony at Charles Town, the English were in a position to assert their dominance over the Westos, who had apparently outlived their usefulness as slave raiders and trading partners.

In early 1680, the Westo War erupted. The causes of the war are tied up in the politics of English Carolina. Essentially, Woodward and the proprietors intended to regulate trade with Indians, while a planter faction known as the Goose Creek Men desired to expand the trade as far inland as possible.[24] To achieve this goal, the Goose Creek Men armed the Savannahs. The Savannahs proceeded to defeat and enslave much of the Westo population. Governor, and proprietor, John Archdale would later write that "the Hand of God was eminently seen in thining the *Indians,* to make room for the *English.* As for Example in *Carolina,* in which were seated Two Potent Nations, called the *Westoes,* and *Sarannah,* which contained many Thousands, who broke out into an unusual Civil War, and thereby reduced themselves into a small Number, and the *Westoes,* the more Cruel of the two, were at the last forced quite out of that Province, and the *Sarannahs* continued good Friends and useful Neighbors to the *English.*"[25] Archdale's most obvious omission is the fact that English traders bore some responsibility for the conflict. The language in the passage owes much to its author's background; he perceived Native Americans as a single race and explicitly called out the role of God in preparing the land for English colonization.

In its fighting, the war itself seems to have been a rather lopsided affair. Hostilities began in the winter of 1679–80 and flared sporadically into the early 1680s. Hundreds of captured Westos were brought to Charles Town and sold into West Indian slavery.[26] The war also appears to have begun with some treachery on the part of white Carolinians. A 1683 letter from the proprietors chided the colonists for the "heads of the Westohs being taken whilst they were in treaty with that Government . . . & put to death in Cold blood & the rest Driven from their country."[27] No firsthand accounts of the actual combat survive, so it's not clear if the reference to heads being taken is literal, and recent historians have been reluctant to speculate too much.[28] Two facts about the Westo War are beyond dispute. First, it dispersed the Westos as a people; splinter groups moved north to Iroquoia and west to what would become Creek country.[29] Second, it resulted in the ascendance of the Savannahs to the role of Carolina's main Indian trading partner, with all the attendant advantages and disadvantages thereof.

The Westo War, and the war with the Kussoes that preceded it, demonstrate another instance of the "Americanization" of the English culture of violence. The English in other parts of North America had recognized something of the complexity of Native American politics and alliances or competition between native communities, and the planters of Carolina were no exception. They sought to exploit preexisting Native American rivalries. The benefits to English Carolina were great, but the behavior was risky, too, since violence could beget violence and move in unpredictable directions. The English at Carolina would employ a similar tactic with the large interior nations in the early eighteenth century.

Not surprisingly, the proprietors—who found out about the Westo War far too late to affect its prosecution or outcome—voiced strong disapproval and placed the blame for the conflict squarely on the white Carolinians: "If friendships had been preserved with ye Westos it would have kept all the neighbouring Indians from dareing to offend you; and if you had protected them from being injured by the Westoes, that protection would have made them love as well as feare you which consideration hath been ye maine inducement of our endeveaours to hold a fayre correspondence wuth ye Westoes by making ourselves usefull to them by trade." The letter quoted above goes on to note, significantly, that "Peace is in the Interest of Planters."[30] In South Carolina's Lowcountry, it would be more accurate to say that war was in the interest of planters, and they knew it. Planters benefited from lands vacated by fleeing Indians, and if two neighboring groups went to war, Carolina's traders could expect an influx of new slaves.

The proprietors also suspected that the Westo War was undertaken for inappropriate reasons. A March 1681 letter reminded the colonists that the proprietors as yet had "no Depositions to prove the matter of fact on which this warr was grounded." As such, they "could not well judg whether this war was made upon a reall necessity for the preservation of the Collony, or to serve the ends of particular men by trade."[31] The difference between "reall necessity" and "the ends of particular men" was not a distinction that Carolina's colonizers were willing to recognize or accept. Carolina in the late seventeenth century survived and turned a profit on an exploitative trade in Indian goods and human beings.

In the aftermath of the war, the Savannahs replaced the Westos as English Carolina's most powerful Indian allies and its most prominent slave raiders. In the late-seventeenth-century Southeast, these two roles coincided. Thomas Newe, a young colonist, described the Savannahs in 1682 as "the most potent Kingdome of the Indians armed by us."[32] This distinction would eventually belong to a third group: the Yamasees.

The Yamasees did not replace the Savannahs overnight. In the 1680s, both communities occupied prime locations to operate between the Indian world of the interior and the English world of Charles Town. In the decades between 1680 and 1710, the story of the Savannahs is fuzzy to a frustrating degree. It is clear that the Savannahs and Carolina saw some advantage in maintaining a relationship, and it is equally clear that Savannahs were beginning to sour on living in the Southeast by the first decade of the eighteenth century, maybe even a family or kin group at a time. John Lawson, in an account of his 1701 trip to the backcountry, described the Savannahs as a "famous, warlike, friendly Nation of Indians."[33]

The proceedings of the Commons House of Assembly refer to the Savannahs during 1707 and 1708 as the "Revolted Savanas" and the "deserted Savanas," and the choice of words is revealing: the Savannahs had revolted, but they had done so by leaving.[34] In essence, the Shawnees, who probably never viewed themselves as under English dominion and therefore were incapable of revolting against it, voted with their feet. Some Savannahs moved to Maryland and Pennsylvania. The latter maintained a reputation for tolerant attitudes toward Native Americans before the shameful Walking Purchase of the 1730s. Shawnee identity was highly adaptable; it did not preclude related communities from dwelling far apart. Nor did it preclude individuals and families from moving between far-flung settlements. Compared to the Westos and Yamasees, the Savannahs seem to have fared the best in their encounter with Carolina colony in its early years.

## Yamasee Genesis and the Early Yamasee-Carolina Alliance

In the 1680s, the Yamasees began their migration to Carolina. The precise origins of the Yamasees, like their language, may never be known, but the basic contours of their migrations are increasingly clear thanks to underused and recently uncovered documents and archaeological sites on the eastern seaboard. By the 1660s, the Yamasees existed in pockets on the fringes of the Spanish mission province of Guale and the more northerly province of Escamaçu. The evidence is scant, but most of it seems to indicate that the Yamasees were an ethnically diverse group of native peoples seeking refuge from raids carried out by Chichimecos (Westos) and others. A 1663 letter written by the Franciscan Carlos de Anguiano placed a string of Yamasee towns "six, eight, four, three, two, and more days distant by road" from Guale—directly between the Chichimecos and the missions.[35] The very looseness of their allegiance to the Spanish helped mark these refugees as Yamasees, since the term came to apply to any number of smaller ethnic groups who, although they were connected to the Spanish through trade, continually refused baptism. As raids intensified, the Yamasees abandoned their outlying villages and moved more solidly into the mission provinces. A 1681 census notes various "aggregations of Yamace Indians" throughout Guale and Mocama; the same source is careful to distinguish between Christian Indians and "pagan Yamazes."[36] In exchange for Spanish military protection, some subjected themselves to the *repartimiento*. Still, the Yamasee-Spanish alliance was a strategic choice on the part of some Yamasees, and when the relationship outlived its usefulness, they left the mission provinces en masse.

The Yamasees moved away from the Spanish missions and replaced the Westos and Savannahs in the Savannah River country and the Sea Islands, wedged in between the Spanish and English. The English welcomed the Yamasees and placed them into the same mental space that had been previously occupied by the Savannahs and Westos. The native world of the Southeast was in flux as the remnants of chiefdoms dispersed, whether as a result of disease or slave raids, and reformulated themselves into new polities, many of them multiethnic. At the regional level, competing empires faced off against each other, but locally, the struggle was carried out by ambitious friars, traders, planters, pirates and their native allies.

From their position near Port Royal, the Yamasees became English Carolina's main trading and raiding partners—in the minds of the Europeans settled at Charles Town, they became the new Westos. The mass migration to South Carolina was a defining moment in the history of the Yamasees. It marked a transformation between two types of identity, a local identification and a Pan-Indian or multiethnic one more suited to the rigors of life between two colonial powers.[37] In a way, the move from Florida to Carolina was a sort of Yamasee middle passage. It demonstrates a link between migration and ethnogenesis that parallels other, better-understood population movements.[38]

The Yamasees arrived in the Sea Islands at about the same time as Lord Henry Cardross was planting his colony of Stuart's Town. In a letter dated March 27, 1685, Lord Cardross and William Dunlop relayed their goals to Sir Peter Colleton, one of the Lords Proprietors of Carolina. In the dream world of long-term colonial goals, the Scots intended to find a Southwest Passage of sorts—a route from Port Royal to New Mexico in an effort to subvert Spanish mining profits, "which if effectuated wold be a matter of vast importance both to you and us."[39] More short-term, pragmatic motives lay behind the conscious effort to befriend the Yamasees, whom the Scots reckoned "the most considerable" of the area's native peoples. The Scottish colonists were blunt about the reasons for the alliance: "We have consented to them that they remaine here during their good behaviour, and the truth is they are so considerable and warlike that we would not doe utherwayes."[40] Cardross also averred that it was in the interest of the Scots and English to keep the large number of Yamasees "effectionit," since they were "Inveterat enemies to the Spainzard."[41] Cardross and Dunlop were probably correct in their assessment of Yamasee strength. At a time when the Scots' population hovered in the fifties and the numbers of English and African people were about fourteen hundred and five hundred respectively, the English slave trader Caleb Westbrooke wrote from Port Royal and estimated the number of Yamasees in the region at "a thousand or more" and expected that figure to rise daily.[42]

Soon after their withdrawal from the Spanish sphere of influence, a force of Yamasees carried out a devastating raid on a mission in Timucua which offers an excellent opportunity to explore the intricacies of native and European violence in the Southeast. A party of Yamasees under Altamaha attacked Santa Catalina de Afuyca (Ajoyca) in 1685 in a fashion that bespoke a potent combination of old enmity, anti-Catholic feeling, and new economic motives provided by the Scots and Westbrooke of Stuart's Town. Niquisalla, a cacique from Guale with prior knowledge of the attack, cited longstanding Yamasee-Timucua hatred as a motivating factor.[43]

When several Yamasees appeared before colonial officials months later in Charles Town, they described a horrific scene: the raiders "burnt severall Townes and in particuler the said Chappell and the Fryers house."[44] The Yamasees, who remained unconverted and recognized by the Spanish and English as pagans and infidels, struck forcefully at the symbols of mission life. The dawn raid resulted in the destruction or theft of religious articles and texts. Yamasee actions that morning seem to have moved beyond the quest for immediate profit. Their destruction of the chapel and friary indicate a forceful rejection of Spanish missionization. The cost in human lives was also dear: fifty Timucuans perished, and twenty-two were carried off as slaves.[45]

Enmity between the Timucuans and Yamasees, and Yamasee mistrust of Catholic intentions, could have developed without any external persuasion. But the looming presence of Carolina's slave market and the actions of Lord Cardross and Caleb Westbrooke also played some role, as evidence before and after the Santa Catalina raid shows. Prior to the attack, John Chaplin reported to Henry Woodward, Carolina's resident Indian expert, that he saw "armes and other things delivered to the Yamases."[46] Woodward reminded the colony's deputy governor that this was a bad idea, since it would inflame tensions between the Spanish and English unnecessarily. It seemed unlikely that the Spanish, should they choose to retaliate from St. Augustine, would distinguish between Scottish and English plantations.[47] The Yamasee testimony given after the raid also mentioned that it was carried out at Westbrooke's suggestion, but this may have been an easy way for the Yamasees to deflect blame. The trader and the Scots had armed the

Yamasees with muskets and swords, and Lord Cardross had paid the Yamasees for the slaves and other booty taken during the assault.[48]

The conflict highlights some divisions between the Scots, the English, and the Lords Proprietors. The Scots had initially settled at Port Royal with the permission of the Lords Proprietors, but shortly thereafter had come into conflict with the English at Charles Town. Both Charles Town and Stuart's Town were under the nominal control of the proprietors, but that meant very little in Carolina. At one point, Henry Woodward had been arrested by the Scots, whose leaders claimed independence from the government at Charles Town. In retaliation for Woodward's detention and the unauthorized Yamasee raid in Timucua, warrants were issued at Charles Town for the arrest of Lord Cardross. James Moore, a leading Indian slaver and proponent of the deregulation of Indian trade in general, was behind the effort.[49] English traders were not upset that the proprietors had been shown up—their disdain for proprietary rule was well established—they were more concerned with the fact that a Scots-Yamasee alliance would deprive the English of the profits from any slaves taken in Yamasee raids. In the opening decade of the eighteenth century, Governor James Moore would get his chance.

The Santa Catalina raid demonstrates the utility of the close study of violence as a way to understand the early colonial Southeast. The Yamasees might have attacked the mission of their own accord. Their disdain for proselytizing Franciscans was well documented. Their rivalry with the Timucuans might have roots even deeper than the fact that the Timucuans were Christian and the Yamasees were not. At the same time, external forces were shaping Yamasee violence. Chief among these was the developing market for Indian slaves at Stuart's Town and Charles Town. The trader Caleb Westbrooke and Lord Cardross did not necessarily provide the main motivation for the raid; for instance, it seems unlikely that they suggested to burn the chapel and friary and take religious texts. Still, their gift of weaponry ensured that the raid would result in a larger number of captives and gave the Yamasees incentive to bring the captives to Stuart's Town, not Charles Town, for sale. Even when the nations of England and Spain were officially at peace, colonizers representing those nations in the American Southeast clashed violently.

Spanish forces sent by Governor Juan Márquez Cabrera fell on the recently abandoned Stuart's Town in 1686 and burned it to the ground. Proceeding to the northeast, they wreaked havoc in several English plantations, carrying off slaves, silver, and a robe taken during the raid on the Santa Catalina mission.[50] The attack slowed English expansion along the coast of

Georgia and put a temporary halt to Yamasee depredations. The events of the 1680s set the stage for the much larger conflict of the first decade of the eighteenth century.

One avenue that requires further exploration is the changing meaning of captivity in eastern Native America. At various points, and for many groups, captivity stopped serving a social purpose and began to serve an economic one. Of course, social and economic motivations cannot be so easily separated. Economics alone are enough to explain why adoption of captives slowed and the sale of captives to slave traders picked up. The answer is probably related to the uncertainties of Native American life in the colonial world. Some groups like the Savannah/Shawnees saw advantages in remaining mobile, not getting attached to their present surroundings. Other groups, most notably the large interior Creek and Cherokee nations, while nominally slave raiders, saw the benefits of remaining rooted and letting refugees from smaller, collapsing polities swell their ranks. One thing is certain: the practice of traveling long distances to secure slaves for eventual sale as forms of chattel property did not exist before extensive contact with Europeans. In the early years of Carolina's white settlement, indigenous communities in the Southeast had to choose between being enslaved by people working for Carolina planters and traders or trading for arms and enslaving their neighbors. These were the kinds of poor choices forced on Native Americans by the English culture of violence radiating out from Carolina.

## Raiding Spanish Florida in the Early Eighteenth Century

War between European powers was nothing out of the ordinary around the turn of the eighteenth century. European imperialism did, however, alter the goals of violence in the Southeast at the same time as it expanded the scope of violence and provided new motivations to fight. Queen Anne's War was the American theater of the larger War of the Spanish Succession, which lasted from 1701 to 1714.

Alan Gallay has referred to impending hostilities between England and the combination of France and Spain as "the worst-kept secret in America."[51] The implications for imperially minded white Carolinians were clear: Florida and Louisiana could combine to thwart Carolina's expansion and dominance. South Carolina's Commons House of Assembly recognized as much. In a letter to the proprietors dated August 28, 1701, the legislature petitioned the proprietors for shot, powder, cutlasses, and field pieces, noting that "a War is already or will immediately break out between the Kingdom of England and the Confederates thereof and the Kingdom of France and

Spain." In the coming conflict, Carolina could be left vulnerable since, in the words of the legislature, it was "a Frontier to the Spanish and French who have threatned to attack us and have lately attempted by their Spies to withdraw the Yamasee Indians from us to them and so to invite the other Indyans to make Warr upon us."[52] Not surprisingly, the petition failed to mention that the English had been meddling in the native Southeast for decades or that Native Americans might choose for themselves when to forge alliances or "make Warr."

The stakes had risen in the Southeast because a new empire was on the scene. The French, all but absent from the region since the 1560s, had returned and established Biloxi in 1699 and Mobile in 1702. The fact that Charles Town's elites, about five hundred miles from Biloxi and Mobile, viewed the French as interlopers demonstrates their aims on a regional—not to say continental—scale. French colonizer Pierre Le Moyne d'Iberville and his younger brother Jean-Baptiste Le Moyne de Bienville had their own ambitious plan for the Southeast. Nicknamed "Projet sur la Caroline," the idea was to weaken English influence over the Southeast with an eye toward isolating and eventually destroying Carolina. French investigations in 1702 illuminated just how devastating the English presence had proven for some Southeastern Indians. In a meeting at Mobile, Iberville learned that from 1690 or so to 1702, Chickasaws armed by the English had killed eighteen hundred Choctaws and enslaved five hundred more.[53] The French tried to persuade Choctaws and Chickasaws to choose peace and ally against the English. The "ultimate plan of the Englishman, after weakening you by means of wars," Iberville wrote, "is to come and seize you in your villages and then send you to be sold somewhere else, in faraway countries from which you can never return, as the English have treated others, you know."[54] It's difficult to imagine a more penetrating assessment of English behavior in the Southeast.

Carolina's slave raiders and traders continued and escalated their assaults on the missions of Florida as well. Between 1701 and 1706, joint Muskogee-Yamasee-English attacks, the most devastating of which were led by Governor James Moore and Deputy Governor Robert Daniel of South Carolina, annihilated the mission provinces of Apalachee and Timucua but fell short of capturing the fortified Castillo de San Marcos of St. Augustine. This war was a windfall for those engaged in the Indian slave trade, including the Yamasees, but its failure to destroy St. Augustine completely and expel the Spanish struck a nerve with some English, who accused Moore of putting personal profit ahead of the good of the colony.[55] One critic called it a "Project of Freebooting under the specious Name of War."[56]

From the perspective of the Spanish, and to an even greater extent the mission Indians, the devastation could hardly have been more traumatic.[57] A joint English-Indian army of about nine hundred men left Charles Town overland and by boat in the fall of 1702 and burned several coastal installations on its way to lay siege to St. Augustine. In 1703, James Moore returned at the head of a private army made up almost entirely of Muskogee speakers to wreak further havoc in the mission province of Apalachee. The proceedings near the town of Ayubale in January 1704 were particularly grisly. Muskogee warriors burned sixteen prisoners, and cut out their eyes, tongues, and ears.[58] Thomas Nairne, who would die by torture at the outset of the Yamasee War, described the English strategy in 1705 when he noted, "We have these two . . . past years been intirely kniving all the Indian Towns in Florida which were subject to the Spaniards and have even accomplished it."[59] Native Americans went to war, but their goals in warfare rarely involved "intirely kniving" whole towns before the English arrived. Even during the longer campaigns, involving the higher risk battles the English preferred, native ideas about violence were not entirely absent. From the Creek perspective, careful, ritually performed torture might have been the proper

**FIG. 8.** This diorama, created by Ned Burns for Ocmulgee National Monument in the years after World War II, shows a joint Muskogee-English army leaving from the Macon Plateau to launch a raid on Spanish missions in Florida. Photograph by Lonnie Davis, courtesy of the National Park Service.

way to take the lives of Florida mission Indians, while the English would have probably preferred that they stayed alive to be sacrificed to sugar plantations on Barbados or elsewhere.[60]

For native communities in the region, the message was clear: English Carolina was the major European player in the American Southeast. Though the English and their Yamasee and Muskogee allies had not taken the heavily fortified heart of St. Augustine, they had burned the town and weakened Spanish religious and civil authority pretty much everywhere else. The early eighteenth century was the height of Yamasee power and Yamasee-English interdependence. The fighting also demonstrated that Yamasees, other native groups, and English, though they conceived of violence in different ways, could work together toward common goals. The English had combined diverse native people into large multiethnic war parties. This included Muskogees from different towns, who may have recognized that they shared important goals or historical experiences in common. It seems likely that English imperialism played a crucial role in Creek nation building in this instance.[61]

The violence of Queen Anne's War also could also be chaotic and point toward unintended consequences. Even groups that were allied with the English were not guaranteed immunity from enslavement in such violent times. Steven Oatis has recently brought to light two incidents in which Carolina traders paid Cherokees to take slaves from Creek towns whose contributions were essential to Carolina's war efforts. Continuing down that road, the legislature reasoned, "may be Very Prejediciall to this Collony by Giveing great disincouragemt to Such of the nations that are in Amity with us to be any further Assisting to this Collony, now in this Time of Warr."[62]

The fighting of the early eighteenth century represents an awakening of sorts on the part of the English at Carolina. The colony's government began to perceive Carolina as a leading edge of empire in the Southeast. Raids in the 1700s served a number of functions. In addition to enriching the men who led them and drawing more slaves to auction at Charles Town, they sought to establish English dominance over a territory contested by multiple European empires. This imperial perspective underlay the criticism directed at James Moore for his inability to vanquish the Spanish completely, even though his mission was a success from a financial standpoint. Moore himself had warned the Commons House of Assembly in August of 1701 that French liberality could turn former native allies into enemies. He also explicitly compared the situation in South Carolina to the violent border between French Canada and New England.[63] The Yamasee War, which forced South Carolina into a defensive position, made it clear that while the perspective of white Carolinians may have expanded, their ability to project imperial power into the interior was limited.

In a broad sense, the cases of the Westos, Savannahs, and Yamasees are indicative of the kind of violence associated with the early phases of white settlement in Carolina, trade and adaptation to the emerging Atlantic market and colonial realities. Trade itself need not be violent, but the type of trade fomented by Carolina among its native neighbors all but precluded long-term peaceful, mutually beneficial relations between the peoples of the Southeast. As William Ramsey has recently shown in the case of the Yamasee War, the very nature of the trade between the English and Native Americans, and its entanglement with all kinds of diplomatic and cultural issues, could itself breed violence.[64]

The sort of violence that took place along Carolina's frontier was neither wholly native nor English in its nature. What happened in South Carolina in the 1670s through the 1730s is a microcosm of what happened when European violence met Native American violence. In the shattered world of the Southeast, indigenous violence reoriented itself to deal with the realities of the plantation and the trading house and eventually was circumscribed by these institutions. This is not to say that the English did not conquer the Southeast. The English conquered the Southeast by subverting forms of violence they perceived as savage; the plantation and trading house were violent institutions, but English planters did not seem to mind the type of violence they could control.

# CHAPTER 7

# Violence in the Era of the Yamasee War

On April 15, 1715, Thomas Nairne, one of South Carolina's leading Indian traders, was put to death at Pocotaligo, the principal Yamasee town. Nairne was one of nearly one hundred white traders killed at the outset of what later historians would call the Yamasee War, but Nairne's death has made headlines in the centuries since because it was public spectacle. According to one account, recalled by an eyewitness who reported it to Carolina's attorney general, George Rodd, Yamasees burst into the place Nairne was sleeping, took him to the town square, tied him up, and burned him slowly to death, perhaps by inserting splinters under his skin and lighting them. Just the night before, Nairne and English negotiators had been working to assure the Yamasees of their peaceful intentions. The morning found the English killed, captured, or running for their lives and the Yamasees poised to lead a complex network of regional alliances, each made up of independent actors, against the English.[1]

Complex factors drove the Yamasees to kill Thomas Nairne, and to dispatch him in the manner they chose, but most of those factors can be traced back to the world of violence that the English created as they exploited the land, resources, and people of the Southeast with scant regard for the possible consequences. In short, the English culture of violence had brought on the Yamasee War. The conflict would eventually include not just Yamasees but also diverse native communities from across the Southeast, white soldiers from North Carolina and Virginia, and African slaves.[2] The costs to South Carolina's white population were high—in terms of percentage of population killed, the Yamasee War may have been more deadly than the now-famous King Philip's War—but the cost to the Yamasees was even higher. Over four hundred white colonists perished during the war, and many fled to the relative safety of Charles Town.[3] The "Yamasee Lands," or "Indian Lands," would remain unoccupied for some time and then would function mainly as a buffer until the establishment of the English colony of Georgia assumed that role.[4] The Native American communities surrounding Charles Town lost thousands of people. The remnants of the Yamasees moved south to the Spanish at St. Augustine. The remnants of those remnants would eventually move with the Spanish when they abandoned that outpost and headed for Cuba and Mexico in 1763.[5] The Yamasees gradually ceased to exist as a political entity, having been wiped off the map by English Carolina and its allied Native peoples, including bands of settlement Indians, Cherokees, and eventually some Creek towns. The upheaval had the long-term effect of helping to consolidate the English conquest of the region, even as it turned the English away from one of the institutions that had made that conquest possible. The war effectively brought an end to Carolina's Indian slave trade.[6]

South Carolina's elites seemed to recognize that trouble with the Indian trade could lead to violence, but the legal evolution of the trade featured a fair amount of trial and error. Laws concerning the trade were bound up in the factional struggle between proprietors, governors, and colonists. By a 1663 charter granted by Charles II, trade with native peoples was the business of the proprietors. Subsequent proprietary proclamations reiterated the point, which seems to indicate that the proprietors were not really in control. In 1707, the Commons House of Assembly made a claim for its supremacy in matters of trade. Sir Nathaniel Johnson, the appointed governor, and his council rejected the measure. The Commons threatened to withhold funds for the defense of Charles Town, and soon the act "For Regulating the Indian Trade and making it Safe to the Public" was in effect. The goal behind the legislation, besides increasing the power of the Commons at the expense of the proprietors, was to limit the sorts of abuses that could lead to violence. The 1707 act also created a board of nine commissioners and the office of Indian agent. The agent was to live in Carolina's native backcountry ten months out of the year.[7]

Thomas Nairne was one of the first men to serve in the position of agent, and his importance to relations between native communities and English Carolina cannot be overstated. Nairne was probably born in northeastern Scotland, but the date and place are not precisely known. Before his arrival in Carolina, at some point prior to 1695, it seems he was a soldier; in his 1710 *Letter from South-Carolina,* Nairne expressed relief at having given up "the unhappy Condition of the Military Imployment" for life as a South Carolina planter. Nairne's landholdings totaled about thirty-six hundred acres on Saint Helena Island, south of Charles Town. Apart from his plantation, Nairne also made money from surveying land for his neighbors and trading. Nairne's previous military training did not go to waste in Carolina, of course. He joined trading and slaving expeditions and commanded troops at several points. Nairne and his contemporary, John "Tuscarora Jack" Barnwell, were planter-warriors well suited to the violent world they helped create.[8] They combined several of the different aspects of the English culture of violence in the Americas. Both were planters, and as such they held slaves under the threat of violence. Given the suddenness of Nairne's death, it's not surprising that his will has not turned up. His widow's estate, whose contents were listed in 1721, included twenty-two African and five Indian slaves.[9] Both also engaged in wide-ranging campaigns, Nairne for the purpose of establishing trade with native nations far to the west and slaving in the Spanish missions to the south and Barnwell at the head of a multiracial army sent by South Carolina to aid North Carolina during the Tuscarora War.

One of Nairne's slaving expeditions took him all the way to central Florida. Nairne accompanied a party of Yamasee warriors on an undated—but probably 1702—slave raid. The route of the raid and an explanatory legend appear in Herman Moll's 1720 *World Described* collection of maps on the map titled "New Map of the North Parts of America." Its legend reads, "Explanation of an Expedition in Florida Neck by Thirty-three Iamesee Indians Accompany'd by Capt. T. Nairn." The raid was difficult, involving six days of rowing and swimming over a deep river, but it was a success. Nairne and the Yamasees took thirty-five slaves and killed thirty-three Florida Indians. On the same raid "a very Numerous body of Indians came against them, they being but 33 men. Yet put them presently to flight; they having no Armes but Harpoos, made of Iron and Fish bones; they were all Painted."[10] Being allied with Carolina brought distinct advantages to the Yamasees, and being connected with the Yamasees benefited Thomas Nairne, at least in 1702.

Nairne had also traveled extensively in the interior Southeast, to the Mississippi in fact, in 1708. The journal he left behind gives some idea of the English imperial mindset and the geographical extent of the Indian slave trade in the first decade of the eighteenth century. Nairne envisioned a wide-ranging network of English trade and settlement. In one letter he expressed the hope that the "English American Empire may not be unreasonably Crampt up."[11] In the early nineteenth century, the United States would bring his expansive vision to life, with devastating results for the region's indigenous peoples. While Nairne was among the Chickasaws he noted that "no imployment pleases the Chicasaws so well as slave catching. A lucky hitt at that besides the Honor procures them a whole Estate at once, one slave brings a Gun, ammunition, horse, hatchet, and a suit of Cloathes, which would not be procured without much tedious toil a hunting."[12]

In a letter to the Earl of Sunderland, also written in 1708, Nairne extolled the "civilizing" effects of the trade in slaves: "The good prices the English Traders give them [Tallapoosas—a Creek town—and Chickasaws] for slaves Encourages them to this trade Extreamly and some men think that it both serves to Lessen their numbers before the French can arm them and it is a more Effectual way of Civilising and Instructing, Then all the efforts used by the French missionaries."[13] From the perspective of Nairne, and probably more of Carolina's English, instructing Southeastern Indians in the ways of the Atlantic market and slave raiding was more important than traditional methods of "civilization." These deceptively simple passages illustrate the nature of the English culture of violence in Carolina in the first decade of the eighteenth century. It was expansive. Nairne had traveled far to the west of Charles Town to lay the groundwork for English trade, which certainly carried the potential for violence. It relied on enslaving Indians, or, more precisely, it armed some Indians and then relied on them to enslave other Indians. Among the Choctaws, Nairne pushed the English case for the destruction of the small nations allied with the French.[14] The English culture of violence was tied to imperial concerns. Nairne, for instance, pointed out "how Just a tittle we have to the Chicasaws, and that by a method the most moderate and equitable that ever dominion was acquired over any rude savage Nation."[15] The notion that the English could claim "title" to a native nation is a fascinating one. In terms of imperial rivalry, Nairne noted that if the numbers of native people were thinned by the trade ("it serves to lessen their numbers"), then the English could gain the upper hand on the French in the struggle for the Southeast. This was a bold, imperialist idea; it was also more than a little incautious. The English people involved were not overly concerned with the possible negative consequences of their actions for their own empire, let alone the native communities who were caught up in these extensive, violent trading networks.

Thomas Nairne was an imperialist, a slave raider, an Indian trader, an observer of native cultures of violence, and a victim of ritual violence. His views on the relationship between the English colony and the native interior deserve a little more scrutiny. He assumed that natives really only reacted to the presence of Europeans in one of two ways: they became subject peoples or they didn't. In 1708, he wrote that the "Cherickee nation" was "now Entirely Subject to us," while the Chickasaws remained frustratingly independent. The situation was temporary, though, and would only obtain until "we have put the French out of any capacity to raise an Indian army," presumably by a combination of gift giving and slave raiding.[16]

Nairne admired the Chickasaws and gained a deep, if biased, understanding of their preparations for war. His journal mentioned the use of "Amulet bages" (presumably medicine pouches). Before elite fighters laid down to camp, their attendants placed their amulets on "Red Targets in a line befor the front fires."[17] Women had a key role to play in Chickasaw violence as well: "10 or Twelve Young women" accompanied each Chickasaw war party and praised men for performing well at combat or, alternately, chided them if they "gave way."[18]

Nairne was an astute recorder of Native American cultures of violence, but his prejudices appear at times. For instance, he criticized Illini slave raiders, "the slyest and most patient men stealers of the World," for practicing what he deemed to be a cowardly method of fighting. But the Chickasaws, and Nairne himself, engaged in a very similar type of violence. Nairne also could not fathom why a large native power hadn't conquered all the nations of the Southeast and created an empire to rival that of the Incas:

> Conquest is neither at some times or in all cases unjust, nor unhappy for these conquered for it had been infinitely better for these infedils, if some powerful tribe had subdued the rest, and brought them under government and to a peaceable life, rather then they should thus have consumed themselves, by their savage quarrells. Thus the Incas of Peru acquiered a Just empire, by making War only against such as were notorious breakers of the Law of nature, whom they brought to be a great nation, liveing peaceable and happy.[19]

We should not expect Nairne to exhibit a particularly deep understanding of the struggles that resulted in the Inca Empire or the civil war that shredded it on the eve of the Spanish invasion. Nairne was only referencing the Incas to make a point: conquest by a powerful and just empire was the best that native peoples of the Southeast could hope for. They might even find such subjection happy and peaceable. And Nairne knew just the empire to fulfill that role.

South Carolina's Commissioners of Indian Trade began meeting at Charles Town in September 1710. Early entries in their journals reveal serious cracks in the regional alliance the English were trying to build and indicate that in matters of trade, English and Indians were often talking past each other. At the commission's second meeting, several people who had been mistakenly enslaved were freed and accusations were leveled at a trader who allegedly stole a young Indian woman from her mother "offering to kill the Mother becaus she would not leve her Daughter behind her."[20]

Alexander Longe posed something of a problem for the Commissioners of the Indian Trade and a fascinating case study in cultures of violence. Long was an Indian trader operating in Cherokee Country in the 1710s and 1720s, and as such he was a representative of the violent trading regime that characterized South Carolina's early years. He was also very close to the Cherokees and operated in Cherokee country during very dangerous times, indicating that he was probably under Cherokee protection. Carolina officials even questioned whether Longe's loyalties lay with the English colony or the Cherokees.

In 1713, Longe committed an act of trade-related violence that the English deemed too extreme. As part of a longstanding feud with the Yuchis, one of whom had apparently partially scalped him ("puled of sum of his Hair"), he blew up a Yuchi with gunpowder and incited the Cherokees to attack the Yuchi town of Chestowe. Some of the defenders of the town chose to kill one another rather than risk "falling into the Hands of the Cherokees."[21] How much encouragement the Cherokees needed to attack the Yuchis is not exactly clear, but the Commissioners of the Indian Trade called for Longe's arrest and the revocation of his license to trade, at which point he ran to Cherokee country, where he remained for the next decade, through the upheavals of the Yamasee War.[22] Longe's act violated South Carolina's loose rules regarding violence (the Yuchis and Carolina were at peace, so they were technically "off limits" for enslavement), but it did not hurt his standing among Cherokees.[23] Longe had begun to understand the Cherokee culture of violence and had expected to be granted asylum in Cherokee country even when he was a wanted man in English Carolina.

In the early 1710s, disputes had already arisen between traders and Yamasees, resulting in the dispatch of an agent specifically to settle differences between Yamasees and traders.[24] The cataclysm between the Yamasees and English was still a few years down the road. In the meantime, Yamasees and others would join white Carolinians in a fight against the Tuscaroras in North Carolina.

## Fighting for North Carolina and Slaves

John Barnwell's Tuscarora War journal, besides being a good read, is helpful in reconstructing the English-Yamasee alliance at a time when it must have been under strain. The good old days of slave raiding in the mission provinces were past, and Yamasee debts were mounting. Barnwell kept his journal fairly regularly, considering the circumstances, and the vivid account of colonial warfare contained therein helps recreate the violent world of the Carolinas in the eighteenth century.

The journal contains an excellent description of the first joint English-Yamasee campaign against the Tuscaroras, including military maneuvers, defeats, and victories. In it, Barnwell also recorded his thoughts on the proper way to fight colonial wars, and he cobbled together a kind of ramshackle racial hierarchy. He believed that certain ethnic groups were better prepared to deal with the rigors of colonial warfare than others. Barnwell's journal also hints at the relationship between manliness and warfare. Most importantly, Barnwell's journal illuminates some crucial aspects of the cultures of violence operating in the eighteenth-century South.

John Barnwell was born in Ireland around 1680 and died in 1724 in Port Royal, South Carolina. He was described by the mayor of Dublin as the "son of a verry good gentleman and gentlewoeman." The mayor went on to say that Barnwell had "extriordinary friends and relasions in this Kingdom" and that he left Ireland in about 1701 "from a humor to goe to travel and for no other reason." Once in South Carolina, Barnwell became master of a four hundred–acre plantation known simply as "Doctors." His land holdings would eventually total sixty-five hundred acres. All this background information aside, it was not because of his high birth, wanderlust, or huge tracts of land that Barnwell became famous; it was his proficiency at frontier warfare and killing Indians that, quite literally, made his name in South Carolina. In 1711 and 1712 he led a major expedition, made up largely of Yamasees, against the Tuscaroras when North Carolina requested South Carolina's aid. His successes in that war that led to the sobriquet "Tuscarora Jack." Barnwell was also a key player in the subsequent Yamasee War.[25]

In 1711, the Tuscaroras and their allies, fed up with the practices of unscrupulous English traders and alarmed by the expansion of Baron de Graffenried's Swiss and German settlement at New Bern, attacked several white settlements and captured John Lawson, the colony's surveyor general, and the baron himself.[26] Although de Graffenried bargained for his freedom, John Lawson quarreled with one of the Tuscarora leaders and was put to death. In the initial attack, the Tuscaroras killed 130 colonists and badly frightened all those who remained. The colonists were not prepared to deal with such hostilities, and the Lords Proprietors back in England did nothing. North Carolina called on Virginia and South Carolina for help. Virginia dissuaded the Upper Tuscaroras and its other Indian allies from joining the war and pledged some financial assistance.[27] South Carolina's response was more aggressive, perhaps because its leading Indian traders and their Native American allies sensed an opportunity. South Carolina raised an army of five hundred Indians (the largest single component was Yamasee, but there were also Catawbas, Cheraws, and other smaller groups involved) and thirty white men to bring relief to North Carolina. The leader of the expedition was John Barnwell. Although the South Carolinians won several important battles, a provision and supply shortage combined with

Yamasee desertions and Barnwell's own wounds to compel Barnwell to agree to terms and move back south. In 1712, a force of about one thousand South Carolina Indians, including three hundred Cherokees, led by James Moore, returned to North Carolina. Moore's larger force was able to finally defeat the Tuscaroras.[28]

On February 4, 1712, John Barnwell's forces camped outside of "Narhantes," or Torhunta, and his journal begins with a list of the contributing communities and the number of men from each one. The Yamasees, Barnwell's neighbors and the largest single group present, numbered eighty-seven. Also included in Barnwell's company were ten "Hog Logees," fifty-six "Apalatchees," and five "Corsaboy." Other native peoples represented in the South Carolina army included Saraws, Saxapahaws, Catawbas, Watterees, and Pedees.[29] This was a remarkably diverse force, and this striking diversity indicates that the old-school narrative of native-white conflict needs to be substantially revised. Throughout American history, native peoples fought on both sides of what white colonists and apologetic historians have labeled "Indian Wars."

The first engagement of the campaign demonstrated that the Yamasees who fought with (not necessarily under) Barnwell were "mettlesome," since they wanted to attack too early, before adequate preparations had been made. At this battle, the majority of the fort's Tuscarora defenders, both male and female, were "put to the sword." The thirty white men who served under Barnwell took up this grisly business, and when it was all over, Barnwell noted that "it was Terror to our own heathen friends to behold us, the word was Revenge, which we made good by the Execution we made of the enemy."[30] It is difficult to conceive how this brutality could be perceived as revenge by Barnwell, since he had lost relatively few men, white, Yamasee, or otherwise, in the battle and had spent the last part of it seeking out the fort's defenders and killing them one by one. Barnwell apparently felt that since the colony at New Bern had been threatened, British people in South Carolina were threatened, or maybe he thought the entire English colonial mission was threatened, and this was enough to justify almost any kind of payback. It is also possible that an inchoate notion of race played some role. Europeans, whether German, Irish, or English, were on one side of a racial divide, and indigenous people were on the other.

The Yamasees and other Native Americans who fought with John Barnwell had their own motives for entering the conflict and for behaving the way they did during it. While Barnwell and the other "Brittains" were busy executing the Tuscaroras, the "Indians got all the slaves & plunder." Dejected, Barnwell noted that "only one girl we gott." This pattern repeats itself time and time again in Barnwell's journal. The Indians plunder, and, as Barnwell lamented, there was "nothing left for the white men but their horses tired & their wounds to comfort them."[31] This distinction between Native American and English goals in war is an important one to note. While the English were concerned with defeating the Tuscaroras militarily, the Yamasees seem to have been interested mainly in "plunder" and slave raiding, not to mention avoiding significant casualties.[32] Yamasees had been trading partners with the English at Charles Town for several decades, and they had become deeply enmeshed in the Indian slave trade. Indian cultures of violence had been influenced by the English presence, but older ways of war had not disappeared entirely. The Yamasees could fight as allies of the English in an imperial war, but do so to increase their own economic standing or garner war honors.

In spite of these sometimes divergent goals, the expedition continued, and Barnwell heaped praise on his Yamasee allies. "The greatest part of our Indians," wrote Barnwell, "are unwilling to proceed into Unknown country, where they may be hem'd in by a numerous enemy and not know how to extricate themselves." The Yamasees were a crucial exception to this rule: "My brave Yamassees told me they would go wherever I led them. They will live and die with me, and Indeed I have that dependance on them that I would not refuse to give battle to the whole Nation of Tuscaruros with them."[33] Two parts of Barnwell's "racial bravery scale" were in place. The "Brittains," as he called them, were at the top, and not too far behind were the Yamasees, who, although they attacked quickly and ran away equally quickly, were nonetheless brave. Note the use of the word "my" to describe the Yamasees. The Yamasees probably did not see themselves as belonging to Barnwell.

The Tuscaroras, not surprisingly, were not nearly so brave, according to Barnwell. He wrote that the Tuscaroras were "extremely cowardly if they have liberty to run. Our Indians outdo the Enemy very much either at bush or Swamp but the Enemy are Fleeter & has the advantage of knowing the country."[34] In the letter dated February 12, 1712, Barnwell described the Tuscaroras as "Skulking dogs" in reference to the shooting of a Seneca man.[35] White British colonists were at the top, followed by the Yamasees, and the Tuscaroras were at the bottom, thus far. Barnwell, of course, was the quintessential frontier warrior, in his mind, and he said as much when he mentioned in passing that, in an attempt at "Extirpating these Indians," he would gladly give his own life, "w'ch for the honour of Carolina I am always ready to sacrifice."[36] One can hardly ignore the mold which Barnwell fits so readily. An early eighteenth-century up-and-coming Irish gentleman, full of notions of honor and masculinity and the not-so-subtle relationship between the two, striding into the arena of colonial warfare, stood ready to prove his worth as a man through the practice of leading troops in battle. He was also a planter, and for at least a handful of white South Carolinians, the roles of planter and warrior appear to have been related.

South Carolina was not attacked during the Tuscarora War, yet Barnwell was ready to sacrifice his life to defend its honor. The early eighteenth century provided ample opportunity for men to prove their mettle fighting "savages" in the wilds of coastal Carolina. The punchline, of course, is that Barnwell returned to South Carolina before he was able to finish the job, and North Carolina's governor questioned his resolve, his honor, and his skill at battle.[37]

Barnwell's plan for attacking Hancock's Town, the main fort of the Tuscaroras, named after King Hancock, was simple and offers some insight into the contempt in which Barnwell held Governor Hyde of North Carolina: "When I come to Hancock's Fort I will offer him a battle, which if refused, I will well view the same, & if I think it practicable, I will have ye hon[r] of finishing the war by taking it. Otherwise I will build a Fort by it and expect the assistance of the pusillanimous Governor of North Carolina."[38]

Barnwell's assessment of the character of North Carolina has a foil in the virtues of South Carolina. As he closed the entry quoted above, he congratulated that colony's governor for the "success of our army hitherto and for the hon[r] & Glory of virtuous South Carolina whose armies are the same winter gathering Laurells from the Cape Florida and from the Bay of Spiritta Sancta even to the Borders of Virginia."[39]

In Barnwell's mind, South Carolina's fights were simple ones of right against wrong. One imagines that the conflict was not quite so basic in the minds of the Tuscaroras and Yamasees who were fighting the war for different reasons. The documentary record reveals no previous enmity between the two groups. The Yamasees may have fought because they were interested in moving farther from the declining Spanish empire and desired to attach themselves to the rising colonial star of the Southeast, the English. Fighting on the side of the English cemented the alliance began in the 1680s with the Yamasee migration and ethnogenesis. There were few better ways to impress the planters and merchants of Charles Town than to ally with them in war and return with English and German booty from Tuscarora villages and Tuscarora slaves to be sold in the West Indies or any of the North American colonies.[40] Their behavior in battle indicates that the Yamasees, though interested in furthering English war aims, also had war aims of their own, namely, returning to South Carolina with as many Tuscarora slaves as possible.

Barnwell recorded Yamasee and English bravery and "skulking" Tuscarora cowardice. The Tuscaroras are not alone at the bottom of the colonial warfare barrel; Barnwell reserved his harshest criticism for the military men of North Carolina. To be sure, the forces of North Carolina suffered when scores of white men of military age were killed in the initial Tuscarora attack; this begs the question of why, when Barnwell expressed his concern over the well-being of war widows and children of dead fathers, he did not make the connection between these survivors and the sixty-seven North Carolina men who showed up without ammunition and in no condition to fight on February 26.[41] From the beginning of the campaign, Barnwell noted that his "scouts made no discovery of any men from North Carolina to joyn me at the place concerted between me and Major Gale."[42] This theme runs throughout the journal. The North Carolinians arrive late, if at all, and fight poorly when they do arrive.

Barnwell's journal entry for March 4, 1712, which describes a hazardous river crossing, also chastises the North Carolinians lyrically as a "Cowardly Country Crew," since they were afraid to cross into Indian territory. Barnwell boasted that "5 South Carolina men . . . went over on the first raft."[43] The Germans accompanying the expedition were deficient in a number of areas. They had some experience with constructing defensive "Fashines," though they were apparently unskilled in their use. The following quotation from the journal illustrates Barnwell's voice and his thoughts on ethnicity and proficiency at war: "The enemy made a terrible fire upon us without the least damage in the world, but this country base, cowardly people hearing the shott strike their Fashines, threw both them & their arms away & run for life, w[ch] not only left themselves exposed but also all those that went under their shelters; this encouraged the enemy to renew the firing, who deservedly shott sev[ll] of them in their arses. In the mean time my brave South Carolina men [and] 23 of this country undauntedly kept their order."[44]

Barnwell's racial hierarchy was finally complete. At the top are the virtuous South Carolinians, next come "my brave Yamasees." The Tuscaroras are "cowardly" and "skulking," and the forces of North Carolina can do no better than running under fire and being "deservedly shott . . . in their arses."

Barnwell's ideas about race and warfare highlight an Anglo-American culture of violence in the second decade of the eighteenth century. Willing to admit that the Yamasees are brave, Barnwell never once describes them as virtuous. This omission is significant. While Indians may be useful to white South Carolinians, they cannot escape the fact that they are still Indians and, as such, incapable of attaining virtue. Later in the eighteenth century, as Native Americans disappeared (the colonists hoped) from the landscape, it became easier to accept Indians as virtuous. Similarly, the Tuscaroras' "skulking" and "cowardly" status is related largely to the fact that they are the enemies of white South Carolinians. Barnwell's attitudes toward the Europeans are very strange, and one has to wonder how much of his attitude toward North Carolina is rhetorical in nature. He idealizes South Carolina, the armies of which pursue evil enemies far beyond the borders of their own adopted homeland. North Carolinians, on the other hand, come in for what would appear to be an undue amount of scorn. The German, Swiss, and English forces of North Carolina had suffered terrible, crushing defeats at the hands of the Tuscaroras, and Barnwell, while he is sympathetic to their plight, shows them relatively little mercy in his journal.

One might question whether Barnwell was advocating a parochial brand of colonization, limited to furthering the military and trade aims of South Carolina alone. Indeed, Steven Oatis, in his book *A Colonial Complex,* uses Barnwell's campaign as an example of what he terms "the arrogance of South Carolina imperialism."[45] On the other hand, Barnwell did describe his campaign as revenge, so even if he placed South Carolina at the head of his list of reasons for going to war, racial solidarity and advancing English empire followed closely. As the campaign progressed, Barnwell was frustrated by the lack of aid from North Carolina. He may have felt that he was going out of his way to help a stricken fellow colony, and receiving very little assistance in doing so. So it was probably not just a mistrust of the Germans and Swiss that fueled Barnwell's resentment; they simply reinforced his image of himself as a lone frontier warrior among the Indians. In one sense, this might not be South Carolina's imperial arrogance so much as Barnwell's alone, or a case study in a broader kind of colonial cockiness. Barnwell was also using the still-developing marker of race to decide who could attain virtue and who could not. Aggressive, intrinsically violent Indians had attacked peace-loving, civilized farmers, and such an insult would not stand. Barnwell, like Thomas Nairne, represents a generation of white men who sought mastery over neighboring natives and black slaves. This class of "planter-warriors" would drive English colonization and help shape an Anglo-American culture of violence.[46]

When we left Tuscarora Jack, he was just beginning to recognize the impossibility of taking Hancock's Town. The last several entries in his journal are a litany of excuses as to why he ultimately failed: his provisions ran out, too many Indians had deserted him, it was too cold, the North Carolina legislature was drinking his health with rum while he dined on cold water and grass. If he had just four more days' provisions he believed he could take the fort and end the war. The list goes on and on, and the journal ends by describing the terms of the peace treaty and with this pathetic plea: "May

So. Carolina flourish when I bleed & suffer. . . . Send some corn to help ye poor Yamassees home."[47]

Upon returning to New Bern, Barnwell expected honors and rewards. Characteristically, Barnwell would likely complain, none were forthcoming.[48] In fact, Governor Hyde thought Barnwell a coward for not pursuing a victory he was so close to obtaining.[49] Barnwell returned to South Carolina, without his honor, disgraced, at least in the minds of North Carolinians. Tuscarora Jack did not leave North Carolina altogether empty handed, though; he captured some Native American slaves under the pretense of peace, and as for his honor, he was able to restore that with his leadership in the fight *against* his "brave Yamasees," his neighbors and former allies, in the Yamasee War.[50]

As mentioned above, a larger Cherokee-English force returned to North Carolina the year after Barnwell's Yamasee campaign and defeated the Tuscaroras. The Carolina-Cherokee army routed the Tuscaroras, destroying the fortified town of Neoheroka in the process.[51] In the battle at Neoheroka, the Tuscaroras suffered hundreds of casualties while the attackers suffered scores, and many of the Tuscarora survivors left the Southeast. Military historian Wayne Lee has argued that the battle at Neoheroka demonstrated that the Tuscaroras were attempting to adapt European-style military fortifications but that this decision had devastating consequences. Tuscaroras were inventive enough to built a bastioned fortification, complete with underground tunnels linking strongholds. Unfortunately, they couldn't match the Carolina army in terms of firepower, and the use of explosives and artillery proved too much to resist.[52]

## The Yamasee War

The study of the Yamasee War has recently broken free from the cozy world of Southeastern Indian history. A handful of dissertations on the war appeared in the late 1990s and early 2000s.[53] William Ramsey's *Journal of American History* article and *The Yamasee War,* Steven Oatis's *Colonial Complex,* Steven Hahn's *Invention of the Creek Nation,* and, most notably, Alan Gallay's *Indian Slave Trade,* awarded the Bancroft Prize, have confirmed the war's renewed importance in early American history.[54] The Yamasee War even has its own debate, and the wrangling over the primary causes of the conflict is not likely to be resolved any time soon, though each new work purports to have the last say.[55]

One recent interpretation of the causes of the Yamasee War is directly related to the English culture of violence, though William Ramsey takes his interpretation in a slightly different direction. He uses his sharp analysis of trade to put the Yamasee War into its proper historical context. This is an important task, and it still leaves room for other historians to use the violent story of Anglo-Indian trade as part of a different story about cultures of violence. Ramsey points out that the nature of the Indian trade itself was capable of leading to violence. Prior interpretations of the conflict blamed the unscrupulousness of individual traders, the failure of regulatory legislation, Yamasee fears of being enslaved, and ecological factors for the war. Few of these recognized that it was the set of cultural assumptions underlying trade—from both native and English sides—that caused the conflagration.[56]

In 1714, as a result of the rivalry between Nairne and John Wright, South Carolina was no longer communicating with Southeastern native America in any kind of official capacity. The messages that were sent were being relayed by individual traders operating independent of any semblance of colonial policy, and violence was the result.[57]

The war itself began with the April 15, Good Friday, 1715, murders of several important Carolina ambassadors in the main Yamasee town of Pocotaligo. Some traders died instantly; Thomas Nairne did not. According to George Rodd, "the wretches ran many pieces of wood through Mr. Nairne, then the pieces of wood were lit."[58] Nairne burned slowly over several days.

The method chosen for Nairne's execution obviously inflamed English passions and added more evidence to the argument that Native Americans were one-dimensional, vicious brutes. The event was probably not so simple from a Yamasee perspective. Though a large body of evidence regarding torture among the Yamasees specifically does not exist, the practice of torture was widespread in the Southeast, and many groups in eastern native America practiced a similar sort of violence. Moreover, the Upper Yamasee towns may have spoken a Muskogean language, so torture practices from that broad cultural group may have had some influence on the Yamasees.[59] Both natives and Europeans took trophies from their defeated enemies. Disembodied heads and headless scalps seem to have transmitted messages across cultural lines in Ireland, on Roanoke, in the interior Southeast, and in the Carolina Lowcountry. These trophies demonstrated mastery of a defeated enemy and in some cases served to warn others of the might of those who had taken the trophies. Torture fulfilled a different role in Native American communities, though. In a wide-ranging study, Georges Sioui suggested that for Native Americans, torture, far from being a dehumanizing act, was the exact opposite. The taking of a human life in this way was, in fact, a profoundly humanizing act. And the fact that such great care was taken in dispatching victims might even be seen as a way of recognizing a common humanity. For many groups, this was a "considered, rational, and necessary act."[60] Among the Creeks, torture served a crucial function: it allowed aggrieved parties to grieve publicly the wrongs done them and it allowed for "the brave to exit this world in a manly fashion," according to historian Kathryn E. Holland Braund.[61] Georges Sioui also noted that for many groups, the ritual death was a way of bringing episodes of violence to a close, of "killing the war itself."[62]

The specifics of Nairne's case would appear to demonstrate a Yamasee culture of war in crisis. Nairne went to bed on April 14, 1715, assuming that whichever parties needed to be assuaged had been assuaged or that at least a crisis had been averted. After Nairne turned in, Yamasee leaders heard evidence of Carolina's two-faced behavior. Nairne's rival, a trader named John Wright, had told a Yamasee headman that the English intended to enslave the Yamasees and added an insult that meant the same thing in multiple cultures of violence: "The Yamasees were like women." Further debate resulted in a change of plans, and Nairne's death was the result.[63]

Nairne had a longtime association with the Yamasees, and one wonders, though it is not possible to prove, if some of the same individuals who joined him in his Florida slaving expedition, or perhaps their relatives, were among those who put Nairne to death or were present at the scene. If so, this would lend weight to the notion that Nairne was given this special death rather than being shot in his bed or otherwise quickly dispatched. So his killing should be seen as an illustration of the Yamasee culture of violence. But unlike other tortures, Nairne's killing didn't end an episode of violence. It started one. This demonstrates that the Yamasee culture of violence had been altered by Europeans. The ritual killing of one man was not enough to counter the offenses that English Carolina had committed over the previous years. More violence was needed to set things straight or restore balance in the Southeast.

In the weeks that followed, other traders, perhaps totaling ninety men, were killed in Indian towns throughout the Southeast. Even groups that would participate nominally in the fighting of the war (the Lower Cherokees, Upper Creeks, Chickasaws, and Choctaws) used the opportunity to kill the traders stationed among them. This indicates a widespread dissatisfaction with the English trading regime. Fighting flared briefly on Carolina's northern frontier, as some Cherokees and Catawbas sacked plantations and attacked a hastily built fort, but the Yamasee War's northern front, which had little to do with the Yamasees, was quiet by the early summer.

Another trader, Seymour Burroughs (Mr. Burage in the Rodd account), was shot twice in the same attack during which Thomas Nairne was captured but managed to swim in the Pocotaligo River and escape to the

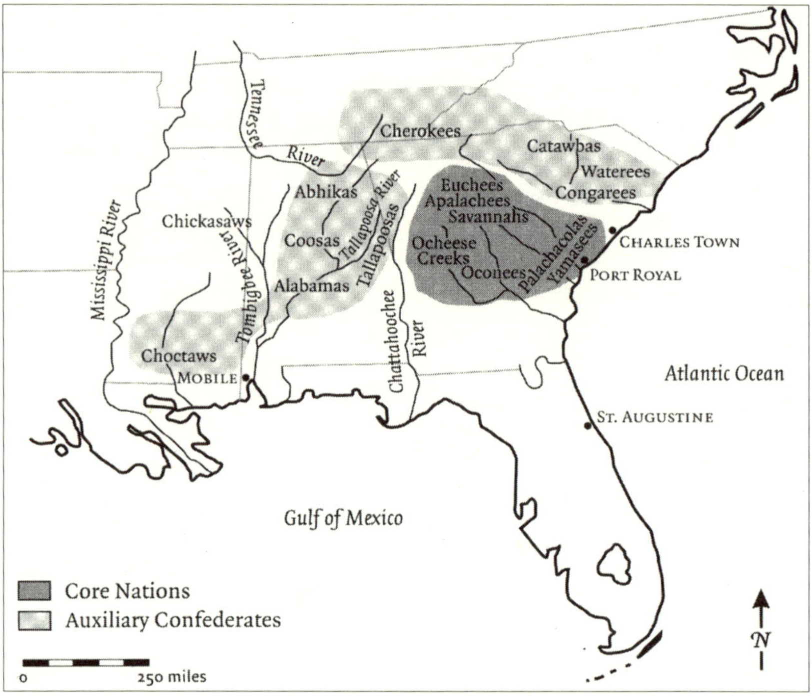


**Map 3.** William Ramsey, author of *The Yamasee War,* demonstrated that far from being a region-wide push to drive the English into the sea, there were varying levels of commitment to the war effort. In both the core nations and auxiliary nations, natives killed the English traders among them. After this coup, though, the auxiliary nations backed off, and in one notable case even went to war against one another. Reproduced from *The Yamasee War* by William Ramsey. Used by permission of the University of Nebraska Press. Copyright 2008 the Board of Regents of the University of Nebraska.

plantation of John Barnwell, who sounded the wider alarm. From the Yamasees' point of view, the initial stages of the conflict were a remarkable success, even a "coup" such as that accomplished by the Powhatans in Virginia and the Tuscaroras in North Carolina: one war party killed more than one hundred colonists and slaves in an assault on St. Bartholomew's Parish, west of Charles Town. As William Ramsey has shown, the initial stages of the war also demonstrate Yamasee goals in the war. After initial successes, the Yamasees retreated in two directions, mirroring the paths they had traveled into Carolina in the 1680s.[64] The Yamasees struck quickly against well-defined targets (the traders and the plantations which they could reach without risking too many casualties) and then fell back, pursued by English soldiers.

The Yamasees who fled toward Florida were relatively easily dealt with by the English, but the group that moved into the interior proved more intractable and launched repeated attacks on English plantations, killing many farm animals—note the symbolic victory over offensive English animals—as part of a large though not region-wide alliance including Yuchis, Savannahs, some Lower Creeks, and Apalachees.[65] Violence continued on the war's southern front and included the Lower Creeks and the originally aggrieved Yamasees. In early 1716, some semblance of normalcy returned with a fresh alliance between Carolina and the Cherokees, and in 1717 Carolina was once again at peace with the Creek towns.[66] Groups of Yamasees continued to attack Carolina's outlying plantations for the next ten years, eventually retreating to the relative safety of the Spanish sphere near St. Augustine. South Carolina's militia counterattacked ferociously. Led by Governor Craven, George Chicken, John Barnwell, and other experienced fighters, the militia managed to regain the momentum of the war within a few months. It bears mentioning that the South Carolina militia was not exactly a clumsy bunch of farmers forced to take up arms. At least in leadership positions, the militia could boast several men of what I referred to above as the "planter-warrior" class.

Dispatches from the war zone reveal that some white Carolinians believed the assault to be an all-out race war and thought the very survival of Charles Town was threatened. Reverend Francis Le Jau referred to the initial attack as a "General Conspiracy of the Indians that Surround us—from the borders of St. Augustin to Cape Fear."[67] George Rodd feared that "they planned to take possession of the whole continent, and to kill or drive out all of us."[68] The General Assembly, among other letter writers, attested to the feeling that white Carolina was "surrounded by numerous Indian Nations that hope by their multitude to make a Prey of this your Majesty's late prosperous and flourishing colony."[69] It is not hard to forgive these initial reporters their terror. Le Jau's parishioners feared for their lives, and Rodd himself had lost his plantation in the first stages of the war, but their reports must be balanced against the fact that some very powerful nations, the Upper Creeks and Cherokees, hardly participated in the war at all. Even the Yamasees probably did not conceive of the war as an all-out effort to drive the English into the sea. Many more Native peoples seemed resigned to the fact that the English were in Carolina for the long haul and sought to benefit from a relationship with them.[70]

"Rodd's Relation" gives a good idea of how crucial the Yamasee War was in the minds of white Carolinians and how "the ruin and destruction of this beautiful land might be prevented." After reminding the proprietors and the king that it was their duty to "lighten the misfortunes of all their subjects and to prevent their estates from falling into the hands of pagans and barbarians," Rodd took on a counterargument, that "one would vainly represent Carolina as a country of little importance." Instead, Rodd averred that if Carolina should fall to Indian control, then the whole continent might be danger. "This country," Rodd reminded his readers, "is worth the trouble of going to war to keep it."[71] For George Rodd and other white planters, Carolina represented English colonization in microcosm, and the use of violence to protect their homes and investments was an entirely appropriate response. Here is another example of the effects of the transfer of the English culture of violence across the Atlantic. The English who fought against the Yamasees and their allies in the 1710s were fighting in defense of their homes. Their immediate predecessors, the first generation of English in Carolina, inhabited a more precarious position. They viewed the climate and soils favorably (one, William Sayle, wrote that he was "never in a sweater clymate then this is")[72] but fretted about their ability to fully take advantage of the richness of the land. After listing all the things that would grow in Carolina, the Council begged "yo$^{r}$ Hono$^{rs}$ shipps to fetch more people that this honor$^{ble}$ designe might not fall for want of an Industrious management."[73] Some perceived themselves to be isolated on the fringe of the English empire. By the 1710s, Carolinians may have still thought themselves isolated, but they had significant emotional and financial ties to American land and were willing to go to war to defend that land. In a short time, the English had gone from being interlopers to considering Carolina a new homeland. In the weeks after Rodd wrote his desperate account, Carolina's armies proved him right. South Carolina was worth "going to war to keep it."

By the 1730s, English Carolina had undergone a massive shift from a sparsely settled network of farms, plantations, and trading houses to a highly profitable economic powerhouse. The transformation made a handful of people at the top of the heap some of the wealthiest folks in British North America. This shift has been covered in other venues, but rarely with an eye to how it affected violence in the Southeast. Some statistics indicate just how important rice was becoming to Carolina. Rice exports began in the 1690s and by 1709 had surpassed the one-million-pound mark. It is no coincidence that 1708 or 1709 is the year that the colony's African population first surpassed that of the English. In 1731, over twenty million pounds of rice were exported, and exports would only drop below this level for a handful of individual years before the outbreak of the War for Independence. In one striking period, the end of the 1730s and the beginning of the 1740s, rice exports rocketed past thirty and forty million pounds per year.[74]

The emergence of a mature plantation economy had a profound effect on all aspects of South Carolina society. It made white planters hunger for land in regions suited to rice production. If they were able to obtain land, they turned their thoughts to labor. The time period between the 1690s, when rice production began, and the 1730s, witnessed vast new tracts of land fall under the control of Carolina. According S. Max Edelson, the "size of English Carolina doubled in the first twenty-five years of the new century [the 1700s]."[75]

In the aftermath of the Yamasee War, one exception to this rule was the so-called Indian Lands. In the first decade of the eighteenth century, the South Carolina Commons House of Assembly had set aside this area, to the southwest of Charles Town, as a sort of reserve for Yamasees. After the Yamasees abandoned the Indian Lands over the course of the 1720s, they remained unclaimed by white people until the settlement of Georgia. What to do with the lands was part of a larger controversy between colonists and proprietors. In 1716, the Commons passed an "Act to Appropriate the Yamasee Lands." The idea behind the legislation was to draw Protestants from around the British Empire to act as a buffer. The proprietors responded by repealing the law and suggesting that Carolina "dissolve the present Assembly and that you forthwith call another Assembly."[76] The proprietors explained their reasoning several months later, instructing the surveyor general to "survey and set out for us our heirs and assigns upon the Yamasee lands . . . fifteen Baronies consisting of 12,000 acres each Barony, one fourth part of each barony must front a river."[77]

How were the Southeast's cultures of violence affected by the expansion of rice production? Part of the answer has to do with the importation of large numbers of African women and men to work rice plantations. In terms of Native American cultures of violence, the difference between the 1670s and the 1730s was profound. The era in which coastal native communities welcomed English arrivals in small numbers had passed. The period that saw Indians relocate to be close to Carolina and its burgeoning Indian slave trade was gone as well. In the 1720s, large interior nations such as the Creeks faced off against a Carolina that barely resembled its colonial roots. English-owned plantations worked by Africans spread out from Charles Town. The English also now actively promoted violence between native peoples with an eye toward expansion, not simply the slaves that might result from such a conflict. The problem, as stated by Joseph Boone, a member of South Carolina's legislature, was in trying to "hold both [Creeks and Cherokees] as our friends, and assist them in Cutting one anothers throats with out offending Either."[78] English colonists had long perceived themselves to be "absolute Masters over the *Indians*," in the words of John Lawson, but beginning in the late 1710s, and certainly by the 1730s, the English came to dominate Indian territory and trade in ways that approached mastery.[79]

One result of the Yamasee War was the end of proprietary rule in South Carolina. More than just a political realignment, the new order put South Carolina's planter class in a position to spread South Carolina's regional influence on its own violent terms. James Moore Jr., the leader of South Carolina's militia and son of the former governor and slave raider, was elected provisional governor as the Commons seized control.[80]

In the aftermath of the Yamasee War, the English put the brakes on an Indian slave trade that had led to regional instability and violence.[81] Of course, several decades of the trade had created deep fault lines in the Native American Southeast and had opened up swaths of territory between the settlement Indians of the coast and the large nations of the interior. The trade had never been unprofitable, but it had outlived its usefulness, and English agents could still turn a profit in native America, at the same time as their cousins took tentative steps to establish plantations somewhat farther inland. The former Yamasee lands were an exception, as described above. After a decade of raids launched from what is now Georgia, the South Carolina legislature moved to restrict the trade.

During the era of the Yamasee War, the English and Yamasees, as well as other groups, inhabited multiple worlds of violence simultaneously. In the interior, the coalescing Creek and Cherokee nations began to recognize the imperial reach of Carolina, which would inform their actions in the years that followed the Yamasee War. Still, the Creeks in particular demonstrated their allegiance to older ways of violence by killing English traders but then limiting their participation in the wider conflict. The Yamasees provide an interesting case study. In the late seventeenth century, they could be seen advancing English imperial interests, but with Yamasee reasons for doing so. Their ritual execution of Thomas Nairne is in keeping with older Native American traditions of violence, but their launch of a wider war in the aftermath of Nairne's death exhibits the influence of the English culture of violence. Speaking of the English, during the Yamasee War, they demonstrated their ability to adapt their style of war to American realities, as they did at an ambush which killed thirty-five Yamasees, but they also used their militia tradition to eliminate the most serious military threats to their presence on the coast.[82] Even without immediately reoccupying the former Yamasee lands, the English hold on the Atlantic Coast was secure, and they could turn their attention to developing a full-blown plantation economy, which rested on its own violent Anglo-American labor regime.

## CHAPTER 8

# American Nations, American Violence

Just a few years ago, finding the exact site of the Stono Rebellion was not all that easy. To be honest, it was impossible, at least for an eager college student stealing half an hour from an all-too-rare family vacation, armed only with the hope that a highway map would be enough and the naïve conviction that something so important could not possibly go without a historical marker. My family indulged this kind of thing, though, so I snapped a few shots of the tall grass near the river by the side of U.S. Highway 17, told myself that I had gotten close enough, and got back in the car. Over the next few years, as I began to consider history and memory more seriously, the apparent desire to forget (or at least not to commemorate) Stono got under my skin.

As it turns out, the site had been designated a National Historic Landmark in 1974, at which time the paperwork had been filled out by Marcia M. Greenlee of the Afro-American Bicentennial Corporation in Washington, D.C. Greenlee's application pointed out that American historical memory about colonial times was flawed and would remain so until the nation complicated its understanding of slavery and resistance to slavery. It was dangerous to continue to believe that "masters and slaves lived in perfect harmony" and that "Blacks were so supine as to submit to slavery without resistance."[1] The site was listed on the National Register, but it took until 2006 to get a highway marker erected. In that year, the Sea Island Farmers Cooperative, a local black farmers' group, welcomed the marker's placement on some of its land next to the highway.[2] In a process that moves excruciatingly slowly, the modern United States is beginning to recognize the role that colonial era violence, whether between enslaved Africans and English planters or Native American nations and European colonial powers, played in the early history of North America.

It is impossible to tell the last part of this story without reference to nations and nationalism. The modern United States has been very successful in downplaying or distorting its violent past to serve a powerful national myth which stressed "settlement" over "conquest" as the method by which the nation spread over the continent. In the era after the Yamasee War, Native

American nations came into sharper focus in the American Southeast. They possessed national territories and created national histories to support their claims on the Southeast. The English nation in the Southeast was also expanding into what is now Georgia, and in the process creating something of a national identity. Though the "English-ness" of the English nation in the Southeast would be called into question violently by the American War for Independence, it is clear that some pieces of an Anglo-American culture of violence lived on and were gathering strength in the late eighteenth century, with a renewed commitment to African slavery and an ever-present hunger for Native lands. In terms of slavery, the 1700s are too early a time period in which to formally delineate a black nation in the American Southeast. But Africans from various regions and cultures were beginning to form an identity that transcended its constituent parts. Though African Americans lacked a national territory, unlike their English owners and Creek and Cherokee neighbors, and though they held on to disparate African identities much longer than most people realize, even in the eighteenth century there was some kind of feeling that moved beyond the local. In some cases this was because the members of African nations were enslaved together: Bambara in Louisiana and BaKongo in South Carolina. In others, people came together across previously existing lines because all they had was each other to help resist an exploitative labor regime and a developing racial caste system.[3]

## Slave Violence, Stono, and Planters' Power

English homes in Carolina symbolized many things, not least of which was the power and wealth of their owners. The connection between architecture and power in similar settings has been established by Rhys Isaac and scholars of material culture. Few studies have explored English houses as arenas of intercultural violence. English plantations became the sites of violence, not only when under attack during the Yamasee War described above but also in labor relations between African slaves and English masters.

The violence of slavery was multifarious. When masters disciplined their slaves, they could be enacting violence of a domestic nature. White men in South Carolina could bring down violence on any number of people, including their wives, children, and social inferiors. But since the violence of slavery crossed racial lines, it had some of the characteristics of intercultural violence as well. African slavery was an integral part of the Anglo-American culture of violence that was taking shape in South Carolina around the turn of the eighteenth century.

The Fundamental Constitutions, which were intended to establish the legal framework for early South Carolina, didn't have too much to do with slavery, and South Carolina's slave laws were a mix of Barbadian influences and trial and error on the part of slaveholders.[4] The trading regime featured in the previous two chapters also involved a fair amount of trial and error, and it caused violence. South Carolina's earliest slave code came from Barbados, as did many of the colony's earliest slaves and their owners. The slave codes regulated the behavior of slaves and established guidelines for the appropriate use of violence on the part of masters. These acts were revised several times in the late seventeenth and early eighteenth centuries. The slave codes were based upon the assumption that Africans were naturally violent. One slave law from 1712 explained that "negroes and other slaves . . . are of barbarous, wild, savage natures" and are "naturally prone" to "disorders, rapines, and inhumanity."[5] The slave codes, then, were to have a taming effect on allegedly savage African and Native American violence. One form of nonviolent resistance, running away out of Carolina, carried a violent penalty: death. For inciting others to run away, slaves were to be whipped and branded. Later codes softened these penalties somewhat, largely for economic reasons. Perpetual short-term runaways, who were assumed *not* to be running away out of Carolina, faced punishments of increasing violence: a public whipping for the first offense, a branding for the second, an ear cut off for the third—and castration for male slaves. Running away five times resulted in the Achilles tendon being severed or death, at which point the loss of slave property would be compensated by public funds.[6]

Slavery was based on coercion and violence, but in order for it to work as a system of labor and remain profitable, negotiation (obviously not between equals in power) had to be present as well. For this reason, slave codes reigned in English violence. The 1712 slave code provided for a fine when a master killed a slave out of "wantoness, or only of bloody-mindedness."[7] White servants who killed slaves could be imprisoned under this law, and the class implications are not too difficult to discern: fines for the master class, prison for poor whites. The 1735 slave code increased the maximum penalty from fifty to five hundred pounds. Slave codes enacted in 1722 and 1735 also noted a form of violence that might be overlooked. If slave owners were not providing their slaves with enough food, they could be fined.[8]

Some of the earliest incidents of slavery-related violence in South Carolina were public, not private. Francis Le Jau recounted one incident of such public violence: "A poor Slavewoman was burnt alive near my door without any positive proof of the Crime she was accused of . . . [she] protested her innocence even to my self to the last."[9] Slaves who committed especially egregious violations of the established order were put to death in public. Many were decapitated afterward, and severed African heads mounted on mileposts and hung on trees were not an uncommon site in early Carolina. The idea behind such displays was to discourage other slaves from engaging in similar practices. Taking trophy heads was standard English practice in Elizabethan Ireland, and in Virginia as well. In one 1732 case, a white man robbed by a runaway slave was ordered by a justice of the peace to behead his assailant. The severed head was then "fix[ed] upon a Pole, and set . . . up in a Cross-Road."[10] When Quash, a fugitive slave who managed to remain at large for seven years, was hanged in 1734, his head was severed and attached to the gallows.[11] The more spectacular the resistance, the more spectacular the grisly display; as the Stono rebels were apprehended and killed, according to one source, "Planters . . . Cutt off their heads and set them up at every Mile Post they came to."[12]

Most violence directed at slaves, while it had the sanction of the state, was not administered by the state. The threat of the lash was universal in Carolina's variant of slavery, and the most common physical form of violence that accompanied slavery was whipping. Robert Olwell, author of *Masters, Slaves, and Subjects,* notes that "because whipping was considered such a routine part of slave management, it was seldom thought worthy of mention by either overseers or masters."[13] Here was a kind of intercultural violence that was so commonplace and legitimate that the people employing it felt little need to describe it or account for it. The violence of slavery of was intercultural and interracial, but it was also highly personal. According to one eighteenth-century observer, the "common Method is to tie [slaves] up by the Hands to the branch of a Tree, so that their Toes can hardly touch the ground." The same observer noted that there was "hardly a Negro but bears the marks of Punishment in large Scars on his Back and Sides."[14] Given such widespread violence, it is not surprising that Africans in colonial South Carolina rose up in greater numbers than in any other mainland English colony.

If early Carolina functioned like every other slave society, it is safe to assume that slave owners forced their slaves to have sex with them. That such coerced sex does not appear too often in the records is not particularly surprising. White planters in Carolina assumed that such relations were among their rights as owners, so, like the use of the lash against slaves, rape was common enough not to mention. It was a widely practiced and legitimate form of intercultural violence in the eyes of the men who committed it. Moreover, the stigma associated with blackness and the benefits of whiteness made it even more unlikely that documentation of coerced interracial sex would make it into the archives and from there into the historical record.[15]

The Stono Rebellion of 1739 has been used to prove a lot of different things over the centuries since it took place, from the survival of African traits in America to the Marxist leanings of black slaves. The example of Stono draws such scrutiny because it was so rare. The basic outline of the events of 1739 is pretty well established. What the rebellion meant for cultures of violence in the Southeast has yet to be determined.

On September 9, 1739, a handful of slaves gathered at the Stono River, a few miles west of Charles Town. The rebels stormed Hutchinson's store, arming themselves and killing the men who were minding the shop. The white men at the store were beheaded and their heads were left on display. The public display of enemies' heads had gained wide currency by 1739. The slave army—whose core consisted of literate, Catholic BaKongo men from the kingdom of Kongo—then marched south, killing whites (though selectively, it must be added) and burning plantations. The rebels signaled their presence with drums and banners and shouted "Liberty!" as they marched. The Black army eventually included between sixty and one hundred people. In a pitched battle, at a plantation now called Battlefield, the slaves engaged South Carolina's militia under the command of Lieutenant Governor William Bull and were dispersed. A week later, Carolina militia caught up with a group of rebels thirty miles to the south of the original engagement and won a second battle.[16]

Some scholars have traced the motivation and behavior of the Stono rebels to Africa, and in recreating an African American culture of violence, this line of questioning is most provocative. John Thornton, a scholar of Africa's role in the creation the Atlantic world, has looked to Africa for the origins of the rebellion. Thornton acknowledges that poor treatment on Carolina plantations was the immediate cause of hostilities. The deeper roots are in the kingdom of Kongo (in modern Angola), a region marked by Catholicism, the speaking of Portuguese, and civil war. Each of these characteristics played some role in the events of 1739. The initial conspirators spoke the same language, which combined Portuguese and African languages, and the behavior of the rebels on the battlefield—the use of banners and drums—indicates some level of organization beyond what would be associated with a simple desire to kill some white people and escape slavery. Thornton remains cautious when it comes to drawing a direct line from Kongo military practice to Carolina slave military practice, but he does note that "a military revolution was altering war in Kongo . . . increasing the size of armies, and replacing the hand-to-hand combat of lances, swords,

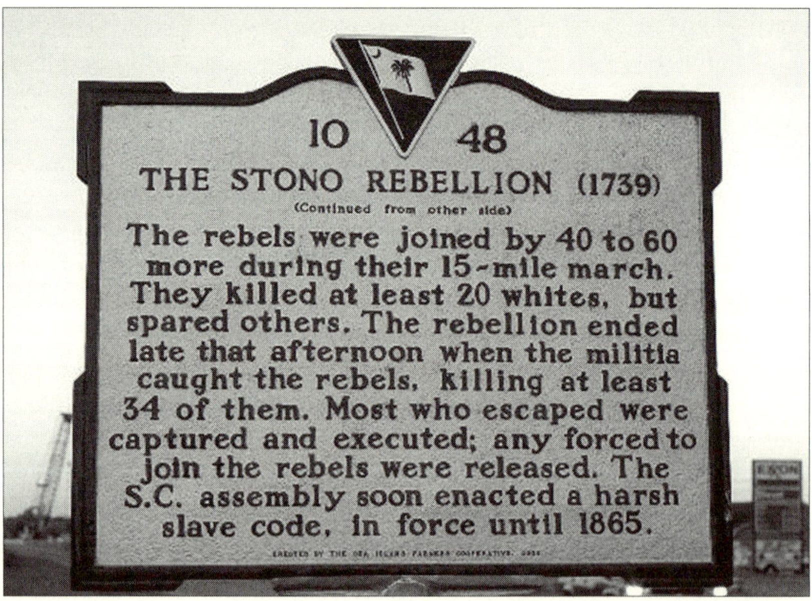


**FIGS. 9 AND 10.** The two sides of the Stono Rebellion historical marker, erected in 2006 by the Sea Island Farmers Cooperative. The text implies that the slave code was a harsh response. While that is true, it also made further efforts to restrict the kind of white violence that some planters felt had led to Stono. From the author's collection.

and axes with the missile combat of muskets."[17] Stephen Williams, author of one of the few primary accounts of the rebellion, noted that the rebels "furnished themselves with Arms and Ammunition," while another firsthand account stated that the slaves "behaved boldly" and "fought stoutly."[18]

The timing of the Stono Rebellion and the behavior of the rebels at various points in the rebellion indicates the persistence of a BaKongo culture of violence in the colonial Southeast. Though the alarm was raised on Sunday, September 9, 1739, and the Carolina militia rushed out of church to counter the growing threat, the rebels had actually begun their struggle on Saturday. And this was no normal Saturday. It coincided with the nativity of the Virgin Mary, who was a central figure in the BaKongo-Catholic hybrid religion so cherished by many BaKongo men and women.[19] One scholar has argued that the people "regarded the Virgin Mary as Christ's female co-chief." Another interpretation links her to the Kongolese conception of the "feminine embodiment of the earth." The army also stopped on the shores of the Edisto River, which didn't make sense from a tactical perspective but was clearly important from a cultural perspective. Perhaps thanks had to be given for prior success and rituals needed to be performed before the next stage of the revolt. One unknown English writer recalled that they "halted in a field, and set to dancing, Singing and beating Drums."[20] The BaKongo army was dispersed shortly thereafter, but it resorted to a skirmishing style of warfare which harassed English Carolina for weeks afterward and had the added psychological benefit of keeping whites in constant fear of renewed hostilities.[21]

In the aftermath of the Stono Rebellion, South Carolina passed a new slave code. The "Act for the better ordering and governing of Negroes and other Slaves" built upon earlier slave codes by limiting already limited black freedoms and went further to curtail the kinds of abuses some white men felt had led to Stono in the first place. Masters were forbidden to force their slaves to work on Sunday and could be fined for such offense. Masters also had to provide "sufficient cloathing, covering or food" for their slaves. The 1740 act set limits on the amount of work that slaves could legally be expected to perform, with some variations seasonally.[22]

It should not be assumed from the previous paragraphs that most African violence in Carolina was channeled into large-scale revolt. Indeed, Stono is a remarkable exception to the kind of violence normally associated with slaves in North America. Africans did resist slavery violently, and in the process, African cultures of violence became an African American culture of violence that formed a major part of the resistance to the institution of slavery. Throughout the eighteenth century, there were very few murders of white masters or overseers by black slaves. Spectacular acts like this were usually suicidal, and their rarity attests to the level of mastery achieved by Carolina's master class. An African American culture of violence took shape in other arenas: violence against property and, more rarely, poisoning.

For slaves to damage the bodies of their masters carried a death sentence, whether immediate or delayed by some legal proceeding. Violence against property could take many forms, including sabotage of plantation equipment and arson. The fact that African American violence was more often directed at things rather than people indicates how thoroughly the English culture of violence had reshaped African cultures of violence. Planters' houses may have been the highest value targets for arsonists—the Anglican missionary Francis Le Jau witnessed a woman burned to death after she was accused of just such a crime, but barns were more likely to be burned. Peter Wood has noticed that as rice production increased, the number of barn fires increased in the months when the heaviest labor was required to clean and barrel rice. Slave codes dealt harshly with even minor incidents of fire-related crime, assigning the death penalty to any slave who burned "rice, corn, or other grain."[23] A cautionary letter to the *South Carolina Gazette* in 1732 warned that "Mr. James Grey work'd his Negroes late in his Barn at Night, and the next Morning before Day, hurried them out again, and when they came to it, found it burnt down to the Ground, and all that was in it."[24] It may have been too difficult or dangerous to strike out directly against slave owners in most cases, but attacking the source of the planters agricultural wealth could hurt the planter's pocketbook and carry symbolic meaning as well.

Poisonings by slaves were rare, so it is not entirely appropriate to treat them on the same level as more everyday forms of violence. But a brief exploration can demonstrate how African cultures of violence became a widely held African American culture of violence. It bears mentioning that slaves poisoned other slaves as well as white masters and that the practice of conjuring did not always relate to violence or intend to harm. As slaves practiced magic and conjured, they drew on a wide array of spiritual sources. Philip Morgan, author of *Slave Counterpoint,* has described this as an "expanded role for the realm of lesser spirits."[25] In the 1750s, white physician Alexander Garden noted that "the Negroes bring their knowledge of the Poisonous Plants, which they use here, with them from their own Country."[26] Poisoning drew on diverse African origins but developed along similar lines throughout English colonies and continued after slaves converted to Christianity, to the chagrin of white people. South Carolina's master class feared slave magic, exaggerated the threat it posed, and sought to legislate it out of existence in 1751. The Commons made it a capital crime for a slave to "teach or instruct another slave in the knowledge of any poisonous root, plant, herb or other sort of poison whatever."[27]

Another episode of violence, this one from the French colonial Southeast, admittedly on the fringe of the current study, shows the long-lived nature of African cultures of violence in the Americas as well as the willingness of Africans to ally themselves with Native Americans. French Louisiana was home to a sizable Bambara population (about four hundred) in the 1730s and 1740s. After the failed Natchez uprising of the early 1730s, which they had joined, Bambaras maintained close ties to Native American nations in the region. Gwendolyn Midlo Hall believes that the Bambara slaves, if they had been able, might have enslaved other groups of Africans in an attempt to recreate the situation that had obtained in their West African homeland. In any event, Bambara slaves garnered reputations for being "particularly defiant" toward the French, according to Hall. The Bambaras were also the inheritors of a "proud military tradition, honed in a long history of warfare against Mandingas and other Muslim peoples."[28] They were the main ethnic group involved in the Samba Bambara slave conspiracy. Samba Bambara, who had been shipped to the Americas in the first place for engaging in rebellion against French power in what is now Senegal, used his considerable linguistic skills to become an interpreter for the Superior Council and an overseer on a large company-run plantation. In 1731, Samba and other Bambaras sent feelers to Native American communities in the region, hoping to build an interracial force that could challenge the French. The revolt failed, and Samba was dismembered. In the aftermath, the French shrewdly armed black militia units, the members of which could be set free for their service to the colony.[29]

Bambaras asserted their own culture of violence at the same time as they recognized the utility of seeking Native American allies in their quest to weaken the French hold on Louisiana. BaKongo soldiers put their trust in Mary as they put the skills they honed on African battlefields to use against the English in Carolina. Most slaves were not BaKongo or Bambara rebels, but the ways in which they fought against slavery in the early eighteenth-century Southeast demonstrate the lingering presence of African cultures of violence and hint at the very beginning of an African American culture of violence.

## Native Nations

Neither the Yamasees, Westos, nor Savannahs remained in the vicinity of Carolina after their forays as slavers and main trading partners of the English operating out of Charles Town. The Westos and Savannahs moved to the north, while the Yamasees reattached themselves to the Spanish south of Carolina. Some groups in the Piedmont region, most famously the Catawbas, adapted well to the colonial realities of the eighteenth century and parlayed alliance with the English into long-term residency within the colony (and eventually the state) of South Carolina. At the same time as the English were planting and trading, Creek and Cherokee polities were coalescing and developing the skills that would allow them to weather the storm of colonization largely intact. Violence was a major part of coalescence. Richard Slotkin has described America's national identity as a series of "regenerations through violence," and I would extend this trend to the Indian nations that came of age in the era of English colonization as well.[30] In the story they told William Bartram in the 1770s, the Creeks emphasized their right to stay on the land, since they had fought for it.

Creeks and Cherokees also came into conflict in the aftermath of the Yamasee War. English Carolina actively fomented Creek-Cherokee rivalry and, in doing so, continued to transform the Southeast's cultures of violence and the Southeast in general. Violence in the Southeast occurred increasingly along lines determined by the English.

Creek and Cherokee towns had gone to war against each other in the past, though not in the same way as they would during the Yamasee War. The difference in the 1710s was that the English had begun taking a larger role in regional affairs, and their very presence had raised the stakes of intergroup conflict. In late 1715, a small army of South Carolinians, led by George Chicken and John Herbert, arrived in Cherokee Country. In January of 1716, the Carolinians came upon a stunning scene. At the site of a failed parlay in the Cherokee town of Tugaloo, Cherokees had killed several Muskogee leaders. George Chicken wrote that "there was 12 Creake Indines come in to Tugaloe and they hade killd them all."[31] The origins of the specific dispute are not known, but the fates of Cherokees and white Carolinians were tied together as a result.

Fighting between Creeks and Cherokees escalated in 1716 and 1717. The killing of so many headmen was not a crime that could go unpunished, and violence began to impact indigenous life to an extent all but unknown before the early eighteenth century. The Cherokees registered some military successes, but their alliance with the English cost them dearly. It didn't help matters that, as dictated by the "cutting one anothers throats" policy, the English stayed out of the most intense fighting between native nations. Cherokees were understandably resentful of the English absence, noting in 1724 that "it brought upon themselves and their families a continued war. . . . Their wives and children have been killed and taken and . . . if it had not been to save the white people they would have been at peace and quietness."[32] The threat of Muskogee violence kept Cherokee men at home when they should have been out trading and hunting.[33]

After the Tugaloo killings, Muskogee warriors attacked Nagouchee, a Lower Cherokee town. In the words of the English trader, perhaps Captain William Hatton, they "Destroyed it, carreing off a abundance of slaves and kill'd most of the Rest of the inhabitance and the next morning before they left the place kill'd three of our Factors in the Path between Chottee and the aforesaid Town they being about a mile asunder."[34] If the trader can be believed, the fact that the Creeks were in the business of destroying towns indicates that something of the all-consuming English style of warfare had become a part of the Creek culture of violence. But older ways lived on as well. Why carry off slaves? The trade out of Carolina was in a shambles in the late 1710s, and they probably could not be sold at market. Perhaps they were Africans belonging to the Cherokees or English who might eventually be ransomed, but there were not too many Africans in Cherokee country in the 1710s.[35] Perhaps they were war captives taken along traditional lines, to be either tortured or adopted, or perhaps some combination of the two. While the deaths of the three traders might be chalked up to the Creek desire to annihilate the English, their killings might have been an attempt to convey a message to the English and Cherokees and could fit older patterns which featured the symbolic use of violence. It should not be assumed that Creeks adopted English-style violence wholesale.

According to Tom Hatley, author of *The Dividing Paths*, the Yamasee War era was seared into the Cherokees' collective memory and oral traditions. The message was clear: alliance with English Carolina was not a relationship among equals, and the scope of warfare brought to the Southeast by the English wreaked havoc on native communities in ways that previous forms had not. Cherokee memory of the Yamasee War strikes a counterpoint to the story told to William Bartram by the Creeks at Ocmulgee in the 1770s.[36] At the same time as English violence conquered the Southeast, it demonstrated to Creeks and Cherokees the utility of forging national identities to resist it. Nationhood, whether English, American, Creek or Cherokee, is not a timeless truth but a historical contingency.

## Violence and Georgia's Beginnings

The establishment of Georgia further solidified the position of the English in the Southeast. The planners of Georgia, like the men who planned Carolina in the previous century, sought to avoid violence, at least of the internal variety. To this end, they prohibited the things that led to Carolina's wealthy but unstable and violent society. In addition to the well-known bans on most large landholdings, African slavery, and distilled spirits, the Georgia Board of Trustees, who governed the colony, also intended to supervise those Britons who traded in Indian country as closely as possible.[37] All of these measures sought to preserve the peace within Georgia's borders. Of course, Georgia itself was a provocation to the Spanish on the Gulf of Mexico and at St. Augustine. The colonists of Georgia would build on the violent traditions of their cousins in South Carolina. They would press imperial aims using a similar culture of violence to that which had developed in South Carolina.

There was at least one major difference between the violence that rocked Carolina from its birth through the 1710s and the violence associated with the establishment of Georgia, however: the Native American context. Carolina had aligned itself with small coastal nations, known collectively as the Cusabos, and had allied with and subsequently alienated a number of more powerful groups, beginning with the Westos in the 1670s, the Savannahs in the late seventeenth century, and the Yamasees by the early eighteenth. Each of these relationships was soured by Carolina's expansionist greed, and each ended in varying degrees of violence.[38]

Georgia's founders faced a very different indigenous political situation. The Yamacraw community which occupied the bluffs overlooking the Savannah River a few miles from its mouth might have appeared at first glance to be a minor player, but its connection to the older Muskogee-speaking towns in the interior made it necessary for the English at Savannah to tread carefully.

As Cusabos had welcomed the appearance of the English in Carolina in the 1670s, Yamacraws welcomed the establishment of Savannah. The parallels are worth noting. Cusabos had been the victims of Westo slave raids and sought alliance with English Carolina as a way to survive in a world increasingly oriented to the English Atlantic. The reorientation of the native Southeast toward the Atlantic was more than a shift in economic priorities, of course, and could be the cause of sweeping cultural change and violence.

Tomochichi, leader of the Yamacraws, appears to have been an exile from the Muskogee town of Apalachicola. One Georgia trustee, the Earl of Egmont, speculated that Tomochichi had been banished from Muskogee country for "cutting down a Popish Chappel, which the French were endeavoring to erect, with design to convert it into a fort."[39] In the late 1720s, the leading Creek town, Coweta, under the guidance of Brims, had been working to establish cordial relations with French colonists operating out of Fort Toulouse.[40] The idea was to remain neutral in the developing struggle between the English and French and thus preserve some measure of Creek autonomy. For threatening the delicate negotiations, and for violating Creek rules governing the use of violence, Tomochichi and scores of others, about one hundred people in all, were exiled to the east. The founding of Georgia provided Tomochichi with the opportunity to improve a damaged reputation.

Since Tomochichi's group was at least somewhat ethnically diverse, comprised of exiles from a number of other Muskogee towns and perhaps some Yamasees as well, the first orders of business were creating a *talwa* and choosing a mico.[41] Talwa is usually translated as "town" in English, but in Muskogee it connotes not just a political structure but also a kind of ethnic group, so its importance to identity formation should not be overlooked.[42] Tomochichi had apparently appointed himself mico of the town. The arrival of the English gave Tomochichi a chance to become a mico in the eyes of the Creeks, and he took full advantage.[43]

The diplomatic rituals performed by Tomochichi and General James Oglethorpe, the foremost of the trustees and architect of the colonization of Georgia, demonstrate that both native and English ways of conducting diplomacy and cultures of violence had changed substantially by the eighteenth century as the peoples had become increasingly familiar with each other. Compare the founding of Georgia with the debacle at Roanoke and the beheading of Wingina. The proceedings at Yamacraw Bluff in February 1733 followed a set of protocols that all parties present appeared to understand on a basic level. The encounter began with a ceremonial exchange of gunfire, which may have alluded to the martial skills of both Yamacraws and English. A Creek soldier wearing white feathers—the color of peace—approached Oglethorpe, stroking him with a feather fan and prepared the way for Tomochichi by dancing and shaking a rattle. One English witness criticized the singing as "a very uncouth Hollowing."[44] The assembled Creek men and women each shook hands with Oglethorpe. Translation services provided by Coosaponakeesa (whom colonists knew as Mary Musgrove) and her husband John Musgrove of Colleton County, Carolina, certainly helped matters. The Musgroves, connected through ties of kinship and marriage to the powerful Muskogee town of Coweta and English Carolina, helped forge a peaceful relationship between that colony and the Muskogee towns, and they would do the same for the Creeks and Georgia in that colony's earliest years.[45]

Peter Gordon, a colonial official, recorded that two warriors preceded Tomochichi, shaking rattles and singing. As Gordon perceived the songs, they "recounted all the warlike exploits of their forefathers, which is all the records they have, and the only methode of handing down to posterity the history of their great men."[46] Following the impressive and history-conscious entrance, Tomochichi asked Oglethorpe for permission to exact revenge for the killing of a relative by the Yuchis: "He would not take revenge without Mr. Oglethorp's concent and approbation."[47] While it is possible that such a request was part of the ritual of alliance building taking place, it was more likely an admission that a persistent English presence in the Southeast had reshaped the cultures of violence in the region profoundly. After all, why would Muskogee people, ostensibly in charge of their own affairs, need permission from an English chieftain to administer justice? Tomochichi's request also indicates that the relationship between Native Americans and English colonists by the 1730s was not a partnership of equals. Tomochichi knew this, but even an alliance with the English in which the Yamacraws were a junior partner had its benefits. Previous initial encounters between the English and Native Americans had been peaceful but had quickly exploded into violence. The difference in the case of Georgia is the fact that the peace lasted longer, probably due to the fact that Native people in the Southeast moved around the developing Anglo-American presence much more cautiously once they recognized the kind of violence the English were capable of unleashing. They had witnessed the expansion of South Carolina and the destruction of mission towns in Florida in the preceding decades.

Tomochichi led off the talks by telling the English exactly what he thought wanted to hear: how great they were. At Yamacraw Bluff, Tomochichi presented Oglethorpe with a buffalo robe painted with an eagle motif. Through a translator (likely John or Mary Musgrove), the Yamacraw leader explained the significance of such a gift, noting that "the eagle signified speed and the buffalo strength." "The English were swift as the bird, and as strong as the beast," Tomochichi continued. Like eagles, "they flew from the utmost parts of the earth." Like the buffalo, "nothing could withstand them."[48] However, English power carried certain obligations as well. Oglethorpe's colony was bound to "love and protect their [the Yamacraws'] little families," since "the feathers of the eagle were soft, and signified love" and "the buffalo's skin [was] warm, and signified protection."[49] The exchange between Tomochichi and Oglethorpe was friendly enough, but it also shows that Tomochichi recognized the geopolitical situation that had come about in the Southeast, whereby the presence of English planters and traders, and their potential for violence, was a given. The rituals that accompanied the establishment of Georgia looked different from Creek and English perspectives, but both parties were satisfied by the outcome. One English witness wrote that the Yamacraws paid "their obedience to Mr. Oglethorpe."[50] It's more likely that

Tomochichi wished to establish a kinlike relationship with the English, so his actions that February day reflected his desire for reciprocity. The English were welcome to plant a colony on land claimed by Yamacraws, but doing so carried certain obligations: trade on reasonable terms and military protection. Over several weeks, Yamacraws and English exchanged ritual gifts and forged an alliance. The earliest meetings were family affairs for Tomochichi. He was accompanied by his wife, Senaukey.[51] Her voice doesn't appear in the records, but her presence might have been intended to convince the English of the Yamacraws' peaceful mindset.

In March 1733, in an attempt to reduce future conflict, Tomochichi and Oglethorpe agreed that Georgia's boundaries would stretch to the Yamacraw village but would not include it. The meeting that sealed the deal featured many of the ceremonial trappings of the earlier talks, such as feather fans, and included a ritual smoke. Tomochichi spoke first, indicating through an interpreter that "they were glad to see him [Oglethorpe], and his people, safely arrived in this country and bid us hearty welcome to Yamacraw." Tomochichi stressed his personal connections: "He was not a stranger to the English" and his "father and grand father had been very well known to them."[52] On a later occasion, his identification with the English went even further. Once, a young Creek man took his own life, though his family believed him to have been murdered by the English and threatened to attack English plantations. Tomochichi stopped them by dramatically confronting them, baring his chest and saying, "If you kill anybody, kill me, for I am an Englishman."[53] Oglethorpe responded, promising friendship and protection, and he made good on these promises a couple of weeks later, when he commissioned two Yamacraw militia companies and armed them.

One can get a sense of the delicate political maneuvering involved in Tomochichi's behavior when a larger, and certainly more legitimate, Muskogee delegation arrived from the interior in May 1733. The main motivation for the invitation was to clear up the concerns over the legitimacy of Georgia's land claim. Previous agreements dating to 1717 and 1732 had closed the area south of the Savannah River to white settlement, and the more prominent Creek towns might justifiably perceive the deal between Oglethorpe and Tomochichi as breaking these earlier understandings. Moreover, Tomochichi had represented himself to the English as a mico. The English translated mico as "chief" or "king," and Tomochichi in their eyes was "King of the Yamacraws." This served both English and Tomochichi's purposes well, but Oglethorpe and the English were shrewd enough to seek negotiations with the older, more powerful Muskogee-speaking towns and sent out feelers to this end. Tomochichi's status in the Muskogee world was tenuous until the spring 1733 arrival of Yahoulakee of Coweta and a delegation of fifty-two leaders drawn from at least eight Muskogee-speaking towns. The delegation included four micos, among whom Oueekachumpa (from Oconee) spoke first. According to one account, he thanked the English for their "kindness to Tomo-chi-chi" and said that the "banished men chose him king."[54] Shortly after this pronouncement, Tomochichi entered the room and was humbled by the presence of so many of his erstwhile countrymen. Yahoulakee, who as "Emperor" Brims' successor was as close as the Creeks could come to a national leader, spoke on behalf of the delegation and suggested that the Yamacraws be allowed "to call the kindred that love them out of each of the Creek towns, that they may come together and make one town."[55] He also suggested that Yamasees be encouraged to come back, so that they might "be buried in peace among their ancestors."[56] Combined, the talks of Oueekachumpa and Yahoulakee legitimized Tomochichi's leadership and formalized the talwa status of Yamacraw. Yahoulakee's reference to the Yamasee kin being buried in peace indicates a desire to get past the hostility of the Yamasee War era. The interplay between Tomochichi and Yahoulakee demonstrates the fluidity and adaptability of eighteenth-century Muskogee politics. Before Yahoulakee's arrival, Tomochichi had been a self-styled mico and Yamacraw had been a talwa of exiles on the very fringe of the Muskogee world. When the Creek delegation left, though, Yamacraw was a full-fledged talwa, and one who would seem to be ideally placed to mediate the relationship between the older towns in the interior and the English town at Savannah.

The talks over land forced the English to concede that the Creeks were a nation, with sovereignty over a large national territory. The Creeks were willing to part with lands they used less often in exchange for the recognition of this sovereignty. Creeks also agreed to return runaway slaves. Oglethorpe crowed to the trustees back in London that he concluded a peace with the Creeks, who were formerly friends to the Spanish and French. He was mistaken in using the past tense, since the Creeks were keeping diplomatic channels open to the French and Spanish at the same time.[57] Still, the meeting of Yahoulakee's delegation and Oglethorpe's English, through the mediation of Tomochichi, symbolizes the beginning of a Muskogee-English alliance, running from Coweta to Savannah (and eventually London), through Yamacraw.

As Oglethorpe and Tomochichi cemented their friendship and the alliance between Yamacraw and English, Oglethorpe was laying plans to secure the southern edge of Great Britain's mainland North American empire. Towns were planted at militarily important sites, and roads extended from Georgia into Carolina, home of a much larger militia. Many of these secondary towns failed, since they were planted with an eye toward military usefulness and no consideration of livability or profitability. Augusta, on the Savannah River, was a notable exception. The garrison stationed there protected the Indian trade with the Creeks.

Some of the ties established in Georgia's earliest years proved short lived. The Yamacraws remained very close to the English, even sending Tomochichi and his nephew Toonahowi to London in 1734. Their tight connection to the English meant that when the English went to war against the Spanish in the War of Jenkins' Ear, the Yamacraws went too. Tomochichi, too old to have been an effective fighter, died just before the war, but Toonahowi killed a Spanish officer and died in a raid on Florida. The Yamacraws lost their talwa status by mid-century, and refugees from the coast rejoined their Muskogee kin in the interior.[58]

The trustees of Georgia and Oglethorpe sought to eliminate one element that had brought violence to Carolina: racial slavery. The prohibition on slavery did not last long, and within two decades of its establishment, Georgia had developed a slave-based plantation economy that reflected the influence of Carolina, even if Georgia planters would never match their neighbors' vast wealth. Oglethorpe and the other trustees had not prohibited slavery because of any particularly benevolent feelings toward Africans. They believed that Georgia's tenuous position, near Spanish Florida, would entice slaves to desert at alarming rates. Oglethorpe also wrote that relying heavily on African labor would weaken white people. The exploitative character of plantation slavery, as it was practiced in South Carolina, was not in keeping with the idealistic beginning Georgia's founders had envisioned. In 1735, England's House of Commons prohibited slavery in Georgia.[59]

Throughout the 1740s, factions in South Carolina and Georgia pressured the trustees and the House of Commons to lift the ban on slavery. White Georgians argued that the absence of slavery kept them from being as prosperous as they could be, and Carolina planters were eager to expand the system that was making them some of the richest men in mainland North America.[60] Illegal importation of slaves began in this time period. The proslavery faction convinced the trustees to overturn the ban in 1750. The trustees managed to win some concessions they hoped would prevent the unbalanced racial situation of Carolina from repeating itself in Georgia. These compromises proved totally unenforceable as slave owners and slaves poured into Georgia. Between 1750 and 1775, Georgia's slave population increased from fewer than five hundred to about eighteen thousand. The expansion of slavery re-created conditions established in South Carolina.

The slaveholder-dominated colonial legislature eventually scrapped Georgia's body of slave laws and replaced them with statutes nearly identical to those of South Carolina.[61]

The creation of Georgia as a buffer zone expanded the English culture of violent plantation and trade farther south and west. Georgia's trustees, led by James Oglethorpe, attempted to moderate some of the characteristics of prior colonization in the Southeast. The prohibition on slavery might have set Georgia apart in this regard. After it failed, Georgia began to resemble South Carolina more closely socially, racially, and in terms of its culture of violence.

The Creek nation was not the sort of political entity that the English envisioned when they agreed that the Creeks constituted a nation. In fact, the Creek definition of "nation" had broadened significantly during this time period. It seems likely that individual Muskogee-speaking towns, each of which had its own territory and customs, might have perceived themselves as constituting more or less autonomous nations in the seventeenth century, even as they traded between towns, and shared certain deep-rooted structures, such as matrilineality and kinship systems. The great achievement of Creek diplomats in the early eighteenth century was to forge a national identity and to maintain a national territory in the face of increasing European, especially English, land pressure.[62]

For their part, when the English named the Creeks a nation, they may have imagined something along the lines of the Cusabos in South Carolina, sometimes referred to as settlement Indians or "our Indians," who posed no military threat whatsoever and fulfilled valuable roles as slave catchers and occasional trading partners. Or something like the Yamacraws, who numbered just over one hundred in 1733 and welcomed the English as the dominant partner in an unequal relationship. The settlement reached by the Muskogees and the English over the course of the 1730s and 1740s ensured that two nations would compete over the Savannah River country and points west. This competition would not be resolved until early in the nineteenth century, by force of arms. Fortunately, the total consolidation of U.S. rule in the region remains illusory. Though American soldiers marched Creek families into exile, recent political developments have demonstrated that the Muscogee (Creek) Nation of Oklahoma remains a force to be reckoned with in middle Georgia, through its Native American Graves Protection and Repatriation Act claims and the Traditional Cultural Property that runs to the south of Ocmulgee National Monument in Macon.

## Back to Ocmulgee

Walking between the mounds at Ocmulgee and climbing them practically forces one to take the long view of history, culture, and the violence that transformed the Southeast and its peoples from the Mississippian era through the 1740s. The Ocmulgee site testifies to the different cultures of violence that have held sway over the Southeast over the centuries. When the mounds were constructed, they were symbols of Mississippian power and chiefly might. Mississippians from these centers went to war for chiefly reasons and believed that violence was one way to restore balance between the Upper World and Lower World in This World. The evidence from smaller Mississippian towns indicates a slightly more egalitarian social structure and culture of violence. When Hernando de Soto's Spanish army moved through the region, he sped the dispersal of Mississippian chiefdoms with a lethal mix of European disease and a style of violence that had not been seen before in the Mississippian world. Subsequent expeditions, such as those undertaken by Luna and Pardo, encountered a world that was in rapid flux, as chiefdoms dispersed and autonomous towns became the dominant polity in the region. Towns still undertook military campaigns and were capable of committing acts of great violence, but they also were judicious in their deployment of forces, careful not to chance losing too many valuable warriors in high-risk affairs. Their conceptions of the proper role of violence had deep roots in the Mississippian era, but how they built upon that cultural legacy varied from linguistic group to linguistic group, and even from town to town.

The Ocmulgee site, according to the Creeks and William Bartram, was the place where the Creeks first "sat down," that is, came into being as a people. They established themselves in the Southeast through violence, and violence played a key role in Native American nation building, helping to answer questions such as who was a Creek and who was a Cherokee in the colonial era. "National" violence, of the sort undertaken by the Creeks and Cherokees during the era of English colonization, could not have existed long before the English arrived, for the simple reason that the people of the autonomous towns of the Southeast didn't necessarily consider themselves members of "nations" and would have been unlikely to spend resources, human or otherwise, in a fight for them.

Native communities moved near the Ocmulgee site to have access to English trade goods. The Lower Creeks, as well as the Westos, Savannahs, and Yamasees, moved closer to English Carolina and did enjoy greater access to valuable goods, but their migrations also brought them into closer contact with the developing Anglo-American culture of violence, with devastating consequences. The Tuscarora and Yamasee Wars of the 1710s showed native communities facing crises of violence, caught between Native American understandings of the proper role of conflict in society and the conquering English culture of violence. Native Americans had held captives before the English arrived but had not sold slaves on an Atlantic market previously. Native Americans had traded goods over long distances before, but the English introduced an especially violent trading regime to the Southeast, transforming native conceptions of violence in the process. It should not be assumed that native communities adopted English ways of violence wholesale, though. Native violence was circumscribed by the English, but it was not eliminated entirely.

The multiethnic polity which the English named the Creeks was a colonial era invention and a powerful response to the stresses which European colonization placed on the indigenous Southeast. By the time the English had cemented their domination over the Southeast, the Creeks had a national territory and were forging a national identity. They were also prepared to defend their nation with violence. By the 1770s, when William Bartram visited Ocmulgee, it is clear that the Creeks had articulated several versions of a national history that staked their claim to the Southeast. According to the stories, they had fought their way into the region and had therefore earned the right to be there, and to stay, regardless of the increasing numbers of white Georgians and their African slaves who flooded Georgia. An 1805 treaty that ceded most of the Creeks' land exempted the mound complex, indicating its significance. Subsequent treaties formally ceded the mound complex and other land holdings in Georgia.[63] The nation building of the eighteenth century would form the basis for the resistance of the Red Sticks in the early nineteenth century. A similar case could be made for the kind of Cherokee nationalism that came of age at a slightly later date, though the nineteenth-century Cherokee resistance to the descendants of the English assumed a different character and took place in courtrooms and newspapers. By the early nineteenth century, the American Southeast was a region of many nations, but one was dominating.

The Anglo-American regional culture of violence was not the same one that had appeared in Ireland and Roanoke in the 1500s. It was a descendant of these forms of violence. English Carolina's style of violence strove to control Indian land and commerce. English Carolina's culture of violence also manifested itself in a system of coerced labor that had the threat of violence at its very core. One cannot overlook the connection between race, "civilization," and violence in early Carolina. White Carolinians were actively engaged in violence, yet they saw their presence as taming a savage land, and with it cultures of violence they perceived as backward or barbarous, whether Native American or African.

The Yamasee War and the Stono Rebellion were turning points in the history of violence in the Southeast. The Yamasee War forced a massive realignment of native polities and sped the nation building of the Creeks and Cherokees, with far-reaching implications. The Stono Rebellion was the first and last major African rebellion in Carolina's history. It is possible to argue that even during the height of the Yamasee War, the survival of Charles Town was never really in question, and that even if the Stono rebels had made it to St. Augustine and freedom, South Carolina's slave-based plantation economy would have continued. These two events do, however, mark the end of an era in which competing visions of violence clashed in Carolina. The approach of this study shows, among other things, that the conquest of the Southeast by the English was a decades-long process. Beginning in the 1670s, the English remade the Southeast along lines which would benefit them. By the end of the 1730s, the conquest was more or less complete.

The English position in the region was strengthened further by the founding of Georgia in the 1730s, and even though Georgia's founders dreamed their colony would buck the trend of the rising plantation South, within a few years Georgia had developed along South Carolinian lines. The Spanish continued to offer sporadic resistance, which came to a head—or at least a piece of one—in the War of Jenkins' Ear (1739–43), but their empire was weakening, and the English and African populations continued to grow rapidly. Conflict between native groups and the English continued, but the peoples in a position to oust the English from the region, the Creeks and Cherokees, could see little benefit in doing so, having become dependent on trade goods and power brokers in their own right.

The area under English control expanded rapidly, and the English put the new land under the plow as quickly as they came to control it. English plantation agriculture, and its attendant African slavery, came to characterize South Carolina. In fact, one Swiss settler, Samuel Dyssli, remarked in 1737 that colonial South Carolina was "more like a Negro country."[64] In 1739, a group of African slaves on the outskirts of Charles Town tried to make that more than just a clever turn of phrase; they rose up against their masters in one of the largest slave revolts in North America. Planters crushed the rebellion, and afterward they instituted a slave code that limited many already circumscribed African American freedoms at the same time as it attempted to modify and limit English violence. This code would become a model for other southern English colonies and exert influence into the nineteenth century.

In the first half of the eighteenth century, the English had placed themselves at the pinnacle of South Carolina society through violence. Their conquest, accomplished by the forces of the plantation and the market, was essentially complete. The English established their dominance over small coastal groups, forcing the survivors of a number of devastating wars to flee to the larger native nations in the interior. Some communities, like the Yamasees, cast their lot with the Spanish, whose influence was declining as the English fanned out south and west from Charles Town. Some groups left the region altogether. The Tuscaroras moved to New York, where they became the Sixth Nation of the Iroquois. Still other native groups joined the English at and around Charles Town, but this was less common in Carolina than it had been in Pennsylvania or New England.

Though Native Americans would continue to resist English encroachment, the struggle rapidly shifted from a fight over land and power to a fight for cultural autonomy in the face of droves of white settlers. Individual slaves would continue to resist their masters, but never again with the concerted effort present at Stono in 1739. Natives and Africans could contest English colonial control, but neither group posed a serious threat to English mastery. The violence of the English plantation had supplanted African and Native American expressions of violence by 1740. Put another way, South Carolina's planter and trader elite had "tamed" violence they saw as savage and primitive to serve their own violent ends. From the 1500s to the 1700s, the people of the Southeast—Native American, European, and African—experienced successive "new worlds" of violence. These various cultures of violence left their marks on America, and not just along the sides of our highways.

# Notes

## Introduction

1. Gregory A. Waselkov and Kathryn E. Holland Braund, *William Bartram on the Southeastern Indians,* by William Bartram (Lincoln: Univ. of Nebraska Press, 1995), 4.
2. U.S. Department of the Interior, National Park Service, "Ocmulgee," n.d.
3. William Bartram, *The Travels of William Bartram,* ed. Francis Harper, Naturalist's Edition (New Haven: Yale Univ. Press, 1958), 34.
4. Most of this information is available on the web site of Ocmulgee National Monument: http://www.nps.gov/ocmu/History.htm/. For information on Ichisi, see Charles Hudson, "The Social Context of the Chiefdom of Ichisi," in *Ocmulgee Archeology, 1936–1986,* ed. David J. Hally (Athens: Univ. of Georgia Press, 1994), 175–80; and Charles Hudson, *Knights of Spain, Warriors of the Sun: Hernando de Soto and the South's Ancient Chiefdoms* (Athens: Univ. of Georgia Press, 1997), esp. 157–62. Other essays in *Ocmulgee Archaeology* deal with material cultural remains left behind by Ocmulgee's inhabitants over the last few thousands of years.
5. Bartram, *Travels of William Bartram,* 35. For the importance of Ocmulgee to the formation of Muskogee identity, see Joseph M. Hall, "Making an Indian People: Creek Formation in the Colonial Southeast, 1590–1735," Ph.D. diss., Univ. of Wisconsin, 2001, 19–21.
6. Bartram, *Travels of William Bartram,* 35.
7. "South Carolina Treaty with the Creeks at Coweta," in Alden T. Vaughan, series ed., *Early American Indian Documents: Treaties and Laws, 1607–1789,* vol. 13, *North and South Carolina Treaties, 1654–1756,* ed. W. Stitt Robinson (Bethesda, Md.: University Publications of America, 2001), 90–91.
8. Michael D. Green, *The Politics of Indian Removal: Creek Government and Society in Crisis* (Lincoln: Univ. of Nebraska Press, 1985), 22.
9. Tom Hatley, *The Dividing Paths: Cherokees and South Carolinians Through the Revolutionary Era* (New York: Oxford Univ. Press, 1995), 26–28.
10. This notion receives more coverage in the conclusion. While it is certainly true that Cherokees and Creeks came from different language families and originated in different parts of North America, it is dangerous to assume that identities such as "Creek," "Cherokee," or "American," for that matter, are

timeless. The Creek nation developed as a response to European colonization and grew in population by incorporating refugees from any number of indigenous communities.

11. "South Carolina Treaty with the Creeks at Coweta," 90.
12. Peter H. Wood, "The Changing Population of the Colonial South: An Overview by Race and Region, 1685–1790," in *Powhatan's Mantle: Indians in the Colonial Southeast,* ed. Peter H. Wood, Gregory A. Waselkov, and M. Thomas Hatley (Lincoln: Univ. of Nebraska Press, 1989), 35–103. Population chart appears on 38–39.
13. "Journal of the Congress at Augusta with the Indians," in Alden T. Vaughan, series ed., *Early American Indian Documents: Treaties and Laws, 1607–1789,* vol. 5, *Virginia Treaties, 1723–1775,* ed. W. Stitt Robinson (Bethesda, Md.: University Publications of America, 1983), 263–303. The reference to past offenses appears on 283.
14. Quoted in Robert M. Weir, *Colonial South Carolina: A History,* 2nd ed. (New York: KTO Press, 1983; Columbia: Univ. of South Carolina Press, 1997), 3.
15. David J. Weber, *The Spanish Frontier in North America* (New Haven: Yale Univ. Press, 1992), 60–65.
16. Lawrence C. Rowland, *Window on the Atlantic: The Rise and Fall of Santa Elena, South Carolina's Spanish City* (Columbia: South Carolina Department of Archives and History, 1990), 28.
17. Weber, *Spanish Frontier in North America,* 142–44.
18. Robert Olwell, *Masters, Slaves, and Subjects: The Culture of Power in the South Carolina Low Country, 1740–1790* (Ithaca: Cornell Univ. Press, 1998), 6–7.
19. Peter H. Wood, *Black Majority: Negroes in Colonial South Carolina from 1670 through the Stono Rebellion* (New York: W. W. Norton, 1974), 278. Harsh public punishments, including branding and castration, declined over the course of the eighteenth century.
20. Ibid., 308–26; John Thornton, "African Dimensions of the Stono Rebellion," *American Historical Review* 96, no. 4 (Oct. 1991): 1101–13.
21. Evan Haefeli, "Kieft's War and the Cultures of Violence in Colonial America," in *Lethal Imagination: Violence and Brutality in American History,* ed. Michael A. Bellesiles (New York: New York Univ. Press, 1999), 17–40, esp. 18. The quotation appears on 35.
22. John Hope Franklin, *The Militant South, 1800–1861* (Cambridge: Harvard Univ. Press, 1956), 13.
23. Though it came out too late to influence my thinking, Carol Smith-Rosenberg's *This Violent Empire: The Birth of an American National Identity* (Chapel Hill:

Univ. of North Carolina Press, 2010) appears to tell a later chapter in the story of the connection between violence and American identity.

24. Clifford Geertz, "Religion as a Cultural System," in *The Interpretation of Cultures,* by Clifford Geertz (New York: BasicBooks, 1973), 89.
25. *Oxford English Dictionary,* 2nd ed., s.v. "Violence." The word has Latin roots (*violentia* indicates vehemence or impetuosity).
26. David Riches, ed., *The Anthropology of Violence* (Oxford: Basil Blackwell, 1986), 8.
27. Bettina E. Schmidt and Ingo W. Schröder, eds., *Anthropology of Violence and Conflict* (London: Routledge, 2001), 6.
28. Neil Whitehead, "On the Poetics of Violence," in *Violence,* ed. Neil Whitehead (Santa Fe, N.M.: School of American Research Press, 2004), 55–77; quotation appears on 68.
29. Herbert E. Bolton and Mary Ross, *The Debatable Land: A Sketch of the Anglo-Spanish Contest for the Georgia Country* (1925; rpt. New York: Russell & Russell, 1968).
30. Verner W. Crane, *The Southern Frontier, 1670–1732* (1928; rpt. New York: Norton, 1981); J. Leitch Wright, *The Only Land They Knew: American Indians in the Old South* (1981; rpt. Lincoln: Univ. of Nebraska Press, 1999).
31. See Claudio Saunt, *A New Order of Things: Power, Property and the Transformation of the Creek Indians, 1733–1816* (Cambridge: Cambridge Univ. Press, 1999), 3–5.
32. Ian K. Steele, *Warpaths: Invasions of North America* (New York: Oxford Univ. Press, 1994). Quotation appears in the preface.
33. Richard Slotkin, *Regeneration Through Violence: The Mythology of the American Frontier, 1600–1860* (1973; rpt. New York: HarperPerennial, 1996), 17.
34. Donald L. Fixico, "Ethics and Responsibilities in Writing American Indian History," in *Natives and Academics: Researching and Writing About American Indians,* ed. Devon A. Mihesuah (Lincoln: Univ. of Nebraska Press, 1998), 84–99. I do not claim to have achieved this balance, but I have tried.
35. Charles Hudson and Carmen Chaves Tesser, eds., *The Forgotten Centuries: Indians and Europeans in the American South, 1521–1704* (Athens: Univ. of Georgia Press, 1994).
36. Robbie Ethridge and Sheri Marie Shuck-Hall, eds., *Mapping the Mississippian Shatter Zone: The Colonial Indian Slave Trade and Regional Instability in the American South* (Lincoln: Univ. of Nebraska Press, 2009). My contribution to that volume traces the role of violence in reshaping the region. The shatter zone framework is a useful one for getting at the changes that took place in

the Southeast. There is a danger in overextending the framework to people outside the reach of Mississippian traditions, though.

37. Joseph Hall, *Zamumo's Gifts: Indian-European Exchange in the Colonial Southeast* (Philadelphia: Univ. of Pennsylvania Press, 2009). Hall's work is especially strong when it comes to presenting a Muskogee perspective on exchange and gift giving.
38. Frederic Gleach, "Controlled Speculation: Interpreting the Saga of Pocahontas and Captain John Smith," in *Reading Beyond Words: Contexts for Native History,* ed. Jennifer S. H. Brown and Elizabeth Vibert (Peterborough, Ont.: Broadview Press, 1996), 21–42.
39. James Merrell provided a critique of ethnohistory in "Some Thoughts on Colonial Historians and American Indians," *William and Mary Quarterly* 46, no. 1 (Jan. 1989): 94–119. Merrell complained that ethnohistorians have ghettoized themselves instead of trying to effect change in the field of colonial history or American history at large. In the preface to James H. Merrell, *The Indians' New World: Catawbas and Their Neighbors from European Contact Through Removal* (Chapel Hill: Univ. of North Carolina Press, 1989), Merrell made the point that Indian history and colonial American history are essentially one and the same. Frederick Hoxie made similarly trenchant points about marginalization in his address "Ethnohistory for a Tribal World," *Ethnohistory* 44, no. 4 (Fall 1997): 595–615.
40. Clifford Geertz, "Thick Description: Toward an Interpretive Theory of Culture" and "Deep Play: Notes on the Balinese Cockfight," in *The Interpretation of Cultures,* by Clifford Geertz (New York: BasicBooks, 1973); Keith Basso, *Wisdom Sits in Places: Landscape and Language Among the Western Apache* (Albuquerque: Univ. of New Mexico Press, 1996); and Julie Cruikshank, Angela Sidney, Kitty Smith, and Annie Ned, *Life Lived Like a Story: Life Stories of Three Yukon Native Elders* (Lincoln: Univ. of Nebraska Press, 1990).
41. Schmidt and Schröder, *Anthropology of Violence and Conflict,* 3–4.
42. Riches, *Anthropology of Violence,* vii.
43. Thanks to the anonymous reviewer who helped me rethink this.
44. For a forceful refutation of this model, see Deborah Poole, "Introduction: Anthropological Perspectives on Violence and Culture—A View from the Peruvian High Provinces," in *Violence, Power, and Cultural Identity in the High Provinces of Southern Peru,* ed. Deborah Poole (Boulder, Colo.: Westview Press, 1994), 1–31.
45. Poole, "Introduction," 1.
46. Michael A. Gomez, *Exchanging Our Country Marks: The Transformation of African Identities in the Colonial and Antebellum South* (Chapel Hill: Univ.

of North Carolina Press, 1998), 51–54; Gwendolyn Midlo Hall, *Africans in Colonial Louisiana* (Baton Rouge: Louisiana State Univ. Press, 1995); and Gwendolyn Midlo Hall, *Slavery and African Ethnicities in the Americas: Restoring the Links* (Chapel Hill: Univ. of North Carolina Press, 2007).

47. The legacy of the Mississippian world receives extensive treatment in Ethridge and Shuck-Hall, *Mapping the Mississippian Shatter Zone,* and a more concise appraisal in James Carson, *Searching for the Bright Path: The Mississippi Choctaws from Prehistory to Removal* (Lincoln: Univ. of Nebraska Press, 1999). There were certain deep structures such as captivity, matrilineality, and conceptions of the sacred that continued to inform the situation in the Southeast long after chiefdoms had passed from the scene.

48. For a good summary, see Wayne E. Lee, "Early American Ways of War: A New Reconnaissance," *Historical Journal* 44, no. 1 (Mar. 2001): 269–89. See also John Grenier, *The First Way of War: American War Making on the Frontier* (Cambridge: Cambridge Univ. Press, 2005); Armstrong Starkey, *European and Native American Warfare, 1675–1815* (Norman: Univ. of Oklahoma Press, 1998); Ronald Dale Karr, "'Why Should You Be So Furious?': The Violence of the Pequot War," *Journal of American History* 85, no. 3 (Dec. 1998): 876–909; and Patrick Malone, *The Skulking Way of War: Technology and Tactics among the New England Indians* (1991; rpt. Lanham, Md.: Madison Books, 2000). For a contrarian view, that English war was not all that profoundly affected by Native military culture, see Guy Chet, *Conquering the American Wilderness: The Triumph of European War in the Colonial Northeast* (Amherst: Univ. of Massachusetts Press, 2003). See also Wayne E. Lee, "Fortify, Fight, or Flee: Tuscarora and Cherokee Defensive Warfare and Military Culture Adaptation," *Journal of Military History* 68, no. 3 (July 2004): 713–70, esp. n. 4 on 715–16.

49. James Brooks, *Captives and Cousins: Slavery, Kinship, and Community in the Southwest Borderlands* (Chapel Hill: Univ. of North Carolina Press, 2002); Jill Lepore, *The Name of War: King Philip's War and the Origins of American Identity* (New York: Alfred A. Knopf, 1998); Peter Silver, *Our Savage Neighbors: How Indian War Transformed Early America* (New York: W. W. Norton, 2008); Ned Blackhawk, *Violence over the Land: Indians and Empires in the Early American West* (Cambridge: Harvard Univ. Press, 2006); and Karl Jacoby, *Shadows at Dawn: A Borderlands Massacre and the Violence of History* (New York: Penguin Press, 2008).

50. Jacoby, *Shadows at Dawn,* 4.

51. This quotation is from George Rodd's "Relation," in *Records in the British Public Record Office Relating to South Carolina, 1663–1782,* vol. 6 (Columbia: South Carolina Department of Archives and History), 74–85 (hereafter,

*Records in the British Public Record Office* cited as *BPRO* with reference to the appropriate volume and page number). The original document is in French (the script is hard to decipher: "Ce Pais vant donc la peine que l'on fasse la guerre pour le conserver"?). Caroline Gordon Richardson translated all the *BPRO* documents in French for her 1947 master's thesis. Caroline Gordon Richardson, "Translations of Correspondence in French in Volumes 1–17 of the Records from the British Public Records Office Owned by the Historical Commission of South Carolina," master's thesis, Univ. of South Carolina, 1947. The phrase "This country is worth the trouble of going to war to keep it" can be found in vol. 6, Tr. 4.

52. It is possible to argue that the Cherokee War was also a war of conquest of sorts. I argue in the conclusion, "American Nations, American Violence," that the process which led to the British forays into Cherokee country was set in motion by earlier events.
53. See Joyce Chaplin, *Subject Matter: Technology, the Body, and Science on the Anglo-American Frontier, 1500–1676* (Cambridge: Harvard Univ. Press, 2001), 7–8. Chaplin argued, very subtly, that the encounter between English and Native Americans could be viewed as a conquest—to the extent that any Native peoples could be entirely conquered—but that scholars have focused on white settlement and native resistance instead.
54. This definition of nationhood leans on Steven C. Hahn, *The Invention of the Creek Nation, 1670–1763* (Lincoln: Univ. of Nebraska Press, 2004), 8.
55. Albert S. Gatschet, *A Migration Legend of the Creek Indians* (Philadelphia, 1884), 244.
56. Ibid., 245–46.
57. Ibid., 248.
58. Ibid., 250.
59. Ibid., 250–51.
60. Ibid., 235–36.
61. Benjamin Hawkins, "A Sketch of the Creek Country in the Years 1798 and 1799," in *The Collected Works of Benjamin Hawkins, 1796–1810,* ed. Thomas Foster (Tuscaloosa: Univ. of Alabama Press, 2003), 82.
62. Ibid., 83.

## Chapter 1

1. This follows the work of Timothy R. Pauketat in *Chiefdoms and Other Archaeological Delusions* (Lanham, Md.: Altamira Press, 2007), 1–30. One classic, and narrow, definition of a chiefdom can be found in Elman R. Service,

*Primitive Social Organization* (New York: Random House, 1962). More recent incarnations include Joyce Marcus and Gary Feinman, eds., *Archaic States* (Santa Fe, N.M.: School of American Research, 1998), 3–13; and L. Antonio Curet, "Issues on the Diversity and Emergence of Middle-Range Societies of the Ancient Caribbean: A Critique," *Journal of Archaeological Research* 11 (2003):1–42.

2. Max Weber, "Politics as a Vocation," in *Max Weber: Essays in Sociology,* ed. and trans. H. H. Gerth and C. Wright Mills (New York: Oxford Univ. Press, 1946), 77–128.
3. Timothy R. Pauketat, *Ancient Cahokia and the Mississippians* (Cambridge: Cambridge Univ. Press, 2004); and Timothy R. Pauketat, *Cahokia: Ancient America's Great City on the Mississippi* (New York: Penguin, 2009) are accessible introductions to Cahokia.
4. Pauketat, *Chiefdoms and Other Archaeological Delusions,* 34.
5. Timothy R. Pauketat, "Cahokian Political Economy," in *Cahokia: Domination and Ideology in the Mississippian World,* ed. Timothy R. Pauketat and Thomas E. Emerson (Lincoln: Univ. of Nebraska Press, 1997), 30–51. Pauketat describes the "Big Bang" on 31–32.
6. Pauketat, *Cahokia,* 1–10; Pauketat, *Ancient Cahokia,* 1–27; Sally A. Kitt Chappell, *Cahokia: Mirror of the Cosmos* (Chicago: Univ. of Chicago Press, 2002), 51–76; Timothy R. Pauketat and Thomas E. Emerson, eds., *Cahokia: Domination and Ideology in the Mississippian World* (Lincoln: Univ. of Nebraska Press, 1997); Thomas E. Emerson, *Cahokia and the Archaeology of Power* (Tuscaloosa: Univ. of Alabama Press, 1997); Bioline Whiting Young and Melvin L. Fowler, *Cahokia: The Great Native American Metropolis* (Urbana: Univ. of Illinois Press, 2000); Robert Hall, "The Cahokia Site and Its People," in *Hero, Hawk, and Open Hand: American Indian Art of the Ancient Midwest and South,* ed. Robert F. Townshend (New Haven: Yale Univ. Press for the Art Institute of Chicago, 2004), 93–104; and George Milner, *The Cahokia Chiefdom: The Archaeology of a Mississippian Society* (Washington, D.C.: Smithsonian Institution Press, 1998), 1–24.
7. The phrase is borrowed from Chappell, *Cahokia,* 51–75.
8. Warren Wittry, "Discovering and Interpreting the Cahokia Woodhenges," in *The Ancient Skies and Sky Watchers of Cahokia: Woodhenges, Eclipses, and Cahokian Cosmology,* ed. Melvin L. Fowler (Milwaukee: Wisconsin Archaeological Society, 1996), 26–35.
9. On Cahokian art in general, see James A. Brown, "The Cahokian Expression: Creating Court and Cult," in *Hero, Hawk, and Open Hand: American Indian Art of the Ancient Midwest and South,* ed. Robert F. Townshend (New Haven:

Yale Univ. Press for the Art Institute of Chicago, 2004), 105–23; and F. Kent Reilly III, "People of Earth, People of Sky: Visualizing the Sacred in Native American Art of the Mississippian Period," 125–137, in the same volume. The Corn Mother pipe was excavated in Arkansas but likely created at Cahokia between 1100 and 1200. Corn Mother iconography and stories associated with Corn Mother were, and are, widespread in native North America. See Reilly, "People of Earth," 125. The Rogan Plates, of which this is one, were excavated by John Rogan in the 1880s. See Adam King, "Power and the Sacred: Mound C and the Etowah Chiefdom," in *Hero, Hawk, and Open Hand: American Indian Art of the Ancient Midwest and South,* ed. Robert F. Townshend (New Haven: Yale Univ. Press for the Art Institute of Chicago, 2004), 150–65.

10. John A. Strong, "The Mississippian Bird-Man Theme in Cross Cultural Perspective," in *The Southeastern Ceremonial Complex: Artifacts and Analysis, the Cottonlandia Conference,* ed. Patricia Galloway (Lincoln: Univ. of Nebraska Press, 1989), 211–38. On the Adena Tablets, see David W. Penney, "The Archaeology of Aesthetics," in *Hero, Hawk, and Open Hand: American Indian Art of the Ancient Midwest and South,* ed. Robert F. Townshend (New Haven: Yale Univ. Press for the Art Institute of Chicago, 2004), 42–55, esp. 44–45.
11. Brown, "Cahokian Expression," 118.
12. Robert L. Hall, "The Cultural Background of Mississippian Symbolism," in *The Southeastern Ceremonial Complex: Artifacts and Analysis, the Cottonlandia Conference,* ed. Patricia Galloway (Lincoln: Univ. of Nebraska Press, 1989), 238–78, esp. 250–51.
13. A detailed assessment of the Upper World and Under World belief systems can be found in Emerson, *Cahokia and the Archaeology of Power,* 220–23.
14. Charles Hudson, *The Southeastern Indians* (Knoxville: Univ. of Tennessee Press, 1976), 122–28.
15. Fred A. Finney and James B. Stoltman, "The Fred Edwards Site: A Case of Stirling Phase Culture Contact in Southwestern Wisconsin," in *New Perspectives on Cahokia: Views from the Periphery,* ed. James B. Stoltman (Madison, Wis.: Prehistory Press, 1991), 229–52; and Timothy R. Pauketat and Thomas Anderson, "Conclusion," in Pauketat and Emerson, *Cahokia,* 269–78, esp. 270–71.
16. David G. Anderson, "The Role of Cahokia in the Evolution of Southeastern Mississippian Society," in Pauketat and Emerson, *Cahokia,* 248–68, esp. 255. On the size of Mississippian chiefdoms, see David J. Hally, "The Territorial Size of Mississippian Chiefdoms," in *Archaeology of Eastern North America: Papers in Honor of Stephen Williams,* Archaeological Report No. 25 (Jackson: Mississippi Department of Archives and History, 1993), 143–68. For the Ca-

hokia estimate, see Melvin L. Fowler, "Cahokia and the American Bottom: Settlement Archaeology," in Bruce D. Smith, ed., *Mississippian Settlement Patterns* (New York: Academic Press, 1978), 455–78.

17. Chappell, *Cahokia,* 62–63; Timothy R. Pauketat and Neal Lopinot, "Cahokia Population Dynamics," in Pauketat and Emerson, *Cahokia,* 103–23, with laborer totals on 103. See Milner, *Cahokian Chiefdom,* for a minimalist view of the earthworks and palisade.
18. Milner, *Cahokian Chiefdom,* 157; Peter Peregrine treats permeability of communities and warfare in "An Archaeological Correlate of War," *North American Archaeologist* 14, no. 2 (1993): 139–51.
19. Emerson, *Cahokia and the Archaeology of Power,* 193 ff.
20. Anderson, "Role of Cahokia," 253–58.
21. Pauketat, *Chiefdoms and Other Archaeological Delusions,* 155–56.
22. Anderson, "Role of Cahokia," 258.
23. Pauketat, *Chiefdoms and Other Archaeological Delusions,* 121–22. For a recent consideration of walls and military developments, see Sissel Schroeder, "Walls as Symbols of Political, Economic, and Military Might," in *Leadership and Polity in Mississippian Society,* ed. Brian M. Butler and Paul D. Welch, Center for Archaeological Investigations, Occasional Paper No. 33 (Carbondale: Southern Illinois Univ., 2006), 115–41.
24. Mound 72 is offset at thirty degrees from the east-west line, one guideline upon which Cahokia was planned. Interestingly, Mound 72 aligns exactly with the summer solstice sunset and the winter solstice sunrise. See Young and Fowler, *Cahokia,* 123–53.
25. See Young and Fowler, *Cahokia,* 123–53; Melvin L. Fowler, "Mound 72 and Early Mississippian at Cahokia," in *New Perspectives on Cahokia: Views from the Periphery,* ed. James B. Stoltman (Madison, Wis.: Prehistory Press, 1991), 1–28; Pauketat, *Cahokia,* 69–84; and Pauketat, *Ancient Cahokia,* 87–93. It may seem at first that human sacrifice would constitute a form of intracultural violence and thereby beyond the scope of this study, but evidence indicates that the victims of the violence that resulted in Mound 72 were from neighboring, possibly subsidiary, groups. Perhaps some shocking acts of intercultural violence helped Cahokian elites maintain their metropolis.
26. Antoine Simon Le Page Du Pratz, *The History of Louisiana* (1774; rpt. New Orleans: Pelican Press, 1941), 335–39.
27. Anderson, "Role of Cahokia," 253.
28. Pauketat, *Ancient Cahokia,* 145–53.
29. Charles Mann, *1491: New Revelations of the Americas Before Columbus* (New York: Alfred A. Knopf, 2005), 259–67; and William I. Woods, "Population

Nucleation, Intensive Agriculture, and Environmental Degradation: The Cahokia Example," *Agriculture and Human Values* 21, nos. 2/3 (June 2004): 151–57.

30. Pauketat, *Ancient Cahokia,* 153–55.
31. Mark Williams, "The Origins of the Macon Plateau Site," in *Ocmulgee Archaeology, 1936–1986,* ed. David A. Hally (Athens: Univ. of Georgia Press, 1994), 130–37; and James Griffin, "Cahokia Interaction with Contemporary Southeastern and Eastern Societies," *Midcontinental Journal of Archaeology* 18 (1993): 3–17. Williams dates the Ocmulgee site between 950 and 1100, but Pauketat dates it to 1100 and argues for its abandonment about 1200 in *Chiefdoms and Other Archaeological Delusions,* 114–15.
32. Timothy K. Perttula, Cathy J. Crane, and James E. Bruseth, "A Consideration of Caddoan Subsistence," in *Southeastern Archaeology* 1, no. 2 (Winter 1982): 89–102; and James Brown, "The Mississippian Period," in *Ancient Art of the American Woodland Indians,* by James Brown, David S. Brose, and David W. Penney (New York: Harry N. Abrams in association with the Detroit Institute of Arts, 1985), 93.
33. John M. Goggin and William C. Sturtevant, "The Calusa: A Stratified, Nonagricultural Society (with Notes on Sibling Marriage)," in *Explorations in Cultural Anthropology: Essays in Honor of George Peter Murdock,* ed. Ward H. Goodenough (New York: McGraw-Hill, 1964), 179–219; Randolph J. Widmer, *The Evolution of the Calusa: A Nonagricultural Chiefdom on the Southwest Florida Coast* (Tuscaloosa: Univ. of Alabama Press, 1988), 1–2; and Brown, "Mississippian Period," 93.
34. Adam King, *Etowah: The Political History of a Chiefdom Capital* (Tuscaloosa: Univ. of Alabama Press, 2003), 114–15; King, "Power and the Sacred," 150–65; Adam King, "Leadership Strategies and the Nature of Mississippian Chiefdoms in Northern Georgia," in *Leadership and Polity in Mississippian Society,* ed. Brian M. Butler and Paul D. Welch, Center for Archaeological Investigations, Occasional Paper No. 33 (Urbana: Southern Illinois Univ., 2006), 73–90; and Pauketat, *Chiefdoms and Other Archaeological Delusions,* 114–18.
35. For early Moundville, see Gregory D. Wilson, *The Archaeology of Everyday Life at Early Moundville* (Tuscaloosa: Univ. of Alabama Press, 2008).
36. Vernon James Knight and Vincas Steponaitis, *Archaeology of the Moundville Chiefdom* (Washington, D.C.: Smithsonian Institution Press, 1998), 60.
37. John H. Blitz, *Ancient Chiefdoms of the Tombigbee* (Tuscaloosa: Univ. of Alabama Press, 1993), 15–16; Pauketat, *Chiefdoms and Other Archaeological Delusions,* 123.

38. Dennis A. Peterson, "A History of Excavations and Interpretations from the Spiro Mounds Site," in *The Southeastern Ceremonial Complex: Artifacts and Analysis, the Cottonlandia Conference,* ed. Patricia Galloway (Lincoln: Univ. of Nebraska Press, 1989), 114–21; and Mallory McCane O'Connor, *Lost Cities of the Ancient Southeast* (Gainesville: Univ. Press of Florida, 1995), 52–65.
39. Maria Ostendorf Smith, "Beyond Palisades: The Nature and Frequency of Deliberate Violent Trauma in the Chickamauga Reservoir of East Tennessee," *American Journal of Physical Anthropology* 121, no. 4 (2003): 303–18.
40. Scott W. Hammerstedt, "Mississippian Status in Western Kentucky: Evidence from the Annis Mound," *Southeastern Archaeology* 24, no. 1 (2005): 11–27.
41. Edmond A. Boudreaux, *The Archaeology of Town Creek* (Tuscaloosa: Univ. of Alabama Press, 2007), 73–113.
42. David H. Dye, "Warfare in the Sixteenth-Century Southeast: The De Soto Expedition in the Interior," in *Columbian Consequences,* vol. 2, *Archaeological and Historical Perspectives on the Spanish Borderlands East,* ed. David Hurst Thomas (Washington, D.C.: Smithsonian Institution Press, 1990), 211–22; quotation appears on 213.
43. Marvin T. Smith, *Coosa: The Rise and Fall of a Southeastern Mississippian Chiefdom* (Gainesville: Univ. Press of Florida, 2000), 94.
44. Charles R. Cobb, "Mississippian Chiefdoms: How Complex?" *Annual Review of Anthropology* 32 (2003): 63–84.
45. Lewis H. Larson Jr., "Functional Considerations of Warfare in the Southeast during the Mississippi Period," *American Antiquity* 37, no. 3 (July 1972): 383–92.
46. Ibid., 389.
47. David G. Anderson, *The Savannah River Chiefdoms: Political Change in the Late Prehistoric Southeast* (Tuscaloosa: Univ. of Alabama Press, 1994), 133–34. The most striking example of this phenomenon is the near-total abandonment of the central Mississippi Valley about1400. See Stephen Williams, "The Vacant Quarter and Other Events in the Lower Valley," in *Towns and Temples Along the Mississippi,* ed. David H. Dye and Cheryl Anne Cox (Tuscaloosa: Univ. of Alabama Press, 1990), 170–80.
48. Jon L. Gibson, "Aboriginal Warfare in the Protohistoric Southeast: An Alternative Perspective," *American Antiquity* 39, no. 1 (Jan. 1974): 130–33; quotation appears on 130.
49. D. Bruce Dickson, "The Yanomamö of the Mississippi Valley? Some Reflections on Larson (1972), Gibson (1974), and Mississippian Period Warfare in the Southeastern United States," *American Antiquity* 46, no. 4 (Oct. 1981):

909–16. Dickson posited that Larson's argument made sense on a strategic level but Gibson's position could work at a tactical level. That is, Mississippian warfare could be seen as a "big picture" struggle for arable land, but individual Mississippians fought for reasons such as those outlined by Gibson: revenge, glory, and the capture of prisoners for ransom. The method I will follow in the next chapter relies more on case studies, though.

50. Anderson, *Savannah River Chiefdoms,* 134–35.
51. Garcilaso de la Vega, *La Florida del Inca,* trans. Charmion Shelby and ed. David Bost, in *The De Soto Chronicles: The Expedition of Hernando de Soto to North America in 1539–1542,* vol. 2, ed. Lawrence A. Clayton, Vernon James Knight, and Edward C. Moore (Tuscaloosa: Univ. of Alabama Press, 1993), 394 (hereafter cited as Garcilaso). "Capaha" is a slightly garbled rendering of Pacaha.
52. Anderson, *Savannah River Chiefdoms,* 100–101.
53. A Gentleman from Elvas, "True Relation of the Hardships Suffered by Governor Hernando de Soto & Certain Portuguese Gentlemen During the Discovery of the Province of Florida," trans. and ed. James Alexander Robinson, in *The De Soto Chronicles: The Expedition of Hernando de Soto to North America in 1539–1542,* vol. 2, ed. Lawrence A. Clayton, Vernon James Knight, and Edward C. Moore (Tuscaloosa: Univ. of Alabama Press, 1993), 85 (hereafter cited as Elvas).
54. Ibid., 106. Incidentally, this was a trick intended to force de Soto to divide his army. Still, it demonstrates that tribute collection was a legitimate reason to go to war.
55. Rodrigo Rangel, "Account of the Northern Conquest and Discovery of Hernando Soto," trans. and ed. John Worth, in *The De Soto Chronicles: The Expedition of Hernando de Soto to North America in 1539–1542,* vol. 1, ed. Lawrence A. Clayton, Vernon James Knight, and Edward C. Moore (Tuscaloosa: Univ. of Alabama Press, 1993), 303 (hereafter cited as Rangel).
56. A translation of Dávila Padilla's account is printed in John R. Swanton, *Early History of the Creek Indians and Their Neighbors* (Washington, D.C.: Smithsonian Institution Press, 1922; Gainesville: Univ. Press of Florida, 1998), 231–39; quotation appears on 232.
57. Anderson, *Savannah River Chiefdoms,* 101–10.
58. David H. Dye, "Feasting with the Enemy: Mississippian Warfare and Prestige-Goods Circulation," in *Native American Interactions: Multiscalar Analyses and Interpretations in the Eastern Woodlands,* ed. Michael S. Nassaney and Kenneth E. Sassaman (Knoxville: Univ. of Tennessee Press, 1995), 289–316.

59. John Blitz, "Mississippian Chiefdoms and the Fission-Fusion Process," *American Antiquity* 64, no. 4 (Oct. 1999): 577–92; quotation appears on 580.

60. George Milner, Eve Anderson, and Virginia G. Smith, "Warfare in Late Prehistoric West-Central Illinois," *American Antiquity* 56, no. 4 (Oct. 1991): 581–603.

61. Mary Lucas Powell, "In the Best of Health? Disease and Trauma Among the Mississippian Elite," in *Lords of the Southeast: Social Inequality and the Native Elites of Southeastern North America,* ed. Alex W. Barker and Timothy R. Pauketat, Archeological Papers of the American Anthropological Association, No. 3 (Washington, D.C.: American Anthropological Association, 1992), 81–98.

62. Pauketat, *Ancient Cahokia and the Mississippians,* 156–57.

63. Jeffrey D. Brain and Philip Phillips, *Shell Gorgets: Styles of the Late Prehistoric and Protohistoric Southeast* (Cambridge: Harvard Univ. Press, 1996), 253–54. Brain and Phillips date the shell gorgets in general much later (one hundred to two hundred years later) than most other sources. If the shell gorget dates from 1350 to 1450, or even the 1500s, this would be an argument in favor of long-term continuity in Mississippian ideas about violence.

64. Patricia Galloway, ed., *The Southeastern Ceremonial Complex: Artifacts and Analysis* (Lincoln: Univ. of Nebraska Press, 1989); Adam King, ed., *Southeastern Ceremonial Complex: Chronology, Content, Context* (Tuscaloosa: Univ. of Alabama Press, 2007); Vernon James Knight Jr., "Farewell to the Southeastern Ceremonial Complex," *Southeastern Archaeology* 25 (2006): 1–5.

65. David Dye, "Art, Ritual, and Chiefly Warfare in the Mississippian Southeast," in *Hero, Hawk, and Open Hand: American Indian Art of the Ancient Midwest and South,* ed. Robert F. Townshend (New Haven: Yale Univ. Press for the Art Institute of Chicago, 2004), 180–205, esp. 197–98.

66. Knight, "Farewell to the Southeastern Ceremonial Complex," 2; Charles R. Cobb and Adam King, "Re-inventing Mississippian Tradition at Etowah, Georgia," *Journal of Archaeological Method and Theory* 12 (2005): 167–92.

67. Vernon James Knight Jr., "The Institutional Organization of Mississippian Religion," *American Antiquity* 51, no. 4 (Oct. 1986): 675–87.

68. Ibid., 677–79.

69. Ibid.

70. Bartram, *Travels,* 288; Waselkov and Braund, *William Bartram on the Southeastern Indians,* 105; and Knight, "Institutional Organization of Mississippian Religion," 683.

71. Emerson, *Cahokia and the Archaeology of Power,* 217; and J. H. Howard, *The Southern Ceremonial Complex and Its Interpretations,* Memoir 6 (Columbia: Missouri Archaeological Society, 1968), 43–44.

72. Hudson, *Knights of Spain, Warriors of the Sun,* 24.
73. Dye, "Feasting with the Enemy," 295–98.
74. David H. Dye, "Warfare in the Protohistoric Southeast, 1500–1700," in *Between Contacts and Colonies: Archaeological Perspectives on the Protohistoric Southeast,* ed. Cameron B. Wesson and Mark A. Rees (Tuscaloosa: Univ. of Alabama Press, 2002), 126–41, esp. 133–34; and David H. Dye, "The Transformation of Mississippian Warfare: Four Case Studies from the Mid-South," in *The Archaeology of Warfare: Prehistories of Raiding and Conquest,* ed. Elizabeth Arkush and Mark W. Allen (Gainesville: Univ. Press of Florida, 2006), 101–42.
75. Chester DePratter, "Late Prehistoric and Early Historic Chiefdoms in the Southeastern United States," Ph.D. diss., Univ. of Georgia, 1983, 44–45.
76. Álvar Núñez Cabeza de Vaca, *The Narrative of Cabeza de Vaca,* ed., trans., and introd. by Rolena Adorno and Patrick Charles Pautz (Lincoln: Univ. of Nebraska Press, 2003), 68 (hereafter cited as Cabeza de Vaca).
77. Cabeza de Vaca, 68; for the incident at Mabila, see Rangel, 293.
78. Elvas, 107–8.
79. Ibid., 109.
80. Ibid., 110.
81. Rangel, 255.
82. Hudson, *Knights of Spain, Warriors of the Sun,* 19; Wayne Van Horne, "The Warclub: Weapon and Symbol in Southeastern Indian Societies," Ph.D. diss., Univ. of Georgia, 1993.
83. John Lawson, *A New Voyage to Carolina,* ed. and with an introduction by Hugh Talmage Lefler (Chapel Hill: Univ. of North Carolina Press, 1967), 44.
84. René Laudonnière, *Three Voyages,* trans. Charles E. Bennett (Tuscaloosa: Univ. of Alabama Press, 2001), 83.
85. Dye, "Art, Ritual, and Chiefly Warfare," 180–205; and David H. Dye, "The Art of War in the Sixteenth-Century Central Mississippi Valley," in *Perspectives on the Southeast: Linguistics, Archaeology and Ethnohistory,* Patricia B. Kwachka (Athens: Univ. of Georgia Press, 1994), 44–60.
86. Dye, "Art, Ritual, and Chiefly Warfare," 191–92, 198.
87. Matthew Restall, *Seven Myths of the Spanish Conquest* (Oxford: Oxford Univ. Press, 2003), 144; and Inga Clendinnen, "'Fierce and Unnatural Cruelty': Cortés and the Conquest of Mexico," *Representations* 33 (Winter 1991): 65–100.
88. Laudonnière, *Three Voyages,* 85.
89. Biedma, 237, in *The De Soto Chronicles: The Expedition of Hernando de Soto to North America in 1539–1542,* vol. 1, 221–46, (hereafter cited as Biedma).
90. Rangel, 298.

91. Wayne Lee has treated the limiting of warfare in eastern North America in "Peace Chiefs and Blood Revenge: Patterns of Restraint in Native American Warfare, 1500–1800," *Journal of Military History* 71, no. 3 (July 2007): 701–41. Though his examples mainly come from later periods, his conclusions seem to make sense when applied to the violence between Spanish and Mississippians.

## Chapter 2

1. For an overview of Spanish activities in the Canaries and their connection to New World colonization, see Alan Taylor, *American Colonies* (New York: Viking, 2001), 28–32.
2. Hudson, *Knights of Spain, Warriors of the Sun,* 3; see also J. H. Elliott, *Imperial Spain, 1469–1716* (1963; rpt. New York: Penguin, 1970).
3. See Restall, *Seven Myths of the Spanish Conquest,* 44–63.
4. Some scholars have argued that the "reconquest" was more myth than reality. See, for instance, Joseph F. O'Callaghan, *Reconquest and Crusade in Medieval Spain* (Philadelphia: Univ. of Pennsylvania Press, 2003), 3. O'Callaghan provides a succinct summary of the Christian campaign for Iberia. If the reconquest was a fiction, it was a powerful one in which many Spanish Christians believed, not to mention one which legitimized their use of violence.
5. For summaries of Spanish military organization and the types of weapons Spanish soldiers wielded, see John Lynch, *Spain, 1516–1598: From Nation State to World Empire* (Oxford: Blackwell, 1991), 106; and William H. Prescott, *The Art of War in Spain: The Conquest of Granada, 1481–1492,* edited and with an introduction by Albert D. McJoynt (Mechanicsburg, Pa.: Stackpole Books, 1995), 16–42.
6. Derek W. Lomax, *The Reconquest of Spain* (London: Longman, 1978), 99–100; Hudson, *Knights of Spain, Warriors of the Sun,* 7; and Elliott, *Imperial Spain,* 32. On the social divisions of Spain, see Bartolomé Bennassar, *The Spanish Character: Attitudes and Mentalities from the Sixteenth to the Nineteenth Century,* trans. Benjamin Keen (1975; rpt. Berkeley and Los Angeles: Univ. of California Press, 1979), 23–24.
7. Elliott, *Imperial Spain,* 32.
8. John Edwards, *The Spain of the Catholic Monarchs, 1474–1520* (Oxford: Blackwell, 2000), 154. Hidalgo status was not permanent. If nobles failed to maintain their horses or weapons, it could be revoked.
9. O'Callaghan, *Reconquest and Crusade,* 125.
10. Lomax, *Reconquest of Spain,* 99–101; John E. Kicza, "Patterns in Early Spanish Overseas Expansion," *William and Mary Quarterly* 49, no. 2 (Apr. 1992): 233.
11. Kicza, "Patterns in Early Spanish Overseas Expansion," 239.

12. Lomax, *Reconquest of Spain,* 99–101.
13. Elena Lourie, "A Society Organized for War: Medieval Spain," in *Crusade and Colonisation: Muslims, Christians, and Jews in Medieval Aragon,* by Elena Lourie (Brookfield, Vt.: Variorum, 1990), 54–76. Originally published in *Past and Present* 35 (Dec. 1966): 54–76.
14. Albert McJoynt, in his introduction to Prescott, *Art of War in Spain,* writes, "The Master of Santiago was one of the six most important men in the government of Castile under the Catholic kings" (56).
15. The testimony appears in Lawrence A. Clayton, Vernon James Knight, and Edward C. Moore, *The De Soto Chronicles: The Expedition of Hernando de Soto to North America in 1539–1542,* vol. 1 (Tuscaloosa: Univ. of Alabama Press, 1993), 470–84.
16. Lomax, *Reconquest of Spain,* 103–4. For information on the Order of Santiago, of which de Soto was a member, see Hudson, *Knights of Spain, Warriors of the Sun,* 6; and Lomax, *Reconquest of Spain,* 109–10. At one battle in the 1230s, defeated Muslims claimed to have seen Santiago waving a sword and a white banner, leading an entire legion dressed in white. See Lomax, *Reconquest of Spain,* 143. Santiago's image and actions changed over time, as described in O'Callaghan, *Reconquest and Crusade,* 193–96.
17. Elliott, *Imperial Spain,* 32.
18. Angus Mackay, *Medieval Spain: From Frontier to Empire, 1000–1500* (London: Macmillan, 1977), 5–7.
19. Rangel, 293.
20. Francesco Guicciardini, "Relazione di Spagna," in *Opere,* ed. Vittorio di Caprariis (Milan: Riccardo Ricciardi, 1961), 29–31; quoted in Benjamin Keen, "Translator's Preface," in Bennassar, *Spanish Character,* xi.
21. Bennassar, *Spanish Character,* 223.
22. Ibid. Bennassar makes the crucial point that honor's days as an entirely positive concept were numbered. About the time of conquest, honor became increasingly viewed as something that required protection, something that could be lost easily, rather than something that could be gained through the accumulation of wealth and victories in battle.
23. Lomax, *Reconquest of Spain,* 104–5.
24. Patricia Seed, *Ceremonies of Possession in Europe's Conquest of the New World: 1492–1640* (Cambridge: Cambridge Univ. Press, 1995), 69–99.
25. Kicza, "Patterns in Early Spanish Overseas Expansion," 230, 238. Obviously, in some areas—for instance, Mexico, Peru, and the North American Southeast—the Spanish never established the kind of domination they sought, and

in others, such as the Canary Islands, they failed to found any significant cities. Having said that, full settlement, like most other ways of going about colonization, should be seen as an ideal. Further, full settlement and the mercantile tradition were not mutually exclusive.

26. Eduardo Aznar Vallejo, "The Conquests of the Canary Islands," in *Implicit Understandings: Observing, Reporting, and Reflecting on the Encounters Between Europeans and Other Peoples in the Early Modern Era,* ed. Stuart B. Schwartz (New York: Cambridge Univ. Press, 1994), 134–56. Edwards, *Spain of the Catholic Monarchs,* 80–87, provides a useful summary of the conquest of the Canary Islands.

27. Juan de Abreu de Galindo, *The History of the Discovery and Conquest of the Canary Islands* (1764) Accessed through *http://www.archive.org/details/historyofdiscove00abre* <September 10, 2010>, 1-2.

28. Ibid., 2.

29. Weber, *Spanish Frontier in North America,* 94. One imagines the collective sigh of relief from the millions of Native people in the Americas upon hearing the good news.

30. Much work remains to be done on the Canary Islands as early experiments in Atlantic colonization. The basic scholarly works, in addition to the Eduardo Aznar Vallejo and Jon Kicza articles and the Abreu manuscript cited above, are Felipe Fernández-Armesto, *The Canary Islands After the Conquest: The Making of a Colonial Society in the Early Sixteenth Century* (Oxford: Clarendon Press, 1982); Silvio A. Zavala, *Las Conquistas de Canarias y América* (Las Palmas: Ediciones del Cabildo Insular de Gran Canaria, 1991), which was a reprint of a 1935 article in *Tierra Firme;* and John Mercer, *The Canary Islanders: Their Prehistory, Conquest, and Survival* (London: Rex Collings, 1980).

31. Christopher Columbus, *The Diario of Christopher Columbus's First Voyage to America, 1492–93,* transcribed and trans. Oliver Dunn and James E. Kelley Jr. (Norman: Univ. of Oklahoma Press, 1989), 67.

32. S. Max Edelson, correspondence with author, Feb. 2006.

33. Columbus, *Diario,* 67–69.

34. Bernal Díaz del Castillo, *The Conquest of New Spain,* trans. J. M. Cohen (London: Viking Penguin, Penguin Classics, 1963), 214–35.

35. See also Inga Clendinnen, "Cortés, Signs, and the Conquest of Mexico," in *The Transmission of Culture in Early Modern Europe,* ed. Anthony Grafton and Ann Blair (Philadelphia: Univ. of Pennsylvania Press, 1990), 87–131. Clendinnen argues that the Spanish were horrified by the Mexicas' culture of violence, which seemed to them to degrade the value of human life.

36. Edelson correspondence.
37. Cabeza de Vaca's published account, which did not appear until 1542, obviously had little effect on de Soto's expedition, which began three years earlier. Still, Cabeza de Vaca's adventures were well known, and, in fact, Cabeza de Vaca turned down an offer to accompany de Soto's entrada, choosing instead the post of governor of Paraguay. See Weber, *Spanish Frontier in North America,* 50.
38. Paul Hoffman, *A New Andalucia and a Way to the Orient: The American Southeast During the Sixteenth Century* (Baton Rouge: Louisiana State Univ. Press, 1990), 41–47.
39. Ponce was entangled in the legal dispute between Diego Columbus and the Crown.
40. There remains some speculation as to the role of a mystical fountain in motivating Ponce's voyage to Florida. Few contemporary sources mention such a fountain, though Oviedo noted the myth of the fountain as the subject of a joke shared by Indians and Spaniards alike, and it may have played some vague role in inspiring voyages of discovery in general. Las Casas argued that slaves were the reason, and King Ferdinand's license "to discover and settle the Islands of Beniny [*Bimini* here refers to any and all northern islands]" instructed Ponce as to the distribution of gold and Indians but makes no mention of a fountain. See letters in David Beers Quinn, *New American World,* 5 vols. (New York: Arno Press, 1979), vol. 1:238–47.
41. Carl Ortwin Sauer, *Sixteenth-Century North America: The Land and the People as Seen by the Europeans* (Berkeley and Los Angeles: Univ. of California Press, 1971), 26–28 and 35.
42. "Oviedo on Juan Ponce de León's Second Voyage," in Quinn, *New American World* 1:246–47.
43. Paul Hoffman provides a detailed account of Ayllón's expeditions and associated lawsuits in *A New Andalucia and a Way to the Orient.* The incident at the Native village is described on 77. Several primary sources, including Charles V's *Capitulaciones* and assorted legal documents, can be found in Beers, *New American World* 1:249–73.
44. Weber, *Spanish Frontier in North America,* 33–37 and 42–45, chronicles early Spanish activities in the Southeast. The *maestre de campo* was an extremely important position. He was outranked only by the *adelantado* and was in charge of matters related to the care of the soldiers and military preparedness in general.
45. Patricia Galloway, "The Incestuous Soto Narratives," in *The Hernando de Soto Expedition: History, Historiography, and "Discovery" in the Southeast,* ed.

Patricia Galloway (Lincoln: Univ. of Nebraska Press, 1997), 11–44. The volume contains several essays that treat the de Soto sources in great detail. The emerging field of de Soto studies has suffered from its overarching desire to combine all four major accounts—Biedma, Rangel/Oviedo, Elvas, and Garcilaso—into some sort of "supertext" that will bring all of de Soto's army's activities and the native Southeast into crisp focus. The term "supertext" comes from David Henige, "'So Unbelievable It Has to Be True': Inca Garcilaso in Two Worlds," in *The Hernando de Soto Expedition: History, Historiography, and "Discovery" in the Southeast,* ed. Patricia Galloway (Lincoln: Univ. of Nebraska Press, 1997), 155–77. "Supertext" appears on 167.

46. Ida Altman, "An Official's Report: The Hernández de Biedma Account," in *The Hernando de Soto Expedition: History, Historiography, and "Discovery" in the Southeast,* ed. Patricia Galloway (Lincoln: Univ. of Nebraska Press, 1997), 3–10.

47. This is not meant to imply that Oviedo became a Dominican as a result of his conversion. In fact, he mistrusted the amount of power held by the Dominican order in general and did not care for Las Casas specifically. This paragraph combines insights from Galloway, "Incestuous Soto Narratives," esp. 12–18, and José Rabasa, "The Representation of Violence in the Soto Narratives," in *The Hernando de Soto Expedition: History, Historiography, and "Discovery" in the Southeast,* ed. Patricia Galloway (Lincoln: Univ. of Nebraska Press, 1997), 380–409.

48. Galloway, "Incestuous Soto Narratives," 18–27; and Martin Malcolm Elbl and Ivana Elbl, "The Gentleman of Elvas and His Publisher," in *The Hernando de Soto Expedition: History, Historiography, and "Discovery" in the Southeast,* ed. Patricia Galloway (Lincoln: Univ. of Nebraska Press, 1997), 45–97.

49. This echoes the sentiments expressed in Henige, "So Unbelievable It Has to Be True," 165. Other considerations of Garcilaso include Galloway, "Incestuous Soto Narratives," 27–39; Lee Dowling, "*La Florida del Inca:* Garcilaso's Literary Sources," in *The Hernando de Soto Expedition: History, Historiography, and "Discovery" in the Southeast,* ed. Patricia Galloway (Lincoln: Univ. of Nebraska Press, 1997), 98–154; and Henige, "So Unbelievable It Has to Be True." This should not be taken as a condemnation of the text. It is a truly extraordinary work and an important indigenous contribution to literature.

50. Galloway, "Incestuous Soto Narratives," 31.

51. Rangel, 278.

52. The controversy over the source of the Elvas narrative is not likely to dissipate any time soon, since each side has its own heavyweight. Patricia Galloway argues that Elvas is based almost entirely on Rangel, citing instances where the two used nearly identical language, similar structures, and pointing out that

Burgos had contact with Oviedo and was familiar with the publishing scene in Seville. Charles Hudson has found "no merit" in Galloway's argument and notes that the Elvas narrative is much longer and includes many instances that occurred after the Rangel narrative left off (these could be treated in Rangel, but those chapters are missing). Hudson is also unconvinced that two different accounts would not use very similar words to describe similar things. After reading both accounts, I lean toward Galloway's perspective, but it seems clear that whoever informed Burgos's Elvas narrative had a lot to add to the story of de Soto's entrada. I treat the two as entirely separate texts in the way that they approach Spanish violence, recognizing that this could just as easily reflect differences between Burgos and Oviedo. For Hudson's critique of Galloway's arguments, see his *Knights of Spain, Warriors of the Sun,* 443–52. In the same section, he also defends the use of Garcilaso against the protestations of Henige.

53. The *capitulación* appears in *De Soto Chronicles* 1:358–364, translated by Buckingham Smith.
54. Rangel, 247–306; quoted material appears on 270–71.
55. Rabasa, "Representation of Violence in the Soto Narratives," 402.
56. Biedma, 232.
57. Elvas, 70.
58. Ibid., 81.
59. Rangel, 288.
60. Elvas, 70.
61. Ibid., 74.
62. Rangel, 284–85.
63. Ibid., 285.
64. Ibid., 289.
65. Elvas, 154.
66. Ibid., 95.
67. Ibid., 68.
68. Ibid., 94.
69. Ibid., 69.
70. Ibid., 126.
71. Ibid., 135.
72. Ibid., 142.
73. Ibid., 152.
74. Rangel, 276. Rangel criticizes the action, noting that "later on all was repaid" (276).

75. Elvas, 146.

76. Rangel, 257.

77. Elvas, 90–91.

78. Ibid., 69.

79. Rangel, 266.

80. Cañete Fragment, 309, in Clayton, Knight, and Moore, *De Soto Chronicles* 1: 307–10.

81. Hudson, *Knights of Spain, Warriors of the Sun,* 148, 235–36.

82. Elvas, 96. De Soto's actions before Atahualpa are described by Paul Hoffman in "Hernando de Soto: A Brief Biography," in Clayton, Knight, and Moore, *De Soto Chronicles* 1:421–59. On 439, Hoffman writes, "De Soto is credited with charging his horse right up to Atahualpa's throne, then causing the beast to rear on its hind legs, froth from its flanks (or mouth) falling on the emperor. Another version has the animal's breath stirring the imperial fringe (the sign of his office) on the man's forehead."

83. Elvas, 96.

84. Biedma, 232.

85. Elvas, 99.

86. Rangel, 292.

87. Hudson, *Knights of Spain, Warriors of the Sun,* 237–38.

88. Rangel, 247–306. The quotation appears on 293. Rangel's account is generally considered one of the most accurate of all the de Soto narratives, but this issue will be discussed in much greater detail later in this chapter.

89. Rangel, 293–94. Incidentally, the pearls had been carried from Cofitachequi, in South Carolina. De Soto intended to use them to prove the value of further colonizing efforts in the Southeast. For students of colonial history, this action may recall the events of the Pequot War of 1637, when English forces surrounded a fort on the Mystic River and burned it, killing the Pequot noncombatants who fled.

90. Elvas, 96–101; and Rangel, 292–94.

91. For the early accounts of the battle at Mabila, see Elvas, 95–104; Biedma, 233–35; and Rangel, 291–95. Recent secondary treatments of the battle appear in Daniel K. Richter, *Facing East from Indian Country: A Native History of Early America* (Cambridge: Harvard Univ. Press, 2001), 24–25; Hudson, *Knights of Spain, Warriors of the Sun,* 242–49; and Steele, *Warpaths,* 14–15.

92. Hudson, *Knights of Spain, Warriors of the Sun,* 244–47.

93. Elvas, 148.

94. Ibid., 156.

95. Biedma, 245.
96. The image can be found online at the Library of Congress's site, http://www.loc.gov/exhibits/1492/images/conquist.jpg/ (accessed Apr. 22, 2007).
97. Rangel, 265.
98. See for instance, José Rabasa, *Writing Violence on the Northern Frontier: The Historiography of Sixteenth-Century New Mexico and Florida and the Legacy of Conquest* (Durham: Duke Univ., 2000), esp. 1–30, for a thought-provoking commentary on the writing of violence and the legacy of colonialism.
99. Elvas; quoted material from 59 and 69, respectively.
100. Ibid., 151–52.
101. Rangel, 261–62.
102. Ibid., 305.
103. Ibid., 256. For more on manliness and womanliness in cultures of violence, see chapter 4, "Violence After the Entrada."
104. Ibid., 267. "Mucio Scévola, the Roman," refers to C. Mucius, or Scaevola, who proved his loyalty to ancient Rome by burning his right hand in a fire. The action impressed his Etruscan captors enough to set Scaevola free and sue for peace with Rome. See Titus Livius, *Early History of Rome* (New York: Modern Library, 1912). Online version at http://etext.virginia.edu/toc/modeng/public/Liv1His.html/ (accessed Jan. 23, 2010).
105. Rangel, 301–3; and Elvas, 136–39.
106. Elvas, 170.
107. Rangel, 302.
108. Two Spaniards who followed in the wake of de Soto, Pardo, and Luna traded more extensively and were generally "more conciliatory" to the people they met, according to Charles Hudson and other scholars. See chapter 5 below, and Charles Hudson, Marvin Smith, David Hally, Richard Polhemus, and Chester DePratter, "Coosa: A Chiefdom in the Sixteenth-Century United States," *American Antiquity* 50, no. 4 (Oct. 1985): 723–37, esp. 732.
109. Rabasa, *Writing Violence,* 184–89; and Weber, *Spanish Frontier in North America,* 78–79.
110. Correspondence with S. Max Edelson helped me recognize this fact and articulate it.

## Chapter 3

1. The best recent treatment of the attack is John T. McGrath, *The French in Early Florida: In the Eye of the Hurricane* (Gainesville: Univ. Press of Florida, 2000). The number of French killed varies widely between the sources, as

do the circumstances surrounding their killing. These wide variances have everything to do with the purpose French narratives about the violence were intended to serve.

2. These sources include Gonzalo Solís de Merás, *Pedro Menéndez de Avilés y la Conquista de la Florida,* ed. and presented by José Manuel Gómez-Tabanera (Oviedo, Spain: Grupo Editorial Asturiano, 1990). Solís was Pedro Menéndez's brother-in-law and accompanied him on his expeditions to Florida. Menéndez's own writings are available in several collections. I have relied most heavily on Eugenio Ruidíaz y Caravia, *La Florida: Su Conquista y Colonización por Pedro Menéndez de Avilés,* 2 vols. (1843; rpt. Madrid: Real Academia de le Historia, 1893); and Pedro Menéndez de Avilés, *Cartas sobre la Florida, 1555–1574,* ed. Juan Carlos Mercado (Madrid: Iberoamericana, 2002). Charles Bennett borrowed the translations of Annie Averett, originally published in A. M. Brooks, *The Unwritten History of St. Augustine* (St. Augustine, Fla., 1909) in his *Laudonnière and Fort Caroline: History and Documents* (1964; rpt. Tuscaloosa: Univ. of Alabama Press, 2001). See Bennett, *Laudonnière and Fort Caroline,* 125.
3. See Charles Gibson, ed., *The Black Legend: Anti-Spanish Attitudes in the Old World and New* (New York: Alfred A. Knopf, 1971); and Roger Schlesinger, *In the Wake of Columbus: The Impact of the New World on Europe, 1492–1650,* 2nd ed. (1996; rpt. Wheeling, Ill.: Harlan Davidson, 2007), 35–45.
4. The "line" in this phrase generally refers to an imaginary line running west of the Azores and south of the Tropic of Cancer. The phrase appears to have entered official diplomatic usage in the Treaty of Vervins (1598), but the thinking behind the phrase was present as soon as the contest for the Americas' resources began and lasted well into the eighteenth century. See Carl Bridenbaugh and Roberta Bridenbaugh, *No Peace Beyond the Line: The English in the Caribbean, 1624–1690* (New York: Oxford Univ. Press, 1972); and Eliga H. Gould, "Lines of Plunder or Crucible of Modernity? Toward a Legal History of the English-Speaking Atlantic, 1660–1825" (paper presented at Seascapes, Littoral Cultures, and Trans-Oceanic Exchanges, Library of Congress, Washington D.C., Feb. 12–15, 2003), http://www.historycooperative.org/proceedings/seascapes/gould.html/ (accessed Feb. 12, 2005).
5. Kris E. Lane, *Pillaging the Empire: Piracy in the Americas, 1500–1750* (Armonk, N.Y.: M. E. Sharpe, 1998), 11–30.
6. For Ayllón, see Hoffman, *New Andalucia,* 3–21.
7. In spite of all of the attempts to rein in war during the sixteenth century, J. A. Fernández-Santamaria makes the point that "war both lay at the basis of every contemporary conception of the state . . . and touched man as an ethical being." See J. A. Fernández-Santamaria, *The State, War and Peace: Spanish*

*Political Thought in the Renaissance, 1516–1559* (Cambridge: Cambridge Univ. Press, 1977), 121.

8. The legal category *bellum Romanum* owed more to a medieval understanding of Roman warfare than to Roman warfare itself. Medieval thinkers manipulated the category to suit their needs, and rulers in the early modern period applied it to wars of conquest and colonization. See Robert Stacey, "Age of Chivalry," in *The Laws of War: Constraints on Warfare in the Western World,* ed. Michael Howard, George J. Andreopoulos, and Mark R. Shulman (New Haven: Yale Univ. Press, 1994), 27–39. The discussion of *bellum Romanum* appears on 27–28.
9. Deut. 20:12–20 (KJV). The directly quoted verse is 16.
10. Quoted in Geoffrey Parker, "Early Modern Europe," in *The Laws of War: Constraints on Warfare in the Western World,* ed. Michael Howard, George J. Andreopoulos, and Mark R. Shulman (New Haven: Yale Univ. Press, 1994), 40–58. Parker discusses Ayala's treatise on 43.
11. Parker, "Early Modern Europe," 43. For a detailed treatment of English theory on colonial violence and its proper deployment, see chapter 5, "Creating English Conquest."
12. Ibid., 44–51.
13. Ibid., 52.
14. Ibid., 46–47.
15. Ibid., 52.
16. The French colony in Brazil, La France Antarctique, tore itself apart over religious infighting: The colony was a joint Protestant-Catholic venture. See Schlesinger, *In the Wake of Columbus,* 36–37.
17. McGrath, *French in Early Florida,* 8–18.
18. Ibid., 13.
19. Ibid., 20–21.
20. Hoffman, *New Andalucia,* 128.
21. Eugene Lyon, *The Enterprise of Florida: Pedro Menéndez de Avilés and the Spanish Conquest of 1565–1568* (Gainesville: Univ. Presses of Florida, 1976), 12. On the Sores attack, see Hoffman, *New Andalucia,* 128–30.
22. McGrath, *French in Early Florida,* 40–44. Other scholars have heightened the role of Protestantism in these colonial ventures. See Laura Fishman, "Old World Images Encounter New World Reality: René Laudonnière," *Sixteenth Century Journal* 26, no. 3 (Autumn 1995): 547–59, esp. 548n6.
23. Whether Ribaut was in England of his own free will or was a prisoner of war has been a matter of some debate. McGrath, *French in Early Florida,* 49–55.

24. Ibid., 33–49; Fishman, "Old World Images," 549.
25. McGrath, *French in Early Florida,* 67; Fishman, "Old World Images," 549–50; and Bennett, *Laudonnière and Fort Caroline,* 7–10.
26. McGrath, *French in Early Florida,* 66.
27. I have left most sixteenth-century language alone. I have replaced "u" with "v" where it made sense to do so, to increase readability in the text (the notes retain original spellings). Thus *Discoueryе* becomes *Discoverye.* Jean Ribaut, *The Whole and True Discouerye of Terra Florida* (London, 1563; rpt. Gainesville: Univ. of Florida Press, 1964).
28. Ribaut, *Whole and True Discouerye,* 53–55. In the twentieth century, replica columns of those left behind by Ribaut were planted near the sites of Charlesfort and Fort Caroline. Both emphasized the Protestant aspects of French Florida. The 1925 column on Parris Island, South Carolina, erected by the U.S. government, contains an engraving of a Bible above the words "religion, freedom, and truth." The inscription mentions that Charlesfort was built as "a refuge for Huguenots and to the glory of France." The commemorative column in Florida, put up by the Daughters of the American Revolution, marks the spot of "the first landing of Protestants on American soil."
29. Corn is not the sole prerequisite for a powerful chiefdom. The Calusas of southwestern Florida, who repelled the intrusion of Juan Ponce de León, killing him, were a highly stratified, organized chiefdom with little to no agriculture. See Goggin and Sturtevant, "Calusa."
30. See René Laudonnière, *Three Voyages,* ed. and with an introduction by Charles Bennett (1975; rpt. Tuscaloosa: Univ. of Alabama Press, 2001), 76. It is unclear whether the "brothers" were blood relations or not, but most scholars believe that they were not. See Jerald T. Milanich, *The Timucua* (Oxford, Eng.: Blackwell, 1996), 48. Perhaps Saturiwa was describing different levels of alliance.
31. Laudonnière, *Three Voyages,* 83 and 119–20.
32. This is definitely true for Mississippian violence, but more difficult to prove for Timucuan violence, since the sources are not as rich.
33. "Thymogona," or "Tymongoua," or any of a number of similarly rendered words, including "Timucua," preferred by modern writers, represent the word for "enemy" used by many of the peoples of northern Florida. Laudonnière, *Three Voyages,* 39–42.
34. Ribaut, *Whole and True Discouerye,* 91. It is possible to argue that early chroniclers exaggerated the productivity of the land in order to draw settlers and soldiers into colonizing schemes. While this sort of thing certainly took place, it seems unlikely that experienced soldiers and sailors such as Laudonnière and Ribaut would keep planting colonies and military outposts in lands they

knew could not sustain them. Their actions support the notion that they believed in Florida's capacity to support large populations. Spanish and English explorers also reported that Florida was a fertile land.

35. The designation of "paramount chief" is a specific archaeological term, and it probably does not apply to Outina. John Worth, a leading archaeologist of the early Southeast, notes that "Outina might have been a strong chief ruling a simple chiefdom of large geographic extent or a weak chief ruling a complex chiefdom consisting of a substantial number of small-scale multiple chiefdoms (or indeed both at the same time)." See John Worth, *Timucuan Chiefdoms of Florida,* 2 vols. (Gainesville: Univ. Press of Florida, 1998), 1:22. Because of the scant evidence, scholars cannot reach a consensus on the nature of Outina's chiefdom. Worth sees a larger chiefdom in decline, while Jerald T. Milanich, author of *Florida Indians and the Invasion from Europe* (Gainesville: Univ. Press of Florida, 1995), refers to both Outina and Saturiwa as "powerful eastern Timucuan chiefs." The quotation appears on 88.
36. Milanich, *Timucua,* 163–64.
37. Paul Hoffman, *Florida's Frontiers* (Bloomington: Indiana Univ. Press, 2002), 48.
38. Seed, *Ceremonies of Possession,* 41–68.
39. Ribaut, *Whole and True Discouerye,* 70.
40. Many are collected in Stefan Lorant, *The New World: The First Pictures of America* (New York: Duell, Sloan and Pearce, 1965).
41. Milanich, *Florida Indians,* 144–45.
42. Ribaut, *Whole and True Discouerye,* 70.
43. Ibid., 82.
44. Bennett, *Laudonnière and Fort Caroline,* 15.
45. Laudonnière, *Three Voyages,* 47. Laudonnière himself would eventually face a crisis in military discipline on his second voyage to Florida.
46. A deposition given later by Guillaume Rouffi—a young man who decided to stay in Florida rather than risk the ocean crossing with inexperienced sailors—mentioned the killing of the captain, but his account makes Albert's murder seem more accidental: "The one who had been left as captain over the others one day struck a soldier with a club, that the soldier drew his sword and in struggling with him killed him." Report of Manrique de Rojas, in Bennett, *Laudonnière and Fort Carolina,* 107–24; quotation appears on 119.
47. Laudonnière, *Three Voyages,* 49–51.
48. Ibid., 58–59.
49. Ibid., 67–68.
50. Ibid., 89–90.

51. Ibid., 82.

52. Ibid., 92.

53. Ibid., 95–106.

54. See Linda Colley, *Captives: Britain, Empire, and the World, 1600–1850* (London: Random House, 2002; New York: Anchor Books, 2004), 37; and Ann Laura Stoler, "Rethinking Colonial Categories: European Communities and the Boundaries of Rule," *Comparative Studies in Society and History* 31, no. 1 (Jan. 1989): 134–61. Stoler's work focuses on nineteenth-century colonialism, which differs in some crucial ways from sixteenth-century colonization. Still, Stoler succeeds in applying a notion of class divisions to colonial situations, and students of early colonization could learn from her example not to ignore ways in which class relations in a colonizing country might affect that country's colonies.

55. Laudonnière, *Three Voyages*, 117–21.

56. Ibid., 119–20.

57. Ibid., 120.

58. Ibid.

59. Ibid.

60. Ibid., 120–21.

61. For more on Timucuan warfare, see John Hann, *A History of the Timucua Indians and Missions* (Gainesville: Univ. Press of Florida, 1996), 41–42. Hann notes, describing the same incident, that the French desire to annihilate Potano was "what the European idea of war was all about."

62. Laudonnière, *Three Voyages*, 124.

63. Ibid., 125.

64. Ibid., 129.

65. Hann, *History of the Timucua Indians*, 45. Hann also provides a more complete translation than Bennett, which presents a more complicated succession ceremony.

66. Laudonnière, *Three Voyages*, 130.

67. Ibid., 142–51.

68. Lyon, *Enterprise of Florida*, 213–19.

69. Ibid., 214.

70. Ruidíaz, *La Florida* 2:324.

71. McGrath, *French in Early Florida*, 178.

72. Ruidíaz, *La Florida* 2:86.

73. Ibid. 2:87.

74. Menéndez, *Cartas sobre la Florida,* 143.

75. Ibid.

76. Grajales claimed responsibility for the sparing of the French Catholics, noting that he "was a sacerdote with the bowels of a man." See Francisco López de Mendoza Grajales, "Memoire of the Happy Result," in Bennett, *Laudonnière and Fort Caroline,* 141–63; quotation appears on 163.

77. Ruidíaz, *La Florida* 2:103.

78. Nicholas Le Challeux, *A true and perfect description, of the last voyage or navigation, attempted by Capitaine Iohn Rybaut deputie and generall for the French men, into Terra Florida, this yeare past. 1565. Truely sette forth by those that returned from thence, wherein are contayned things as lame[n]table to heare as they have bene cruelly executed* (London, 1566), Early English Books Online, http://eebo.chadwyck.com.proxy2.library.uiuc.edu/search/full_rec?SOURCE=pgimages.cfg&ACTION=ByID&ID=99842600&FILE=./session/1177469680_24193&SEARCHSCREEN=CITATIONS&VID=7267&PAGENO=15&ZOOM=FIT&VIEWPORT=&SEARCHCONFIG=config.cfg&DISPLAY=ALPHA&HIGHLIGHT_KEYWORD=undefined/ (accessed Apr. 24, 2007), C3.

79. Henri Lancelot Voisin, "Stranger Things Are Yet to Come," translated in Bennett, *Laudonnière and Fort Caroline,* 79–86; quotation appears on 86.

80. Ibid.

81. McGrath, *French in Early Florida,* 162 and 175.

82. His parents and brother were all Catholics, but there is a lack of decisive evidence regarding his personal religious leanings. See Woodbury Lowery, *The Spanish Settlements Within the Present Limits of the United States: Florida, 1562–1574* (New York: G. P. Putnam's Sons, 1905), 2:324n3.

83. Quoted in McGrath, *French in Early Florida,* 163.

84. Ibid., 164.

85. Rowland, *Window on the Atlantic,* 28.

86. "The *Primrose* Journal of Drake's Voyage: Florida and Virginia," in Quinn, *New American World* 3:306.

87. Ibid.

88. Ibid., 3:307.

89. Rowland, *Window on the Atlantic,* 28.

90. Joseph Dalton to Lord Ashley, Sept. 9, 1670, in *The Shaftesbury Papers,* ed. Langdon Cheves (1897; rpt. Charleston: Tempus, for the South Carolina Historical Society, 2000), 183.

91. Jerald T. Milanich, *Laboring in the Fields of the Lord: Spanish Missions and Southeastern Indians* (Washington, D.C.: Smithsonian Institution Press, 1999), 112–15; and Luís de Gerónimo de Oré, "The Martyrs of Florida, 1513–1616," *Franciscan Studies* 18 (July 1936): 73–75; direct quotation appears on 73.
92. Red ocher pigment decorated ancient chunky stones, and some scholars have connected the chunky game to ritual and warfare. See Hudson, *Southeastern Indians,* 392; and Pauketat, *Cahokia,* 42 . In the twenty-first century, the Muscogee Red Stick Society honors the valor of Creek combat veterans. See http://www.creekcombatveterans.org/ (accessed Jan. 29, 2010).
93. Oré, "Martyrs of Florida"; and Milanich, *Laboring in the Fields,* 112–15.
94. Amy Turner Bushnell, *Situado and Sabana: Spain's Support System for the Presidio and Mission Provinces of Florida,* Anthropological Papers of the American Museum of Natural History, No. 74 (Athens: Univ. of Georgia Press, 1994), 65.
95. Quoted in ibid., 66.
96. Milanich, *Laboring in the Fields,* 115.

## Chapter 4

1. Edward Rothstein, "Who Should Tell History: The Tribes or the Museums?" *New York Times,* Dec. 21, 2004, sec. E.
2. See Patricia Galloway, *Choctaw Genesis, 1500–1700* (Lincoln: Univ. of Nebraska Press, 1997); and Carson, *Searching for the Bright Path;* Ethridge and Shuck-Hall, *Mapping the Mississippian Shatter Zone;* Hudson and Tesser, *Forgotten Centuries;* Bonnie G. McEwan, ed., *Indians of the Greater Southeast: Historical Archaeology and Ethnohistory* (Gainesville: Univ. Press of Florida, 2000); Robbie Ethridge and Charles Hudson, eds., *The Transformation of the Southeastern Indians, 1540–1760* (Jackson: Univ. Press of Mississippi, 2002); and Cameron B. Wesson and Mark A. Rees, eds., *Between Contacts and Colonies: Archaeological Perspectives on the Protohistoric Southeast* (Tuscaloosa: Univ. of Alabama Press, 2002).
3. Hudson, *Southeastern Indians,* 206; and Carson, *Searching for the Bright Path,* 9.
4. Paul Kelton has suggested that the role of epidemic disease in depopulation has been chronically misunderstood. He places the first smallpox epidemics in the interior Southeast about the turn of the eighteenth century. See Paul Kelton, "The Great Southeastern Smallpox Epidemic, 1696–1700," in Ethridge and Hudson, *Transformation of the Southeastern Indians,* 21–38.
5. This perspective has informed the study of the African slave trade for some time. Diverse groups of West and West-Central Africans held on to pieces

of their identities at the same time as they fashioned a new one based on the situation in which they found themselves. Old ways of looking at the world may have been lost or transformed, but something new and powerful was formed in the process: a collective racial identity that was crucial to resisting enslavement. See Gomez, *Exchanging Our Country Marks.* Gwendolyn Midlo Hall has recently argued for the persistence of distinct African ethnicities in *Slavery and African Ethnicities in the Americas.*

6. Joshua Piker, *Okfuskee: A Creek Indian Town in Colonial America* (Cambridge: Harvard Univ. Press, 2004).
7. Weber, *Spanish Frontier in North America,* 67; and Priestley, "Historical Introduction" to *The Luna Papers.* The makeup of the party caused Velasco some consternation: He was concerned that it contained too many people—especially Africans, mestizos, Indians, and women—who would be a drain on the expedition's resources. See *The Luna Papers: Documents Relating to the Expedition of Don Tristán de Luna y Arellano for the Conquest of La Florida in 1559–1561,* 2 vols., trans. and ed. Herbert Ingram Priestley (Deland: Florida State Historical Society, 1928), vol. 1:55.
8. Luis de Velasco to Tristán de Luna, Oct. 25, 1559, in *Luna Papers* 1:67.
9. The soldiers' testimony was taken on Española in August 1661. See *Luna Papers* 2:289, 291, and 305.
10. The evidence for the purchase of corn comes from the same body of soldiers' testimony cited above. See ibid. 2:307.
11. Letter of Fray Pedro de Feria, in ibid. 2:327.
12. Charles Hudson, "A Coosa-Spanish Alliance in Sixteenth-Century Georgia," *Georgia Historical Quarterly* 72, no. 4 (1988): 599–626.
13. Quotations from an officer's (*sargento mayor*) letter to Spanish officials, summer 1660, in *Luna Papers* 1:211.
14. Letters and petitions dated June and July 1560; *Luna Papers* 1:133, 139, 141, 143.
15. *Luna Papers* 1:161.
16. Weber, *Spanish Frontier in North America,* 68.
17. "Long" Bandera Relation, trans. and annotated by Paul Hoffman, in *The Juan Pardo Expeditions: Exploration of the Carolinas and Tennessee, 1566–1568,* by Charles Hudson (Washington, D.C.: Smithsonian Institution Press, 1990), 267. As Hudson points out, the dry, legal language of Bandera's relation pales in comparison to the de Soto narratives, but it contains a wealth of specific information about towns that's lacking from the more dramatic accounts of the 1530s and 1540s.
18. Ibid., 270.
19. Ibid., 271.

20. Quotation from "Pardo Relation," in *The Juan Pardo Expeditions: Exploration of the Carolinas and Tennessee, 1566–1568,* by Charles Hudson (Washington, D.C.: Smithsonian Institution Press, 1990), 314.
21. Charles Hudson, *The Juan Pardo Expeditions: Exploration of the Carolinas and Tennessee, 1566–1568* (Washington, D.C.: Smithsonian Institution Press, 1990), 105–8.
22. Ibid., map 144.
23. Ibid., 176.
24. See David G. Moore, Robin A. Beck Jr., and Christopher Rodning, "Afterword," in *Juan Pardo Expeditions: Exploration of the Carolinas and Tennessee, 1566–1568,* by Charles Hudson, rev. ed. (Tuscaloosa: Univ. of Alabama Press, 2005), 343–49; "The History of the Berry Site," Archaeology at Warren Wilson College, http://www.warren-wilson.edu/~arch/berryhistory/ (accessed Jan. 30, 2010); and Marion Blackburn, "Spain's Appalachian Outpost: Failed Ambitions for a North American Empire," *Archaeology* 62, no. 4 (July–Aug. 2009): 38–43. Thanks to Ashley Self for bringing the Blackburn article to my attention.
25. Paul Kelton, *Epidemics and Enslavement: Biological Catastrophe in the Native American Southeast, 1492–1715* (Lincoln: Univ. of Nebraska Press, 2007).
26. Hudson, *Knights of Spain, Warriors of the Sun,* 421.
27. Hudson, *Juan Pardo Expeditions,* rev. ed., 64.
28. Hudson, *Knights of Spain, Warriors of the Sun,* 425; and Marvin T. Smith, "Aboriginal Depopulation in the Postcontact Southeast," in Hudson and Tesser, *Forgotten Centuries,* 257–75.
29. Hudson explained the logic behind using "coalescent society," as opposed to "tribe" or "nation," to describe Native American political developments during this time period in *Knights of Spain, Warriors of the Sun,* 435.
30. Hahn, *Invention of the Creek Nation,* 21–23.
31. The entry of three Native American groups, the Westos, Savannahs, and Yamasees, into the Atlantic economy is treated in detail in chapter 5, "English Violence in the Southeast." On population maintenance through "mourning wars," see Daniel K. Richter, *The Ordeal of the Longhouse: The Peoples of the Iroquois League in the Era of European Colonization* (Chapel Hill: Univ. of North Carolina Press, 1992), 145.
32. This should not be taken to mean that the Ochessees who lived at Ocmulgee were descended from the people who built it. They were in all likelihood the heirs of a Mississippian era pottery tradition known as Western Lamar. Though their immediate prior location was in the province of Apalachicola on the Chattahoochee River, their deep roots may be traced to Coosa, Shine

II, or Stewart phase developments. See Vernon James Knight Jr., "The Formation of the Creeks," in Hudson and Tesser, *Forgotten Centuries,* 373–92. For the period just before Nairne's visit, see John E. Worth, "The Lower Creeks: Origins and Early History," in McEwan, *Indians of the Greater Southeast,* 265–98.

33. Thomas Nairne, *Nairne's Muskhogean Journals: The 1708 Expedition to the Mississippi River,* ed. Alexander Moore (Oxford: Univ. Press of Mississippi, 1988), 44.
34. Jean-Bernard Bossu, *Travels Through That Part of North America Formerly Called Louisiana* (London, 1771), http://www.archive.org/stream/travelsthroughth01boss#page/296/mode/2up (accessed Sept. 11, 2010), vol. 1: 296. See also Carson, *Searching for the Bright Path,* 19; and Galloway, *Choctaw Genesis.*
35. Hahn, *Invention of the Creek Nation,* 20.
36. Ibid.
37. Nairne, *Nairne's Muskhogean Journals,* 32.
38. Ibid.
39. See Hahn, *Invention of the Creek Nation;* Hudson, *Southeastern Indians;* Ethridge and Hudson, *Transformation of the Southeastern Indians;* Wesson and Rees, *Between Contacts and Colonies;* and McEwan, *Indians of the Greater Southeast.* See also Knight, "Formation of the Creeks."
40. Christopher B. Rodning, "Reconstructing the Coalescence of Cherokee Communities in Southern Appalachia," in Ethridge and Hudson, *Transformation of the Southeastern Indians,* 155–75; quoted material is from 161. See also Gerald F. Schroedl, "Cherokee Ethnohistory and Archaeology from 1540 to 1838," in McEwan, *Indians of the Greater Southeast,* 204–41.
41. For origins of the term "Cherokee," which some suppose to be Muskogean, see Raymond Fogelson, "Cherokee in the East," in William C. Sturtevant, gen. ed., *Handbook of North American Indians,* vol. 14, *Southeast,* ed. Raymond Fogelson (Washington, D.C.: Smithsonian Institution Press, 2004), 337–53, esp. 349.
42. Raymond Fogelson, "Cherokee Notions of Power," in *The Anthropology of Power,* ed. Raymond Fogelson and Richard Adams (New York: Academic Press, 1977), 85–95.
43. Clan membership, a prerequisite for Cherokee identity, was inherited from one's mother. Theda Perdue, *Cherokee Women: Gender and Culture Change, 1700–1835* (Lincoln: Univ. of Nebraska Press, 1998), 42; Carolyn Ross Johnston, *Cherokee Women in Crisis: Trail of Tears, Civil War, and Allotment, 1838–1907* (Tuscaloosa: Univ. of Alabama Press, 2003), 11–35; and Sarah Hill, *Weaving*

*New Worlds: Southeastern Cherokee Women and Their Basketry* (Chapel Hill: Univ. of North Carolina Press, 1997), 27.

44. Johnston, *Cherokee Women in Crisis,* 13.
45. Perdue, *Cherokee Women,* 53–55.
46. Ibid., 36.
47. Ibid., 38, 53–54. Men who crossed the strict gender boundary were not lauded but ridiculed. War Women also had the power to free captives.
48. Alexander Longe, "A Small Postscript on the Ways and Manners of the Indians Called Cherokees," ed. David Corkran, *Southern Indian Studies* 21 (Oct. 1969): 6–49. The quotation appears on 46.
49. *Colonial Records of South Carolina: Documents Relating to Indian Affairs, 1750–1754,* 2 vols., ed. William L. McDowell Jr. (1958; rpt. Columbia: South Carolina Department of Archives and History, 1992), 1:177.
50. Quoted in Hann, *History of the Timucua Indians,* 207; emphasis added.
51. See the last chapter of Galloway's *Choctaw Genesis* for a narrative overview of the process by which Mississippians became Choctaws.
52. Carson, *Searching for the Bright Path,* 12–13.
53. Ibid., 14–15.
54. Ibid., 15.
55. Robin A. Beck Jr., "Catawba Coalescence and the Shattering of the Carolina Piedmont, 1540–1575," in Ethridge and Shuck-Hall, *Mapping the Mississippian Shatter Zone,* 114–41.
56. "Long" Bandera Relation, 267.
57. Walter Williams, *The Spirit and the Flesh: Sexual Diversity in American Indian Culture* (Boston: Beacon Press, 1992). The word *berdache,* from Arabic by way of French, carries a connotation of sexual slavery. The role is more complicated than that.
58. Hudson, *Juan Pardo Expeditions,* rev. ed., 99. The engraving can be seen at http://www.csulb.edu/~aisstudy/woodcuts/001_001_0005_1335.jpg/ (accessed Jan. 30, 2010).
59. James Adair, *The History of the American Indians,* ed. Kathryn Holland Braund (1775; rpt. Tuscaloosa: Univ. of Alabama Press, 2003), 193.
60. Vernon James Knight Jr., "The Institutional Organization of Mississippian Religion," *American Antiquity* 51, no. 4 (Oct. 1986): 675–87, esp. 682.
61. Carson, *Searching for the Bright Path,* 18–19.
62. These Tuckabatchee plates were described by various individuals in the eighteenth and nineteenth centuries. They were carried by the people of Tuckabatchee on their forced removal to Indian Territory in the nineteenth century.

Old Bracket, when he was simply Bracket, was involved in the decision of the Creeks not to pursue the Yamasee War beyond its initial stages or join any kind of alliance to remove the English from Carolina entirely. He figured prominently in the Anglo-Creek alliance described in the Introduction and chapters 6 and 7. See Adair, *History of the American Indians,* 209 and 506. See Hahn, *Invention of the Creek Nation,* 249.

63. Dye, "Warfare in the Protohistoric Southeast," 126–41, esp. 135–40.
64. See Frederic W. Gleach, *Powhatan's World and Colonial Virginia: A Conflict of Cultures* (Lincoln: Univ. of Nebraska Press, 2000), 4, 148–58; and Lee, "Peace Chiefs and Blood Revenge."
65. Several groups present in the early Carolina region, including the Westos, Savannahs, and Yamasees, were not indigenous to the area. Their motivations for migration, and their connection to the colonial slave trade and other forms of violence are treated in chapter 6.

## Chapter 5

1. Gleach, *Powhatan's World and Colonial Virginia,* 97–102; and Michael Leroy Oberg, *The Head in Edward Nugent's Hand: Roanoke's Forgotten Indians* (Philadelphia: Univ. of Pennsylvania Press, 2008).
2. Hiram Morgan, "The Colonial Venture of Sir Thomas Smith in Ulster, 1571–1575," *Historical Journal* 28, no. 2 (June 1985): 261–78. It is not surprising that Smith, a leading classical scholar in *A Discourse of the Commonweal of this Realm of England* (London, 1549), would look to Roman antecedents. He references Strongbow's conquest in an "anonymous" letter; see I. B. Gentleman [Thomas Smith], *A Letter Sent by I. B. Gentleman vnto his very frende Maystet* [*sic*] *R. C. Esquire vvherin is conteined a large discourse of the peopling & inhabiting the cuntrie called the Ardes, and other adiacent in the north of Ireland, and taken in hand by Sir Thomas Smith one of the Queenes Maiesties priuie Counsel, and Thomas Smith Esquire, his sonne* (London, 1572), Early English Books Online, http://gateway.proquest.com.proxy2.library.uiuc.edu/openurl?ctx_ver=Z39.88-2003&res_id=xri:eebo&rft_id=xri:eebo:citation:99836219/ (accessed Apr. 25, 2007), 14.
3. William Strachey, *Historie of Travaile into Virginia Britania,* ed. R. H. Major, Works Issued by the Hakluyt Society, vol.6 (1612; rpt. London: Hakluyt Society, 1849), 18. Other early seventeenth-century advocates of colonization, including William Crashaw and Robert Johnson, also made the connection between the benefits of Roman conquest and English activities in Virginia.
4. Nicholas Canny, "The Origins of Empire: An Introduction," in *The Origins of Empire: British Overseas Enterprise to the Close of the Seventeenth Century,*

ed. Nicholas Canny (Oxford: Oxford Univ. Press, 1998), 8–9. Canny cites a number of reasons for lack of English interest in the Americas, including a desire to complete earlier conquests closer to home, the generally conservative bent of merchants, and, after the onset of militant Protestantism, the desire to spread the faith in areas technically under Crown control.

5. Gleach, *Powhatan's World and Colonial Virginia*, 87.
6. Anthony Pagden, *Lords of All the World: Ideologies of Empire in Spain, Britain and France, c. 1500–c. 1800* (New Haven: Yale Univ. Press, 1995), 29.
7. For distinctions between English, Spanish, French, Dutch, and Portuguese methods of establishing dominion, see Seed, *Ceremonies of Possession.*
8. Canny, "Origins of Empire," 7. For the history of early colonization within the British Isles, see R. R. Davies, *The First English Empire: Power and Identities in the British Isles, 1093–1343* (Oxford: Oxford Univ. Press, 2000); R. R. Davies, *Domination and Conquest: The Experience of Ireland, Scotland, and Wales, 1100–1300* (Cambridge: Cambridge Univ. Press, 1990); Marjorie Chibnall, *Anglo-Norman England, 1066–1166* (London: Basil Blackwell, 1986); Robin Frame, *The Political Development of the British Isles, 1100–1400* (Oxford: Oxford Univ. Press, 1990); and J. C. Holt, *Colonial England, 1066–1215* (London: Hambledon Press, 1997). For a recent narrative of early Britain, see Simon Schama, *A History of Britain: At the Edge of the World? 3000 B.C.–A.D. 1603* (New York: Hyperion, 2000). The descriptor "English" has often taken a back seat to "Anglo-French" or "Anglo-Norman" in assigning ethnicity to the people that planted colonies in late medieval Britain. Anglo-French and Anglo-Norman accurately describe the leadership and chroniclers, but the majority of people doing the colonizing were English. Between 1100 and 1300, Norman and French identities weakened, and a unified English identity coalesced. The shift was apparent to English and non-English people alike. See Davies, *First English Empire*, esp. 143–45.
9. John McGurk, *The Elizabethan Conquest of Ireland: The 1590s Crisis* (Manchester: Manchester Univ. Press, 1997), 51–76.
10. One scholar notes about three thousand deaths from starvation and says that Charles Blount Mountjoy's forces "killed anyone they came across." See S. J. Connolly, *Contested Island: Ireland, 1460–1630* (New York: Oxford Univ. Press, 2007), 252–54.
11. Katharine Simms, "The Norman Invasion and the Gaelic Recovery," in *The Oxford History of Ireland*, ed. R. F. Foster (Oxford: Oxford Univ. Press, 1992), 44–87; and Nicholas Canny, "Early Modern Ireland, c. 1500–1700," in *The Oxford History of Ireland*, ed. R. F. Foster (Oxford: Oxford Univ. Press, 1992), 88–133.

12. Canny argues that Ireland did not necessarily prepare British people for overseas colonization. Activities in Ireland probably slowed colonial involvement elsewhere and made that involvement more English. While such activities may have slowed colonial involvement across the Atlantic, they helped form the moral, economic, and ideological justifications for colonizing voyages to the Americas.
13. Thomas Churchyard, *The miserie of Flaunders, calamitie of Fraunce, misfortune of Portugall, vnquietnes of Irelande, troubles of Scotlande: and the blessed state of England* (London, 1579), Early English Books Online, http://gateway.proquest.com.proxy2.library.uiuc.edu/openurl?ctx_ver=Z39.88-2003&res_id=xri:eebo&rft_id=xri:eebo:citation:99840763/ (accessed Apr. 25, 2007), i. It is possible to overstate the connection between Protestantism and the beginnings of the British empire. David Armitage argues subtly that Hakluyt's writings are more classicist than Protestant. See Armitage, *The Ideological Origins of the British Empire* (Cambridge: Cambridge Univ. Press, 2000), 77.
14. Martial law appealed to English governors because it was inexpensive and horrifying. Martial law cost so little to implement because holders of royal commissions could confiscate rebels' property, and redistribute it to officers in their small armies. See David Edwards, "Beyond Reform: Martial Law and the Tudor Reconquest of Ireland," *History Ireland* 5, no. 2 (Summer 1997): 16–21. Martial law would also figure prominently in an early set of rules governing the Jamestown colony, 1611's *Lawes Divine, Morall, and Martiall.* On Ireland during Elizabeth's reign, see McGurk, *Elizabethan Conquest of Ireland;* Hiram Morgan, *Tyrone's Rebellion: The Outbreak of the Nine Years War in Tudor Ireland* (Suffolk, UK: Boydell Press, 1993); and William Palmer, *The Problem of Ireland in Tudor Foreign Policy, 1485–1603* (Suffolk, UK: Boydell Press, 1994).
15. Canny, "Early Modern Ireland," 103–4.
16. Canny, *The Elizabethan Conquest of Ireland: A Pattern Established, 1565–1576* (New York: Barnes & Noble, 1976), 145–46; and David Edwards, "The Butler Revolt of 1569," *Irish Historical Studies* 38, no. 111 (May 1993): 228–55.
17. Thomas Churchyard, *A Generall Rehearsall of Warres, called Churchyardes choise wherein is fiue hundred seuerall seruices of land and sea as seiges, battailes, skirmiches, and encounters* (London, 1579), Early English Books Online, http://gateway.proquest.com.proxy2.library.uiuc.edu/openurl?ctx_ver=Z39.88-2003&res_id=xri:eebo&rft_id=xri:eebo:citation:99843573 150/ (accessed Apr. 25, 2007), 150.
18. Ibid., 145.
19. Though *View of the Present State of Ireland* was officially published in 1633, Edmund Spenser's opinions had circulated among the English in Ireland and at court since the late sixteenth century. Spenser himself was among the English who fled Munster during the Nine Years' War.

20. Nicholas Canny, *Making Ireland British, 1580–1650* (Oxford: Oxford Univ. Press, 2001), 44, 49; and Edmund Spenser, *A View of the State of Ireland,* ed. Andrew Hadfield and Willy Maley (1663; rpt. Oxford: Blackwell, 1997).
21. Richard Beacon, *Solon His Folie, or a Politique Discourse touching the Reformation of common-weales conquered, declined, or corrupted* (London, 1594), ed. and annotated by Clare Carroll and Vincent Carey (Binghamton, N.Y.: Medieval and Renaissance Texts and Studies, 1996), xxvi–xxvii.
22. John Derricke, *The Image of Irelande* (1581; rpt. Edinburgh, 1883), plates V and VI.
23. Ibid., plate VI.
24. Canny, *Elizabethan Conquest,* 123; and Steven G. Ellis, "The Tudors," in *A Military History of Ireland,* ed. Thomas Bartlett and Keith Jeffrey (Cambridge: Cambridge Univ. Press, 1996), 116–35.
25. Canny, *Making Ireland British,* 83.
26. Bartolomé de Las Casas, *The Spanish Colonie, or Briefe chronicle of the acts and gestes of the Spaniardes in the West Indies, called the newe world, for the space of xl. yeeres: written in the Castilian tongue by the reuerend Bishop Bartholomew de las Cases or Casaus, a friar of the order of S. Dominicke* (London, 1583), Early English Books Online, http://gateway.proquest.com.proxy2.library.uiuc.edu/openurl?ctx_ver=Z39.88-2003&res_id=xri:eebo&rft_id=xri:eebo:citation:99840647/ (accessed Apr. 25, 2007).
27. The term "Black Legend" was coined by Spanish journalist Julián Juderías in 1912. Anti-Spanish sentiment is much, much older. See William S. Maltby, *The Black Legend in England: The Development of Anti-Spanish Sentiment, 1558–1660* (Durham, N.C.: Duke Univ. Press, 1971); Gibson, *Black Legend;* and Benjamin Keen, "The Black Legend Revisited: Assumptions and Realities," *Hispanic American Historical Review* 49, no. 4 (1969): 703–19.
28. Richard Hakluyt, *Discourse on Western Planting,* ed. David B. Quinn and Alison M. Quinn (London: Hakluyt Society, 1993), 11. David Armitage has argued that Protestantism took a back seat to other factors, namely, Hakluyt's desire to increase England's power and wealth at the expense of Spain. See Armitage, *Ideological Origins of the British Empire,* 61–99.
29. Hakluyt, *Discourse on Western Planting,* 59.
30. The list can be found in ibid., 123.
31. A reference to soldiers trained in the "late warres of Fraunce and Falunders" appears in ibid., 119.
32. For a concise treatment of the "charters as violence" theory, see Christopher Tomlins, "In a Wilderness of Tigers: Violence, the Discourse of English Colonizing, and the Refusals of American History," *Theoretical Inquiries in Law* 4, no. 2 (July 2003): 450–90, esp. 474. In a recent interpretation, Stuart Banner,

author of *How the Indians Lost Their Land: Law and Power on the Frontier* (Cambridge: Harvard Univ. Press, 2005), has explained the process of dispossession anew. Banner views land sales, usually under some form of duress, as a piece of the English conquest of the eastern half of North America.

33. April Lee Hatfield, *Atlantic Virginia: Intercolonial Relations in the Seventeenth Century* (Philadelphia: Univ. of Pennsylvania Press, 2004), provides a good look at the connections between Virginia and the Atlantic world.
34. Gleach, *Powhatan's World and Colonial Virginia,* 101.
35. It is not clear whether Wingina was actually planning such an attack. Wingina was rightfully wary of several English attempts to draw him into a trap. See ibid., 101; David Beers Quinn, *Set Fair for Roanoke: Voyages and Colonies, 1584–1606* (Chapel Hill: Univ. of North Carolina Press), 124–27; and Karen Ordahl Kupperman, *Roanoke: The Abandoned Colony* (Totowa, N.J.: Rowman & Allenheld, 1984), 85–87.
36. Interestingly, Lane's account describes the man and youth who chased Wingina into the woods and beheaded him as Irish. Ralph Lane recorded his version of events in *Ralph Lane's Discourse on the First Colony.* This appears in Hakluyt's *Principall Navigations* (London, 1589) and in David Beers Quinn, ed., *The Roanoke Voyages, 1584–1590* (London: Hakluyt Society, 1955), 2:255–94. The battle occurs on 286–88; Oberg describes the lead-up and killing in detail in *The Head in Edward Nugent's Hand,* 81–100.
37. Thomas Hariot, *A Brief and True Report of the Discovery of the New Found Land of Virginia,* 24. The first edition appeared in London in 1588. Theodor de Bry published Hariot's work in English, Latin, German, and French, with drawings by John White, at Frankfurt in 1590. See Thedor de Bry, *Thomas Hariot's Virginia* (Ann Arbor: University Microfilms, 1966). The 1590 edition also contains some of John White's drawings of Picts. The reason for their inclusion is not clear, although it may have been an attempt to compare the lifeways of early British people with Native Americans.
38. Hariot, *Brief and True Report,* 28.
39. Ibid., 30. Gesa Mackenthun treats Hariot and Lane in *Metaphors of Dispossession: American Beginnings and the Translation of Empire, 1492–1637* (Norman: Univ. of Oklahoma Press, 1997), 141–62. Mackenthun argues that although Lane and Hariot differ in their outlook—Lane's discourse was paranoid, Hariot's was optimistic—they share some crucial elements. Both texts assume native treachery, for instance.
40. A brief biography of Crashaw can be found at St. John's College Library, University of Cambridge, http://www.joh.cam.ac.uk/library/special_collections/early_books/pix/provenance/crashaw/crashaw.htm/ (accessed May 27, 2010).

41. William Crashaw, *A sermon preached in London before the right honorable the Lord Lawarre, Lord Governour and Captaine Generall of Virginea and others of his Maiesties Counsell for that kingdome, and the rest of the aduenturers in that plantation At the said Lord Generall his leaue taking of England his natiue countrey, and departure for Virginea, Febr. 21. 1609,* (London, 1609), Early English Books Online, http://gateway.proquest.com.proxy2.library.uiuc.edu/openurl?ctx_ver=Z39.88-2003&res_id=xri:eebo&rft_id=xri:eebo:citation:99844721/ (accessed Apr. 25, 2007), G4. The Spanish did not present a threat, according to Crashaw, because they had not claimed Virginia proper. This was not the case, of course, as the Spanish had established a mission at Jacán, on Chesapeake Bay, in the 1570s. The French were more inclined to follow the lead of the English and settle near them, rather than challenge their settlements in Virginia.
42. Ibid., H2.
43. Ibid., F4. The entrance of the Hebrews into Canaan was not exactly a peaceful process and might be described as a conquest. See, for instance, Joshua 24:11 (KJV), in which various tribes resisted the Hebrews and God "delivered them into your hand."
44. Robert Johnson, *Nova Britannia offering most excellent fruites by planting in Virginia: exciting all such as be well affected to further the same* (London, 1609), Early English Books Online, http://gateway.proquest.com.proxy2.library.uiuc.edu/openurl?ctx_ver=Z39.88-2003&res_id=xri:eebo&rft_id=xri:eebo:citation:22924007/ (accessed Apr. 25, 2007), C2.
45. Ibid., C3.
46. George Percy, *A Trewe Relation, Colonial Williamsburg Journal,* Winter 2007, http://www.history.org/Foundation/journal/Winter07/A%20Trewe%20Relation.pdf/ (accessed Apr. 25, 2007), 11.
47. Ibid., 12.
48. Ibid.
49. Edward Waterhouse, *A declaration of the state of the colony and affaires in Virginia With a relation of the barbarous massacre in the time of peace and league treacherously executed by the natiue infidels vpon the English, the 22 of March last* (London, 1622), Early English Books Online, http://gateway.proquest.com.proxy2.library.uiuc.edu/openurl?ctx_ver=Z39.88-2003&res_id=xri:eebo&rft_id=xri:eebo:citation:99846899/ (accessed Apr. 25, 2007). The best recent interpretation can be found in Gleach, *Powhatan's World and Colonial Virginia,* 148–58.
50. Waterhouse, *Declaration,* 22.
51. Chaplin, *Subject Matter,* 81.

52. Ibid., 254.
53. Seed, *Ceremonies of Possession,* 17.
54. *Oxford English Dictionary,* 2nd ed., s.v. "pale." The word appeared in the 1300s and was eventually used to describe a fence made up of pales and the area enclosed by such a fence. The "Pale," in reference to the English settlement in Ireland, first appeared in the 1580s. See Seed, *Ceremonies of Possession,* 21.
55. Canny, "Origins of Empire," 32.
56. Banner, *How the Indians Lost Their Land,* 1–8. Banner does not imply that the deals were always fair, of course, and he is careful to point out that seemingly innocuous land deals were made under the crushing pressure of colonial power relationships.
57. Gleach, *Powhatan's World and Colonial Virginia.* Gleach summarizes Powhatan trade on pp. 54–60 and English trade on pp. 65–70. References to trade prohibitions and restrictions appear on 163, 165, and 171–72.
58. On Indian dependence, see ibid., 172–73.
59. William Ramsey, *The Yamasee War: A Study of Culture, Economy, and Conflict in the Colonial South* (Lincoln: Univ. of Nebraska Press, 2008).
60. Betty Wood, *The Origins of American Slavery: Freedom and Bondage in the English Colonies* (New York: Hill and Wang, 1997), 40–56.
61. Richard S. Dunn, *Sugar and Slaves: The Rise of the Planter Class in the English West Indies, 1624–1713* (Chapel Hill: Univ. of North Carolina Press, 1972), 245–46. See also Hilary McD. Beckles, "The 'Hub of Empire': The Caribbean and Britain in the Seventeenth Century," in *The Origins of Empire: British Overseas Enterprise to the Close of the Seventeenth Century,* ed. Nicholas Canny (Oxford: Oxford Univ. Press, 1998), 218–40, esp. 228n29.
62. Dunn, *Sugar and Slaves,* 246.
63. Richard Ligon, *A true & exact history of the island of Barbados illustrated with a mapp of the island, as also the principall trees and plants there, set forth in their due proportions and shapes, drawne out by their severall and respective scales : together with the ingenio that makes the sugar, with the plots of the severall houses, roomes, and other places that are used in the whole processe of sugar-making* (London, 1657), Early English Books Online, http://gateway.proquest.com.proxy2.library.uiuc.edu/openurl?ctx_ver=Z39.88-2003&res_id=xri:eebo&rft_id=xri:eebo:citation:12703788/ (accessed Apr. 25, 2007), 46; Roger D. Abrahams and John F. Szwed, eds., *After Africa: Extracts from British Travel Accounts and Journals of the Seventeenth, Eighteenth, and Nineteenth Centuries Concerning the Slaves, Their Manners, and Customs in the British West Indies* (New Haven: Yale Univ. Press, 1983); K. R. Andrews, "The English in the Caribbean, 1560–1620," in *The Westward Enterprise:*

*English Activities in Ireland, the Atlantic, and America, 1480–1650,* ed. K. R. Andrews, N. P. Canny, and P. E. H. Hair. (Detroit: Wayne State Univ. Press, 1979), 103–23; Bridenbaugh and Bridenbaugh, *No Peace Beyond the Line;* Gary A. Puckrein, *Little England: Plantation Society and Anglo-Barbadian Politics, 1627–1700* (New York: New York Univ. Press, 1984); David Eltis, *The Rise of African Slavery in the Americas* (Cambridge: Cambridge Univ. Press, 2000); and J. H. Parry et al., *A Short History of the West Indies* (New York: St. Martin's Press, 1987).

64. Puckrein, *Little England,* 79. Quotations from Henry Drax's "Instructions" appear on 78 and 79.
65. David Eltis, *The Rise of African Slavery in the Americas* (Cambridge: Cambridge Univ. Press, 2000), 193–223.
66. Ethridge and Shuck-Hall, *Mapping the Mississippian Shatter Zone.*
67. James Walvin, *Black Ivory: Slavery in the British Empire,* 2nd ed. (1992; rpt. Oxford: Blackwell, 2001), 205.
68. It bears mentioning that corporal punishment at this time was not limited to slaves. Outside of the military, English men used violence to discipline women and children at home, as well as social inferiors and disorderly workers in more public settings.
69. Ira Berlin, *Many Thousands Gone: The First Two Centuries of Slavery in North America* (Cambridge: Belknap Press of Harvard Univ. Press, 1998), 115–16. Philip D. Morgan, *Slave Counterpoint: Black Culture in the Eighteenth-Century Chesapeake and Lowcountry* (Chapel Hill: Univ. of North Carolina Press, 1998), 263, confirms this interpretation.
70. S. T. Ansell, "Legal and Historical Aspects of the Militia," *Yale Law Review* 26, no. 6 (Apr. 1917): 471–80. For the system's roots in Saxon times, see 472–73.
71. For overviews of this period in English military history, see Jeremy Black, *European Warfare, 1494–1660* (London: Routledge, 2002), esp. 153–59; Mark Charles Fissel, *English Warfare, 1511–1642* (London: Routledge, 2001), esp. 282–303; M. J. Braddick, "An English Military Revolution?" *Historical Journal* 36, no. 4 (Dec. 1993): 965–75; and M. J. Braddick, "The English Government, War, Trade, and Settlement, 1625–1688," in *The Origins of Empire: British Overseas Enterprise to the Close of the Seventeenth Century,* ed. Nicholas Canny (Oxford: Oxford Univ. Press, 1998), 286–308.
72. Braddick, "English Government," 286.
73. Barbara Donagan has treated the former in her "Atrocity, War Crime, and Treason in the English Civil War," *American Historical Review* 99, no. 4 (Oct. 1994): 1137–66. See also her articles "Codes and Conduct in the English Civil War," *Past and Present* 118 (Feb. 1998): 65–95, and "Halcyon Days and the

Literature of War: England's Military Education before 1642," *Past and Present* 147 (May 1995): 65–100.

74. Rhys Isaac, *The Transformation of Virginia, 1740–1790* (Chapel Hill: Univ. of North Carolina Press, 1982), 104–7.
75. Ibid., 107.
76. Sally Hadden, *Slave Patrols: Law and Violence in Virginia and the Carolinas* (Cambridge: Harvard Univ. Press, 2001). The statutes are cited on 11–12.
77. Fissel, *English Warfare,* 282.
78. Gleach, *Powhatan's World and Colonial Virginia,* 87.

## Chapter 6

1. Gene Waddell, "Cusabo," in William C. Sturtevant, gen. ed., *Handbook of North American Indians,* vol. 14, *Southeast,* ed. Raymond Fogelson (Washington, D.C.: Smithsonian Institution Press, 2004), 254–64. "Cusabo" is a blanket term applied to eighteen distinct communities which split time between the coast and towns farther inland.
2. Laudonnière, *Three Voyages,* 26–51; quoted material appears on 26.
3. Waddell, "Cusabo," 259.
4. Ethridge and Shuck–Hall, *Mapping the Mississippian Shatter Zone.*
5. See Alan Gallay, *The Indian Slave Trade: The Rise of the English Empire in the American South, 1670–1717* (New Haven: Yale Univ. Press, 2002), 51–52; *Journals of the Grand Council* (Columbia: South Carolina Department of Archives and History, 1907), Sept./Oct. 1671; Gene Waddell, *Indians of the South Carolina Lowcountry, 1562–1751* (Spartanburg, S.C.: Reprint Company, 1980); and Waddell, "Cusabo," 254–64.
6. "Mr. Carteret's Relation," in *The Shaftesbury Papers,* ed. Langdon Cheves (1897; rpt. Charleston: Tempus Publishing for the South Carolina Historical Society, 2000), 165–71; quotation appears on 168–69.
7. For the origins of the Westos, see Eric Bowne, *The Westo Indians: Slave Traders of the Early Colonial South* (Tuscaloosa: Univ. of Alabama Press, 2005), esp. 37–53; John T. Juricek, "The Westo Indians," *Ethnohistory* 11, no. 2 (Spring 1964): 134–73; Marvin T. Smith, *Archaeology of Aboriginal Culture Change* (Gainesville: Univ. Press of Florida, 1987), 131–32; and Gallay, *Indian Slave Trade,* 41–42.
8. Bushnell, *Situado and Sabana,* 134–35.
9. Richter, *Ordeal of the Longhouse,* 32–38; and Daniel K. Richter, "War and Culture: The Iroquois Experience," *William and Mary Quarterly,* 3rd ser., 40, no. 4 (Oct. 1983): 528–59.

10. Richter, *Ordeal of the Longhouse,* 62; Smith, *Archaeology,* 132; and Bowne, *Westo Indians,* 39–41 and 49–52. Most of these accounts can be traced to Jesuit relations of life in New France.
11. See Gallay, *Indian Slave Trade,* 41–43; Bowne, *Westo Indians,* 72–75; John Worth, *The Struggle for the Georgia Coast: An Eighteenth-Century Spanish Retrospective on Guale and Mocama,* Anthropological Papers of the American Museum of Natural History, no. 75 (New York: American Museum of Natural History, 1995), 17; and Maureen Meyers, "From Refugees to Slave Traders: The Transformation of the Westo Indians," in Ethridge and Shuck-Hall, *Mapping the Mississippian Shatter Zone,* 81–103.
12. It bears mentioning that the phrase "labor shortage" is relative in this usage. Carolina's planters needed labor to turn the sort of profit they believed befitted the climate of their new colony.
13. Woodward's *Faithfull Relation of My Westoe Voiage* was written in December 1674. It appears in A. S. Salley Jr., ed., *Narratives of Early Carolina, 1650–1708* (New York: Charles Scribner's Sons, 1911; New York: Barnes & Noble, 1939 and 1959), 125–34, and as "Woodwards Westo Discovery," in *The Shaftesbury Papers,* ed. Langdon Cheves (1897; rpt. Charleston: Tempus, for the South Carolina Historical Society, 2000), 456–62.
14. Woodward, *Faithfull Relation,* in Salley, *Narratives of Early Carolina,*133.
15. Though it is not mentioned explicitly, these could have been undertaken for the purposes of slaving and taking dressed skins; this would repeat a pattern established by the Five Nations in previous decades.
16. Woodward, *Faithfull Relation,* in Salley, *Narratives of Early Carolina,* 134. This should not be taken to mean that Anthony Ashley Cooper, Lord Shaftesbury, ever resided at the plantation—he just owned it.
17. Stephen Bull to Lord Ashley, Sept. 12, 1670, in *The Shaftesbury Papers,* ed. Langdon Cheves (1897; rpt. Charleston: Tempus, for the South Carolina Historical Society, 2000). Quotation appears on 194.
18. Bowne, *Westo Indians,* 79; and Crane, *Southern Frontier,* 6.
19. Eric Bowne, "'Caryinge awaye their Corne and Children': The Effects of Westo Slave Raids on the Indians of the Lower South," in Ethridge and Shuck-Hall, *Mapping the Mississippian Shatter Zone,* 104–14; and Matthew Jennings, "Violence in a Shattered World," 272–94, in the same volume.
20. As important as the Shawnees were to nineteenth-century American history, it is surprising so little has been written about them in earlier time periods. See James H. Howard, *Shawnee! The Ceremonialism of a Native Indian Tribe and Its Cultural Background* (Athens: Ohio Univ. Press, 1981), esp. 1–23; Jerry E. Clark, *The Shawnee* (Lexington: Univ. Press of Kentucky, 1993), esp. 5–27;

and Erminie Wheeler-Voegelin and Helen Hornbeck Tanner, *Indians of Ohio and Indiana Prior to 1795,* vol. 1 (New York: Garland, 1974), esp. 30–37. For Shawnee divisions in the Southeast, see Stephen Warren and Randolph Noe, "'The Greatest Travelers in America': Shawnee Survival in the Shatter Zone," in Ethridge and Shuck-Hall, *Mapping the Mississippian Shatter Zone,* 163–87.

21. June Namias, "Captives," and Theda Perdue, "Slavery," in *Encyclopedia of North American Indians: Native American History, Culture, and Life from Paleo-Indians to the Present,* ed. Frederick E. Hoxie (Boston: Houghton Mifflin, 1996), 99–101 and 596–98, respectively.
22. Bowne, *Westo Indians,* 85. Given the Shawnees' history of organized, methodical migrations, this explanation makes sense.
23. Woodward, *Faithfull Relation,* in Salley, *Narratives of Early Carolina,* 133–34.
24. Gallay, *Indian Slave Trade,* 60–61.
25. John Archdale, "A New Description of That Fertile and Pleasant Province of Carolina" (1707), in *Historical Collections of South Carolina,* ed. B. R. Carroll (New York: Harper & Brothers, 1836), 85–120; quotation on 88–89.
26. Bowne, *Westo Indians,* 100; and Wright, *Only Land They Knew,* 107.
27. Proprietors to Government and Council in Charles Town, Sept. 30, 1683, *BPRO* 1:256.
28. Accounts of the war, such as they are, can be found in Chapman Milling, *Red Carolinians* (Chapel Hill: Univ. of North Carolina Press, 1940), 82–83; Crane, *Southern Frontier,* 18–21; and Gallay, *Indian Slave Trade,* 57–58.
29. Bowne, *Westo Indians,* 106–7.
30. Craven, Albemarle, Shaftesbury, and P. Colleton to the Governor and Council att [*sic*] Ashley River, Feb. 21, 1680/81, *BPRO* 1:104–5.
31. Craven, Shaftesbury, and P. Colleton to the Governor and Council att [*sic*] Ashley River in Carolina, Mar. 7, 1680/81, *BPRO* 1:115–20; quotations on 115.
32. Thomas Newe, "Letters of Thomas Newe," in Salley, *Narratives of Early Carolina,* 177–87; quotation on 182.
33. Lawson, *New Voyage to Carolina,* 48. For a useful discussion of colonial authors' propensity to employ "warlike" to describe people, see Gallay, *Indian Slave Trade,* 173–75.
34. *Journals of the Commons House of Assembly,* 78 vols., ed. A. S. Salley Jr. (Columbia: Historical Commission of South Carolina, 1926–41), June 5, 1707–July 19, 1707 (hereafter cited as *JCHA,* with appropriate dates); references to the revolt and desertion of the Savannahs are on 26, 27, and 28. Gallay relied on these journals in *Indian Slave Trade,* 210–12. The Savannahs may have been fleeing Catawba attacks; it's also possible they recognized the danger of getting drawn too close to Carolina's Indian trade.

35. Fray Carlos Anguiano, letter of April 1663, trans. John E. Worth, in *The Struggle for the Georgia Coast: An Eighteenth-Century Spanish Retrospective on Guale and Mocama,* Anthropological Papers of the American Museum of Natural History No. 75 (Athens: Univ. of Georgia Press, 1995), 92. The term "Chichimeco" has led to a fair amount of confusion, since it was applied to raiding groups throughout northern New Spain. In the seventeenth-century Southeast, the term referred to the people known to the English as Westos (Richahecrians or Ricohockrians).
36. Captain Francisco de Fuentes, 1681 Census of Guale and Mocama, trans. John E. Worth, in Worth, *Struggle for the Georgia Coast,* 101. This should not imply that the Yamasees integrated themselves fully into the mission system. For the best overviews of late-seventeenth-century Yamasee life, see Worth's introductory essay to *Struggle for the Georgia Coast* and Gallay's *Indian Slave Trade.*
37. Bradley Schrager, "Yamasee Indians and the Challenge of Spanish and English Colonialism in the North American Southeast, 1660–1715," Ph.D. diss., Northwestern Univ. 2001, 71–72.
38. See, for instance, Merrell, *Indians' New World;* and Galloway, *Choctaw Genesis.* James Carson touches on several recent interpretations in *Searching for the Bright Path,* 9–11.
39. Lord Henry Cardross and William Dunlop to Peter Colleton, Mar. 27, 1685, quoted in George Pratt Insh, "Arrival of the Cardross Settlers," *South Carolina Historical and Genealogical Magazine* 30, no. 2 (Apr. 1929): 69–80; quotation appears on 75. See also Insh, "The *Carolina Merchant:* Advice of Arrival," *Scottish Historical Review* 25 (1928): 99–108. This calls to mind Juan Pardo's assignment to trace a road from South Carolina to Zacatecas.
40. Cardross and Dunlop to Colleton, quoted in Insh, "Arrival of the Cardross Settlers," 76.
41. Ibid.
42. The population figures come from Wood, "Changing Population of the Colonial South," 46. Westbrooke's letter, dated February 21, 1685, can be found in *BPRO* 2:8–9.
43. Bushnell, *Situado and Sabana,* 166–67.
44. "The Examination of Severall Yamasse Indians," *BPRO* 2:66.
45. Ibid.
46. Henry Woodward to John Godfrey (Deputy Governor), Mar. 21, 1685, *BPRO* 2:49.
47. When the Spanish retaliated in 1686, they did attack both Stuart's Town and several English plantations farther to the north. See Worth, *Struggle for the Georgia Coast,* 46.

48. "The Examination of Severall Yamasee Indians," *BPRO* 2:66; see also Bushnell, *Situado and Sabana,* 166–67, and Worth, *Struggle for the Georgia Coast,* 45–46.
49. Gallay, *Indian Slave Trade,* 79–80.
50. Worth, *Struggle for the Georgia Coast,* 146–71.
51. Gallay, *Indian Slave Trade,* 135.
52. Legislature to John Earl of Bath and the rest of the true and Absolute Lords and Proprietors of the Province of Carolina, *BPRO* 5:35. The date for the document can be found in Milling, *Red Carolinians,* 105.
53. Crane, *Southern Frontier,* 71–72; Daniel H. Usner Jr., *Indians, Settlers, and Slaves in a Frontier Exchange Economy* (Chapel Hill: Univ. of North Carolina Press, 1992), 18; and Gallay, *Indian Slave Trade,* 130–32.
54. Pierre Le Moyne d'Iberville, *Iberville's Gulf Journals,* trans. and ed. Richebourg Gaillard McWilliams (Tuscaloosa: Univ. of Alabama Press, 1981), 172. Quoted in Gallay, *Indian Slave Trade,* 131–32.
55. Gallay, *Indian Slave Trade,* 135–48. The city of St. Augustine was burned, but Carolina's army failed to take the Castillo San Marcos before it withdrew.
56. John Ash, "The Present State of Affairs in Carolina," 1706, in Salley, *Narratives of Early Carolina,* 267–76. Beyond this description, the tenor of which was shared by others, Ash's account is of minimal value. Ash and Moore were on opposite sides of a bitter factional struggle.
57. See *Firestorm and Ashes: The Siege of 1702,* vol. 39 of *El Escribano: St. Augustine Journal of History,* 2002; Gallay, *Indian Slave Trade,* 135–48; Mark F. Boyd, Hale G. Smith, and John W. Griffin, *Here They Once Stood: The Tragic End of the Apalachee Missions* (Gainesville: Univ. of Florida Press, 1951); Crane, *Southern Frontier,* 71–107; Hann, *History of the Timucua Indians,* 268–95; Worth, *Timucuan Chiefdoms of Spanish Florida,* 140–46; Charles W. Arnade, *The Siege of St. Augustine in 1702,* University of Florida Monographs, Social Sciences, no. 3, Summer 1959 (Gainesville: Univ. of Florida Press, 1959); and Steven Oatis, "'To Eat Up a Village of White Men': Anglo-Indian Designs on Mobile and Pensacola, 1705–1715," *Gulf South Historical Review* 14, no. 1 (Fall 1998): 104–19. Overviews of mission life appear in Milanich, *Florida Indians;* Bonnie G. McEwan, ed., *The Spanish Missions of La Florida* (Gainesville: Univ. Press of Florida, 1993); and John Hann and Bonnie G. McEwan, *The Apalachee Indians and Mission San Luis* (Gainesville: Univ. Press of Florida, 1998).
58. For a blow-by-blow account of Moore's activities, see the list of destroyed missions in Boyd, Smith, and Griffin, *Here They Once Stood,* 11–13. The torture testimony comes from a July 8, 1704, letter by Manuel Solana to Governor Zúñiga at San Luis (50–55). See also John E. Worth, "Razing Florida: The

Indian Slave Trade and the Devastation of Spanish Florida, 1659–1715," in Ethridge and Shuck-Hall, *Mapping the Mississippian Shatter Zone,* 295–311.

59. Nairne quoted in Crane, *Southern Frontier,* 81.
60. Wayne Lee argues that even in the era of increasing casualties and higher levels of violence, native notions about the limiting of conflict and its proper conduct persisted, even if they were muted. See Lee, "Peace Chiefs and Blood Revenge," 701.
61. Hahn, *Invention of the Creek Nation,* describes the nation as a colonial era phenomenon.
62. Steven J. Oatis, *A Colonial Complex: South Carolina's Frontiers in the Era of the Yamasee War, 1680–1730* (Lincoln: Univ. of Nebraska Press, 2004), 53; *JCHA,* Apr. 29, 1703.
63. *JCHA,* Aug. 13, 1701.
64. Ramsey, *Yamasee War;* William L. Ramsey, "'Something Cloudy in Their Looks': The Origins of the Yamasee War Reconsidered," *Journal of American History* 90, no. 1 (June 2003): 44–75, esp. n. 5. For works that treat the significance of trade, see Joel Martin, "Southeastern Indians and the English Trade in Skins and Slaves," in Hudson and Tesser, *Forgotten Centuries,* 304–24; James Merrell, "'Our Bond of Peace': Patterns of Intercultural Exchange in the Carolina Piedmont, 1650–1750," in *Powhatan's Mantle: Indians in the Colonial Southeast,* ed. Peter Wood, Gregory Waselkov, and M. Thomas Hatley (Lincoln: Univ. of Nebraska Press, 1989), 196–222; and Kathryn Holland Braund, *Deerskins and Duffels: Creek Indian Trade with Anglo-America, 1685–1815* (Lincoln: Univ. of Nebraska Press, 1993). As Ramsey points out, the study of the fur trade has produced one of the best such works: Richard White's *The Middle Ground: Indians, Empires, and Republics in the Great Lakes Region, 1650–1815* (Cambridge: Cambridge Univ. Press, 1992).

## Chapter 7

1. Secondary accounts of the execution rely on George Rodd's "Relation," which the *Calendar of State Papers* describes as a letter "to his Employer in London (forwarded by him to the King)." From "America and West Indies: May 1715, 1–15," *Calendar of State Papers Colonial, America and West Indies, vol. 28: 1714–1715* (1928): 161–82, http://www.british-history.ac.uk/report.aspx?compid=73961/ (accessed Feb. 1, 2010). The original, in French, can be found in *BPRO* 6:74–85. Caroline Gordon Richardson produced a translation in "Translations of Correspondence in French." Ramsey, *Yamasee War,* relies solely on Rodd, while Oatis, *Colonial Complex,* and Hahn, *Invention of the Creek Nation,* supplement this with a Spanish source. The main addition from the Spanish source is the information that a woman visited the town in the

predawn hours. Oatis, *Colonial Complex,* 112–39, argues that the notion that region-wide alliance acted in concert to destroy Carolina is a Carolina-manufactured myth.

2. Oatis, *Colonial Complex,* 146; Ramsey, *Yamasee War.*
3. Ramsey, *Yamasee War,* 2.
4. S. Max Edelson, *Plantation Enterprise in Colonial South Carolina* (Cambridge: Harvard Univ. Press, 2006), 52.
5. John E. Worth, "Yamasee," in William C. Sturtevant, gen. ed., *Handbook of North American Indians,* vol. 14, *Southeast,* ed. Raymond Fogelson (Washington, D.C.: Smithsonian Institution Press, 2004), 245–53.
6. Ramsey, *Yamasee War,* 171–81.
7. The act can be found in Thomas Cooper and David J. McCord, eds., *Statutes at Large of South Carolina* (Columbia, S.C., 1837), 2:309–16. See Crane, *Southern Frontier,* 147–52.
8. Thomas Nairn[e], *A Letter from South Carolina; Giving an Account of the Soil, Air, Product, Trade, Government, Laws, Religion, People, Military Strength, &c of that Province* (London, 1710), Eighteenth Century Collections Online, http://galenet.galegroup.com.proxy2.library.uiuc.edu/servlet/ECCO, Gale Document Number CW105826075/ (accessed Apr. 25, 2007), 4.
9. For the racial makeup of the slave population, see Ramsey, *Yamasee War,* 173. For Nairne's biography, see Alexander Moore, introduction to Nairne, *Nairne's Muskhogean Journals,* 3–31; and Walter Edgar and N. Louise Bailey, *Biographical Directory of the South Carolina House of Representatives,* vol. 2, *The Commons House of Assembly, 1692–1775* (Columbia: Univ. of South Carolina Press, 1977), 491–92. A brief Barnwell biography can be found on 52–54 of the *Biographical Dictionary.* I have not seen Barnwell's will, and those who have note that Barnwell's main wealth was in land, but in order to be elected to the Commons House of Assembly after 1721, one had to own at least ten slaves, and Barnwell was elected to the last of his several terms after this law was in place.
10. An online version of the map is available at the University of Georgia Library, http://www.libs.uga.edu/darchive/hargrett/maps/1720m6.jpg/ (accessed Apr. 25, 2007).
11. Nairne, *Nairne's Muskhogean Journals,* 73.
12. Ibid., 47–48.
13. Ibid., 75–76.
14. Moore, introduction to Nairne, *Nairne's Muskhogean Journals,* 15.
15. Nairne, *Nairne's Muskhogean Journals,* 49.
16. Ibid., 76, 50; Gallay, *Indian Slave Trade,* 176–77.

17. Nairne, *Nairne's Muskhogean Journals,* 42. Note the appearance of the color red in this context.
18. Ibid., 43.
19. Ibid., 58.
20. *Journals of the Commissioners of the Indian Trade, 1710–1718,* ed. W. L. McDowell (Columbia: South Carolina Archives Department, 1955), Sept. 21, 1710 (hereafter cited as *JCIT* with a reference to the date of the proceeding).
21. *JCIT,* May 4–6, 1714.
22. Long, "Small Postscript," 3–49, esp. 3.
23. Ramsey, *Yamasee War,* 83–87.
24. *JCIT,* Mar. 9, 1711.
25. What little we do know about John Barnwell can be found in Edgar and Bailey, *Biographical Directory of the South Carolina House of Representatives,* vol. 2, esp. 52–57; and Barnwell Rhett Hayward and A. S. Salley Jr., "Barnwell of South Carolina," *South Carolina Historical Magazine* 2, no. 1 (Jan. 1901): 46–88. All of the other secondary sources seem to lean heavily on these two, particularly the 1901 *SCHM* article. Barnwell also drafted a farsighted township plan for South Carolina, but he died before it could be implemented. Although his own religious inclinations are unclear, he sided with the dissenters against the High Church party during the crisis over the establishment of the Church of England in 1704–7 and for this stand temporarily lost his access to patronage. Although the church was eventually established, the Dissenters gained control of the legislature and he was back in.
26. Wayne Lee explains the debate over the causes of the war in "Fortify, Fight, or Flee," 713–70, esp. 731.
27. Barnwell believed upon reaching one of these Upper Tuscarora towns that the Virginians had "begged a most ignominious neutrality of these cowardly miscreants," who for their neutrality got goods at a cheap rate and were allowed to have their children be brought up at "the College."
28. The large majority of the Tuscaroras moved slowly north to join the Five Nations in the 1720s. Some North Carolina communities claim to be descended from Tuscaroras who did not make the move. The story of the Tuscarora War has been retold a number of times. See Milling, *Red Carolinians;* Douglas LeTell Rights, *The American Indian in North Carolina* (Durham, N.C.: Duke Univ. Press, 1947); Hugh T. Lefler and William S. Powell, *Colonial North Carolina: A History* (New York: Charles Scribner's Sons, 1973); and Merrell, *Indians' New World.* The North Carolina Department of Archives and History has published two relevant pamphlets: Theda Perdue, *Native Carolinians: The Indians of North Carolina* (Raleigh, 1985) and E. Lawrence Lee, *Indian Wars*

*in North Carolina, 1663–1673* (Raleigh, 1997). The war receives some treatment in histories of South Carolina as well.

29. John Barnwell, "The Journal of John Barnwell," *Virginia Magazine of History and Biography* 5 (Apr. 1898): 391–402, esp. 392–94. The second half of Barnwell's Tuscarora War journal was published in *Virginia Magazine of History and Biography* 6 (July 1898): 42–55 (hereafter cited as Barnwell's journal, with reference to appropriate page numbers).
30. Ibid., 395. There is a parallel here with the shock expressed by Massachusetts Bay Colony's native allies at the carnage at the fort on the Mystic River during the Pequot War.
31. Ibid.
32. For some thoughts on differing goals in European and Native American ways of war, see Perdue, *Cherokee Women,* esp. 86–114; and Starkey, *European and Native American Warfare,* esp. 17–56. These works mention Tuscaroras and Yamasees only in passing, but they do provide insights into the ways that other Native American peoples perceived armed conflict.
33. Barnwell's journal, 396–97.
34. Ibid., 397.
35. Ibid., 398.
36. Ibid., 397.
37. This simplifies a debate among historians concerning the feasibility of Barnwell taking Hancock's Town. Generally, historians writing from the North Carolina documents side with Governor Hyde, who chastised Barnwell for failing to prevail. Historians working in the South Carolina archives have been kinder, mostly because they are relying on Barnwell's journal.
38. Barnwell's journal, 398.
39. Ibid.
40. Nor were Native American slaves exclusively for export; in 1708, about the time South Carolina's African population first surpassed that of whites, fully one-quarter of the slaves working in South Carolina were Indians. Robert Weir makes this point forcefully in his *Colonial South Carolina.*
41. Barnwell's journal, 43.
42. Ibid., 394.
43. Ibid., 44.
44. Ibid., 45.
45. Oatis, *Colonial Complex,* 87. This imperial arrogance strikes me as more of a widespread European trait rather than a South Carolina–specific attribute. Of course, there were variations between the English colonies in terms of

their dates of settlement, the motivations for their development, and their reliance on African slavery, among other factors. I perceive the differences between the Carolinas' versions of colonization more as a difference in degrees rather than fundamental principles. South Carolina's version of colonization was arrogant, to be sure, but every type of colonization could be seen as arrogant to some extent.

46. Both Barnwell and Nairne had roots outside of England: in Ireland and Scotland, respectively. Once in Carolina, they both advanced imperial interests.
47. Barnwell's journal, 49–55; quotation appears on 55.
48. Rights, *American Indian in North Carolina,* 56.
49. Lee, *Indian Wars in North Carolina,* 31.
50. Baron de Graffenried described this event: "This so unchristian act very properly embittered the rest of the Tuscarora and Carolina Indians very much, although heathens, so that they no longer trusted the Christians." Quotation taken from Rights, *American Indian in North Carolina,* 56.
51. Lee, "Fortify, Fight, or Flee," 743–44.
52. Ibid. Lee attributes this to a poor decision to gather too many Tuscaroras in place, based upon an imperfectly applied adaptation of European fortification practices.
53. Schrager, "Yamasee Indians and the Challenge of Spanish and English Colonialism"; Steven Oatis, "A Colonial Complex: South Carolina's Changing Frontiers in the Era of the Yamasee War, 1680–1730," Ph.D. diss., Emory Univ., 1999; William Ramsey, "'Heathenish Combination': The Natives of the North American Southeast During the Era of the Yamasee War," Ph.D. diss., Tulane Univ., 1998; David Rayson, "'A Great Matter to Tell': Indians, Europeans, and Africans From the Mississippian Era Through the Yamasee War in the North American Southeast, 1550–1720," Ph.D. diss., Univ. of Minnesota, 1996; and Richard Durschlag, "The First Creek Resistance: Transformations in Creek Indian Existence and the Yamasee War, 1670–1730," Ph.D. diss., Duke Univ., 1995.
54. Ramsey, "Something Cloudy in Their Looks"; Ramsey, *Yamasee War;* Gallay, *Indian Slave Trade;* Oatis, *Colonial Complex;* and Hahn, *Invention of the Creek Nation.*
55. Ramsey, "Something Cloudy in their Looks," begins by tracing the debate from Verner Crane onward.
56. Ibid., 45–46.
57. Ramsey, *Yamasee War,* 90–97.
58. Rodd, "Relation," 74–85; Richardson, "Translations of Correspondence in French," Tr. 4.

59. On Yamasee language, see Worth, "Yamasee," 245.
60. Georges Sioui and Sheila Fischman, *For an Amerindian Autohistory: An Essay on the Foundations of a Social Ethic* (1992; rpt. Montreal: McGill-Queen's Univ. Press, 1995), 54–56; quoted material on 55.
61. Kathryn E. Holland Braund, "The Creek Indians, Blacks, and Slavery," *Journal of Southern History* 57, no. 4 (Nov. 1991): 601–36; quotation on 602. See also Joel Martin, *Sacred Revolt: The Muscogee's Struggle for a New World* (Boston: Beacon Press, 1991), 19, 27–28.
62. Sioui, *For an Amerindian Autohistory,* 54.
63. Ramsey, *Yamasee War,* 96. The quotation comes from the only document in a Yamasee voice which explains Yamasee motivations for fighting. Ramsey discovered the long-lost letter from the "Huspah King" enclosed in another letter (see 227–28).
64. Ibid., 116–17.
65. Francis Le Jau, *The Carolina Chronicle of Dr. Francis Le Jau, 1706–1717* (Berkeley and Los Angeles: Univ. of California Press, 1956), 161; and Ramsey, *Yamasee War,* 122.
66. Hatley, *Dividing Paths,* 31, 68.
67. Le Jau, *Carolina Chronicle,* 152.
68. Rodd, "Relation," 74–85; Richardson, "Translations of Correspondence in French," Tr. 6.
69. *BPRO* 6:86.
70. Ramsey posits a two-tiered alliance, wherein larger interior nations killed many traders but otherwise participated minimally in the war. See Ramsey, *Yamasee War,* 127–56.
71. Rodd, "Relation," 74–85; Richardson, "Translations of Correspondence in French," Tr. 8–9.
72. "The Council to the Proprietors," n.d. (between June 27 June and July 4, 1670), in *The Shaftesbury Papers,* ed. Langdon Cheves (1897; rpt. Charleston: Tempus, for the South Carolina Historical Society, 2000), 175.
73. Ibid., 176.
74. Judith A. Carney, "Rice Milling, Gender, and Slave Labour," *Past and Present* 153 (Nov. 1996): 108–34.
75. Edelson, *Plantation Enterprise,* 135.
76. *BPRO* 7:146; Oatis, *Colonial Complex,* 164.
77. *BPRO* 7:183.
78. *BPRO* 7:75.

79. Lawson, *New Voyage to Carolina,* 10. John Lawson spoke too soon in his own case; he was put to death by Tuscaroras in the opening stages of that war.
80. Weir, *Colonial South Carolina,* 101.
81. Gallay, *Indian Slave Trade,* 345–51.
82. Ramsey, *Yamasee War,* 119.

## Chapter 8

1. South Carolina Department of Archives and History, "National Register Properties in South Carolina, Stono River Slave Rebellion Site, Charleston County (off U.S. Hwy. 17, Rantowles vicinity)," National Register of Historic Places, http://www.nationalregister.sc.gov/charleston/S10817710075/index.htm (accessed Feb. 5, 2010). Original National Register form available at http://www.nationalregister.sc.gov/charleston/S10817710075/S10817710075.pdf/ (accessed Feb. 5, 2010).
2. "The Stono Rebellion," Historical Marker Database, http://www.hmdb.org/marker.asp?marker=14855/ (accessed Feb. 5, 2010).
3. A most influential treatment of nations and nationhood can be found in Benedict Anderson, *Imagined Communities: Reflections on the Origin and Spread of Nationalism* (1983; rpt. New York: Verso, 2006).
4. The Fundamental Constitutions did contain the instruction that "every Freeman of Carolina shall have absolute power and authority over Negro slaves, of what opinion or Religion soever." See A. Leon Higginbotham Jr., *In the Matter of Color: Race and the American Legal Process,* vol. 1, *The Colonial Period* (Oxford: Oxford Univ. Press, 1980), 163.
5. Ibid., 167; Thomas Cooper and David J. McCord, eds., *Statutes at Large of South Carolina* (Columbia, S.C., 1840), 7:352.
6. Higginbotham, *In the Matter of Color,* 167; Cooper and McCord, *Statutes at Large of South Carolina* 7:352. See also Wood, *Black Majority,* 278.
7. Higginbotham, *In the Matter of Color,* 189; Cooper and McCord, *Statutes at Large of South Carolina* 7:353–54.
8. Higginbotham, *In the Matter of Color,* 191.
9. Wood, *Black Majority,* 135; Le Jau, *Carolina Chronicle,* 55.
10. Wood, *Black Majority,* 283.
11. Ibid., 284.
12. Mark M. Smith, *Stono: Documenting and Interpreting a Southern Slave Revolt* (Columbia: South Carolina Press, 2005), 8.
13. Olwell, *Masters, Slaves, and Subjects,* 189.

14. Wood, *Black Majority,* 279.
15. That the documentation of such forced sex is lean is not terribly surprising: no evidence has ever turned up of a white man being convicted of raping an enslaved woman between 1700 and the 1860s. The topic of forced sex between masters and slaves is a crucial and complicated one that deserves fuller treatment beyond the narrow focus of this study. Masters had many tools—including brute force—at their disposal to coerce enslaved women to have sex with them. Some relied on other forms of persuasion as well. Though enslaved women were unable to wholly avoid being raped, they were not without some modicum of human agency in the situation. There are documented cases, albeit outside of colonial Carolina, of enslaved women exacting promises in exchange for coerced sex, or forcing the rapes out into the open. See Sharon Block, *Rape and Sexual Power in Early America* (Chapel Hill: Univ. of North Carolina Press, 2006), 64–73, and Gwyn Campbell, Suzanne Miers, and Joseph C. Miller, eds., *Women and Slavery,* vol. 2: *The Modern Atlantic* (Athens: Ohio Univ., 2008).
16. Smith, *Stono,* xiii; James Carson, *Making an Atlantic World: Circles, Paths and Stories from the Colonial South* (Knoxville: Univ. of Tennessee Press, 2007), 112–15; and Wood, *Black Majority,* 308–26.
17. Thornton, "African Dimensions of the Stono Rebellion," 1101–13; quotation appears on 1109.
18. Smith, *Stono,* 15.
19. Smith, in an article collected in *Stono,* notes that the rebels were slightly off. They had timed their rebellion by the Julian, rather than the Gregorian, calendar. See Smith, *Stono,* 117.
20. "Account of the Negroe Insurrection in South Carolina," in Smith, *Stono,* 13–15; quoted material on 15.
21. Smith, *Stono;* Carson, *Making an Atlantic World,* 112–15; and Wood, *Black Majority,* 308–26. Carson points out the style of violence preferred by the rebels.
22. Smith, *Stono,* 20–27.
23. Wood, *Black Majority,* 293; Cooper and McCord, *Statutes at Large of South Carolina* 7:402.
24. *South Carolina Gazette,* Oct. 14, 1732, quoted in Wood, *Black Majority,* 293.
25. Morgan, *Slave Counterpoint,* 612.
26. Ibid., 617.
27. Cooper and McCord, *Statutes at Large of South Carolina* 7:423.
28. Berlin, *Many Thousands Gone,* 81.

29. Hall, *Africans in Colonial Louisiana*, 103; and Berlin, *Many Thousands Gone*, 89.
30. Slotkin, *Regeneration Through Violence.*
31. George Chicken, "Journal of Colonel George Chicken," *City of Charleston, Year Book—1894* (Charleston, S.C.: Walker, Evans and Cogswell, 1894), 345.
32. Quoted in Hatley, *Dividing Paths*, 27.
33. Oatis, *Colonial Complex*, 189.
34. Rena Vassar, "Some Short Remarkes on the Indian Trade in the Charikees and in Management thereof since the Year 1717," *Ethnohistory* 8, no. 4 (Autumn 1961): 401–23; quoted material appears on 414.
35. Tiya Miles, *Ties that Bind: The Story of an Afro-Cherokee Family in Slavery and Freedom* (Berkeley and Los Angeles: Univ. of California Press, 2005), 28–29.
36. Hatley, *Dividing Paths*, 28.
37. James Oglethorpe, *Some Account of the Design of the Trustees for Establishing Colonys [sic] in America*, ed. Rodney Baine and Phinizy Spalding (Athens: Univ. of Georgia Press, 1990), xv.
38. Matthew Jennings, "Violence in a Shattered World," in Ethridge and Shuck-Hall, *Mapping the Mississippian Shatter Zone*, 272–94.
39. Quoted in Hahn, *Invention of the Creek Nation*, 152.
40. Ibid., 152–53.
41. Ibid., 153–54.
42. Green, *Politics of Indian Removal.*
43. Hahn, *Invention of the Creek Nation*, 149–85, esp. 157–60.
44. Thomas Causton to his Wife, 1733, in *General Oglethorpe's Georgia: Colonial Letters, 1733–1743*, ed. Mills Lane (Savannah, Ga.: Beehive Press, 1975), 9. White, of course, was the color most closely associated with civil leadership and peace in the Muskogee world.
45. Sweet, *Negotiating for Georgia*, 24–39; Hahn, *Invention of the Creek Nation*, 154–55.
46. Alden Vaughan, series ed., *Early American Indian Documents: Treaties and Laws, 1607–1789*, vol. 9, *Georgia and Florida Treaties, 1763–1776*, ed. John T. Juricek (Bethesda, Md.: University Publications of America, 2001), 9.
47. Juricek, *Georgia and Florida Treaties*, 9.
48. James Oglethorpe, "A Curious Account of the Indians," in Juricek, *Georgia and Florida Treaties*, 9–10.
49. Ibid.
50. Peter Gordon's journal, in Juricek, *Georgia and Florida Treaties*, 9.

51. Thomas Causton to his Wife, in *General Oglethorpe's Georgia: Colonial Letters, 1733–1743,* ed. Mills Lane (Savannah, Ga.: Beehive Press, 1975), 9.
52. Quoted in Sweet, *Negotiating for Georgia,* 32.
53. *South Carolina Gazette,* July 7, 1733; quoted in Hahn, *Invention of the Creek Nation,* 156.
54. Charles C. Jones, *Historical Sketch of Tomo-Chi-Chi, Mico of the Yamacraws* (Albany, N.Y.: Joel Munsell, 1868), 30.
55. Ibid.
56. Ibid., 31.
57. Hahn, *Invention of the Creek Nation,* 156–58.
58. Ibid., 173–85.
59. Betty Wood, *Slavery in Colonial Georgia* (Athens: Univ. of Georgia Press, 1984).
60. Ibid., 24–43.
61. Ibid., 74–109.
62. See Hahn, *Invention of the Creek Nation,* esp. 229–77. For nationalism and identity in general, see Anderson, *Imagined Communities.* On national identities among Native American peoples, see Nancy Shoemaker, *A Strange Likeness: Becoming Red and White in Eighteenth-Century North America* (New York: Oxford Univ. Press, 2004), 6–8.
63. National Park Service, "Ocmulgee," n.d.
64. Samuel Dyssli, a Swiss settler, wrote from Charles Town to his family on December 3, 1737. The letter appears in "Swiss Settlers in South Carolina," *South Carolina Historical and Genealogical Magazine,* ed. R. W. Kelsey, 22, no. 3 (July 1922): 85–91. The quotation appears on 90.

# Bibliography

## Primary Sources

*A 17th Century Letter of Gabriel Diaz Vara Calderón, Bishop of Cuba, Describing the Indians and Indian Missions of Florida.* Washington, D.C.: Smithsonian Institution Press, 1936.

Abrahams, Roger D., and John F. Szwed, eds. *After Africa: Extracts from British Travel Accounts and Journals of the Seventeenth, Eighteenth, and Nineteenth Centuries Concerning the Slaves, their Manners, and Customs in the British West Indies.* New Haven: Yale Univ. Press, 1983.

Abreu de Galindo, Juan de. *The History of the Discovery and Conquest of the Canary Islands.* London: George Glas, 1764. Eighteenth Century Collections Online. http://galenet.galegroup.com.proxy2.library.uiuc.edu/servlet/ECCO/. Gale Document Number CW103754529. Accessed Apr. 25, 2007.

Adair, James. *The History of the American Indians.* Edited and with an introduction by Kathryn E. Holland Braund. 1775. Rpt. Tuscaloosa: Univ. of Alabama Press, 2005.

*Alonso de Posada Report, 1686: A Description of the Area of the Present Southern United States in the Seventeenth Century.* Trans. and ed. Alfred Barnaby Thomas. Pensacola, Fla.: Perdido Bay Press, 1982.

Bartram, William. *The Travels of William Bartram.* Ed. Francis Harper. Naturalist's Edition. New Haven: Yale Univ. Press, 1958.

———, *William Bartram on the Southeastern Indians,* ed. Gregory A. Waselkov and Kathryn E. Holland Braund. Lincoln: Univ. of Nebraska Press, 1995.

Beacon, Richard. *Solon His Follie, or A Politique Discourse touching the Reformation of common-weales conquered, declined, or corrupted.* 1594. Rpt. Binghamton, N.Y.: Medieval and Renaissance Texts and Studies, 1996.

Bennett, Charles E. *Laudonnière and Fort Caroline: History and Documents.* Gainesville: Univ. of Florida Press,1964; Tuscaloosa: Univ. of Alabama Press, 2001.

Bossu, Jean-Bernard. *Travels Through That Part of North America Formerly Called Louisiana.* 2 vols. London, 1771. http://www.archive.org/stream/travelsthroughth01boss#page/296/mode/2up.

Cabeza de Vaca, Álvar Núñez. *The Narrative of Cabeza de Vaca.* Edited, translated, and with an introduction by Rolena Adorno and Patrick Charles Pautz. Lincoln: Univ. of Nebraska Press, 2003.

*The Carolina Chronicle of Dr. Francis Le Jau, 1706–1717.* Ed. Frank J. Klingberg. Berkeley and Los Angeles: Univ. of California Press, 1956.

Carroll, B. R., ed. *Historical Collections of South Carolina.* 2 vols. New York: Harper & Brothers, 1836.

del Castillo, Bernal Díaz. *The Conquest of New Spain,* trans. J. M. Cohen. London: Viking Penguin, 1963.

Cheves, Langdon, ed. *The Shaftesbury Papers.* 1897. Rpt. Charleston: Tempus for the South Carolina Historical Society, 2000.

Churchyard, Thomas. *A Generall Rehearsall of Warres, called Churchyardes choise wherein is fiue hundred seuerall seruices of land and sea as seiges, battailes, skirmiches, and encounters.* London, 1579. Early English Books Online. http://gateway.proquest.com.proxy2.library.uiuc.edu/openurl?ctx_ver=Z39.88-2003&res_id=xri:eebo&rft_id=xri:eebo:citation:99843573/. Accessed Apr. 25, 2007.

———. *The miserie of Flaunders, calamitie of Fraunce, misfortune of Portugall, vnquietnes of Irelande, troubles of Scotlande: and the blessed state of England.* London, 1579. Early English Books Online. http://gateway.proquest.com.proxy2.library.uiuc.edu/openurl?ctx_ver=Z39.88-2003&res_id=xri:eebo&rft_id=xri:eebo:citation:99840763/. Accessed Apr. 25, 2007.

*City of Charleston, Year Book—1894.* Charleston, S.C.: Walker, Evans and Cogswell, 1984.

Clayton, Lawrence A., Vernon James Knight, and Edward C. Moore, eds. *The De Soto Chronicles: The Expedition of Hernando de Soto to North America in 1539–1542.* 2 vols. Tuscaloosa: Univ. of Alabama Press, 1993.

*Colonial Records of North Carolina.* 10 vols. Ed. William L. Saunders. Raleigh, N.C.: Josephus Daniels, 1886–90.

*Colonial Records of North Carolina.* Second Series. *Records of the Executive Council.* 3 vols. Ed. Robert J. Cain. Raleigh, N.C.: Division of Archives and History, 1984, 1988, and 1994.

*Colonial Records of South Carolina: Documents Relating to Indian Affairs, 1750–1754.* 2 vols. Ed. William L. McDowell Jr. 1958. Rpt. Columbia: South Carolina Department of Archives and History, 1992.

*Colonial Records of South Carolina: Documents Relating to Indian Affairs, 1754–1765.* Ed. William L. McDowell Jr. 1970. Rpt. Columbia: South Carolina Department of Archives and History, 1992.

*Colonial Records of South Carolina: Journals of the Commissioners of the Indian Trade, 1710–1718.* Ed. William L. McDowell. Columbia: South Carolina Archives Department, 1955.

Columbus, Christopher. *The Diario of Christopher Columbus's First Voyage to America, 1492–93.* Transcribed and translated by Oliver Dunn and James E. Kelley Jr. Norman: Univ. of Oklahoma Press, 1989.

Cooper, Thomas, and David J. McCord, eds. *Statutes at Large of South Carolina.* 10 vols. Columbia, S.C., 1836–41.

Crashaw, William. *A sermon preached in London before the right honorable the Lord Lawarre, Lord Governour and Captaine Generall of Virginea.* London, 1609. Early English Books Online. http://gateway.proquest.com.proxy2.library.uiuc.edu/openurl?ctx_ver=Z39.88-2003&res_id=xri:eebo&rft_id=xri:eebo:citation:99844721/. Accessed Apr. 25, 2007.

De Bry, Theodor. *Thomas Hariot's Virginia.* 1590. Rpt. Ann Arbor: University Microfilms, 1966.

Derricke, John. *The Image of Irelande.* 1581. Rpt. Edinburgh, 1883.

Díaz del Castillo, Bernal. *The Conquest of New Spain.* Translated by J. M. Cohen. London: Viking Penguin, Penguin Classics, 1963.

*Documentos Históricos de La Florida y La Luisiana.* Madrid: Librería General de Victoriano Suárez, 1912.

*Documents Concerning English Voyages to the Spanish Main, 1569–1580.* Works Issued by the Hakluyt Society, second series, vol. 71. London: Hakluyt Society, 1932.

"Documents Concerning Rev. Samuel Thomas, 1702–1707." *South Carolina Historical and Genealogical Magazine* 5. no. 1 (Jan. 1904): 21–99.

*Early American Indian Documents: Treaties and Laws, 1607–1789.* Gen ed. Alden T. Vaughan. Bethesda, Md.: University Publications of America, 2001.

*An Early Florida Adventure Story by Fray Andrés de San Miguel.* Translated by John H. Hann. Gainesville: Univ. Press of Florida, 2001.

Gatschet, Albert S. *A Migration Legend of the Creek Indians.* Philadelphia, 1888.

Gentleman, I. B. [Thomas Smith.] *A Letter Sent by I. B. Gentleman vnto his very frende Maystet* [*sic*] *R. C. Esquire vvherin is conteined a large discourse of the peopling & inhabiting the cuntrie called the Ardes, and other adiacent in the north of Ireland, and taken in hand by Sir Thomas Smith one of the Queenes Maiesties priuie Counsel, and Thomas Smith Esquire, his sonne.* London, 1572. Early English Books Online. http://gateway.proquest.com.proxy2.library.uiuc.edu/openurl?ctx_ver=Z39.88-2003&res_id=xri:eebo&rft_id=xri:eebo:citation:99836219/. Accessed Apr. 25, 2007.

Gerónimo de Oré, Luís. *The Martyrs of Florida, 1513–1616.* Translated by Maynard Geiger. Franciscan Studies, No. 18. July 1936.

Hakluyt, Richard. *Discourse on Western Planting.* Ed. David B. Quinn and Alison M. Quinn. London: Hakluyt Society, 1993.

Hariot, Thomas. *A Brief and True Report of the Discovery of the New Found Land of Virginia.* 1588. Rpt. Ann Arbor: University Microfilms, 1966.

Hawkins, Benjamin. *The Collected Works of Benjamin Hawkins, 1796–1810.* Ed. Thomas Foster. Tuscaloosa: Univ. of Alabama Press, 2003.

Hudson, Charles. *The Juan Pardo Expeditions: Exploration of the Carolinas and Tennessee, 1566–1568*. Washington, D.C.: Smithsonian Institution Press, 1990. Rev. ed., Tuscaloosa: Univ. of Alabama Press, 2005.

*Iberville's Gulf Journals*. Trans. and ed. Richebourg Gaillard McWilliams. University: Univ. of Alabama Press, 1981.

Johnson, Robert. *Nova Britannia offering most excellent fruites by planting in Virginia: exciting all such as be well affected to further the same*. London, 1609. Early English Books Online. http://gateway.proquest.com.proxy2.library.uiuc.edu/openurl?ctx_ver=Z39.88-2003&res_id=xri:eebo&rft_id=xri:eebo:citation:22924007/. Accessed Apr. 25, 2007.

"Journall: Capt. Dunlop's Voyage to the Southward, 1687." Contributed by J. G. Dunlop. Notes by Mabel L. Weber. *South Carolina Historical and Genealogical Magazine* 30, no. 3 (July 1929): 127–33.

*Journal of Colonel John Herbert, Commissioner of Indian Affairs for the Province of South Carolina, October 17, 1727, to March 19, 1727/8*. Ed. A. S. Salley Jr. Columbia: Historical Commission of South Carolina, 1936.

"Journal of John Barnwell." *Virginia Historical Magazine* 6, no. 1 (July 1898): 42–55.

*Journals of the Commons House of Assembly*. 78 vols. Ed. A. S. Salley Jr. Columbia: Historical Commission of South Carolina, 1926–41.

*Journals of the Grand Council, 1671–1680*. Columbia: South Carolina Department of Archives and History, 1907.

Kimber, Edward. *A Relation or Journal of a Late Expedition to the Gates of St. Augustine on Florida*. 1744. Rpt. Boston: Charles E. Goodspeed, 1935.

Lane, Mills, ed. *General Oglethorpe's Georgia: Colonial Letters, 1733–1743*. Savannah, Ga.: Beehive Press, 1975.

Laudonnière, René. *Three Voyages*. Translated with an introduction and notes by Charles E. Bennett, foreword by Jerald T. Milanich. Gainesville: Univ. Presses of Florida, 1975; Tuscaloosa: Univ. of Alabama Press, 2001.

Lawson, John. *A New Voyage to Carolina*. Edited and with an introduction and notes by Hugh Talmage Lefler. 1709. Rpt. Chapel Hill: Univ. of North Carolina Press, 1967.

Le Challeux, Nicolas. *A true and perfect description, of the last voyage or navigation, attempted by Capitaine John Rybaut deputie and generall for the French men, into Terra Florida, this yeare past. 1565*. London, 1566. Early English Books Online. http://gateway.proquest.com.proxy2.library.uiuc. edu/openurl?ctx_ver=Z39.88-2003&res_id=xri:eebo&rft_id=xri:eebo:citation:99842600/. Accessed Apr. 25, 2007.

"Letters from John Stewart to William Dunlop." Contributed by J. G. Dunlop, note by Mabel L. Webber. *South Carolina Historical and Genealogical Magazine* 32, no. 1 (Jan. 1931): 1–174.

Ligon, Richard. *A true & exact history of the island of Barbados.* London, 1657. Early English Books Online. http://gateway.proquest.com.proxy2.library.uiuc.edu/openurl?ctx_ver=Z39.88-2003&res_id=xri:eebo&rft_id=xri:eebo:citation:12703788/. Accessed Apr. 25, 2007.

Longe, Alexander. "A Small Postscript on the ways and maners of the Nashon of Indians called Charikees." Ed. David H. Corkran. *Southern Indian Studies* 31 (Oct. 1969): 3–49.

Lorant, Stefan. *The New World: The First Pictures of America.* New York: Duell, Sloan and Pearce, 1965.

*The Luna Papers: Documents Relations to the Expedition of Don Tristán de Luna y Arellano for the Conquest of La Florida in 1559–1561.* 2 vols. Trans. and ed. Herbert Ingram Priestley. Deland: Florida State Historical Society, 1928.

Lyon, Eugene. *The Enterprise of Florida: Pedro Menéndez de Avilés and the Spanish Conquest of 1565–1568.* Gainesville: Univ. Presses of Florida, 1976.

Mason, John. *Brief History of the Pequot War.* 1736. Ann Arbor: University Microfilms, 1966.

Menéndez de Avilés, Pedro. *Cartas sobre la Florida, 1555–1574.* Ed. Juan Carlos Mercado. Madrid: Iberoamericana, 2002.

Merrens, H. Roy, ed. *The Colonial South Carolina Scene: Contemporary Views, 1697–1774.* Columbia: Univ. of South Carolina Press, 1977.

Murray, James C. *Spanish Chronicles of the Indies: Sixteenth Century.* New York: Twayne, 1994.

Nairn[e], Thomas. *A Letter from South Carolina; Giving an Account of the Soil, Air, Product, Trade, Government, Laws, Religion, People, Military Strength, &c of that Province.* London, 1710. Eighteenth Century Collections Online. http://galenet.galegroup.com.proxy2.library.uiuc.edu/servlet/ECCO/. Gale Document Number CW105826075. Accessed Apr. 25, 2007.

*Nairne's Muskhogean Journals: The 1708 Expedition to the Mississippi River.* Edited with an introduction by Alexander Moore. Jackson: Univ. Press of Mississippi, 1988.

*Narratives of Early Carolina, 1650–1708.* Ed. Alexander S. Salley Jr. New York: Charles Scribner's Sons, 1911; New York: Barnes & Noble, 1959.

Oglethorpe, James. *Some Account of the Design of the Trustees for Establishing Colonys [sic] in America.* Ed. Rodney Baine and Phinizy Spalding. Athens: Univ. of Georgia Press, 1990.

Quinn, David Beers. *New American World: A Documentary History of North America to 1612.* 5 vols. New York: Arno Press, 1979.

———. *The Roanoke Voyages, 1584–1590.* London: Hakluyt Society, 1955.

———. *Set Fair for Roanoke: Voyages and Colonies, 1584–1606.* Chapel Hill: Univ. of North Carolina Press, 1985.

*Records in the British Public Record Office Relating to South Carolina, 1663–1782.* 37 vols. Columbia: South Carolina Department of Archives and History.

*The Records of the Virginia Company of London.* 4 vols. Washington, D.C.: Government Printing Office, 1906–35.

Ribaut, Jean. *The Whole and True Discouerye of Terra Florida.* Facsimile of 1563 London ed. Gainesville: Univ. Press of Florida, 1964.

Richardson, Caroline Gordon. "Translations of Correspondence in French in Volumes 1–17 of the Records from the British Public Records Office Owned by the Historical Commission of South Carolina." Master's thesis, Univ. of South Carolina, 1947.

Ruidíaz y Caravia, Eugenio. *La Florida: Su Conquista y Colonización por Pedro Menéndez de Avilés.* 2 vols. Madrid: Hijos de J. A. García, 1893.

Sidney, Philip. *Miscellaneous Prose of Sir Philip Sidney.* Ed. Katherine Duncan Jones and Jan Van Dorsten. Oxford: Oxford Univ. Press, 1973.

Smith, John. *Captain John Smith: A Select Edition of His Writings.* Ed. Karen Ordahl Kupperman. Chapel Hill: Univ. of North Carolina Press, 1988.

———. *The Generall Historie of Virginia, New-England, and the Summer Isles.* 1624. Ann Arbor: University Microfilms, 1966.

Solís de Merás, Gonzalo. *Pedro Menéndez de Avilés y la Conquista de la Florida.* Original text dates to the sixteenth century. Oviedo, Spain: Grupo Editorial Asturiano, 1990.

*South Carolina Gazette.* Charleston, 1732–75.

*Southeastern Indians: Life Portraits, A Catalogue of Pictures, 1540–1860.* Ed. Emma Lila Funderburk. 1958. Rpt. Tallahassee: Rose Printing, 1996.

*Spanish Borderlands Sourcebooks.* 27 vols. Gen. ed. David Hurst Thomas. New York: Garland, 1991.

*Spanish Documents Concerning English Voyages to the Caribbean, 1527–1568.* Works Issued by the Hakluyt Society, Second Series, vol. 62. London: Hakluyt Society, 1928.

Spenser, Edmund. *A View of the Present State of Ireland.* Ed. Andrew Hadfield and Willy Maley. 1633. Rpt. Oxford: Blackwell, 1997.

Strachey, William. *Historie of Travaile into Virginia.* Original text dates to c. 1612. Works Issued by the Hakluyt Society, vol. 6. London: Hakluyt Society, 1849.

*Travels in the American Colonies.* Ed. Newton D. Mereness. New York: Macmillan, 1916.

Underhill, John. *Newes from America.* London, 1638. Early English Books Online. http://gateway.proquest.com.proxy2.library.uiuc.edu/openurl?ctx_ver=Z39.88-2003&res_id=xri:eebo&rft_id=xri:eebo:citation:99846827/. Accessed Apr. 25, 2007.

*Warrants for Lands in South Carolina, 1672–1711.* Ed. A. S. Salley Jr. Columbia: Univ. of South Carolina Press, 1973.

Waterhouse, Edward. *A declaration of the state of the colony and affaires in Virginia With a relation of the barbarous massacre in the time of peace and league.* London, 1622. Early English Books Online. http://gateway.proquest.com.proxy2.library.uiuc.edu/openurl?ctx_ver=Z39.88-2003&res_id=xri:eebo&rft_id=xri:eebo:citation:99846899/. Accessed Apr. 25, 2007.

Williams, George W., ed. "Letters to the Bishop of London from the Commissaries in South Carolina." *South Carolina Historical Magazine* 78, no. 1 (Jan. 1977): 1–31.

## Secondary Sources

Addington, Larry H. *The Patterns of War Through the Eighteenth Century.* Bloomington: Indiana Univ. Press, 1990.

Anderson, David G. *The Savannah River Chiefdoms: Political Change in the Late Prehistoric Southeast.* Tuscaloosa: Univ. of Alabama Press, 1994.

Anderson, Fred, and Andrew Cayton. *The Dominion of War: Empire and Liberty in North America, 1500–2000.* New York: Viking, 2005.

Andrews, Kenneth R. *The Spanish Caribbean: Trade and Plunder, 1530–1630.* New Haven: Yale Univ. Press, 1978.

Andrews, K. R. "The English in the Caribbean, 1560–1620." In *The Westward Enterprise: English Activities in Ireland, the Atlantic, and America, 1480–1650,* ed. K. R. Andrews, N. P. Canny, and H. E. P. Hair, 103–23. Detroit: Wayne State Univ. Press, 1979.

Ansell, S. T. "Legal and Historical Aspects of the Militia." *Yale Law Review* 26, no. 6 (Apr. 1917): 471–80.

Arkush, Elizabeth, and Mark W. Allen, eds. *The Archaeology of Warfare: Prehistories of Raiding and Conquest.* Gainesville: Univ. Press of Florida, 2006.

Armitage, David. *The Ideological Origins of the British Empire.* Cambridge: Cambridge Univ. Press, 2000.

Arnade, Charles W. *The Siege of St. Augustine in 1702.* University of Florida Monographs, Social Sciences, No. 3. Gainesville: Univ. Press of Florida, 1959.

Axtell, James. *The Indians' New South: Cultural Change in the Colonial Southeast.* Baton Rouge: Louisiana State Univ. Press, 1997.

Banner, Stuart. *How the Indians Lost Their Land: Law and Power on the Frontier.* Cambridge: Harvard Univ. Press, 2005.

Barker, Alex W., and Timothy R. Pauketat, eds. *Lords of the Southeast: Social Inequality and the Native Elites of Southeastern North America.* Archeological Papers of the American Anthropological Association, No. 3. Washington, D.C.: American Anthropological Association, 1992.

Basso, Keith. *Wisdom Sits in Places: Landscape and Language Among the Western Apache.* Albuquerque: Univ. of New Mexico Press, 1996.

Bender, Thomas. *A Nation Among Nations: America's Place in World History.* New York: Hill and Wang, 2006.

Bennassar, Bartolomé. *The Spanish Character: Attitudes and Mentalities form the Sixteenth to the Nineteenth Century.* Translated by Benjamin Keen. Berkeley and Los Angeles: Univ. of California Press, 1979.

Berlin, Ira. *Many Thousands Gone: The First Two Centuries of Slavery in North America.* Cambridge: Belknap Press of Harvard Univ. Press, 1998.

Black, Jeremy. *European Warfare, 1494–1660.* London: Routledge, 2002.

Blackhawk, Ned. *Violence over the Land: Indians and Empires in the Early American West.* Cambridge: Harvard Univ. Press, 2006.

Blitz, John H. *Ancient Chiefdoms of the Tombigbee.* Tuscaloosa: Univ. of Alabama Press, 1993.

———. "Mississippian Chiefdoms and the Fission-Fusion Process." *American Antiquity* 64, no. 4 (Oct. 1999): 577–92.

Bolton, Herbert E., and Mary Ross. *The Debatable Land: A Sketch of the Anglo-Spanish Contest for the Georgia Country.* 1925. Rpt. New York: Russell & Russell, 1968.

Bolton, S. C. "South Carolina and the Reverend Doctor Francis Le Jau: Southern Society and the Conscience of an Anglican Missionary." *Historical Magazine of the Protestant Episcopal Church* 40, no. 1 (Mar. 1971): 63–80.

Boudreaux, Edmond A. *The Archaeology of Town Creek.* Tuscaloosa: Univ. of Alabama Press, 2007.

Bowne, Eric. *The Westo Indians: Slave Traders of the Early Colonial South.* Tuscaloosa: Univ. of Alabama Press, 2005.

Boyd, Mark F., Hale G. Smith, and John W. Griffin. *Here They Once Stood: The Tragic End of the Apalachee Missions.* Gainesville: Univ. of Florida Press, 1951.

Braddick, M. J. "An English Military Revolution?" *Historical Journal* 36, no. 4 (Dec. 1993): 965–75.

Brain, Jeffrey D., and Philip Phillips, *Shell Gorgets: Styles of the Late Prehistoric and Protohistoric Southeast.* Cambridge: Harvard Univ. Press, 1996.

Braund, Kathryn E. Holland. *Deerskins and Duffels: Creek Indian Trade with Anglo-America, 1685–1815.* Lincoln: Univ. of Nebraska Press, 1993.

Bridenbaugh, Carl, and Roberta. *No Peace Beyond the Line: The English in the Caribbean, 1624–1690.* New York: Oxford Univ. Press, 1972.

Brooks, James. *Captives and Cousins: Slavery, Kinship, and Community in the Southwest Borderlands.* Chapel Hill: Univ. of North Carolina Press, 2002.

Brown, James, David S. Brose, and David W. Penney. *Ancient Art of the American Woodland Indians.* New York: Harry N. Abrams in association with the Detroit Institute of Arts, 1985.

Brown, Jennifer S. H., and Elizabeth Vibert, eds. *Reading Beyond Words: Contexts for Native History.* Peterborough, Ont.: Broadview Press, 1996.

Brown, Philip M. "Early Indian Trade in the Development of South Carolina: Politics, Economics, and Social Mobility During the Proprietary Period, 1670–1719." *South Carolina Historical Magazine* 76, no. 3 (July 1975): 118–28.

Brumfiel, Elizabeth M., and John W. Fox, eds. *Factional Competition and Political Development in the New World.* Cambridge: Cambridge Univ. Press, 1994.

Bull, Kinloch. "Barbadian Settlers in Early Carolina: Historiographical Notes." *South Carolina Historical Magazine* 96, no. 4 (Oct. 1995): 329–39.

Bushnell, Amy Turner. *Situado and Sabana: Spain's Support System for the Presidio and Mission Provinces of Florida.* Anthropological Papers of the American Museum of Natural History, No. 74. Athens: Univ. of Georgia Press, 1994.

Butler, Brian M., and Paul D. Welch. *Leadership and Polity in Mississippian Society.* Center for Archaeological Investigations, Occasional Paper No. 33. Carbondale: Southern Illinois Univ., 2006.

Calloway, Colin G. *New Worlds for All: Indians, Europeans, and the Remaking of Early America.* Baltimore: Johns Hopkins Univ. Press, 1997.

Canny, Nicholas. *The Elizabethan Conquest of Ireland: A Pattern Established, 1565–1576.* New York: Barnes & Noble, 1976.

———. "The Ideology of English Colonization: From Ireland to America." *William and Mary Quarterly* 30, no. 4 (Oct. 1973): 575–98.

———. *Making Ireland British, 1580–1650.* Oxford: Oxford Univ. Press, 2001.

———, ed. *The Oxford History of the British Empire.* 5 vols. Oxford: Oxford Univ. Press, 1989.

Canny, Nicholas, and Anthony Pagden, eds. *Colonial Identity in the Atlantic World, 1500–1800.* Princeton: Princeton Univ. Press, 1987.

Carney, Judith. "Rice Milling, Gender, and Slave Labour in Colonial South Carolina." *Past and Present* 153 (Nov. 1996): 108–34.

Carney, Judith A. "From Hands to Tutors: African Expertise in the South Carolina Rice Economy." *Agricultural History* 67, no. 3 (Summer 1993): 1–30.

Carson, James Taylor. *Making an Atlantic World: Circles, Paths, and Stories from the Colonial South.* Knoxville: Univ. of Tennessee Press, 2007.

———. *Searching for the Bright Path: The Mississippi Choctaws from Prehistory to Removal.* Lincoln: Univ. of Nebraska Press, 1999.

Cave, Alfred A. *The Pequot War.* Amherst: Univ. of Massachusetts Press, 1996.

Chappell, Sally A. Kitt. *Cahokia: Mirror of the Cosmos.* Chicago: Univ. of Chicago Press, 2002.

Chaplin, Joyce E. *Subject Matter: Technology, the Body, and Science on the Anglo-American Frontier, 1500–1676.* Cambridge: Harvard Univ. Press, 2001.

Chet, Guy. *Conquering the American Wilderness: The Triumph of European War in the Colonial Northeast.* Amherst: Univ. of Massachusetts Press, 2003.

Chibnall, Marjorie. *Anglo-Norman England, 1066–1166.* London: Basil Blackwell, 1986.

Clark, Jerry E. *The Shawnee.* Lexington: Univ. Press of Kentucky, 1993.

Clendinnen, Inga. "'Fierce and Unnatural Cruelty': Cortés and the Conquest of Mexico." *Representations* 33 (Winter 1991): 65–100.

Cobb, Charles R. "Mississippian Chiefdoms: How Complex?" *Annual Review of Anthropology* 32 (2003): 63–84.

Cobb, Charles R., and Adam King. "Re-inventing Mississippian Tradition at Etowah, Georgia." *Journal of Archaeological Method and Theory* 12 (2005): 167–92.

Coclanis, Peter A. "Bitter Harvest: The South Carolina Low Country in Historical Perspective." *Journal of Economic History* 45, no. 2 (June 1985): 251–59.

———. "Rice Prices in the 1720s and the Evolution of the South Carolina Economy." *Journal of Southern History* 48, no. 4 (Nov. 1982): 531–44.

———. "The Rise and Fall of the South Carolina Low Country: An Essay in Economic Interpretation." *Southern Studies* 24 (Summer 1985): 143–66.

Coleman, Kenneth. *Colonial Georgia: A History.* New York: Charles Scribner's Sons, 1976.

———. "The Southern Frontier: Georgia's Founding and the Expansion of South Carolina." *Georgia Historical Quarterly* 56, no. 2 (1972): 163–74.

Colley, Linda. *Captives: Britain, Empire, and the World, 1600–1850.* London: Random House, 2002; New York: Anchor Books, 2004.

Connolly, S. J. *Contested Island: Ireland, 1460–1630.* New York: Oxford Univ. Press, 2007.

Copp, Roberta V. H. "A Discovery, an Encounter, an Exchange: The Spanish and the English in South Carolina." *Proceedings of the South Carolina Historical Association,* 1993, 48–56.

Corkran, David H. *The Creek Frontier, 1540–1783.* Norman: Univ. of Oklahoma Press, 1967.

Covington, James W. "Apalachee Indians, 1704–1763." *Florida Historical Quarterly* 50 (Apr. 1972): 366–84.

———. *The Seminoles of Florida.* Gainesville: Univ. Press of Florida, 1993.

———. "Some Observations concerning the Florida-Carolina Indian Slave Trade." *Florida Anthropologist* 20, nos. 1–2 (Mar.–June 1967).

———. "Stuart's Town, the Yamasee Indians and Spanish Florida." *Florida Anthropologist* 21, no. 1 (Mar. 1968): 8–13.

———. "The Yamasee Indians in Florida: 1715–1763." *Florida Anthropologist* 23, no. 3 (Sept. 1970): 119–28.

Crane, Verner W. *The Southern Frontier, 1670–1732.* Durham, N.C.: Duke Univ. Press, 1928; New York: Norton, 1981.

Crass, David Colin, Bruce R. Penner, and Tammy R. Forehand. "Gentility and Material Culture on the Carolina Frontier." *Historical Archaeology* 33, no. 3 (Fall 1999): 14–31.

Craven, Wesley Frank. *The Southern Colonies in the Seventeenth Century, 1607–1789.* Baton Rouge: Louisiana State Univ. Press, 1970.

Cronon, William. *Changes in the Land: Indians, Colonists, and the Ecology of New England.* New York: Hill and Wang, 1983.

Cruikshank, Julie, Angela Sidney, Kitty Smith, and Annie Ned. *Life Lived Like a Story: Life Stories of Three Yukon Native Elders.* Lincoln: Univ. of Nebraska Press, 1990.

Curet, L. Antonio. "Issues on the Diversity and Emergence of Middle-Range Societies of the Ancient Caribbean: A Critique." *Journal of Archaeological Research* 11 (2003):1–42

Davies, R. R. *Domination and Conquest: The Experience of Ireland, Scotland, and Wales, 1100–1300.* Cambridge: Cambridge Univ. Press, 1990.

———. *The First English Empire: Power and Identities in the British Isles, 1093–1343.* Oxford: Oxford Univ. Press, 2000.

DePratter, Chester. "Late Prehistoric and Early Historic Chiefdoms in the Southeastern United States." Ph.D. diss., Univ. of Georgia, 1983.

Dickson, D. Bruce. "The Yanomamö of the Mississippi Valley? Some Reflections on Larson (1972), Gibson (1974), and Mississippian Period Warfare in the Southeastern United States." *American Antiquity* 46, no. 4 (Oct. 1981): 909–16.

Dobson, David. *Scottish Emigration to Colonial America, 1607–1785.* Athens: Univ. of Georgia Press, 1994.

Donagan, Barbara. "Atrocity, War Crime, and Treason in the English Civil War." *American Historical Review* 99, no. 4 (Oct. 1994): 1137–66.

———. "Codes and Conduct in the English Civil War." *Past and Present* 118 (Feb. 1998): 65–95.

———. "Halcyon Days and the Literature of War: England's Military Education before 1642." *Past and Present* 147 (May 1995): 65–100.

Drenna, Robert D., and Carlos A. Uribe, eds. *Chiefdoms in the Americas.* Lanham, Md.: Univ. Press of America, 1987.

Dunaway, Wilma A. "The Southern Fur Trade and the Incorporation of Southern Appalachia into the World Economy, 1690–1763." *Review of the Fernand Braudel Center* 17, no. 2 (Spring 1994): 215–42.

Dunlop, J. G. "Spanish Depredations, 1686." *South Carolina Historical and Genealogical Magazine* 30, no. 2 (Apr. 1929): 81–89.

Dunn, Richard S. "The English Sugar Islands and the Founding of South Carolina." *South Carolina Historical Magazine* 72 (Apr. 1971): 81–93.

———. *Sugar and Slaves: The Rise of the Planter Class in the English West Indies, 1624–1713.* Chapel Hill: Univ. of North Carolina Press, 1972.

Durschlag, Richard. "The First Creek Resistance: Transformations in Creek Indian Existence and the Yamasee War, 1670–1730." Ph.D. diss., Duke Univ., 1995.

Dye, David H. H. Dye, "Warfare in the Sixteenth-Century Southeast: The de Soto Expedition in the Interior." In *Columbian Consequences*. Vol. 2, *Archaeological and Historical Perspectives on the Spanish Borderlands East*, ed. David Hurst Thomas, 211–22. Washington, D.C.: Smithsonian Institution Press, 1990.

Edelson, S. Max. *Plantation Enterprise in Colonial South Carolina*. Cambridge: Harvard Univ. Press, 2006.

Edgar, Walter. *South Carolina: A History*. Columbia: Univ. of South Carolina Press, 1998.

Edgar, Walter, and N. Louise Bailey, eds. *Biographical Directory of the South Carolina House of Representatives*. Vol. 2, *The Commons House of Assembly, 1692–1775*. Columbia: Univ. of South Carolina Press, 1977.

Edwards, David. "Beyond Reform: Martial Law and the Tudor Reconquest of Ireland." *History Ireland* 5, no. 2 (Summer 1997): 16–21.

———. "The Butler Revolt of 1569." *Irish Historical Studies* 38, no. 111 (May 1993): 228–55.

Edwards, John. *The Spain of the Catholic Monarchs, 1474–1520*. Oxford: Blackwell, 2000.

Eliades, David K. "The Indian Policy of Colonial South Carolina, 1670–1763." Ph.D. diss., Univ. of South Carolina, 1981.

Elliott, J. H. *Imperial Spain, 1469–1716*. New York: Edward Arnold, 1963; New York: Penguin, 1990.

———. *The Old World and the New, 1492–1650*. Cambridge: Cambridge Univ. Press, 1970.

Ellis, Steven G. "The Tudors." *A Military History of Ireland*. Ed. Thomas Bartlett and Keith Jeffrey. Cambridge: Cambridge Univ. Press, 1996. 116–35.

Eltis, David. *The Rise of African Slavery in the Americas*. Cambridge: Cambridge Univ. Press, 2000.

Emerson, Thomas E. *Cahokia and the Archaeology of Power*. Tuscaloosa: Univ. of Alabama Press, 1997.

Ethridge, Robbie, and Charles Hudson, eds. *The Transformation of the Southeastern Indians, 1540–1760*. Jackson: Univ. Press of Mississippi, 2002.

Ethridge, Robbie, and Sheri Marie Shuck-Hall, eds. *Mapping the Mississippian Shatter Zone: The Colonial Indian Slave Trade and Regional Instability in the American South*. Lincoln: Univ. of Nebraska Press, 2009.

Ewen, Charles R., and John H. Hann. *Hernando de Soto Among the Apalachee: The Archaeology of the First Winter Encampment*. Gainesville: Univ. Press of Florida, 1998.

Ferguson, R. Brian, and Neil L. Whitehead, eds. *War in the Tribal Zone: Expanding States and Indigenous Warfare*. Santa Fe, N.M.: School of American Research Press, 1992.

Fernández-Armesto, Felipe. *Before Columbus: Exploration and Colonization from the Mediterranean to the Atlantic, 1229–1492.* Philadelphia: Univ. of Pennsylvania Press, 1987.

———. *The Canary Islands After the Conquest: The Making of a Colonial Society in the Early Sixteenth Century.* Oxford: Clarendon Press, 1982.

Fernández-Santamaria, J. A. *The State, War and Peace: Spanish Political Thought in the Renaissance, 1516–1559.* Cambridge: Cambridge Univ. Press, 1977.

*Firestorm and Ashes: The Siege of 1702.* Vol. 39 of *El Escribano: St. Augustine Journal of History,* 2002.

Fishman, Laura. "Old World Images and New World Encounters: René Laudonnière and the Timucuans of Florida." *Sixteenth Century Journal* 26, no. 3 (Autumn 1995): 547–59.

Fissel, Mark Charles. *English Warfare, 1511–1642.* London: Routledge, 2001.

Foster, R. F., ed. *The Oxford History of Ireland.* Oxford: Oxford Univ. Press, 1992.

Fowler, Melvin, ed. *The Ancient Skies and Sky Watchers of Cahokia: Woodhenges, Eclipses, and Cahokian Cosmology.* Milwaukee: Wisconsin Archaeological Society, 1996.

Frame, Robin. *The Political Development of the British Isles, 1100–1400.* Oxford: Oxford Univ. Press, 1990.

Franklin, John Hope. *The Militant South, 1800–1861.* Cambridge: Harvard Univ. Press, 1956.

Gallay, Alan. *The Indian Slave Trade: The Rise of the English Empire in the American South, 1670–1717.* New Haven: Yale Univ. Press, 2002.

Galloway, Patricia. *Choctaw Genesis, 1500–1700.* Lincoln: Univ. of Nebraska Press, 1995.

———, ed. *The Hernando de Soto Expedition: History, Historiography, and "Discovery" in the Southeast.* Lincoln: Univ. of Nebraska Press, 1997.

———, ed. *The Southeastern Ceremonial Complex: Artifacts and Analysis / The Cottonlandia Conference.* Lincoln: Univ. of Nebraska Press, 1989.

Gannon, Michael. "The New Alliance of History and Archaeology in the Eastern Spanish Borderlands." *William and Mary Quarterly* 49, no. 2 (Apr. 1992): 321–34.

Geertz, Clifford. *The Interpretation of Cultures.* New York: Basic Books, 1973.

George, Kenneth M. *Showing Signs of Violence: The Cultural Politics of a Twentieth-Century Headhunting Ritual.* Berkeley and Los Angeles: Univ. of California Press, 1996.

Gibson, Charles, ed. *The Black Legend: Anti-Spanish Attitudes in the Old World and New.* New York: Alfred A. Knopf, 1971.

Gibson, John L. "Aboriginal Warfare in the Protohistoric Southeast: An Alternative Perspective." *American Antiquity* 39, no. 1 (Jan. 1974): 130–33.

Girard, René. *Violence and the Sacred.* Translated by Patrick Gregory. 1972. Rpt. Baltimore: Johns Hopkins Univ. Press, 1977.

Gleach, Frederic W. *Powhatan's World and Colonial Virginia: A Conflict of Cultures.* Lincoln: Univ. of Nebraska Press, 2000.

Goggin, John M., and William C. Sturtevant. "The Calusa: A Stratified, Nonagricultural Society (with notes on sibling marriage)." In *Explorations in Cultural Anthropology: Essays in Honor of George Peter Murdock*, ed. Ward H. Goodenough, 179–219. New York: McGraw-Hill, 1964.

Gomez, Michael A. *Exchanging Our Country Marks: The Transformation of African Identities in the Colonial and Antebellum South.* Chapel Hill: Univ. of North Carolina Press, 1998.

Goodyear, Albert C., III, and Glen T. Hanson, eds. *Studies in South Carolina Archaeology: Essays in Honor of Robert L. Stephenson.* Columbia: South Carolina Institute of Archaeology and Anthropology / Univ. of South Carolina, 1989.

Gould, Eliga H. "Lines of Plunder or Crucible of Modernity? Toward a Legal History of the English-Speaking Atlantic, 1660–1825." Paper presented at Seascapes, Littoral Cultures, and Trans-Oceanic Exchanges, Library of Congress, Washington, D.C., Feb. 12–15, 2003.

Grafton, Anthony, and Ann Blair, eds. *The Transmission of Culture in Early Modern Europe.* Philadelphia: Univ. of Pennsylvania Press, 1990.

Green, Michael D. *The Politics of Indian Removal: Creek Government and Society in Crisis.* Lincoln: Univ. of Nebraska Press, 1985.

Green, William G. "The Search for Altamaha: The Archaeology of an Early 18th Century Yamasee Indian Town." Master's thesis, Univ. of South Carolina, 1991.

Greene, Jack P. "Colonial South Carolina and the Caribbean Connection." *South Carolina Historical Magazine* 88, no. 4 (1987): 192–210.

Greene, Jack P., Rosemary Brana-Shute, and Randy J. Sparks, eds. *Money, Trade, and Power: The Evolution of Colonial South Carolina's Plantation Society.* Columbia: Univ. of South Carolina Press, 2001.

Greene, Jack P., and J. R. Pole, eds. *Colonial British America: Essays in the New History of the Early Modern Era.* Baltimore: Johns Hopkins Univ. Press, 1984.

Grenier, John. *The First Way of War: American War Making on the Frontier.* Cambridge: Cambridge Univ. Press, 2005.

Griffin, James. "Cahokia Interaction with Contemporary Southeastern and Eastern Societies." *Midcontinental Journal of Archaeology* 18 (1993): 3–17.

Haan, Richard L. "The 'Trade Do's Not Flourish as Formerly': The Ecological Origins of the Yamasee War of 1715." *Ethnohistory* 28, no. 4 (Fall 1982): 341–58.

Hadden, Sally E. *Slave Patrols: Law and Violence in Virginia and the Carolinas.* Cambridge: Harvard Univ. Press, 2001.

Haefeli, Evan. "Kieft's War and the Cultures of Violence in Colonial America." In *Lethal Imagination: Violence and Brutality in American History,* ed. Michael A. Bellesiles, 17–40. New York: New York Univ. Press, 1999.

Hahn, Steven C. *The Invention of the Creek Nation, 1670–1763.* Lincoln: Univ. of Nebraska Press, 2004.

Hall, Gwendolyn Midlo. *Africans in Colonial Louisiana.* Baton Rouge: Louisiana State Univ. Press, 1995.

———. *Slavery and African Ethnicities in the Americas: Restoring the Links.* Chapel Hill: Univ. of North Carolina Press, 2007.

Hall, Joseph M. "Making an Indian People: Creek Formation in the Colonial Southeast, 1590–1735." Ph.D. diss., Univ. of Wisconsin, 2001.

———. *Zamumo's Gifts: Indian-European Exchange in the Colonial Southeast.* Philadelphia: Univ. of Pennsylvania Press, 2009.

Hally, David J., ed. *Ocmulgee Archaeology, 1936–1986.* Athens: Univ. of Georgia Press, 1994.

———. "The Territorial Size of Mississippian Chiefdoms." In *Archaeology of Eastern North America: Papers in Honor of Stephen Williams,* 143–68. Archaeological Report No. 25. Jackson: Mississippi Department of Archives and History, 1993.

Hammerstedt, Scott W. "Mississippian Status in Western Kentucky: Evidence from the Annis Mound." *Southeastern Archaeology* 24, no. 1 (2005): 11–27.

Hann, John H. *A History of the Timucua Indians and Missions.* Gainesville: Univ. Press of Florida, 1996.

———. "Late Seventeenth-Century Forebears of the Lower Creeks and Seminoles." *Southeastern Archaeology* 15, no. 1 (Summer 1996): 66–80.

———. "Twilight of the Mocamo and Guale Aborigines as Portrayed in the 1695 Spanish Visitation." *Florida Historical Quarterly* 56, no. 1 (July 1987): 1–24.

———, ed. *Missions to the Calusa.* Gainesville: Univ. of Florida Press, 1991.

———, ed. "St. Augustine's Fallout from the Yamasee War." *Florida Historical Quarterly* 68, no. 2 (Oct. 1989): 180–200.

Hann, John H., and Bonnie G. McEwan. *The Apalachee Indians and Mission San Luis.* Gainesville: Univ. Press of Florida, 1998.

Harvey, Henry. *History of the Shawnee Indians, from the Year 1681 to 1854, Inclusive.* Cincinnati: Ephraim Morgan and Sons, 1855.

Hatfield, April Lee. *Atlantic Virginia: Intercolonial Relations in the Seventeenth Century.* Philadelphia: Univ. of Pennsylvania Press, 2004.

Hatley, Tom. *The Dividing Paths: Cherokees and South Carolinians through the Revolutionary Era.* New York: Oxford Univ. Press, 1995.

Hayward, Barnwell Rhett, and A. S. Salley Jr. "Barnwell of South Carolina." *South Carolina Historical Magazine* 2, no. 1 (Jan. 1901): 46–88.

Higginbotham, A. Leon, Jr. *In the Matter of Color: Race and the American Legal Process: The Colonial Period.* Oxford: Oxford Univ. Press, 1978.

Higginbotham, Don. "The Early American Way of War: Reconnaissance and Appraisal." *William and Mary Quarterly* 44, no. 2 (Apr. 1987): 230–73.

Hill, Sarah. *Weaving New Worlds: Southeastern Cherokee Women and Their Basketry.* Chapel Hill: Univ. of North Carolina Press, 1997.

Hinderaker, Eric, and Peter C. Mancall. *At the Edge of Empire: The Backcountry in British North America.* Baltimore: Johns Hopkins Univ. Press, 2003.

Hirsh, Adam J. "The Collision of Military Cultures in Seventeenth-Century New England." *Journal of American History* 74, no. 4 (Mar. 1998): 1187–1212.

Hoffman, Paul E. "Did Coosa Decline Between 1541 and 1560?" *Florida Anthropologist.* 50, no. 1 (Mar. 1997): 25–30.

———. *Florida's Frontiers.* Bloomington: Indiana Univ. Press, 2002.

———. *A New Andalucia and a Way to the Orient: The American Southeast During the Sixteenth Century.* Baton Rouge: Louisiana State Univ. Press, 1990.

Holt, J. C. *Colonial England, 1066–1215.* London: Hambledon Press, 1997.

Hoskins, Janet, ed. *Headhunting and the Social Imagination in Southeast Asia.* Stanford, Calif.: Stanford Univ. Press, 1996.

Howard, James H. *Shawnee! The Ceremonialism of a Native Indian Tribe and Its Cultural Background.* Athens: Ohio Univ. Press, 1981.

Howard, J. H. *The Southern Ceremonial Complex and its Interpretations.* Columbia: Missouri Archaeological Society, 1968.

Hoxie, Frederick. "Ethnohistory for a Tribal World." *Ethnohistory* 44, no. 4 (Fall 1997): 595–615.

Hoxie, Frederick E., ed. *Encyclopedia of North American Indians: Native American History, Culture, and Life from Paleo-Indians to the Present.* Boston: Houghton Mifflin, 1996.

Hudson, Charles. *Conversations with the High Priest of Coosa.* Chapel Hill: Univ. of North Carolina, 2003.

———. "A Coosa-Spanish Alliance in Sixteenth-Century Georgia." *Georgia Historical Quarterly* 72, no. 4 (1988): 599–626.

———. *Knights of Spain, Warriors of the Sun: Hernando de Soto and the South's Ancient Chiefdoms.* Athens: Univ. of Georgia Press, 1997.

———. *The Southeastern Indians.* Knoxville: Univ. of Tennessee Press, 1976.

Hudson Charles, Marvin Smith, David Hally, Richard Polhemus, and Chester DePratter. "Coosa: A Chiefdom in the Sixteenth-Century Southeastern United States." *American Antiquity* 50, no. 4 (Oct. 1985): 723–37.

Hudson, Charles, and Carmen Chaves Tesser, eds. *The Forgotten Centuries: Indians and Europeans in the American South, 1521–1704.* Athens: Univ. of Georgia Press, 1994.

Insh, George Pratt. "Arrival of the Cardross Settlers." *South Carolina Historical and Genealogical Magazine* 30, no. 2 (Apr. 1929): 69–80.

———. "The *Carolina Merchant:* Advice of Arrival." *Scottish Historical Review* 25 (1928): 99–108.

Isaac, Rhys. *The Transformation of Virginia, 1740–1790.* Chapel Hill: Univ. of North Carolina Press, 1982.

Ivers, Larry E. *British Drums on the Southern Frontier: The Military Colonization of Georgia, 1733–1749.* Chapel Hill: Univ. of North Carolina Press, 1974.

Jackson, W. R., Jr. "Early Florida Through Spanish Eyes." University of Miami Hispanic-American Studies No. 12. Coral Gables, Fla.: Univ. of Miami Press, 1954.

Jacoby, Karl. *Shadows at Dawn: A Borderlands Massacre and the Violence of History.* New York: Penguin Press, 2008.

Jennings, Francis. *The Invasion of America: Indians, Colonialism, and the Cant of Conquest.* Chapel Hill: Univ. of North Carolina Press, 1975.

Johnson, David Lee. "The Yamasee War." Master's thesis, Univ. of South Carolina, 1980.

Johnson, James Turner. *The Just War Tradition and the Restraint of War: A Moral and Historical Inquiry.* Princeton: Princeton Univ. Press, 1981.

Johnston, Carolyn Ross. *Cherokee Women in Crisis: Trail of Tears, Civil War, and Allotment, 1838–1907.* Tuscaloosa: Univ. of Alabama Press, 2003.

Jones, Charles C. *Historical Sketch of Tomo-Chi-Chi, Mico of the Yamacraws.* Albany, N.Y.: Joel Munsell, 1868.

Josephy, Alvin M. *Now that the Buffalo's Gone.* New York: Knopf, 1982.

Juricek, John T. "The Westo Indians." *Ethnohistory* 11, no. 2 (Spring 1964): 134–73.

Karr, Ronald Dale. "'Why Should You Be So Furious?' The Violence of the Pequot War." *Journal of American History* 85, no. 3 (Dec. 1998): 876–909.

Keen, Benjamin. "The Black Legend Revisited: Assumptions and Realities." *Hispanic American Historical Review* 49, no. 4 (Nov. 1969): 703–19.

Kelsey, R. W., ed. "Swiss Settlers in South Carolina." *South Carolina Historical and Genealogical Magazine* 22, no. 3 (July 1922): 85–91.

Kelton, Paul. *Epidemics and Enslavement: Biological Catastrophe in the Native American Southeast, 1492–1715.* Lincoln: Univ. of Nebraska Press, 2007.

Kicza, John E. "Patterns in Early Spanish Overseas Expansion." *William and Mary Quarterly* 49, no. 2 (Apr. 1992): 229–53.

King, Adam. *Etowah: The Political History of a Chiefdom Capital.* Tuscaloosa: Univ. of Alabama Press, 2003.

Klingberg, Frank J. "The Indian Frontier in South Carolina as Seen by the S.P.G. Missionary." *Journal of Southern History* 5, no. 4 (Nov. 1939): 479–500.

Knight, Vernon James, Jr. "Farewell to the Southeastern Ceremonial Complex," *Southeastern Archaeology* 25 (2006): 1–5.

———. "The Institutional Organization of Mississippian Religion." *American Antiquity* 51, no. 4 (Oct. 1986): 675–87.

———, and Vincas Steponaitis, *Archaeology of the Moundville Chiefdom*. Washington, D.C.: Smithsonian Institution Press, 1998.

Kupperman, Karen Ordahl. *Roanoke: The Abandoned Colony.* Totowa, N.J.: Rowman & Allenheld, 1984.

Kwachka, Patricia B., ed. *Perspectives on the Southeast: Linguistics, Archaeology and Ethnohistory.* Athens: Univ. of Georgia Press, 1994.

Lafferty, Robert H., III. "An Analysis of Prehistoric Southeastern Fortifications." Master's thesis, Southern Illinois Univ., 1973.

Landers, Jane. *Black Society in Spanish Florida.* Urbana: Univ. of Illinois Press, 1999.

Lane, Kris E. *Pillaging the Empire: Piracy in the Americas, 1500–1750.* Armonk, N.Y.: M. E. Sharpe, 1998.

Larson, Lewis H. "Functional Considerations of Warfare in the Southeast during the Mississippi Period." *American Antiquity* 37, no. 3 (July 1972): 383–92.

*The Late Prehistoric Southeast: A Source Book.* Ed. Chester B. DePratter. New York: Garland, 1986.

Lawson, Sarah. *A Foothold in Florida: The Eye-Witness Account of Four Voyages Made by the French to that Region.* East Grinstead, UK: Antique Atlas Publications, 1992.

Lee, E. Lawrence. *Indian Wars in North Carolina, 1663–1673.* Raleigh: North Carolina Department of Archives and History, 1997.

Lee, Wayne. "Early American Ways of War: A New Reconnaissance." *Historical Journal* 44, no. 1 (Mar. 2001): 269–89.

———. "Fortify, Fight, or Flee: Tuscarora and Cherokee Defensive Warfare and Military Culture Adaptation." *Journal of Military History* 68, no. 3 (July 2004): 713–70.

———. "Peace Chiefs and Blood Revenge: Patterns of Restraint in Native American Warfare, 1500–1800." *Journal of Military History* 71, no. 3 (July 2007): 701–41.

Lefler, Hugh T., and William S. Powell. *Colonial North Carolina: A History.* New York: Charles Scribner's Sons, 1973.

Lepore, Jill. *The Name of War: King Philip's War and the Origins of American Identity.* New York: Alfred A. Knopf, 1998.

Lesser, Charles H. *South Carolina Begins: The Records of a Proprietary Colony, 1663–1721.* Columbia: South Carolina Department of Archives and History, 1995.

Lewis, Kenneth E. "The Metropolis and the Backcountry: The Making of a Colonial Landscape on the South Carolina Frontier." *Historical Archaeology* 33, no. 3 (Fall 1999): 3–13.

Littlefield, Daniel C. *Rice and Slaves: Ethnicity and the Slave Trade in Colonial South Carolina.* Baton Rouge: Louisiana State Univ. Press, 1981; Urbana: Univ. of Illinois Press, 1991.

Livius, Titus. *Early History of Rome.* New York: Modern Library, 1912.

Lockhart, James. *The Men of Cajamarca: A Social and Biographical Study of the First Conquerors of Peru.* Austin: Univ. of Texas Press, 1972.

Lomax, Derek W. *The Reconquest of Spain.* London: Longman, 1978.

Louis, William Roger, ed. in chief. *The Oxford History of the British Empire.* 5 vols. Oxford: Oxford Univ. Press, 1998.

Lourie, Elena. *Crusade and Colonisation: Muslims, Christians, and Jews in Medieval Aragon.* Brookfield, Vt.: Variorum, 1990.

Lowery, Woodbury. *The Spanish Settlements within the Present Limits of the United States, 1513–1561.* 2 vols. New York: G. P. Putnam's Sons, 1911.

Lynch, John. *Spain, 1516–1598: From Nation State to World Empire.* Oxford: Blackwell, 1991.

MacCaffrey, Wallace T. *Elizabeth I: War and Politics, 1588–1603.* Princeton: Princeton Univ. Press, 1992.

MacKay, Angus. *Spain in the Middle Ages: From Frontier to Empire, 1000–1500.* London: Macmillan, 1977.

Mackenthun, Gesa. *Metaphors of Dispossession: American Beginnings and the Translation of Empire, 1492–1637.* Norman: Univ. of Oklahoma Press, 1997.

Malone, Patrick M. *The Skulking Way of War: Technology and Tactics Among the New England Indians.* Plymouth Plantation, 1991; Lanham, Md.: Madison Books, 2000.

Maltby, William S. *The Black Legend in England: The Development of Anti-Spanish Sentiment, 1558–1660.* Durham, N.C.: Duke Univ. Press, 1971.

Mann, Charles. *1491: New Revelations of the Americas Before Columbus.* New York: Alfred A. Knopf, 2005.

Marcus, Joyce, and Gary Feinman, eds., *Archaic States.* Santa Fe, N.M.: School of American Research, 1998.

Matteson, Robert S. "Francis Le Jau in Ireland." *South Carolina Historical Magazine* 78, no. 2 (Apr. 1977): 83–91.

McCusker, John J., and Russell R. Menard. *The Economy of British North America, 1607–1789.* Chapel Hill: Univ. of North Carolina Press, 1985.

McEwan, Bonnie G., ed. *Indians of the Greater Southeast: Historical Archaeology and Ethnohistory.* Gainesville: Univ. Press of Florida, 2000.

———, ed. *The Spanish Missions of La Florida.* Gainesville: Univ. Press of Florida, 1993.

McGrath, John T. *The French in Early Florida: In the Eye of the Hurricane.* Gainesville: Univ. Press of Florida, 2000.

McGurk, John. *The Elizabethan Conquest of Ireland: The 1590s Crisis.* Manchester, UK: Manchester Univ. Press, 1997.

McKivergan, David Andrew, Jr. "Migration and Settlement Among the Yamasee in South Carolina." Master's thesis, Univ. of South Carolina. 1991.

Menard, Russell R. "Financing the Lowcountry Export Boom: Capital and Growth in Early South Carolina." *William and Mary Quarterly* 51, no. 4 (Oct. 1994): 659–76.

Mercer, John. *The Canary Islanders: Their Prehistory, Conquest, and Survival.* London: Rex Collings, 1980.

Merrell, James H. *The Indians' New World: Catawbas and their Neighbors from European Contact through the Era of Removal.* Chapel Hill: Univ. of North Carolina Press, 1989.

———. "Natives in a New World: The Catawba Indians of Carolina, 1650–1800." Ph.D. diss., Johns Hopkins Univ., 1982.

———. "Some Thoughts on Colonial Historians and American Indians." *William and Mary Quarterly* 46, no. 1 (Jan. 1989): 94–119.

Mihesuah, Devon A., ed. *Natives and Academics: Researching and Writing about American Indians.* Lincoln: Univ. of Nebraska Press, 1998.

Milanich, Jerald T. *Florida Indians and the Invasion from Europe.* Gainesville: Univ. Press of Florida, 1995.

———. *Laboring in the Fields of the Lord: Spanish Missions and Southeastern Indians.* Washington, D.C.: Smithsonian Institution Press, 1999.

———. *The Timucua.* Oxford: Blackwell, 1996.

Milanich, Jerald T., and Charles Hudson. *Hernando de Soto and the Indians of Florida.* Gainesville: Univ. Press of Florida, 1993.

Milanich, Jerald T., and Samuel Proctor, eds. *Tacachale: Essays on the Indians of Florida and Southeastern Georgia during the Historic Period.* Gainesville: Univ. Presses of Florida, 1978.

Miles, Tiya. *Ties that Bind: The Story of an Afro-Cherokee Family in Slavery and Freedom.* Berkeley and Los Angeles: Univ. of California Press, 2005.

Milling, Chapman J. *Red Carolinians.* Chapel Hill: Univ. of North Carolina Press, 1940; Columbia: Univ. of South Carolina Press, 1969.

Milner, George R. *The Cahokia Chiefdom: The Archaeology of a Mississippian Society.* Washington, D.C.: Smithsonian Institution Press, 1998.

Milner, George R., Eve Anderson, and Virginia G. Smith. "Warfare in Late Prehistoric West-Central Illinois." *American Antiquity* 56, no. 4 (Oct. 1991): 581–603.

Moore, Alexander. "Daniel Axtell's Account Book and the Economy of Early South Carolina." *South Carolina Historical Magazine* 95, no. 4 (Oct. 1994): 280–301.

Morgan, Edmund S. *American Slavery, American Freedom: The Ordeal of Colonial Virginia.* New York: Norton, 1975.

Morgan, Hiram. "The Colonial Venture of Sir Thomas Smith in Ulster, 1571–1575." *Historical Journal* 28, no. 2 (June 1985): 261–78.

———. *Tyrone's Rebellion: The Outbreak of the Nine Years War in Tudor Ireland.* Bury St. Edmunds, Suffolk: St. Edmundsbury Press, 1993.

———, ed. *Political Ideology in Ireland, 1541–1641.* Dublin: Four Courts Press, 1999.

Morgan, Philip D. *Slave Counterpoint: Black Culture in the Eighteenth-Century Chesapeake and Lowcountry.* Chapel Hill: Univ. of North Carolina Press, 1998.

Muller, Jon. *Mississippian Political Economy.* New York: Plenum Press, 1997.

Murga Sanz, Vicente. *Juan Ponce de León.* San Juan: Ediciones de la Universidad de Puerto Rico, 1959.

Nash, Gary B. "The Image of the Indian in the Southern Colonial Mind." *William and Mary Quarterly* 29, no. 2 (Apr. 1972): 197–230.

———. *Red, White and Black: The Peoples of Early America.* Englewood Cliffs, N.J.: Prentice-Hall, 1974.

Nash, R. C. "South Carolina and the Atlantic Economy in the Late Seventeenth and Eighteenth Centuries." *Economic History Review* 45, no. 4 (Nov. 1992): 677–702.

Nassaney, Michael S., and Kenneth E. Sassaman, eds. *Native American Interactions: Multiscalar Analyses and Interpretations in the Eastern Woodlands.* Knoxville: Univ. of Tennessee Press, 1995.

O'Callaghan, Joseph F. *Reconquest and Crusade in Medieval Spain.* Philadelphia: Univ. of Pennsylvania Press, 2003.

O'Connor, Mallory McCane. *Lost Cities of the Ancient Southeast.* Gainesville: Univ. Press of Florida, 1995.

Oatis, Steven. "A Colonial Complex: South Carolina's Changing Frontiers in the Era of the Yamasee War, 1680–1730." Ph.D. diss., Emory Univ., 1999.

Oatis, Steven J. *A Colonial Complex: South Carolina's Frontiers in the Era of the Yamasee War, 1680–1730.* Lincoln: Univ. of Nebraska Press, 2004.

———. "'To Eat Up a Village of White Men': Anglo-Indian Designs on Mobile and Pensacola, 1705–1715." *Gulf South Historical Review* 14, no. 1 (Fall 1998): 104–19.

Oberg, Michael. *Dominion and Civility: English Imperialism and Native America, 1585–1685.* Ithaca: Cornell Univ. Press, 1999.

———. *The Head in Edward Nugent's Hand: Roanoke's Forgotten Indians.* Philadelphia: Univ. of Pennsylvania Press, 2008.

Ohlmeyer, Jane. "Seventeenth-Century Ireland and the New British and Atlantic Histories." *American Historical Review* 104, no. 2 (Apr. 1999): 446–62.

Oliphant, John. *Peace and War on the Cherokee Frontier, 1756–1763.* Baton Rouge: Louisiana State Univ. Press, 2001.

Olwell, Robert. *Masters, Slaves, and Subjects: The Culture of Power in the South Carolina Low Country, 1740–1790.* Ithaca, N.Y.: Cornell Univ. Press, 1998.

Otto, John Solomon. "Livestock-Raising in Early South Carolina, 1670–1700: Prelude to the Rice Plantation Economy." *Agricultural History* 61, no. 4 (Fall 1987): 13–24.

Paar, Karen Lynn. "'To Settle is to Conquer': Spaniards, Native Americans and the Colonization of Santa Elena in Sixteenth-Century Florida." Ph.D. diss., Univ. of North Carolina. 1999.

Pagden, Anthony. *European Encounters with the New World: From Renaissance to Romanticism.* New Haven: Yale Univ. Press, 1993.

———. *Lords of All the World: Ideologies of Empire in Spain, Britain and France, c. 1500–c. 1800.* New Haven: Yale Univ. Press, 1995.

Palmer, William. *The Problem of Ireland in Tudor Foreign Policy, 1485–1603.* Woodbridge, UK: Boydell Press, 1994.

Parramore, Thomas C. "The Tuscarora Ascendancy." *North Carolina Historical Review* 59, no. 4 (Oct. 1982): 307–26.

———. "With Tuscarora Jack on the Back Path to Bath." *North Carolina Historical Review* 64, no. 2 (Apr. 1997): 115–38.

Parry, J. H. *The Age of Reconnaissance.* London: Weidenfeld and Nicolson, 1963.

Parry, J. H., et al. *A Short History of the West Indies.* New York: St. Martin's Press, 1987.

Pauketat, Timothy R. *Ancient Cahokia and the Mississippians.* Cambridge: Cambridge Univ. Press, 2004.

———. *Cahokia: Ancient America's Great City on the Mississippi.* New York: Penguin, 2009

———. *Chiefdoms and Other Archaeological Delusions.* Lanham, Md.: Altamira Press, 2007.

———, and Thomas E. Emerson, eds. *Cahokia: Domination and Ideology in the Mississippian World.* Lincoln: Univ. of Nebraska Press, 1997.

Pearson, Edward A. "'A Countryside Full of Flames': A Reconsideration of the Stono Rebellion and Slave Rebelliousness in the Early Eighteenth-Century South Carolina Lowcountry." *Slavery and Abolition* 17, no. 2 (Aug. 1996): 22–50.

Pennington, Edgar Legare. "The Reverend Francis Le Jau's Work Among Indians and Negro Slaves." *Journal of Southern History* 1, no. 4 (Nov. 1935): 442–58.

Penrose, Boies. *Travel and Discovery in the Renaissance, 1420–1620.* New York: Cambridge Univ. Press, 1952.

Perdue, Theda. *Cherokee Women: Gender and Culture Change, 1700–1835.* Lincoln: Univ. of Nebraska Press, 1998.

———. *Native Carolinians: The Indians of North Carolina.* Raleigh: North Carolina Department of Archives and History, 1985.

Peregine, Peter N. "An Archaeological Correlate of War." *North American Archaeologist* 14, no. 2 (1993): 139–51.

———. *Mississippian Evolution: A World-System Perspective.* Madison: Prehistory Press, 1992.

Peristiany, J. G. *Honour and Shame: The Values of Mediterranean Society.* Chicago: Univ. of Chicago Press, 1966.

Perttula, Timothy, Cathy J. Crane, and James E. Bruseth. "A Consideration of Caddoan Subsistence." *Southeastern Archaeology* 1, no. 2 (Winter 1982): 89–102.

Philips, Charles F., Jr. "Captain Enriquez: Dr. Henry Woodward and the World of the Early Carolina Indian Trade." Master's thesis, College of Charleston, 2002.

Piker, Joshua. *Okfuskee: A Creek Indian Town in Colonial America.* Cambridge: Harvard Univ. Press, 2004.

Poole, Deborah, ed. *Violence, Power, and Cultural Identity in the High Provinces of Southern Peru.* Boulder, Colo.: Westview Press, 1994.

Prescott, William H. *The Art of War in Spain: The Conquest of Granada, 1481–1492,* ed. with introd. by Albert D. McJoynt. Mechanicsburg, Pa.: Stackpole Books, 1995.

Puckrein, Gary A. *Little England: Plantation Society and Anglo-Barbadian Politics, 1627–1700.* New York: New York Univ. Press, 1984.

Rabasa, José. *Writing Violence on the Northern Frontier: The Historiography of Sixteenth-Century New Mexico and Florida and the Legacy of Conquest.* Durham, N.C.: Duke Univ. Press, 2000.

Ramsey, William L. "'Heathenish Combination': The Natives of the North American Southeast During the Era of the Yamasee War." Ph.D. diss., Tulane Univ., 1998.

———. "'Something Cloudy in Their Looks': The Origins of the Yamasee War Reconsidered." *Journal of American History* 90, no. 1 (June 2003): 44–75.

———. *The Yamasee War: A Study of Culture, Economy, and Conflict in the Colonial South.* Lincoln: Univ. of Nebraska Press, 2008.

Rayson, David. "'A Great Matter to Tell:' Indians, Europeans, and Africans From the Mississippian Era Through the Yamasee War in the North American Southeast, 1550–1720." Ph.D. diss., Univ. of Minnesota, 1996.

Restall, Matthew. *Seven Myths of the Spanish Conquest.* Oxford: Oxford Univ. Press, 2003.

Riches, David., ed. *The Anthropology of Violence.* Oxford: Basil Blackwell, 1986.

Richter, Daniel K. *Facing East from Indian Country: A Native History of Early America.* Cambridge: Harvard Univ. Press, 2001.

———. *The Ordeal of the Longhouse: The Peoples of the Iroquois League in the Era of European Colonization*. Chapel Hill: Univ. of North Carolina Press, 1992.

———. "Whose Indian History?" *William and Mary Quarterly* 50, no. 2 (Apr. 1993): 379–93.

Rights, Douglas LeTell. *The American Indian in North Carolina*. Durham, N.C.: Duke Univ. Press, 1947.

Rogozinski, Jan. *A Brief History of the Caribbean: From the Arawak and the Carib to the Present*. New York: Facts on File, 1992.

Roper, L. H. *Conceiving Carolina: Proprietors, Planters, and Plots, 1662–1729*. New York: Palgrave Macmillan, 2004.

Rosaldo, Michelle Z. *Knowledge and Passion: llongot Notions of Self and Social Life*. Cambridge: Cambridge Univ. Press, 1980.

Rosaldo, Renato. *Ilongot Headhunting, 1883–1974: A Study in Society and History*. Stanford, Calif.: Stanford Univ. Press, 1980.

Rose, Jerome C., Barbera A. Burnett, Michael S. Nassaney, and Mark W. Blauer. "Paleopathology and the Origins of Maize Agriculture in the Lower Mississippi Valley and Caddoan Culture Areas." In *Paleopathology at the Origins of Agriculture*, ed. Mark Nathan Cohen and George J. Armelagos, 393–424. New York: Academic Press, 1984.

Rose, Willie Lee. *Slavery and Freedom*. New York: Oxford Univ. Press, 1982.

Rothstein, Edward. "Who Should Tell History: The Tribes or the Museums?" *New York Times*, Dec. 21, 2004, sec. E.

Rowland, Lawrence S. *Window on the Atlantic: The Rise and Fall of Santa Elena, South Carolina's Spanish City*. Columbia: South Carolina Department of Archives and History, 1990.

Salisbury, Neal. "The Indians' Old World: Native Americans and the Coming of Europeans." *William and Mary Quarterly* 53 (July 1996): 435–58.

———. *Manitou and Providence: Indians, Europeans, and the Making of New England, 1500–1643*. New York: Oxford Univ. Press, 1982.

Sauer, Carl Ortwin. *Sixteenth-Century North America: The Land and People as Seen by the Europeans*. Berkeley and Los Angeles: Univ. of California Press, 1971.

Saunt, Claudio. *A New Order of Things: Power, Property and the Transformation of the Creek Indians, 1733–1816*. Cambridge: Cambridge Univ. Press, 1999.

Schama, Simon. *A History of Britain: At the Edge of the World? 3000 B.C.–A.D. 1603*. New York: Hyperion, 2000.

Scheper-Hughes, Nancy, and Philippe Bourgois, eds. *Violence in War and Peace: An Anthology*. Malden, Mass.: Blackwell, 2004.

Schlesinger, Roger. *In the Wake of Columbus: The Impact of the New World on Europe, 1492–1650*. 2nd ed. 1996. Rpt. Wheeling, Ill.: Harlan Davidson, 2007.

Schmidt, Bettina E., and Ingo W. Schröder. *Anthropology of Violence and Conflict*. London: Routledge, 2001.

Schrager, Bradley. "Yamasee Indians and the Challenge of Spanish and English Colonialism in the North American Southeast, 1660–1715." Ph.D. diss., Northwestern Univ., 2001.

Schwartz, Stuart B., ed. *Implicit Understandings: Observing, Reporting, and Reflecting on the Encounters Between Europeans and Other Peoples in the Early Modern Era.* Cambridge: Cambridge Univ. Press, 1994.

Seed, Patricia. *Ceremonies of Possession in Europe's Conquest of the New World, 1492–1640.* Cambridge: Cambridge Univ. Press, 1995.

Service, Elman R. *Primitive Social Organization.* New York: Random House, 1962.

Shaffer, Lynda Norene. *Native Americans Before 1492: The Moundbuilding Centers of the Eastern Woodlands.* Armonk, N.Y.: M. E. Sharpe, 1992.

Shoemaker, Nancy. *A Strange Likeness: Becoming Red and White in Eighteenth-Century North America* (New York: Oxford Univ. Press), 2004.

Shy, John. "The Cultural Approach to the History of War." *Journal of Military History* 57, no. 5 (Oct. 1993): 13–26.

Silver, Peter. *Our Savage Neighbors: How Indian War Transformed Early America.* New York: W. W. Norton, 2008.

Silver, Timothy. *A New Face on the Countryside: Indians, Colonists, and Slaves in South Atlantic Forests, 1500–1800.* Cambridge: Cambridge Univ. Press, 1990.

Simmons, William S. "Cultural Bias in the New England Puritans' Perception of Indians." *William and Mary Quarterly* 38, no. 1 (Jan. 1981): 56–72.

Slotkin, Richard. *Regeneration Through Violence: The Mythology of the American Frontier, 1600–1860.* Middletown, Conn.: Wesleyan Univ. Press, 1973; New York: HarperCollins, 1996.

Smith-Rosenberg, Carol. *This Violent Empire: The Birth of an American National Identity.* Chapel Hill: Univ. of North Carolina Press, 2010.

Smith, Bruce D., ed. *Mississippian Settlement Patterns.* New York: Academic Press, 1978.

Smith, Maria Ostendorf. "Beyond Palisades: The Nature and Frequency of Deliberate Violent Trauma in the Chickamauga Reservoir of East Tennessee." *American Journal of Physical Anthropology* 121, no. 4 (2003): 303–18.

Smith, Mark M. *Stono: Documenting and Interpreting a Southern Slave Revolt.* Columbia: Univ. of South Carolina Press, 2005.

Smith, Marvin T. *The Archaeology of Aboriginal Culture Change: Depopulation during the Early Historic Period.* Gainesville: Univ. Press of Florida, 1987.

———. *Coosa: The Rise and Fall of a Southeastern Mississippian Chiefdom.* Gainesville: Univ. Press of Florida, 2000.

Snapp, J. Russell. *John Stuart and the Struggle for Empire on the Southern Frontier.* Baton Rouge: Louisiana State Univ. Press, 1996.

Spalding, Phinizy. *Oglethorpe in America.* Chicago: Univ. of Chicago Press, 1977.

Starkey, Armstrong. *European and Native American Warfare, 1675–1815.* Norman: Univ. of Oklahoma Press, 1998.

Steele, Ian K. *Warpaths: Invasions of North America.* New York: Oxford Univ. Press, 1994.

Stine, Linda F., with Martha Zierden, Lesley Drucker, and Christopher Judge, eds. *Carolina's Historical Landscapes: Archaeological Perspectives.* Knoxville: Univ. of Tennessee Press, 1997.

Stoler, Ann Laura. "Rethinking Colonial Categories: European Communities and the Boundaries of Rule." *Comparative Studies in Society and History* 31, no. 1 (Jan. 1989): 134–61.

Stoltman, James B., ed. *Archaeology of Eastern North America: Papers in Honor of Stephen Williams.* Jackson: Mississippi Department of Archives and History, 1993.

———, ed. *New Perspectives on Cahokia: Views from the Periphery.* Madison, Wis.: Prehistory Press, 1991.

Sturtevant, William C., gen. ed. *Handbook of North American Indians.* Vol.14, *Southeast,* ed. Raymond D. Fogelson. Washington, D.C.: Smithsonian Institution Press, 2004.

Styrna, Christine A. "The Winds of War and Change: The Impact of the Tuscarora War on Proprietary North Carolina, 1690–1729." Ph.D. diss., College of William and Mary. 1990.

Suttles, William C., Jr. "African Religious Survivals as Factors in American Slave Revolts." *Journal of Negro History* 56, no. 2 (Apr. 1971): 97–104.

Swanton, John R. *Early History of the Creek Indians and Their Neighbors.* Washington, D.C.: Smithsonian Institution Press, 1922; Gainesville: Univ. Press of Florida, 1998.

———. *The Indians of the Southeastern United States.* Smithsonian Institution, Bureau of American Ethnology, Bulletin 137. 1946. Rpt. New York: Greenwood, 1969.

———. *Myths and Tales of the Southeastern Indians.* Washington, D.C.: Smithsonian Institution Press, 1929; Norman: Univ. of Oklahoma Press, 1995.

Taussig. Michael. *The Nervous System.* New York: Routledge, 1992.

———. *Shamanism, Colonialism, and the Wild Man: A Study in Terror and Healing.* Chicago: Univ. of Chicago Press, 1987.

Taylor, Alan. *American Colonies.* New York: Viking, 2001.

Taylor, William B., and Franklin Pease, G.Y., eds. *Violence, Resistance, and Survival in the Americas: Native Americans and the Legacy of Conquest.* Washington, D.C.: Smithsonian Institution Press, 1994.

Thomas, David Hurst. *St. Catherine's: An Island in Time.* Atlanta: Georgia Humanities Council, 1988.

Thomas, Nicholas. *Colonialism's Culture: Anthropology, Travel, and Government.* Princeton: Princeton Univ. Press, 1994.

Thornton, John. "African Dimensions of the Stono Rebellion." *American Historical Review* 96, no. 4 (Oct. 1991): 1101–13.

Tomlin, Christopher. "In a Wilderness of Tigers: Violence, the Discourse of English Colonizing, and the Refusals of American History." *Theoretical Inquiries in Law* 4, no. 2 (July 2003): 450–90.

Townsend, Richard F. *Hero, Hawk, and Open Hand: American Indian Art of the Ancient Midwest and South.* New Haven: Yale Univ. Press, 2004.

Trexler, Richard C. *Sex and Conquest: Gendered Violence, Political Order, and the European Conquest of the Americas.* Ithaca: Cornell Univ. Press, 1995.

U.S. Department of the Interior. National Park Service. "Ocmulgee." N.d.

Usner, Daniel H., Jr. *Indians, Settlers, and Slaves in a Frontier Exchange Economy: The Lower Mississippi Valley Before 1783.* Chapel Hill: Univ. of North Carolina Press, 1992.

Van Horne, Wayne. "The Warclub: Weapon and Symbol in Southeastern Indian Societies." Ph.D. diss., Univ. of Georgia, 1993.

Waddell, Gene. "Cofitachequi: A Distinctive Culture." *Ethnohistory* 52, no. 2 (Spring 2005): 333–69.

———. *Indians of the South Carolina Lowcountry, 1562–1751.* Spartanburg, S.C.: Reprint Company, 1980.

Waldman, Melissa Anderson. "A History of Remembering: The French and Spanish in Florida, 1562–1565." Ph.D. diss., Univ. of Michigan, 2000.

Walvin, James. *Black Ivory: Slavery in the British Empire.* 2nd ed. New York: HarperCollins, 1992; Oxford: Blackwell, 2001.

Waring, Joseph J. *The First Voyage and Settlement at Charles Town.* Columbia: Univ. of South Carolina Press, 1970.

Waterhouse, Richard. "England, the Caribbean, and the Settlement of Carolina." *Journal of American Studies* 9, no. 3 (1975): 259–81.

Wax, Darold D. "'The Great Risque We Run': The Aftermath of the Rebellion at Stono, South Carolina, 1739–1745." *Journal of Negro History* 67, no. 2 (Summer 1982): 136–47.

Weber, David J. *New Spain's Far Northern Frontier.* Albuquerque: Univ. of New Mexico Press, 1979.

———. *The Spanish Frontier in North America.* New Haven: Yale Univ. Press, 1992.

Weber, Max. *Max Weber: Essays in Sociology,* ed. and trans. H. H. Gerth and C. Wright Mills. New York: Oxford Univ. Press, 1946.

Weddle, Robert S. *Spanish Sea: The Gulf of Mexico in North American Discovery, 1500–1685.* College Station: Texas A&M Univ. Press, 1985.

Weir, Robert M. *Colonial South Carolina: A History.* New York: KTO Press, 1982; Columbia: Univ. of South Carolina Press, 1997.

Wesson, Cameron B. "Chiefly Power and Food Storage in Southeastern North America." *World Archaeology* 31, no. 1 (June 1999): 145–64.

Wesson, Cameron B., and Mark A. Rees. *Between Contacts and Colonies: Archaeological Perspectives on the Prehistoric Southeast.* Tuscaloosa: Univ. of Alabama Press, 2002.

Whayne, Jeannie, ed. *Cultural Encounters in the Early South: Indians and Europeans in Arkansas,* Fayetteville: Univ. of Arkansas Press, 1995.

Wheeler-Voegelin, Erminie. *Indians of Ohio and Indiana Prior to 1795.* 2 vols. New York: Garland, 1974.

White, Richard. *The Middle Ground: Indians, Empires, and Republics in the Great Lakes Region, 1650–1815.* Cambridge: Cambridge Univ. Press, 1992.

Whitehead, Neil L., ed. *Violence.* Santa Fe: School of American Research Press, 2004.

Wickman, Patricia Riles. *The Tree that Bends: Discourse, Power, and the Survival of the Maskókî People.* Tuscaloosa: Univ. of Alabama Press, 1999.

Widmer, Randolph J. *The Evolution of the Calusa: A Nonagricultural Chiefdom on the Southwest Florida Coast.* Tuscaloosa: Univ. of Alabama Press, 1988.

"William Dunlop's Mission to St. Augustine in 1688." Contributed by J. G. Dunlop. *South Carolina Historical and Genealogical Magazine* 34, no. 1 (Jan. 1933): 1–30.

Williams, Mark, and Gary Shapiro, eds. *Lamar Archaeology: Mississippian Chiefdoms in the Deep South.* Tuscaloosa: Univ. of Alabama Press, 1990.

Williams, Stephen. "The Vacant Quarter and Other Events in the Lower Valley." *Towns and Temples Along the Mississippi.* Ed. David H. Dye and Cheryl Anne Cox. Tuscaloosa: Univ. of Alabama Press, 1990. 170–80.

Williams, Walter. *The Spirit and the Flesh: Sexual Diversity in American Indian Culture.* Boston: Beacon Press, 1992.

Williamson, Margaret Holmes. *Powhatan Lords of Life and Death: Command and Consent in Seventeenth-Century Virginia.* Lincoln: Univ. of Nebraska Press, 2003.

Willis, William S. "Divide and Rule: Red, White and Black in the Southeast." *Journal of Negro History* 48, no. 3 (July 1963): 157–76.

Wilson, Gregory D. *The Archaeology of Everyday Life at Early Moundville.* Tuscaloosa: Univ. of Alabama Press, 2008.

Wood, Betty. *The Origins of American Slavery: Freedom and Bondage in the English Colonies.* New York: Hill and Wang, 1997.

———. *Slavery in Colonial Georgia, 1730–1775.* Athens: Univ. of Georgia Press, 1984.

Wood, Peter H. *Black Majority: Negroes in Colonial South Carolina from 1670 through the Stono Rebellion.* New York: Norton, 1975.

Wood, Peter, Gregory A. Waselkov, and M. Thomas Hatley, eds. *Powhatan's Mantle: Indians in the Colonial Southeast.* Lincoln: Univ. of Nebraska Press, 1989.

———. *Powhatan's Mantle: Indians in the Colonial Southeast.* Rev. ed. Lincoln: Univ. of Nebraska Press, 2006.

Woods, William I. "Population Nucleation, Intensive Agriculture, and Environmental Degradation: The Cahokia Example." *Agriculture and Human Values* 21, nos. 2–3 (June 2004): 151–57.

Worth, John E. *The Struggle for the Georgia Coast: An Eighteenth-Century Spanish Retrospective on Guale and Mocama.* Anthropological Papers of the American Museum of Natural History, No. 75. Athens: Univ. of Georgia Press, 1995.

———. *The Timucuan Chiefdoms of Spanish Florida.* 2 vols. Gainesville: Univ. Press of Florida, 1998.

Wright, J. Leitch, Jr. *Creeks and Seminoles: The Destruction and Regeneration of the Muscogulge People.* Lincoln: Univ. of Nebraska Press, 1986.

———. *The Only Land They Knew: American Indians in the Old South.* New York: Free Press, 1981; Lincoln: Univ. of Nebraska Press, 1999.

———. "Spanish Reaction to Carolina." *North Carolina Historical Review* 41, no. 1 (Oct. 1964): 464–76.

Young, Bioline Whiting, and Melvin Fowler. *Cahokia: The Great Native American Metropolis.* Urbana: Univ. of Illinois Press, 2000.

Young, Jeffrey Robert. *Domesticating Slavery: The Master Class in Georgia and South Carolina, 1670–1837.* Chapel Hill: Univ. of North Carolina Press, 1999.

Zavala, Silvio A. *Las Conquistas de Canarias y América.* Las Palmas: Ediciones del Cabildo Insular de Gran Canaria, 1991. Originally published in 1935 in *Tierra Firme.*

———. *Estudios Indianos.* Mexico City: El Colegio Nacional, 1948.

# Index

Page numbers in **boldface** refer to illustrations.